CONTRACT LAW: CASES AND MATERIALS

JENS DAMMANN

Jens Dammann
Contract Law: Cases and Materials
Second Edition

ISBN-13: 979-8-9898469-2-4

Formatted with Vellum

CONTENTS

PREFACE

This casebook allows students to gain an understanding of the legal doctrines of contract law even before coming to class. Thus, it frees up class time for the discussion of more challenging topics such as the efficiency and fairness of legal rules and fine-grained analyses of cases and hypotheticals.

The main focus of this casebook is on the common law of contracts. Regarding the Uniform Commercial Code, this casebook covers mostly sections 2-205 (firm offer rule) and 2-207 (battle of the forms).

I owe special thanks to those who helped with editing and proofreading the manuscript for this book. They include, in alphabetical order, Marie Baldwin, Jael Dammann, Jorn Dammann, Alexandra Friedman, Ashley Schneider, and Timothy Shyu.

Comments are welcome. Please send them to jdammann@law.utexas.edu.

Jens Dammann
The University of Texas School of Law
Austin, TX 78703, USA

CHAPTER 1
FUNDAMENTALS

I. The Big Picture

When one person (the plaintiff) sues another (the defendant) the plaintiff asserts a claim against the defendant. Importantly, the law may grant such claims for any number of reasons. When analyzing legal cases, it is essential to distinguish between various potential areas of law a plaintiff may use to hold the defendant liable. Sometimes, multiple grounds for liability may exist in the same case. For example, if a cosmetic surgeon carelessly maims a patient on the operating table, the patient may have both contractual and tort claims against the surgeon. It is essential to clearly distinguish between the claims because different rules apply to claims based on different areas of law. Below are some examples of the areas of law under which a plaintiff may assert a claim.

A. Torts

In a civilized society, some actions that harm your fellow citizens are perfectly acceptable. For example, as a general rule, you can build a house on your property, even if it obstructs your neighbor's view. However, other actions that harm your fellow citizens are illegal, and if you take these actions anyway, you commit a so-called "tort," and you may have to pay damages. For example, you commit a tort if you carelessly kick a soccer ball through your neighbor's window, thereby breaking the glass. In your torts class, you will learn—or you already have learned—more about which actions constitute torts and which ones do not. The critical point to remember is that in case of a tort, we generally make the defendant pay because they have wronged the plaintiff in a way that society deems unacceptable.

B. Contracts

Another reason why the defendant may have to pay money to the plaintiff may lie in a breach of contract. In that case, the defendant must pay because the defendant has promised something and has broken that promise.[1] To put it succinctly, contract law is the law of broken promises.

> **Example.** Assume you have entered into a valid contract with your neighbor, promising not to build any building on your property. If you do so anyway, you are liable for breach of contract. Note that you have not committed a tort. After all, it is generally legal to build on your property. However, you have broken your promise, and for that, you are held liable. In this case, the basis of your liability is not a tort but a so-called breach of contract.
>
> But wait a minute, you could say. Why is there no tort? After all, you have wronged someone, namely your neighbor, by breaking your promise. True, but torts are actions that are wrong regardless of whether a promise was breached. In this case, you have wronged someone only because you broke your promise. That "wrong" is a breach of contract, not a tort.

Could you commit both a tort and a breach of contract at the same time? Of course! Imagine you have entered into a contract to protect another person's house while that person is on vacation, but then you carelessly break a window by kicking a soccer ball through it. In that case, you have breached the contract because you promised to protect the house. At the same time,

1. See, e.g., Wausau Tile, Inc. v. Cnty. Concrete Corp., 593 N.W.2d 445, 451 (Wis. 1999) (noting that "contract law rests on bargained-for obligations, while tort law is based on legal obligations"); Daanen & Janssen, Inc. v. Cedarapids, Inc., 573 N.W.2d 842, 846 (Wis. 1998) ("Contract law rests on obligations imposed by bargain. The law of contracts is designed to effectuate exchanges and to protect the expectancy interests of parties to private bargained-for agreements. . . .The law of torts, on the other hand, rests on obligations imposed by law. Tort law is rooted in the concept of protecting society as a whole from physical harm to person or property.") (internal citation omitted).

you have committed a tort because negligently damaging another person's property constitutes a tort.

As you may have guessed by now, the idea of holding people to their promises is the central concept of the law of contracts. Essentially, a contract is a promise for the breach of which the legal system provides a remedy.[2] We will discuss the word "remedy" later on, but, in straightforward terms, a remedy is anything that the court can do to help "right the wrong." One example of a remedy is awarding the plaintiff damages.

C. Unjust Enrichment

Yet another reason why the plaintiff may have a claim against the defendant lies in the principles governing unjust enrichment. In the case of unjust enrichment, the plaintiff does not base their claim on a contract. Nor does the plaintiff argue that the defendant has wronged them. Instead, the defendant has been enriched at the plaintiff's expense, and we consider this state of affairs to be intolerably unjust.

> **Example.** Assume that someone is lying unconscious on the street, and a physician wanders by and manages to resuscitate them. In that case, there is no contract: the unconscious person never asked to be saved. Furthermore, there is no tort. After all, what did the unconscious person ever do to the physician? However, it would be terribly unfair if the unconscious person did not have to pay the physician for services rendered. Why should the unconscious person get a free ride just because they were unconscious? Furthermore, if the law does not allow the physician to demand payment, the physician might be far less eager to help in the future.

As you may guess, there are many cases where it is not at all obvious whether a particular situation is sufficiently unjust to warrant a claim based on unjust enrichment. Unjust enrichment claims are much rarer than breach of contract claims.

---

2. Restatement (Second) of Contracts § 1.

D. Family Relationships

A COMPLETELY DIFFERENT reason for why someone might owe money lies within a family relationship. For example, a parent may owe child support. In this case, the parent has not wronged the child. Nor has the parent entered into a contract with the child. We cannot even say that the parent is unjustly enriched at the child's expense (however enriching you may find your offspring to be). Instead, the family relationship provides the basis for holding the parent liable.[3]

II. Sources of Law

For the most part, contract law is state law rather than federal law. There are various sources of contract law.

A. Common Law

Much of contract law takes the form of common law. Under the rule of stare decisis, courts are expected to follow the rulings of courts that have decided like cases in the past. These earlier decisions are called "precedents," and a precedent is binding if the court in question must follow that precedent. However, the binding effect of precedents has limits. To start, courts are not bound by the decisions of courts in other jurisdictions.[4] Thus, if a California state court sets a precedent, Texas state courts are not required to follow that precedent. Even within the same jurisdiction, higher courts do not have to follow precedents set by lower courts.[5] Moreover, courts on the same level do

---

3. Cf. Carroll Cnty. Dept. of Soc. Services v. Edelmann, 577 A.2d 14, 23 (Md. 1990) ("By nature and by law, [parenthood] confers rights and imposes duties. One of the most basic of these is the obligation of the parent to support the child until the law determines that he is able to care for himself."); Brooks v. Brooks, 386 So. 2d 472, 474 (Ala. Civ. App. 1980) ("Generally, parents owe a legal duty to support minors because children are unable to, and do not, support themselves, requiring many years for developing, education, training and maturing before they can become reasonably self-sufficient.").

4. E.g., Kott v. City of Fairbanks, 661 P.2d 177, 183 (Alaska 1983); State v. Davis, 12 A.3d 1271, 1274 (N.H. 2010).

5. Cf. Collins v. Cmmw., 824 S.E.2d 485, 491 n.5 (Va. 2019) ("When applied vertically, stare decisis protects the hierarchy of judicial power by precluding a lower court from declaring the law to be any different from what a higher court's case-specific holding has already declared it to be.").

not have to follow each other's precedents.[6] For example, a federal district court is not bound by the precedents of another federal district court.[7] Are courts bound by their own former decisions? That question is more complicated. In principle, high courts and intermediate appellate courts will seek to respect their own precedents.[8] However, given adequate reasons, a court can "overrule" its own precedents,[9] though it should ideally do so only rarely.[10]

B. Statutory Law

Statutes are another import source of contract law. One particularly important example is the Uniform Commercial Code ("UCC"). Article 2 of the UCC governs contracts for the sale of goods, so it is a highly important provision of contract law. The Uniform Commercial Code is state law rather than federal law, and it is "uniform" because most states have a set of identical statutory provisions. The Uniform Commercial Code was drafted under the guidance of the National Conference of Commissioners on Uniform State Laws ("NCCUSL") and the American Law Institute ("ALI").[11] Pennsylvania was the first state to enact the UCC in in 1953, effective July 1, 1954.[12] Other states quickly followed suit. Today, Article 2 of the UCC, which governs the sale of goods, has been enacted in forty-nine states and the District of Columbia, Louisiana being the sole holdout.[13] Louisiana has not enacted Article 2 of the UCC because of its civil law tradition.[14]

---

6. See, e.g., Georgia v. Pres. of the U.S., 46 F.4th 1283, 1304 (11th Cir. 2022) (holding that "one circuit's decisions are not binding on the others, and a district court's decisions do not bind other district courts, other judges on the same court, or even the same judge in another case").
7. See, e.g., Phelps v. State, 532 S.W.3d 437, 443 n. 6 (Tex. App.—Texarkana 2017).
8. E.g., U.S. v. Meyers, 200 F.3d 715, 720 (10th Cir. 2000); Frederick Schauer, Stare Decisis-Rhetoric and Reality in the Supreme Court, 2018 S. Ct. Rev. 121, 125 (2018).
9. E.g., Alaska Pub. Interest Research Group v. State, 167 P.3d 27, 44 (Alaska 2007).
10. Cf. Frederick Schauer, Stare Decisis-Rhetoric and Reality in the Supreme Court, 2018 S. Ct. Rev. 121, 126 (2018) ("the idea of stare decisis is that judges of a court will, presumptively even if not conclusively, follow the previous decisions of that court--by hypothesis and by definition no higher in the judicial hierarchy--even if and when they think the previous decisions are mistaken").
11. E.g., Samuel Williston, The Law of Sales in the Proposed Uniform Commercial Code, 63 Harv. L. Rev. 562, 562 (1950).
12. Pa. Stat. Ann. Tit. 12A (1954).
13. E.g. Larry A. DiMatteo, Fifty Years of Contract Law Scholarship in the American Business Law Journal, 50 Am. Bus. L.J. 105, 158 n. 15 (2013).
14. Id.

C. The Restatement (Second) of Contracts

The Restatement (Second) of Contracts is not a statute. Instead, it is a document that purports to summarize ("restate") existing case law.[15] The Restatement is authored by the American Law Institute, an organization consisting of professors, judges, and other legal scholars. The Restatement is not binding, but it has substantial influence because it is considered an excellent summary of existing case law.[16]

D. International Law

In 1980, various countries, including the United States, entered into a multilateral treaty on the law applicable to sales contracts between persons in different countries. This treaty is called the Convention on Contracts for the International Sale of Goods ("CISG").[17]

When does the CISG apply? Essentially, there are five requirements. First, the transaction must be a sale of goods.[18] Second, both parties must be merchants.[19] Third, both parties must have their place of business in a country that is a party to CISG.[20] Fourth, the parties' places of business must

---

15. Adam J. Levitin et. al., The Faulty Foundation of the Draft Restatement of Consumer Contracts, 36 Yale J. on Reg. 447, 448 (2019).

16. That the Restatement (Second) of Contracts is highly influential is not in doubt. See, e.g., H. Holmes, The Freedom Not to Contract, 60 Tul. L. Rev. 751, 754 (1986) (calling it "the most influential contemporary authority" in the law of contracts). Courts typically characterize the Restatement (Second) of Contracts as persuasive authority. See, e.g., Williamson v. Guentzel, 584 N.W.2d 20, 24 (Minn. App. 1998) ("Restatements of the law are persuasive authority only and are not binding unless specifically adopted in Minnesota by statute or case law."). But see Adam J. Levitin et. al., The Faulty Foundation of the Draft Restatement of Consumer Contracts, 36 Yale J. on Reg. 447, 448–49 (2019) (noting that "[w]hile Restatements purport to simply 'restate' the law, that is to summarize it, they inevitably involve choices about how the law is restated") (internal citation omitted).

17. United Nations Convention on Contracts for the International Sale of Goods, opened for signature Apr. 11, 1980, S. Treaty Doc. No. 98-9 (1983), 1489 U.N.T.S. 3 (eff. Jan. 1, 1988) [hereinafter CISG].

18. CISG art. 1 (1).

19. CISG, art. 2(a) (providing that "This Convention does not apply to sales: (a) of goods bought for personal, family or household use, unless the seller, at any time before or at the conclusion of the contract, neither knew nor ought to have known that the goods were bought for any such use").

20. Id. art. 1(a) (providing that "This Convention applies to contracts of sale of goods between parties whose places of business are in different States: (a) when the States are Contracting States. . .").

be in different countries.[21] For example, CISG does not apply where one U.S. merchant transacts with another U.S. merchant. And fifth, the parties must not have opted out of the CISG.[22] This last requirement is quite significant in practice. Very often, the parties will stipulate in their contract that the substantive law of one of their countries, or even the substantive law of a third country, shall apply.[23] For example, a U.S. merchant and a German merchant may include a provision in their contract stating that the contract shall be governed by English law.

21. Id.

22. Id. art. 6 (providing that "[t]he parties may exclude the application of this Convention").

23. See, e.g., John F. Coyle, The Role of the CISG in U.S. Contract Practice: An Empirical Study, 38 U. Pa. J. Int'l L. 195, 239 (2016) (presenting empirical evidence that "U.S. companies routinely choose to exclude the CISG").

CHAPTER 2
CONTRACT FUNDAMENTALS

I. Introduction

A contract is essentially a promise or a set of promises that the law will enforce.[1] But not every promise creates legally binding obligations. Rather, for a promise to be legally binding, we typically need two elements: mutual assent and consideration.[2]

The parties typically reach mutual assent through offer and acceptance.[3] However, this method is not the only means of achieving mutual assent. For

---

1. See the definition in Restatement (Second) of Contracts § 1. See also Mag Const. Co. v. McLean Cnty., 181 N.W.2d 718, 722 (N.D. 1970) ("A contract is a promise or set of promises, for the breach of which the law gives a remedy, or the performance of which the law recognizes as a duty.")(internal citation omitted).

2. Restatement (Second) of Contracts § 17. See, e.g., Cuppy v. Gen. Acc. Fire & Life Assur. Corp., 378 S.W.2d 629, 632 (Ky. 1964)(holding that "[e]very contract requires mutual assent and consideration")(internal citation omitted); Reichert v. Keefe Commissary Network, L.L.C., No. C17-5848RBL, 2018 WL 2018452, at *1 (W.D. Wash. May 1, 2018)("In order for a promise or set of promises to be legally enforceable, there must be mutual assent and consideration.")(internal citation omitted). There are exceptions to this rule. As we will see in later chapters, there are some cases in which a one-sided promise is binding even though it is not supported by consideration. See Restatement (Second) of Contracts §§ 82-94.

3. Rossi v. U. of Utah, 496 P.3d 105, 112 (Utah 2021); Rucker v. Taylor, 828 N.W.2d 595, 602 (Iowa 2013); Restatement (Second) of Contracts § 22(1). Cf. McMillon v. City of Kalamazoo, 983 N.W.2d 79, 81 (Mich. 2023)(" Mutuality of agreement requires a valid offer and an acceptance."); Angel, Tr. for Gobsmack Gift Tr. v. Tauch, 642 S.W.3d 481, 488 (Tex. 2022), reh'g denied (Apr. 22, 2022) ("Among the most foundational doctrines in the Anglo-American legal tradition is that an offer and an acceptance are two indispensable elements of a binding and enforceable contract.").

example, if a neutral third person suggests an agreement, and both parties simultaneously agree, the mutual assent requirement is satisfied as well.[4]

As a general rule, the formation of a contract also requires "consideration." Consideration requires a bargain, a quid-pro-quo, where each side gives to induce the other side to give.[5]

> **Example.** A promises to paint B's house, and, in return, B promises to pay A $1000. The consideration for A's promise to paint the house is B's promise to pay the $1000 and vice versa.

II. Misunderstandings

The parties typically achieve mutual assent via offer and acceptance.[6] The acceptance must match the offer.[7] To determine if the parties have reached mutual assent, we need to ascertain the meaning of their conduct, including their statements and non-verbal conduct.

> **Example.** Tom asks Bob whether Bob wants to mow Tom's lawn in exchange for $100, and Bob simply nods without saying a word. A contract has been formed, even though Bob has remained entirely silent.

In the best-case scenario, a party's statement expresses exactly what the party means to say. In other words, ideally, the offeror's intended meaning (= the meaning that the offeror wanted his words or conduct to convey) is the same as the objective meaning (= the meaning that a reasonable observer

---

4. Restatement (Second) of Contracts § 22 cmt. a. Cf. Pres. Capital Corp. v. Reale, 652 A.2d 489, 492–93 (Conn. 1994)(holding that "'[a]manifestation of mutual assent may be made even though neither offer nor acceptance can be identified and even though the moment of formation cannot be determined.'")(internal citation omitted).

5. Read Restatement (Second) of Contracts §§ 17, 71(2). See, e.g., Belanger v. Yorke, 226 A.3d 215, 223 (Me. 2020)(holding that a "return promise is bargained for if it is sought by the promisor in exchange for his promise and is given by the promisee in exchange for that promise.")(citing section 71(2) of the Restatement (Second) of Contracts). There are exceptions to this rule. As we will see in later chapters, there are some cases in which a one-sided promise is binding even though it is not supported by consideration. See Restatement (Second) of Contracts §§ 82-94.

6. Rossi v. U. of Utah, 496 P.3d 105, 112 (Utah 2021); Rucker v. Taylor, 828 N.W.2d 595, 602 (Iowa 2013); Restatement (Second) of Contracts § 22(1).

7. E.g., Shell Oil Co. v. Kelinson, 158 N.W.2d 724, 728 (Iowa 1968); Restatement (Second) of Contracts § 50 (1).

with the same information as the other party would attribute to the offeror's words or conduct).

However, sometimes, the intended meaning and the objective meaning diverge. In that case, the governing legal principle depends on whether the other party has or has not understood the speaker's intended meaning.

If the other party has correctly understood what the speaker meant to say, the law looks to the intended rather than the objective meaning.[8] After all, if both parties share the same understanding—even one that deviates from the objective meaning—there is no reason for the law to impose a meaning that differs from the parties' shared understanding. It is a foundational principle of interpretation that if one party correctly understands the other party's intended meaning, that meaning is the one that counts. In later chapters, we will see that this principle does not necessarily hold in the case of written contracts. The reason is that legal writings are meant to promote legal certainty. However, without a written contract, there is no basis for dismissing a shared understanding in interpreting a contract.

In the second scenario, the parties do not understand each other correctly. For example, the offeror may "offer to sell his used statutory supplement for $10" and may mean U.S. dollars, whereas the offeree may think the offer refers to Australian dollars. In that case, a misunderstanding between the parties exists, and the law has to decide which, if any, of the two meanings prevails.

The law's intuitive solution is to focus on whether one or both parties can be blamed for the misunderstanding.[9] Assume that there are two parties, Alpha and Beta. If Alpha understood Beta's intended meaning, but Beta was unaware of Alpha's intended meaning, Beta's intended meaning prevails.[10] Similarly, if neither party knew of the other's intended meaning, but Alpha had reason to know what Beta meant, whereas Beta had no reason to know

8. Restatement (Second) of Contracts § 21 (1). This become more complicated when the agreement is in writing, an issue that we will discuss in context with the so-called parol evidence rule.
9. Read Restatement (Second) of Contracts § 21 (1).
10. Read Restatement (Second) of Contracts § 21 (1). See, e.g., Toysrus.com, L.L.C. v. Amazon.com Kids, Inc., No. A-3391-06T2, 2009 WL 747898, at *17 (N.J. Super. App. Div. Mar. 24, 2009) (holding that a "court can construe a contract in accord with an objectively reasonable meaning that is in fact held by the first party while the second party knew or had reason to know that the first party held such an understanding"); United Rentals, Inc. v. RAM Holdings, Inc., 937 A.2d 810, 836 (Del. Ch. 2007)(holding that "a court may consider the subjective understanding of one party that has been objectively manifested and is known or should be known by the other party").

what Alpha meant, Beta's meaning is the one that counts.[11] The principle of favoring the "innocent" party in these situations is known as the "forthright negotiator principle."[12]

Question. Alpha and Omega are Austin residents, and they negotiate the sale of a used car. Alpha offers to sell the car for "ten dollars" and means U.S. dollars. Omega, who has just returned from his vacation in Sydney, thinks that Alpha is referring to Australian dollars. Which meaning prevails?

Answer. The term "dollars" has to be interpreted as referring to U.S. dollars. Because the contract is being negotiated in Austin, Texas, and both parties are Austin residents, Alpha had no reason to think that Omega would understand the term dollar to refer to Australian dollars. On the other hand, Omega should have understood that it was referring to U.S. dollars. Therefore, Alpha's intended meaning ("U.S. dollars") prevails.

What if both parties are equally blameless or blameworthy? For example, each party should have understood what the other meant. Or neither party had reason to understand what the other party meant. Given that in these situations, there is no reason to prefer one party's intended meaning over the other party's intended meaning, neither of the parties' meanings prevails, and no contract is formed.[13]

Question. Alpha and Beta are Houston merchants. Alpha offers to sell Beta "all of the grain loaded on the ship *Last Hope* that is currently traveling from Hamburg, Germany, to Galveston, Texas, for $10,000,000." Beta answers, "I accept." Neither party knew or had reason to know that two ships fit this description, one sailing under the Panamanian flag, the other sailing under

---

11. Read Restatement (Second) of Contracts § 21 (1).

12. E.g., Toysrus.com, L.L.C. v. Amazon.com Kids, Inc., No. A-3391-06T2, 2009 WL 747898, at *17; United Rentals, Inc. v. RAM Holdings, Inc., 937 A.2d 810, 836 (Del. Ch. 2007); GOT I, LLC v. XRT, Inc., No. 1:16-CV-38-MHC, 2019 WL 12529019, at *1 (N.D. Ga. Mar. 11, 2019).

13. Restatement (Second) of Contracts § 21 (1). See, e.g., Hill-Shafer Partn. v. Chilson Fam. Tr., 799 P.2d 810, 816 (Ariz. 1990)(holding that "[a]s long as the misunderstandings of the parties are reasonable under the specific circumstances of the case, a court may properly find a lack of mutual assent"); Roach v. Caudle, No. S-10657, 2004 WL 42600, at *6 (Alaska Jan. 7, 2004)(holding that "[a] material misunderstanding may prevent the formation of a contract when 'the parties meant materially different things and neither knew or had reason to know of the others' meaning, or if each knew or had reason to know of the others' meaning'")(internal citation omitted).

the Peruvian flag. Alpha meant the ship sailing under the Panamanian flag. Beta meant the ship sailing under the Peruvian flag. Have the parties formed a contract?

Answer. At first glance, it may look like the parties had reached mutual assent via offer and acceptance. However, there is a misunderstanding between the parties, and neither party can be blamed. Therefore, neither meaning prevails, and no mutual assent has been reached.

Considering the different scenarios, you will arrive at the following rules for interpreting a party's statement.

Alpha	Beta	Which meaning prevails?
Alpha meant X.	Beta understood that Alpha meant X.	X
Alpha meant X and had no reason to believe Beta had a different understanding.	Beta thought that Alpha meant Y and had no reason to think that Alpha had a different understanding.	Neither
Alpha meant X and had no reason to believe Beta would have a different understanding.	Beta thought that Alpha meant Y but should have known that Alpha meant X.	X
Alpha meant X and had no reason to believe Beta would have a different understanding.	Beta thought that Alpha meant Y and had no reason to think that Alpha had a different understanding.	Neither
Alpha meant X but should have realized that Beta would understand Alpha's statement to mean Y.	Beta thought that Alpha meant Y and had no reason to think that Alpha had a different understanding.	Y
Alpha meant X but should have realized that Beta would understand Alpha's statement to mean Y.	Beta thought that Alpha meant Y but should have known that Alpha meant X.	Neither

Of course, these rules may require you to figure out what the parties "should have" understood. What the parties should have understood is what we call the "objective" or "reasonable" meaning. That is because each party can be expected to behave reasonably, and so the meaning that a reasonable observer with the same information as a particular party *would have* attached is the meaning that that party *should have* attached.[14] One more practice question may help to illustrate this point further.

Question. S owns two houses. One house is located on First Street and is painted blue. The other is located on Second Street and is painted green. Unfortunately, S is colorblind and thinks the house on First Street is green and the house on Second Street is blue. The house on First Street is worth about $1,000,000. The house on Second Street is worth about $2,000,000.

S decides to sell the house on First Street. He sends B a letter offering to sell "the green house" for $1,000,000. B is aware of S's mistake and knows that S wants to sell the house on First Street. He writes back: "I accept your offer to sell me your house on First Street for $1,000,000." Have the parties reached mutual assent?

Answer. The answer is "yes." In the case at hand, mutual assent exists even though "objectively" offer and acceptance do not seem to refer to the same thing.

Consider, first, the meaning we must attach to S's offer. Because B was aware of the meaning intended by S—he knew that S wanted to sell the house on First Street—, there was no misunderstanding. The intended meaning (=offer to sell the house on First Street) trumps the objectively reasonable meaning (= offer to sell the house on Second Street).

Next, consider B's acceptance. The reasonable meaning of B's letter is that B wanted to buy the house on First Street, and there is no reason to deviate from this reasonable meaning since it is also the intended meaning. Therefore, B's acceptance matches S's offer.

---

14. See, e.g., Glob. Modular, Inc. v. Kadena P., Inc., 222 Cal. Rptr. 3d 819, 828 (Cal. App. 4th Dist. 2017)(defining the "objectively reasonable meaning" as "what [the party] should have understood the [contract] to mean at the time of contracting").

CHAPTER 3
OFFER

An offer is the manifestation of a will to enter into a contract.[1] In practice, determining the existence of an offer can be challenging. One common challenge is determining whether a party wanted to enter into a contract or merely intended a social obligation. Another is to distinguish offers from statements and inquiries of a merely preliminary nature that are made in preparation of a later contract. Finally, there may be cases where the speaker was only trying to make a joke, but the other party thought they were speaking in earnest.

I. Social obligations

Commitments among family members and friends are often meant to create mere social obligations and are not enforceable as contracts. For example, if you promise your friend to come to a party or if you promise your parents to travel home for Thanksgiving, you probably do not expect to be taken to court if you fail to show up, and it would not be reasonable for the promisee to interpret your conduct as intending a legal commitment. However, the reasonable interpretation depends on the circumstances of the individual case. Factors such as a promise's economic importance, its formal nature, or

1. See Restatement (Second) of Contracts § 24

its potential to induce reliance on the part of the promisee, may all point in the direction of a legal promise rather than a merely social one.

II. Preliminary Statements

Sometimes parties expect to enter into a contract in the future but are still conducting preliminary negotiations. In other words, they are not yet ready to enter into a binding agreement. If, under the general principles of interpretation, a statement is merely preliminary in nature, it does not constitute an offer.[2]

> **Example.** Alpha wants to buy a car. The dealer shows Alpha various models (without indicating prices), and they talk about one particular used SUV. Alpha asks the dealer whether they might be willing to part with it for a price below $2,000. In this scenario, unless both parties understood Alpha's question to be an offer, Alpha has not made an offer. That is because a reasonable party in the dealer's shoes would understand that Alpha is merely trying to gather information. After all, Alpha has not even named a specific price. Moreover, even after learning the price, a typical buyer will often want to discuss other matters such as warranties before making a purchasing decision.

A. Written contracts

Distinguishing preliminary statements from offers can be particularly challenging if the parties have expressed the intention to commit their agreement to writing. In such cases, the parties frequently negotiate the content orally before drawing up a written document. Accordingly, the question arises of whether or not a binding agreement exists before the parties sign the document. To resolve this question, you should proceed in two steps.[3]

First, ask yourself whether the parties both intended the same thing: if both parties wanted to be bound before they signed the document, mutual assent has been reached. If neither party meant for the oral agreement to be binding prior to the signing of the written document, the parties' oral agreement does not constitute a contract.

---

2. Restatement (Second) of Contracts § 26.
3. Cf. Restatement (Second) of Contracts § 21.

Second, if the parties differed concerning how they perceived the agreement, you apply the reasonable person standard: how would a reasonable person have interpreted the parties' behavior? Would a reasonable observer have concluded that the parties wanted their oral statements to be binding even before the written document was set up or not?

B. Invitation to make offers

Sometimes conduct aimed at creating a contract does not constitute an offer but merely an invitation to make an offer ("invitatio ad offerendum"). There are no hard and fast rules as to when a statement constitutes an invitation to make offers and when it constitutes an offer. Advertisements in newspapers or other media are typically mere invitations to make offers.[4] But depending on the circumstances, a different interpretation may be warranted.[5]

> **Example.** Alpha runs an ad in the local newspaper announcing that Alpha wants to sell their 1992 Ford Escort for a price of $2000. If this advertisement were interpreted as an offer, Alpha might open his mailbox to find that hundreds of willing buyers have accepted his offer, meaning that Alpha would have contractual obligations to all of them. Obviously, this is not what Alpha intended. Therefore, a reasonable observer would understand Alpha was merely inviting readers to submit offers to buy the car.

C. Incomplete Statements

What if someone expresses the desire to enter into a contract but fails to clarify all the terms that the contract is supposed to have? For example, what if you "offer" to sell your car for $2000 but do not state when you are willing to deliver it? Such situations present two problems.

First and foremost, there is the question of whether the court will find an offer to have been made. If a statement does not mention essential terms of the intended contract—such as the type of service to be rendered—a reason-

---

4. Id. § 33 ct. c.
5. See Lefkowitz v. Great Minneapolis Surplus Store, Inc., 86 N.W.2d 689, 692 (Minn. 1957) (holding that an advertisement listing various goods and their prices and stating "first come, first served" constituted an offer).

person *may* well have to conclude that the "offeror" does not want to enter into a bargain quite yet. Read section 33(3) of the Restatement (Second) of Contracts.

This rule makes a lot of sense. For example, assume that a used-car dealer shows you a car, and even before the dealer has mentioned the price, you state that you "really like the car" and want to buy it. In this case, a reasonable person would presumably conclude that despite expressing your intention to buy the car, you did not want to make an offer at this point.

So how do you know if the potential offeror wanted to make an offer or not? As always, you need to look at all the facts of the case. The more incomplete a statement is, the less likely it is to constitute an offer in the legal sense.

Assume that the court concludes that the offeror's conduct manifests the will to enter into a contract even though the offer was incomplete. Can the offeree create an enforceable contract by accepting such an offer? For example, assume that someone offers to rent an apartment without specifying the rent, the street, or even the city. Read sections 33(1) and 33(2) of the Restatement (Second) of Contracts.

III. Jokes

Sometimes, what appears to be an offer may simply be intended as a joke. In that case, the general principles on interpretation apply. In effect, this means that the conflict between different meanings is resolved at the expense of the more blameworthy party.[6]

> **Example.** George, a law student, meets his old college buddy Joe, who, instead of attending law school, joined a high-tech startup. To George's chagrin, George drives a battered old Ford, whereas Joe drives a sleek new Maserati. Joe notices George's distraught look and jokingly says: "Hey, how about a deal: my Maserati for your Ford." Without hesitation, George responds, "Deal. Here are the keys." Have the parties formed a contract? The answer is no because in light of the circumstances and the difference in price, George either knew or should have known that Joe was only joking. Hence, there is no offer.

6. See Restatement (Second) of Contracts § 21(1) (summarizing the relevant rules).

Example. Assume that Alpha "offers" to sell Beta his 1973 Volkswagen Beetle for $400. Alpha is only joking and expects Beta to understand the joke. However, Beta takes Alpha's words seriously and says, "I accept." Have the parties formed a contract? The answer is yes. A price of $400 is not all that unusual for an old car. Therefore, barring particular circumstances that should have alerted Beta to the fact that Alpha was only joking, there is a valid offer.

Lonergan v. Scolnick

California District Court of Appeal, 129 Cal.App.2d 179 (1955)

BARNARD, Presiding Justice.

This is an action for specific performance or for damages in the event specific performance was impossible.

The complaint alleged that on April 15, 1952, the parties entered into a contract whereby the defendant agreed to sell, and plaintiff agreed to buy a 40-acre tract of land for $2,500; that this was a fair, just and reasonable value of the property; that on April 28, 1952, the defendant repudiated the contract and refused to deliver a deed; that on April 28, 1952, the property was worth $6,081; and that plaintiff has been damaged in the amount of $3,581. The answer denied that any contract had been entered into, or that anything was due to the plaintiff.

By stipulation, the issue of whether or not a contract was entered into between the parties was first tried, reserving the other issues for a further trial if that became necessary. The issue as to the existence of a contract was submitted upon an agreed statement, including certain letters between the parties, without the introduction of other evidence.

The stipulated facts are as follows: During March, 1952, the defendant placed an ad in a Los Angeles paper reading, so far as material here, 'Joshua Tree vic. 40 acres, * * * need cash, will sacrifice.' In response to an inquiry resulting from this ad the defendant, who lived in New York, wrote a letter to the plaintiff dated March 26, briefly describing the property, giving directions as to how to get there, stating that his rock-bottom price was $2,500 cash, and further stating that 'This is a form letter.' On April 7, the plaintiff wrote a letter to the defendant saying that he was not sure he had found the property, asking for its legal description, asking whether the land was all level or whether it included certain jutting rock hills, and suggesting a certain bank as escrow agent 'should I desire to purchase the land.' On April 8, the defendant wrote to the plaintiff saying 'From your description you have found the property'; that this bank 'is O.K. for escrow agent'; that the land was fairly level; giving the legal description; and then saying, 'If you are really interested, you will have to decide fast, as I expect to have a buyer in the next week or so.' On April 12, the defendant sold the property to a third party for $2,500. The plaintiff received the defendant's letter of April 8 on April 14. On April 15 he wrote to the defendant thanking him for his letter 'confirming that I was on the right land', stating that he would immediately proceed to have the escrow opened and would deposit $2,500 therein 'in conformity with your offer', and asking the defendant to forward a deed with his instructions to the escrow agent. On April 17, 1952, the plaintiff started an escrow and placed in the hands of the escrow agent $100, agreeing to furnish an additional $2,400 at an unspecified time, with the provision that if the escrow was not closed by May 15, 1952, it should be completed as soon thereafter as possible unless a written demand for a return of the money or instruments was made by either party after that date. It was further stipulated that the plaintiff was ready and willing at all times to deposit the $2,400.

The matter was submitted on June 11, 1953. On July 10, 1953, the judge filed a memorandum opinion stating that it was his opinion that the letter of April 8, 1952, when considered with the previous correspondence, constituted an offer of sale which offer was, however, qualified and conditioned upon prompt acceptance by the plaintiff; that in spite of the condition thus imposed, the plaintiff delayed more than a week before notifying the defendant of his acceptance; and that since the plaintiff was aware of the necessity of promptly communicating his acceptance to the defendant his delay was not the prompt action required by the terms of the offer. Findings of fact were filed on October 2, 1953, finding that each and all of the statements in the agreed statement are true, and that all allegations to the contrary in the complaint are untrue. As conclusions of law, it was found that the plaintiff and defendant did not enter into a contract as alleged in the complaint or otherwise, and that the defendant is entitled to judgment against the plaintiff. Judgment was entered accordingly, from which the plaintiff has appealed.

The appellant contends that the judgment is contrary to the evidence and to the law since the facts, as found, do not support the conclusions of law upon which the judgment is based. . . . In his briefs the appellant assumes that an offer was made by the defendant, and confined his argument to contending that the evidence shows that he accepted that offer within a reasonable time.

There can be no contract unless the minds of the parties have met and mutually agreed upon some specific thing. This is usually evidenced by one party making an offer which is accepted by the other party. Section 25 of the Restatement of the Law on Contracts reads:

'If from a promise, or manifestation of intention, or from the circumstances existing at the time, the person to whom the promise or manifestation is addressed knows or has reason to know that the person making it does not intend it as an expression of his fixed purpose until he has given a further expression of assent, he has not made an offer.'

The language used in Niles v. Hancock, 140 Cal. 157, 73 P. 840, 842, 'It is also clear from the correspondence that it was the intention of the defendant that the negotiations between him and the plaintiff were to be purely preliminary,' is applicable here. The correspondence here indicates an intention on the part of the defendant to find out whether the plaintiff was interested, rather than an intention to make a definite offer to the plaintiff. The language used by the defendant in his letters of March 26 and April 8 rather clearly discloses that they were not intended as an expression of fixed purpose to make a definite offer, and was sufficient to advise the plaintiff that some further expression of assent on the part of the defendant was necessary.

The advertisement in the paper was a mere request for an offer. The letter of March 26 contains no definite offer, and clearly states that it is a form letter. It merely gives further particulars, in clarification of the advertisement, and tells the plaintiff how to locate the property if he was interested in looking into the matter. The letter of April 8 added nothing in the way of a definite offer. It merely answered some questions asked by the plaintiff, and stated that if the plaintiff was really interested he would have to act fast. The statement that he expected to have a buyer in the next week or so indicated that the defendant intended to sell to the first-comer, and was reserving the right to do so. From this statement, alone, the plaintiff knew or should have known that he was not being given time in which to accept an offer that was being made, but that some further assent on the part of the defendant was required. Under the language used the plaintiff was not being given a right to act within a reasonable time after receiving the letter; he was plainly told that the defendant intended to sell to another, if possible, and warned that he would have to act fast if he was interested in buying the land.

Regardless of any opinion previously expressed, the court found that no contract had been entered into between these parties, and we are in accord with the court's conclusion on that controlling issue. The court's construction of the letters involved was a reasonable one, and we think the most reasonable one, even if it be assumed that another construction was possible.

The judgment is affirmed.

GRIFFIN and MUSSELL, JJ., concur.

NOTES AND QUESTIONS

*A. **Specific performance.*** The Lonergan court notes that the case "is an action for specific performance or for damages in the event specific performance was impossible." In contract law, damages are the general remedy, while specific performance is granted only if damages are deemed inadequate.[7] One significant application of this rule involves contracts for the sale of land. Because land is considered unique, damages are insufficient to compensate the buyer.[8] Consequently, the buyer is generally entitled to specific performance.[9] What accounts for the impossibility of specific performance in Lonergan?

B. Consideration. The formation of a contract generally requires mutual assent and consideration.[10] Mutual assent is typically achieved via offer and acceptance, and the acceptance must match the offer.[11] Consideration requires a bargain ("quid-pro-quo").[12] If a contract had been formed in Lonergan, the promise to convey the land would have served as consideration for the promise to pay the purchase price and vice versa.

C. Invitation to make offers. An offer requires the manifestation of an intent to enter into a contract.[13] Advertisements in newspapers or other media do

7. See Restatement (Second) of Contracts § 359(1).
8. Id. § 360 ct. e.
9. Id.
10. See id. § 17
11. See id. §§ 22; 50 (1).
12. Id. §§ 71, 72.
13. See id. § 24.

not usually constitute offers; rather, they merely invite readers to make offers.[14] Several arguments support this conclusion. First, the advertising party is typically interested in limiting the number of contracts they enter into. For example, a landlord advertising an apartment for rent may be looking for only one tenant. If the advertisement constituted an offer, it could be accepted by multiple parties, creating contracts that the advertising party has no hope of fulfilling. Second, many advertisements involve situations in which the advertising party reasonably wants to gather additional information about potential contractual parties before deciding whether or not to enter into a contract. To continue our previous example, the landlord may want to check an applicant's references and credit history before accepting them as a tenant. Third, considering an advertisement's space and design constraints, the advertiser often has an interest in concluding a contract with a more complete set of contractual terms.[15]

D. Preliminary statements. Statements of a preliminary nature that merely prepare the bargain do not constitute offers.[16] The Lonergan court notes that the language used in the letters dated March 26 and April 8 "rather clearly discloses that they were not intended" as offers. Do you share the court's view? Why or why not?

E. Meeting of the minds. The Lonergan court states that "[t]here can be no contract unless the minds of the parties have met." That is a common way of referring to the mutual assent requirement, but is this expression potentially misleading?

---

14. See id. § § 33 ct. c; but see Lefkowitz v. Great Minneapolis Surplus Store, Inc., 86 N.W.2d 689, 692 (Minn. 1957) (holding that an advertisement listing various goods and their prices and stating "first come, first served" constituted an offer).

15. See id. § 33 ct. c.

16. See id. § 24.

CHAPTER 4
ACCEPTANCE BY PROMISE

I. Introduction

Mutual assent is typically reached through offer and acceptance.[1] An acceptance is the offeree's manifestation of his assent to the offer's terms.[2] To form a contract, the acceptance must occur in a manner that the offeror has either invited or required.[3]

II. The Matching Principle

Under the matching principle, the acceptance must assent to the offer's terms.

---

1. Rossi v. U. of Utah, 496 P.3d 105, 112 (Utah 2021); Rucker v. Taylor, 828 N.W.2d 595, 602 (Iowa 2013); Restatement (Second) of Contracts § 22(1). Cf. McMillon v. City of Kalamazoo, 983 N.W.2d 79, 81 (Mich. 2023) ("Mutuality of agreement requires a valid offer and an acceptance."); Angel, Tr. for Gobsmack Gift Tr. v. Tauch, 642 S.W.3d 481, 488 (Tex. 2022), reh'g denied (Apr. 22, 2022) ("Among the most foundational doctrines in the Anglo-American legal tradition is that an offer and an acceptance are two indispensable elements of a binding and enforceable contract.").
2. E.g., Rossi v. U. of Utah, 496 P.3d 105, 112 (Utah 2021) (internal citation omitted); Valdez Fisheries Dev. Ass'n, Inc. v. Alyeska Pipeline Serv. Co., 45 P.3d 657, 666 (Alaska 2002) (internal citation omitted); Fed. Nat. Mortg. Ass'n v. Hafer, 351 P.3d 622, 630 (Idaho 2015) (internal citation omitted); Indus. Products Intern., Inc. v. Emo Trans, Inc., 962 P.2d 983, 988 (Colo. App. 1997), as modified on denial of reh'g (Dec. 26, 1997) (internal citation omitted); Gaskins v. Swope Ventures, Inc., 645 F. Supp. 3d 682, 687 (W.D. Ky. 2022), appeal dismissed (May 19, 2023) (internal citation omitted); Restatement (Second) of Contracts § 50(1);
3. E.g., Fed. Nat. Mortg. Ass'n v. Hafer, 351 P.3d 622, 630 (Idaho 2015); Restatement (Second) of Contracts § 50(1).

The offeree has not accepted if the offeree's acceptance is conditioned upon the offeror assenting to different or additional terms. Instead, the offeree's reply constitutes a so-called counteroffer, that is, a rejection of the original offer coupled with a new offer.[4]

The matching principle must be applied carefully. If the offeree's reply *insists* on different or additional terms, it constitutes a counter-offer, not an acceptance. In contrast, if the offeree's reply expresses unconditional assent to the offer and merely *suggests* additional or different terms, the offeree has accepted the offer.[5] In that case, the offeree both accepts the offer's terms—thereby creating a contract—and creates an offer to modify that contract through the suggestion of different or additional terms. It is up to the original offeror to decide whether to accept this offer to modify the contract.

Example. Alpha offers to paint Beta's house in exchange for $2000. Beta replies: "OK, but only if you agree to use only eco-friendly paint." Have the parties reached mutual assent? No. Alpha has made an offer. However, Beta's reply has insisted on an additional term concerning the use of eco-friendly paint. Therefore, Beta's response is not an acceptance but a counteroffer. Unless Alpha accepts this counteroffer, no contract is formed.

Example. Alpha offers to paint Beta's house in exchange for $2000. Beta replies: "OK, you have a deal. By the way, it would be truly awesome if you could agree to use only eco-friendly paint." Have the parties reached mutual assent? Yes. Alpha has made an offer, and Beta has accepted that offer without insisting on additional or different terms. Admittedly, Beta has suggested using eco-friendly paint, but this is a mere suggestion, which does not call Beta's unconditional acceptance into question.

---

4. E.g., Unified Sch. Dist. No. 446, Indep., Kansas v. Sandoval, 286 P.3d 542, 546 (Kan. 2012); Restatement (Second) of Contracts § 59(1).

5. See, e.g., Agema v. City of Allegan, 826 F.3d 326, 333 (6th Cir. 2016) (holding that "when there is an unequivocal acceptance that makes additional requests, the acceptance is still valid"); John's Insulation, Inc. v. Siska Const. Co., Inc., 671 F. Supp. 289, 293 (S.D.N.Y. 1987) (holding that requests or suggestions do not turn an acceptance into a counteroffer); Figueroa v. Prospct Billiards Corp., No. 118CV2144VECKHP, 2019 WL 3415985, at *4 (S.D.N.Y. July 12, 2019), report and recommendation adopted sub nom. Figueroa v. Prospect Billiards Corp., No. 18-CV-2144 (VEC), 2019 WL 3408867 (S.D.N.Y. July 29, 2019) (holding that suggestions, requests, or overtures are not counteroffers).

The distinction between a counteroffer and an unconditional acceptance combined with an offer to modify the contract matters beyond the question of whether the offeree's reply creates a contract. It also has important implications for how we interpret the original offeror's subsequent conduct.

If the offeree's reply constituted a counteroffer rather than an acceptance and the original offeror—who is now the counterofferee—nonetheless renders his performance, the counterofferee's performance can be viewed as an acceptance of the counteroffer.[6] After all, if the counterofferee did want to accept the counteroffer, why would they render their performance.

By contrast, if the offeree has accepted the offeror's offer and has merely suggested different or additional terms, then the original offeror's subsequent performance typically does not amount to an acceptance of the suggested different or additional terms. After all, the original offeror now has a contractual obligation to perform. Therefore, it makes sense for the offeror to perform even if the offeror has no intention to assent to the different or additional terms suggested by the offeree. Accordingly, we can interpret the offeror's performance as an acceptance of any suggested different or additional terms only if exceptional circumstances justify such an interpretation.

> **Example.** Alpha offers to paint Beta's house in exchange for $2000. Beta replies: "OK, but only if you agree to use eco-friendly paint." The next day, Alpha starts painting Beta's house. Is there a contract, and, if so, does that contract include a duty to use eco-friendly paint?
>
> Alpha made an offer to paint Beta's house. Instead of accepting that offer, Beta insisted on an additional term concerning the use of eco-friendly paint and thereby made a counteroffer. When Alpha began to paint Beta's house, he thereby made it clear that he wanted to accept Beta's counteroffer. After all, why else would he have started painting the house? Therefore, Alpha's performance created a contract based on Beta's counteroffer, and since this contract was based on Beta's counteroffer, it included a duty to use eco-friendly paint. This answer would not change if Alpha failed to use eco-friendly paint. Instead, using "regular" paint constitutes a breach of contract.

---

6. See, e.g., AAA Const. of Missoula, LLC v. Choice Land Corp., 264 P.3d 709, 714 (Mont. 2011) (holding that if party's reply constituted a counteroffer, counterofferee "accepted that counteroffer through its performance of its contractual obligations"); Long v. Allen, 906 P.2d 754, 756 (N.M. App. 1995) (holding that performance amounted to acceptance of counteroffer).

Example. Alpha offers to paint Beta's house in exchange for $2000. Beta replies: "OK, you have a deal. By the way, it would be truly awesome if you could agree to use only eco-friendly paint." The next day, Alpha starts painting Beta's house. Is there a contract, and, if so, does that contract include a duty to use eco-friendly paint?

Have the parties reached mutual assent? Yes. Alpha has made an offer, and Beta has accepted that offer without insisting on additional or different terms. Admittedly, Beta has suggested using eco-friendly paint, but this is a mere suggestion, which does not call Beta's unconditional acceptance into question.

But did the additional term concerning the eco-friendly paint become part of the contract? No. Alpha had a contractual obligation to paint Beta's house. Therefore, absent exceptional circumstances, the fact that Alpha painted Beta's house does not indicate that Alpha wanted to assent to Beta's additional term.

III. The Power of Acceptance

The offer bestows on the offeree the so-called power of acceptance.[7] The power of acceptance is the power to create a contract by accepting the offer. Unsurprisingly, there are various ways to terminate the power of acceptance. They include the death of either party, either party's loss of capacity to enter into contracts, lapse of time, direct or indirect revocation, rejection, and counteroffer.[8]

A. Death or Incapacity

Either party's death or loss of capacity to contract terminates the offeree's

7. Foxboro Co., Inc. v. Soft Sys. Engr., Inc., 894 F. Supp. 48, 51 (D. Mass. 1995); McClure Ins. Agency v. Hudson, 377 S.W.2d 814, 816 (Ark. 1964); Ellison v. Premier Salons Intern., Inc., 164 F.3d 1111, 1114 (8th Cir. 1999); Restatement (Second) of Contracts § 35.

8. E.g., Great Lakes Commun. Corp. v. AT&T Corp., 124 F. Supp. 3d 824, 836 (N.D. Iowa 2015); Restatement (Second) of Contracts § 36.

power of acceptance.[9] For example, a person loses the capacity to contract if they are placed under guardianship.[10]

B. Lapse of time

The offeror is the master of the offer.[11] Accordingly, the offer can impose a deadline for accepting the offer.[12] If the offer does not specify the time for acceptance, the offeree has a reasonable time to accept the offer.[13] A reasonable time depends on the circumstances.[14] For example, if you are dealing with services for which the price typically changes quickly, the "reasonable time" will be very short. Once the time for acceptance has passed, the power of acceptance terminates.[15]

> **Question.** Alpha sends a letter to Beta, offering to paint Beta's house for $3000. Beta reads the letter and mails their acceptance the next day. Assuming that the applicable common law corresponds exactly to the Restatement (Second) of Contracts, have the parties formed a contract?
>
> **Answer.** The formation of a contract requires mutual assent and consideration. Mutual assent is typically achieved via offer and acceptance. Alpha made an offer, and Beta attempted to accept that offer. However, the question is

---

9. Restatement (Second) of Contracts § 48. See, e.g., De Kovessey v. Coronet Properties Co., 508 N.E.2d 652, 655 (N.Y. 1987) (holding that offeree's death terminates power of acceptance); J. L. Lester & Son, Inc. v. Smith, 280 S.E.2d 732, 733 (Ga. 1981) (holding that power of acceptance is terminated by death of offeror and death of offeree); Union Tr. and Sav. Bank v. State Bank, 188 N.W.2d 300, 304 (Iowa 1971) (holding that appointment of conservator terminated power of acceptance); J.L. Prop. Owners Assn., Inc. v. Schnurr, 336 So. 3d 291, 301 (Fla. 4th Dist. App. 2022) (holding that death of either offeror or offeree terminates power of acceptance).
10. Restatement (Second) of Contracts § 12.
11. Auto Glass Exp., Inc. v. Hanover Ins. Co., 975 A.2d 1266, 1273 (Conn. 2009); Van Schoiack v. U.S. Liab. Ins. Co., 133 A.2d 509, 514 (Pa. 1957).
12. Childs v. Adams, 909 S.W.2d 641, 645 (Ark. 1995); Est. of Cox by Cox v. Dunakey & Klatt, P.C., 893 N.W.2d 295, 303 (Iowa 2017); Restatement (Second) of Contracts § 41(1).
13. Arduini v. Bd. of Educ. of Pontiac Tp. High Sch., Dist. 90, Livingston Cnty., 441 N.E.2d 73, 76 (Ill. 1982); Provencal v. Vermont Mut. Ins. Co., 571 A.2d 276, 278 (N.H. 1990); Keller v. Bones, 615 N.W.2d 883, 888 (Neb. 2000); Scoular Co. v. Denney, 151 P.3d 615, 618 (Colo. App. 2006), as modified on denial of reh'g (Dec. 14, 2006); Restatement (Second) of Contracts § 41(1).
14. Provencal v. Vermont Mut. Ins. Co., 571 A.2d 276, 278 (N.H. 1990); Restatement (Second) of Contracts § 41(2).
15. Est. of Cox by Cox v. Dunakey & Klatt, P.C., 893 N.W.2d 295, 303 (Iowa 2017); Keller v. Bones, 615 N.W.2d 883, 888 (Neb. 2000); Restatement (Second) of Contracts § 41(1).

whether Beta's power of acceptance had already been terminated by lapse of time. An offer that does not specify the time for acceptance can be accepted within a reasonable time, and what is reasonable depends on the circumstances. Here, Alpha made an offer to paint a house, and providers of that service do not usually change their prices on a daily basis. Moreover, nothing in Alpha's offer conveyed any sense of urgency. Therefore, it was reasonable for Beta to accept the next day. Moreover, that conclusion is not called into question by the rule in section 41(3) of the Restatement (Second) of Contracts. According to section 41(3), if the offeror sent his offer by mail, an acceptance mailed on the same day that the offer was received is reasonable unless the circumstances indicate otherwise. This rule is only meant to create a safe haven: if the acceptance is mailed before midnight, it is reasonable. Conversely, section 41(3) is not meant to imply that accepting offers at a later time is unreasonable.

C. Revocation

As a general rule, the offeror can terminate the offeree's power of acceptance by revoking their offer.[16] The law distinguishes between direct and indirect revocation.

A direct revocation occurs if and when the offeree receives a communication from the offeror indicating that the offeror is no longer willing to enter into the contract.[17] Direct revocation takes effect on receipt, not on dispatch.[18]

Question. Alpha offers Beta to paint Beta's house for $100. The next day, Alpha regrets his offer and mails a letter revoking the offer. Before Beta receives the letter, but after Alpha had dispatched the letter, Beta calls Alpha and tells him he accepts Alpha's offer. Have the parties formed a contract?

---

16. E.g., Angel, Tr. for Gobsmack Gift Tr. v. Tauch, 642 S.W.3d 481, 488 (Tex. 2022), reh'g denied (Apr. 22, 2022)("If an offeror revokes an offer before acceptance, the offeree's power of acceptance terminates."); Normile v. Miller, 326 S.E.2d 11, 18 (N.C. 1985) (holding that "[i]t is a fundamental tenet of the common law that an offer is generally freely revocable"); Restatement (Second) of Contracts §§ 36(1)(c), 42, 43.

17. E.g., Angel, Tr. for Gobsmack Gift Tr. v. Tauch, 642 S.W.3d 481, 488 (Tex. 2022), reh'g denied (Apr. 22, 2022); Carter v. Galardi S. Enterprises, Inc., No. 1:14-CV-2812-WBH, 2015 WL 11605177, at *2 (N.D. Ga. Sept. 14, 2015); Restatement (Second) of Contracts § 42.

18. E.g., Carter v. Galardi S. Enterprises, Inc., No. 1:14-CV-2812-WBH, 2015 WL 11605177, at *2 (N.D. Ga. Sept. 14, 2015); Restatement (Second) of Contracts § 42.

Answer. The formation of a contract requires mutual assent and consideration. Mutual assent is typically achieved through offer and acceptance. Alpha made an offer, and Beta attempted to accept that offer. However, the question is whether, at the time of acceptance, Beta's acceptance had already been terminated through direct revocation. Alpha made an attempt to revoke, but his communication was only received—and hence only took effect—after Beta had already accepted the offer. Therefore, the mutual assent requirement is met. Moreover, the consideration requirement is satisfied, since Alpha's offer to paint serves as consideration for Beta's promise to pay and vice versa. In sum, the parties have formed a contract.

The power of acceptance is terminated through indirect revocation if and when (1) the offeror's conduct is inconsistent with the intention to form the contract and (2) the offeree obtains reliable information of that conduct.[19] Information is reliable if "a reasonable person acting in good faith would believe" it.[20]

Question. Alpha owns an apartment complex and offers Beta a lease for one of the apartments. While Beta is still considering the offer, he drives by the apartment complex and witnesses Alpha using a flamethrower to burn down the whole building. The next day, Beta calls Alpha and states that he, Beta, accepts the contract. Have the parties reached mutual assent?

Answer. Mutual assent is typically achieved through offer and acceptance. Alpha made an offer, and Beta attempted to accept that offer. However, by the time that Beta tried to accept, he had already lost his power of acceptance via indirect revocation: Alpha's burning the building down was inconsistent with the intention to enter into the contract, and Beta obtained reliable information of Alpha's conduct when he witnessed Alpha's actions.

---

19. Normile v. Miller, 326 S.E.2d 11, 18 (N.C. 1985); Angel, Tr. for Gobsmack Gift Tr. v. Tauch, 642 S.W.3d 481, 489-95 (Tex. 2022), reh'g denied (Apr. 22, 2022) (internal citation omitted); Mitchell v. Brimer, No. CIV.A. 1117 (SUSSEX), 1987 WL 5319, at *3 (Del. Ch. Jan. 12, 1987); Restatement (Second) of Contracts § 43.

20. Angel, Tr. for Gobsmack Gift Tr. v. Tauch, 642 S.W.3d 481, 489 (Tex. 2022), reh'g denied (Apr. 22, 2022) (internal citation omitted); see Restatement (Second) of Contracts § 43 cmt. d.

D. Rejection

The offeree's rejection terminates the offer, unless the offeror has indicated that the offer shall remain open despite the rejection.[21]

E. Counteroffer

A counteroffer is an offer that relates to the same matter as the offer, but substitutes the bargain proposed by the offeror with a different one.[22] The offeror's counteroffer terminates his power of acceptance,[23] unless either party has indicated an intention that the original offer shall stay open.[24]

Question. Alpha calls Beta and says: "Hi Beta, I offer to paint your house for $1,000." Beta replies: "I offer to cut your lawn for $200." Does Beta still have the power of acceptance regarding Alpha's offer?

Answer. Beta no longer has the power of acceptance if he made a counteroffer. However, for Beta's offer to qualify as a counteroffer, it would have to concern the same matter as Alpha's offer, while substituting a different bargain for the one proposed by Alpha. However, Alpha's and Beta's offers concerned entirely different matters. Accordingly, Beta's offer does not constitute a counteroffer and therefore did not terminate Beta's power of acceptance. It follows that Beta still has the power of acceptance.

Question. Alpha calls Beta and offers to paint Beta's house for $1000." Beta replies: "If you are willing to do it for $800, then you got yourself a deal.

---

21. Restatement (Second) of Contracts § 38. See, e.g., NDC, LLC v. Wisconsin Dept. of Transp., 874 N.W.2d 347 (Wis. App. 2015) (finding that power of acceptance was terminated by acceptance); Scoular Co. v. Denney, 151 P.3d 615, 618 (Colo. App. 2006), as modified on denial of reh'g (Dec. 14, 2006) (holding that "an offer may be accepted within a reasonable time unless the offer has been revoked by the offeror or rejected by the offeree"); Collins v. Thompson, 679 F.2d 168, 171 (9th Cir. 1982) (holding that rejection terminates power of acceptance unless offeree indicates he wants to think more about offer).
22. Rybin Inv. Co., Inc. v. Wade, 316 N.W.2d 744, 746 (Neb. 1982); Restatement (Second) of Contracts § 39(1).
23. Cavallo v. Lewis, 473 A.2d 338, 340 (Conn. App. 1984); Miller v. Flegenheimer, 161 A.3d 524, 532 (Vt. 2016); Al Dente, LLC v. Consiglio, 157 A.3d 743, 754 (Conn. App. 2017); Muise v. Verhave, 9 N.E.3d 868 (Mass. App. 2014); Restatement (Second) of Contracts § 36(1)(a).
24. Muise v. Verhave, 9 N.E.3d 868 (Mass. App. 2014); Restatement (Second) of Contracts § 36 (1)(a).

Otherwise, no deal." Does Beta still have the power of acceptance regarding Alpha's offer.

Answer. Beta no longer has the power of acceptance. Beta's reply to Alpha concerned the same matter, but substituted the proposed bargain with a different one. Therefore, Beta's reply constitutes a counteroffer, which terminated Beta's power of acceptance.

IV. When Does an Acceptance Take Effect?

A question of great practical importance centers on when the offeree's acceptance takes effect. In particular, this issue becomes relevant if the offeror tries to revoke the offer. Generally, once the acceptance has taken effect, it is too late to revoke the offer. In other words, once the acceptance becomes effective, you no longer need to worry about the power of acceptance. There are other limitations on the offeror's power of revocation, which we will discuss later.

So, when does acceptance take effect? If offeror and offeree communicate face to face, acceptance takes effect instantaneously. The same is true if the parties use a medium which allows for "instantaneous two-way communication," such as the telephone.[25] If an acceptance is sent via mail or a comparable medium such as carrier services, the acceptance takes effect on dispatch.[26] This principle is known as the "mailbox rule."[27] Whether the mailbox rule applies to acceptances via email remains controversial.[28]

---

25. Restatement (Second) of Contracts § 64; see Shehane v. Station Casino, 3 P.3d 551, 554 (Kan. App. 2000) (holding that "[w]hen that act is the acceptance of an offer during a telephone conversation, the contract is 'made' where the acceptor speaks his or her acceptance").

26. Restatement (Second) of Contracts § 63; see, e.g., Cochran v. Norkunas, 919 A.2d 700, 714 (Md. 2007) (mail); Worms v. Burgess, 620 P.2d 455, 457 (Okla. App. Div. 1 1980) (mail);

27. E.g., Hogan v. Pat's Peak Skiing, LLC, 121 A.3d 827, 73 (N.H. 2015); Tippett v. Daly, 10 A.3d 1123, 1133 (D.C. App. 2010).

28. See, e.g., Lasagne A. Wilhite, Promoting E-Legal Behavior: Litigation and Counseling the Best Way to Approach E-Legal Issues Is to Be Mindful of the Nuances of Contract Law That Are Unique to Electronic Behavior, 20 PRAC. LITIGATOR 45, 48 (January 2009) (arguing that the mailbox rule generally applies to email because of the potential delays inherent in communication via email); Amelia Rawls, Contract Formation in an Internet Age, 10 COLUM. SCI. & TECH. L. REV. 200, 231 (2009) (arguing against the application of the mailbox rule to modern forms of electronic communications including email).

Question. Alpha sends Beta a letter saying: "I offer to lend you my car during the spring break in exchange for $300." Beta receives the letter on Friday morning. He writes a letter saying: "I accept your offer." Beta puts the letter in the mail on Friday afternoon. On Friday evening, Alpha calls Beta and says: "I revoke my offer." On Saturday, Alpha gets Beta's letter. Have the parties formed a contract?

Answer. The formation of a contract requires mutual assent and consideration. In this case, the critical question is whether the parties have reached mutual assent. Alpha made an offer by letter, and Beta attempted to accept that offer by way of another letter. But did Beta still have the power of acceptance? Under the so-called "mailbox rule," acceptance takes effect on dispatch. When Beta mailed the letter, Alpha had not yet revoked his offer, meaning that Beta still had the power of acceptance.

Note that the mailbox rule contains certain traps for the unwary. For the mailbox rule to apply, the acceptance must bear the correct address.[29] Yet if the purported acceptance bears the wrong address, acceptance still occurs on dispatch if the acceptance is received no later than it would have been received in case of proper dispatch.[30]

V. Who Can Accept an Offer?

An offer can only be accepted by the person invited to provide the consideration.[31]

Example. Alpha offers Beta to paint Beta's house for $1,000. Gamma learns of this offer and tells Alpha that he, Gamma, accepts the offer. Alpha and Gamma have not entered into a contract. Gamma was not invited to provide the consideration and therefore could not accept Alpha's offer.

Example. Alpha, Beta, and Gamma meet. Alpha, who is notoriously broke, wants to rent Beta's car for the weekend. Beta knows that Alpha is broke but

29. Republic of Sudan v. Harrison, 139 S. Ct. 1048, 1057 (2019); Woods v. Woods, 830 P.2d 1372, 1374 (Okla. 1992); Restatement (Second) of Contracts § 66.
30. Nafstad v. Merchant, 228 N.W.2d 548, 551 (Minn. 1975); Restatement (Second) of Contracts § 67.
31. Restatement (Second) of Contracts § 52.

also knows that Alpha's brother Gamma is wealthy. Therefore, Beta tells Alpha: "I am willing to let you have my car over the weekend for $300, but only if your brother Gamma promises to pay the $300." In this case, the consideration that Beta seeks in exchange for his promise to let Alpha use his car is *Gamma's promise* to pay. Therefore, it is Gamma, not Alpha, who has been asked to provide the consideration for Beta's promise, meaning that only Gamma can accept Beta's offer.

Example. Alpha, Beta, and Gamma meet. Alpha, who is notoriously broke, wants to rent Beta's car for the weekend. Beta knows that Alpha is broke but also knows that Alpha's brother Gamma is wealthy. Therefore, Beta tells Alpha: "I am willing to let you have my car over the weekend for $300, but only if you promise that Gamma will pay the $300." In this case, the consideration sought in exchange for Beta's promise to let Alpha use Beta's car is *Alpha's promise* that Gamma will pay. Therefore, Alpha has been asked to provide the consideration, meaning that Alpha can accept Beta's promise.

VI. The Manner of Acceptance

The offeror is the "master of his offer" and can specify how the offer is to be accepted.[32] Accordingly, the acceptance has to comply with the offeror's specifications to form a contract.[33] The offeror's restrictions regarding the manner, time, or place of acceptance do not have to be reasonable. For example, if the offeror states that acceptance requires a letter written in Vulcan and mailed during a full moon, the acceptance must comply with these requirements. If the offeror does not prescribe a particular manner of acceptance, the offeree can accept in any reasonable way.[34]

While these principles are not complicated, their practical application can be challenging. This is because it can be unclear whether the offeror means to impose binding restrictions regarding the manner of acceptance or whether the offeror merely intends to make non-binding suggestions.

If the offer mentions a particular mode of acceptance, it does not necessarily follow that the offeror wants to limit the offeree to this mode of accep-

32. See Restatement (Second) of Contracts § 32(1).
33. Restatement (Second) of Contracts § 60(1).
34. Restatement (Second) of Contracts § 32.

It is also possible that the offeror, rather than prescribing a specific manner of acceptance, merely intends to suggest one possible way of accepting the offer without precluding other ways. Mere suggestions regarding the manner of acceptance do not prevent the offeree from accepting in a different manner.[35]

Unfortunately, in real life, it can be challenging to figure out whether the offeror intended a prescription or a suggestion. As a general guideline, you should not be too quick to assume that the offeror intends a prescription simply because the offer mentions a particular mode of acceptance. Especially in cases where the offeror had no discernible interest in limiting the offeree to the particular manner of acceptance mentioned in the offer, you can often conclude that the reference to a particular manner of acceptance constitutes a mere suggestion.

> **Question.** Alpha sends Beta an email offering to paint Beta's house in exchange for $2000. The email ends with the words: "If you want to accept this offer, just call or email me." That same afternoon, Alpha happens to meet Beta at the local supermarket. Beta says: "Hi Alpha, good to see you. I accept your offer." Have Alpha and Beta reached mutual assent?

> **Answer.** Mutual assent is typically achieved through offer and acceptance. Alpha made an offer, and Beta accepted that offer. While Beta neither called nor emailed Alpha, these modes of acceptance were mere suggestions. There is no reason to believe that Alpha wanted to preclude Beta from accepting the offer in other ways. In particular, one cannot argue that Alpha wanted to preclude any manner of acceptance that did not provide Alpha with hard evidence in case of later disagreements. After all, a mere phone call would not have created such hard evidence either. It follows that the reference to an email or phone call reasonably had to be understood as a mere suggestion regarding the manner of acceptance.

VII. Acceptance by Silence

As a general rule, silence does not constitute assent.[36] However, this rule is not without exceptions. Read section 69 of the Restatement (Second) of

35. Restatement (Second) of Contracts § 60(2).
36. Restatement (Second) of Contracts § 50.

Contracts. In particular, silence constitutes assent if it is reasonable for the offeror to expect a notification if the latter does not wish to accept the offer.[37] For example, perhaps the parties have, in the course of their dealings, developed a practice under which the offeree notifies the offeror that he (the offeree) does not want to accept the offer.

Normile v. Miller

Supreme Court of North Carolina, 313 N.C. 98 (1985)

FRYE, Justice.

Defendant Hazel Miller owned real estate located in Charlotte, North Carolina. On 4 August 1980, the property was listed for sale with a local realtor, Gladys Hawkins. On that same day, Richard Byer, a real estate broker with the realty firm Gallery of Homes, showed the property to the prospective purchasers, Plaintiffs Normile and Kurniawan. Afterwards, Byer helped plaintiffs prepare a written offer to purchase the property. A Gallery of Homes form, entitled "DEPOSIT RECEIPT AND CONTRACT FOR PURCHASE AND SALE OF REAL ESTATE," containing blanks for the insertion of terms pertinent to the purchasers' offer, was completed in quadruplicate and signed by Normile and Kurniawan. One specific standard provision in Paragraph 9 included a blank that was filled in with the time and date to read as follows: "OFFER & CLOSING DATE: Time is of the essence, therefore this offer must be accepted on or before 5:00 p.m. Aug. 5th 1980. A signed copy shall be promptly returned to the purchaser."

Byer took the offer to purchase form to Gladys Hawkins, who presented it to defendant. Later that evening, Gladys Hawkins returned the executed form to Byer. It had been signed under seal by defendant, with several changes in the terms having been made thereon and initialed by defendant. The primary changes made by defendant were an increase in the earnest money deposit ($100 to $500); an increase in the down payment due at closing ($875 to $1,000); a decrease in the unpaid principal of the existing mortgage amount ($18,525 to $18,000); a decrease in the term of the loan from seller (25 years to

37. Restatement (Second) of Contracts § 69(a).

20 years); and a purchaser qualification contingency added in the outer margin of the form.

That same evening, Byer presented defendant's counteroffer to Plaintiff Normile. Byer testified in his deposition that Normile did not have $500 for the earnest money deposit, one of the requirements of defendant's counteroffer. Also, Byer stated that Normile did not "want to go 25 [sic] years because he wanted lower payments." Byer was under the impression at this point that Normile thought he had first option on the property and that "nobody else could put an offer in on it and buy it while he had this counteroffer, so he was going to wait awhile before he decided what to do with it." Normile, however, neither accepted or rejected the counteroffer at this point, according to Byer. When this meeting closed, Byer left the pink copy of the offer to purchase form containing defendant's counteroffer with Normile. Byer stated that he thought that Normile had rejected the counteroffer at this point.

At approximately 12:30 a.m. on 5 August, Byer went to the home of Plaintiff Segal, who signed an offer to purchase with terms very similar to those contained in defendant's counteroffer to Plaintiffs Normile and Kurniawan. This offer was accepted, without change, by defendant.

Later that same day, at approximately 2:00 p.m., Byer informed Plaintiff Normile that defendant had revoked her counteroffer by commenting to Normile, "[Y]ou snooze, you lose; the property has been sold." Prior to 5:00 p.m. on that same day, Normile and Kurniawan initialed the offer to purchase form containing defendant's counteroffer and delivered the form to the Gallery of Homes' office, along with the earnest money deposit of $500.

Separate actions were filed by plaintiff-appellants and -appellee seeking specific performance. Plaintiff Segal's motion for consolidation of the trials was granted. Defendant, in her answer, recognized the validity of the contract between her and Plaintiff Segal. However, because of the action for specific performance commenced by Plaintiffs Normile and Kurniawan, defendant contended that she was unable to legally convey title to Plaintiff Segal. Both plaintiffs filed a motion for summary judgment. Plaintiff Segal's motion for summary judgment was granted by the trial court, and defendant was ordered to specifically perform the contract to convey the property to Segal. Plaintiffs Normile and Kurniawan appealed to the Court of Appeals from the trial court's denial of their motion for summary judgment. That court unanimously affirmed the trial court's actions. Discretionary review was allowed by this Court on petition of Plaintiffs Normile and Kurniawan.

I.

The first issue on this appeal is whether a time limit within which an offer must be accepted that is contained in a prospective purchaser's written offer to purchase real property becomes a term of the seller's subsequent counteroffer, transforming the counteroffer into an option contract or irrevocable offer for the time stated if signed under seal. We conclude that it does not.

Plaintiff-appellants argue that the counteroffer made by Defendant Miller to plaintiff-appellants became a binding and irrevocable option to purchase within the time for acceptance contained in their original offer to purchase. Essentially, plaintiff-appellants argue that the Court of Appeals was incorrect in holding that defendant's counteroffer was not an irrevocable option because the "promise to hold the offer open until 5:00 p.m., 5 August 1980, was not supported by consideration, ..." Normile, 63 N.C.App. at 694, 306 S.E.2d at 150.

As a preliminary matter, it is obvious that the thrust of both the Court of Appeals' and plaintiff-appellants' arguments center around their analysis of whether or not the counteroffer from Defendant Miller to plaintiff-appellants constituted a binding and enforceable option contract for the period of time for acceptance stated and contained in plaintiff-appellants' original offer to purchase form. This basic proposition seems to be premised upon the inaccurate notion that Defendant Miller's "counteroffer provided that the offer would remain open until 5:00 p.m. on 5 August 1980...." Normile, 63 N.C.App. at 693, 306 S.E.2d at 149. This same misconception is reflected in plaintiff-appellants' brief where they state, without citing any legal authority:

It is basic that when one party makes another a written offer which the offeree changes in some respects, signs and returns, the offer becomes a counteroffer by the original offeree to the original offeror, which consists of the altered provisions and all of the unaltered provisions of the original offer. Thus, since the time limitation for acceptance was not altered, one of the provisions of the counteroffer was that the time for its acceptance would terminate at 5:00 p.m. August 5, 1980.

The counteroffer, being under seal, constituted a binding option to sell, irrevocable during the stated time limitation for its acceptance, and enforceable by specific performance upon its acceptance. (emphasis added).

We do not agree that defendant's counteroffer to plaintiffs-appellants subsumed all the provisions of the original offer from the prospective purchasers. To effectively explain this conclusion, we begin with a brief description of how a typical sale of real estate is consummated. The broker, whose primary duty is to secure a ready, willing, and able buyer for the seller's property, generally initiates a potential sale by procuring the prospective purchaser's signature on an offer to purchase instrument. . . .

Usually, this offer to purchase is a printed form with blanks that are filled in and completed by the broker. Among the various clauses contained in such an instrument, it is not uncommon for the form to contain "a clause stipulating that the seller must accept the offer and approve the sale within a certain specified period of time, ... The inclusion of a date within which the seller must accept simply indicates that the offer will automatically expire at the termination of the named period if the seller does not accept before then."

. . .

In the instant case, the offerors, plaintiffs-appellants, submitted their offer to purchase defendant's property. This offer contained a Paragraph 9, requiring that "this offer must be accepted on or before 5:00 p.m. Aug. 5th 1980." Thus, the offeree's, defendant-seller's, power of acceptance was controlled by the duration of time for acceptance of the offer. Restatement (Second) of Contracts § 35 (1981). . . . It is axiomatic that a valid contract between two parties can only exist when the parties "assent to the same thing in the same sense, and their minds meet as to all terms." . . . This assent, or meeting of the minds, requires an offer and acceptance in the exact terms and that the acceptance must be communicated to the offeror. . . . "If the terms of the offer are changed or any new ones added by the acceptance, there is no meeting of the minds and, consequently, no contract." . . . This counteroffer amounts to a rejection of the original offer. . . .

The question then becomes, did defendant-seller accept plaintiff-appellants' offer prior to the expiration of the time limit contained within the offer? We conclude that she did not. The offeree, defendant-seller, changed the original offer in several material respects, most notably in the terms regarding payment of the purchase price. . . . This qualified acceptance was in reality a rejection of the plaintiff-appellants original offer because it was coupled with certain modifications or changes that were not contained in the original offer. . . . Additionally, defendant-seller's conditional acceptance amounted to a counteroffer to plaintiff-appellants. "A counter-offer is an offer made by an offeree to his offeror relating to the same matter as the original offer and proposing a substituted bargain differing from that proposed by the original offer." Restatement . . . § 39. Between plaintiff-appellants and defendant-seller there was no meeting of the minds, since the parties failed to assent to the same thing in the same sense.

In substance, defendant's conditional acceptance modifying the original offer did not manifest any intent to accept the terms of the original offer, including the time-for-acceptance provision, unless and until the original offeror accepted the terms included in defendant's counteroffer. The offeree, by failing to unconditionally assent to the terms of the original offer and instead qualifying his acceptance with terms of his own, in effect says to the original offeror, "I will accept your offer; provided you [agree to my proposed terms]." . . . Thus, the time-for-acceptance provision contained in plaintiff-appellants' original offer did not become part of the terms of the counteroffer. And, of course, if they had accepted the counteroffer from defendant, a binding purchase contract, which would have included the terms of the original offer and counteroffer, would have then resulted. . . .

It is generally recognized that "[a]n 'option' is a contract by which the owner agrees to give another the exclusive right to buy property at a fixed price within a specified time." . . . In effect, an owner of property agrees to hold his offer open for a specified period of time. . . . This option contract must also be supported by valuable consideration. . . . Disregarding the issue of consideration, it is more significant that defendant's counteroffer did not contain any promise or agreement that her counteroffer would remain open for a specified period of time. . . .

There is no language indicating that defendant-seller in any way agreed to sell or convey her real property to plaintiff-appellants at their request within a specified period of time. There is, however, language contained within the prospective purchasers' offer to purchase that does state, "DESCRIPTION: I/we Michael M. Normile and Wawie Kurniawan hereby agree to purchase from the sellers, ..." and "this offer must be accepted on or before 5:00 p.m. Aug. 5th 1980." (Emphasis added.) Nowhere is there companion language to the effect that Defendant Miller "hereby agrees to sell or convey to the purchasers" if they accept by a certain date.

Therefore, regardless of whether or not the seal imported the necessary consideration, we conclude that defendant-seller made no promise or agreement to hold her offer open. Thus, a necessary ingredient to the creation of an option contract, i.e., a promise to hold an offer open for a specified time, is not present. Accordingly, we hold that defendant's counteroffer was not transformed into an irrevocable offer for the time limit contained in the original offer because the defendant's conditional acceptance did not include the time-for-acceptance provision as part of its terms and because defendant did not make any promise to hold her counteroffer open for any stated time.

II.

The foregoing preliminary analysis of both the Court of Appeals' opinion and plaintiff-appellants' argument in their brief prefaces what we consider to be decisive of the ultimate issue to be resolved. Basic contract principles effectively and logically answer the primary issue in this appeal. That is, if a seller rejects a prospective purchaser's offer to purchase but makes a counteroffer that is not accepted by the prospective purchaser, does the prospective purchaser have the power to accept after he receives notice that the counteroffer has been revoked? The answer is no. The net effect of defendant-seller's counteroffer and rejection is twofold. First, plaintiff-appellants' original offer was rejected and ceased to exist. . . . Secondly, the counteroffer by the offeree requires the original offeror, plaintiff-appellants, to either accept or reject. . . .

Accordingly, the next question is, did plaintiff-appellants, the original offerors, accept or reject defendant-seller's counteroffer?

Plaintiff-appellants in their brief seem to answer this question when they state, "At the time Byer presented the counteroffer to Normile, Normile neither accepted nor rejected it...." Therefore, plaintiff-appellants did not manifest any intent to agree to or accept the terms contained in defendant's counteroffer. Normile instead advised Byer that he, though mistakenly, had an option on the property and that it was off the market for the duration of the time limitation contained in his original offer. . . . Although Normile's mistaken belief that he had an option is unfortunate, he still failed to express to Byer his agreement to or rejection of the counteroffer made by defendant-seller. . . . Plaintiff-appellants . . . did not accept, either expressly or by conduct, defendant's counteroffer. In addition to disagreeing with the change in payment terms, Normile stated to Byer that "he was going to wait awhile before he decided what to do with [the counteroffer]." Neither did plaintiffs explicitly reject defendant's counteroffer. Instead, plaintiff-appellants in this case chose to operate under the impression, though mistaken, that they had an option to purchase and that the property was "off the market." Absent either an acceptance or rejection, there was no meeting of the minds or mutual assent between the parties, a fortiori, there was no contract. . . .

It is evident from the record that after plaintiff-appellants failed to accept defendant's counteroffer, there was a second purchaser, Plaintiff-appellee Segal, who submitted an offer to defendant that was accepted. This offer and acceptance between the latter parties, together with consideration in the form of an earnest money deposit from plaintiff-appellee, ripened into a valid and binding purchase contract.

By entering into the contract with Plaintiff-appellee Segal, defendant manifested her intention to revoke her previous counteroffer to plaintiff-appellants. "It is a fundamental tenet of the common law that an offer is generally freely revocable and can be countermanded by the offeror at any time before it has been accepted by the offeree." . . . Restatement, . . . § 42. The revocation of an offer terminates it, and the offeree has no power to revive the offer by any subsequent attempts to accept. . . .

Generally, notice of the offeror's revocation must be communicated to the offeree to effectively terminate the offeree's power to accept the offer. It is enough that the offeree receives reliable information, even indirectly, "that the offeror had taken definite action inconsistent with an intention to make the contract." . . . In this case, plaintiff-appellants received notice of the offeror's revocation of the counteroffer in the afternoon of August 5, when Byer saw Normile and told him, "[Y]ou snooze, you lose; the property has been sold." Later that afternoon, plaintiff-appellants initialed the counteroffer and delivered it to the Gallery of Homes, along with their earnest money deposit of $500. These subsequent attempts by plaintiff-appellants to accept defendant's revoked counteroffer were fruitless, however, since their power of acceptance had been effectively terminated by the offeror's revocation. Restatement . . . § 36. Since defendant's counteroffer could not be revived, the practical effect of plaintiff-appellants' initialing defendant's counteroffer and leaving it at the broker's office before 5:00 p.m. on August 5 was to resubmit a new offer. This offer was not accepted by defendant since she had already contracted to sell her property by entering into a valid, binding, and irrevocable purchase contract with Plaintiff-appellee Segal.

For the reasons stated herein, the decision of the Court of Appeals is MODIFIED and AFFIRMED.

VAUGHN, J., did not participate in the consideration or decision of this case.

. . .

NOTES AND QUESTIONS

*A. **The matching principle.*** Under common law, an acceptance must match the offer.[38] A reply to an offer that contains additional or different terms constitutes a counteroffer rather than an acceptance.[39] By contrast, mere suggestions or requests for better terms that accompany an unconditional acceptance do not prevent the contract from being formed.[40]

*B. **Counteroffers and the power of acceptance.*** As a general rule, a counteroffer terminates the offeree's power of acceptance.[41] However, either party can avert this outcome by manifesting a contrary intention.[42] Can you contemplate scenarios in which the offeror might rationally want the offeree to retain the power of acceptance even after the offeree has made a counteroffer?

*C. **Direct v. indirect revocation.*** Offers can be revoked directly or indirectly. The offeror can revoke their offer directly by communicating to the offeror that they no longer intend to enter into the contract.[43] A direct revocation takes effect on receipt.[44] For an indirect revocation, it is sufficient that (1) the offeror engages in conduct that is inconsistent with an intent to conclude the contract and (2) the offeree obtains reliable about this change.[45] In *Normile v. Miller*, the court concludes that the defendant revoked her counteroffer before the plaintiff-appellants accepted it. Does the court categorize the defendant's revocation as direct or indirect?

*D. **Deadlines and options.*** In *Normile v. Miller*, the court rejects the argument that the seller's counteroffer was irrevocable until 5:00 p.m. on August 5, 1980. To understand the court's reasoning, it is helpful to distinguish between two related but distinct types of terms that the offeror can include in his offer:

---

38. Restatement (Second) of Contracts § 50.
39. Id. § 59.
40. Id. § 61. See, e.g., Ebline v. Campbell, 121 A.2d 828, 831 (Md. 1956), modified, 121 A.2d 928 (Md. 1956) (distinguishing a reply that contains different or additional terms and therefore constitutes a counteroffer from "a mere inquiry regarding the possibility of better terms . . . or a comment upon the terms of the offer"); Al Dente, LLC v. Consiglio, 157 A.3d 743, 754 (Conn. App. 2017) (holding that mere "comments and suggestions do not constitute a counteroffer").
41. Restatement (Second) of Contracts § 39(2).
42. Restatement (Second) of Contracts § 39(2).
43. Restatement (Second) of Contracts § 42(2).
44. Restatement (Second) of Contracts § 40.
45. Restatement (Second) of Contracts § 42.

(1) a time or date by which the offer must be accepted ("deadline"),[46] and (2) a promise to keep the offer open for a specified duration ("option").[47] If the offer imposes a deadline, the offeree's power of acceptance terminates automatically once the deadline has passed.[48] In contrast, if the offer grants an option, the offeror cannot terminate the power of acceptance by revocation before the option has expired.[49] Crucially, granting an option does not imply the imposition of a deadline, and, likewise, imposing a deadline does not imply the grant of an option.

*E. **Option contracts.*** A contract in which the offeror promises to keep their offer open is termed an option contract.[50] It is imperative not to confuse the option contract, in which a party promises to keep their offer open, with the main contract that results if the offeree accepts the relevant offer. The option and main contracts are separate and therefore require separate consideration. For example, assume that, in the case at hand, Hazel had offered to sell her property to Normile for $1,000,000 and that Hazel and Normile had agreed that Hazel was obligated to keep the offer open for ten days in exchange for Normile's promise to pay $100. If Normile had accepted Hazel's offer to buy the property within ten days, that acceptance would have created the main contract, i.e., the contract for the sale of Hazel's property. The consideration for Hazel's promise to convey her property (in the main contract) would have been the promise to pay the $1,000,000. The consideration for Hazel's promise to keep her offer open would have been the promise to pay the $100.

*F. **Creating option contracts.*** As a general rule, an option contract, like any other contract, is binding only if it meets the general requirements for contract formation: mutual assent and consideration. However, for option contracts, the law provides numerous exceptions to this general rule. Some of these rules dispense with both the mutual assent requirement and the consideration requirements, allowing option contracts to be created by one-sided promises unsupported by consideration. Read sections 87 and 90 of the Restatement (Second) of Contracts and section 2-205 of the Uniform

46. The offeror is free to specify a deadline by which the offer has to be accepted. Restatement (Second) of Contracts § 41.

47. For the promise to keep the offer open to be binding it must either be supported by consideration, Restatement (Second) of Contracts § 25, or the promise must fall into one of the categories in which consideration is not required. See comment E.

48. Restatement (Second) of Contracts § 25.

49. Restatement (Second) of Contracts § 25.

50. Restatement (Second) of Contracts § 25.

Commercial Code (UCC). In one case, the law does not even require a promise to form an option contract. Read section 45 of the Restatement (Second) of Contracts.

CHAPTER 5
ACCEPTANCE BY PERFORMANCE

The offeror can specify how the offer is to be accepted.[1] In that case, the acceptance must comply with the prescribed manner of acceptance in order for a contract to be formed.[2] In particular, the offeror can demand that the offeree render the desired performance to accept the offer.[3]

In case of doubt, an offer is construed as giving the offeree a choice between acceptance by promise and acceptance by performance.[4] However, specific categories of offers, such as rewards and bonus programs, have tradi-

---

1. Restatement (Second) of Contracts § 30. See, e.g., Olsen v. Johnston, 301 P.3d 791, 794 (Mont. 2013) ("As master of the offer, however, the offeror may limit the time, place, or manner in which an offeree can accept").
2. Restatement (Second) of Contracts § 60. See, e.g., BMW of N.A., LLC v. Mini Works, LLC, 166 F. Supp. 3d 976, 982 (D. Ariz. 2010) ("If an offer prescribes these terms, then the offeree must comply with them in order to create a contract"); Olsen v. Johnston, 301 P.3d 791, 794 (Mont. 2013) (holding that "an offeror that prescribes an exclusive mode of acceptance does not consent to be bound by the contract unless the offeree communicates acceptance in that particular manner").
3. Restatement (Second) of Contracts § 32.
4. Restatement (Second) of Contracts § 32. See Smith v. 21st Cent. Nat. Fuels, LLC, No. CV 3:14-12507, 2016 WL 1465431, at *8 (S.D.W. Va. Apr. 14, 2016) (applying the rule that, when in doubt, an offer allows both acceptance by promise and acceptance by performance); Tober v. CDC Realty, L.L.C., No. 2 CA-CV 2007-0044, 2008 WL 4613913, at *9 (Ariz. App. 2d Div. Jan. 24, 2008) (applying the rule that in case of doubt, an offer allows both acceptance by promise and acceptance by performance).

been interpreted to necessitate acceptance through performance, even in the absence of explicit stipulation to that effect.[5]

Boswell v. Panera Bread Company

United States Court of Appeals, Eighth Circuit, 879 F.3d 296 (2018)

ARNOLD, Circuit Judge

The central issue in this contracts case is whether certain at-will employees can hold their employer, Panera, LLC, to its promise to pay them a bonus. The district court thought so and granted summary judgment to the employees. We agree and affirm.

In an effort to recruit and retain general managers for its restaurants, Panera created a program under which qualifying managers were eligible to receive a relatively large one-time bonus, among other emoluments.

A few years after creating the program, Panera asked the managers to sign an employment agreement that incorporated a compensation plan providing that the one-time bonus would be paid about five years after the manager executed the agreement. The amount of the bonus depended heavily on the profitability of the manager's restaurant over the final two years of the five-year period. To receive the bonus, the manager had to be a manager under the program on the date when the bonus was payable.

Panera decided in 2010 that it would set a $100,000 cap on the amount of the bonus because the bonuses would otherwise be too costly. Panera informed its managers of the cap in 2011 and explained that it would become effective in January 2012. Panera received no complaints about the cap until 2014 when one of the managers under the program, Mark Boswell, raised

---

5. Simmons v. U.S., 308 F.2d 160, 164 (4th Cir. 1962) ("The offer of a prize or reward for doing a specified act, like catching a criminal, is an offer for a unilateral contract."); Bahr v. Tech. Consumer Products, Inc., 601 Fed. Appx. 359, 365 (6th Cir. 2015) (treating bonus plan as "an offer for a unilateral contract"); Campbell v. Mercer, 33 S.E. 871, 872 (Ga. 1899) ("A reward is a recompense or premium offered by the government or an individual for special or extraordinary services to be performed. Until acceptance by performance of the services, it is a mere proposition, which may be accepted by any part of the public, if it be offered to the public, or by any particular person or class of persons, if such proposition is made to them.") (internal citation omitted).

concerns shortly before he received his bonus. Boswell and two other managers, David Lutton and Vickie Snyder, then sued Panera for breach of contract on behalf of themselves and a class of similarly situated managers, maintaining that Panera had violated the agreements by imposing the cap. Panera responded that the parties had orally terminated and replaced—or, in legal parlance, novated—the agreement because the managers, by their words and actions, assented to a new agreement containing the cap. Panera also asserted that the managers had waived any claims they had regarding the cap by continuing to work without complaint or were estopped from raising any claims about it because it was too late. . . . The parties agree that we apply Missouri substantive law in this diversity case. . . .

As the district court correctly pointed out, an employer's "promise to pay a bonus in return for an at-will employee's continued employment is an offer for a unilateral contract." See Cook v. Coldwell Banker, 967 S.W.2d 654, 657 (Mo. Ct. App. 1998). An offeror in a unilateral contract receives performance, rather than a promise, as consideration in return for the offeror's promise. Id.

The question that arises at this point is whether Panera could modify or terminate the terms of its offer to pay the one-time bonus by imposing a cap on it. Generally, an offeror can withdraw an offer at any time before the offeree accepts it. Id. But the Missouri Court of Appeals has said several times that a party may not revoke an offer to make a unilateral contract after the offeree has substantially performed it because the offeree, at that point, has supplied consideration to make the contract enforceable against the offeror to the extent it has been performed, see id., and because "great injustice may arise" if the offeror can revoke an offer after the offeree has spent time and expense in performing. See 1 Williston on Contracts § 5:13 (4th ed. 2017). Panera takes issue with the district court's conclusion that all the managers in the class had substantially performed under the offer as a matter of law so as to render the offer irrevocable. We do not think, though, that the Supreme Court of Missouri, if confronted with the issue, would conclude that the offeree of a unilateral-contract offer must render a substantial part of the requested performance to make the offer irrevocable. We think it would conclude instead that an offeree must merely begin performance, and since each of the managers in the class here had at least begun performing under the offer, we conclude that Panera could not modify the offer terms as to any manager.

Panera has not brought to our attention any decision by the Supreme

Court of Missouri regarding how much performance is necessary to make a unilateral-contract offer unmodifiable. It is true that the Missouri Court of Appeals has said on several occasions that "substantial" performance is required, see, e.g., Cook, 967 S.W.2d at 657, but only decisions of a state's highest court can bind us on questions of state law: Though decisions of state intermediate courts can be persuasive, they are not controlling. DeCoursey, 822 F.3d at 476. The Missouri Court of Appeals appears to have derived the substantial-performance principle from a treatise that said with respect to unilateral-contract offers that "the offeror is bound by a contract just as soon as the offeree has rendered a substantial part of that requested performance." See Coffman Indus., Inc. v. Gorman–Taber Co., 521 S.W.2d 763, 772 (Mo. Ct. App. 1975) (quoting 1 Corbin on Contracts § 49 (1963)). That court has since repeated that locution in other cases, but we conclude that, if presented with the issue, the Supreme Court of Missouri would resolve the matter differently.

For one thing, Corbin has abandoned the locution, now saying that "the offeror is bound by a contract just as soon as the offeree has rendered part of the requested performance." 1 Corbin on Contracts § 2.29 (rev. ed. 1993 & Supp. 2017). In addition, the two other authorities the Coffman court relied on in adopting the substantial-performance principle do not help establish that substantial performance is required. Nowhere in the single case that the Coffman court cites does the word "substantial" ever appear, see Am. Publ'g & Engraving Co. v. Walker, 87 Mo. App. 503 (Mo. Ct. App. 1901), and the other treatise that Coffman cites provides that "the offeror becomes bound from the time performance is begun." See 1 Williston on Contracts § 60A (3d ed. 1958). The current version of that treatise adopts the same principle. See 1 Williston on Contracts § 5:13 (4th ed. 2017). Comment d to § 45 of the Restatement (Second) of Contracts agrees that it is "the beginning of performance" that renders the offer of a unilateral contract binding so that the offeror cannot revise its terms, and the Supreme Court of Missouri routinely finds the Restatement (Second) of Contracts persuasive. See, e.g., State ex rel. Vincent v. Schneider, 194 S.W.3d 853, 858–59 (Mo. 2006) (en banc). Based on the current state of the law, therefore, we think that the Supreme Court of Missouri, if faced with the question, would conclude that the offeree's beginning of performance would render the offer irrevocable. So Panera's imposition of the cap would be an ineffective attempt to modify its unilateral-contract offer.

Panera maintains, though, that no matter when a unilateral-contract offer becomes irrevocable as a general matter, in this specific instance Panera expressly reserved the power to revoke or modify its offer. It argues that it reserved that power by conditioning the payment of the bonus on the managers' continued employment, a matter that Panera controlled since the employment was at will. . . .

In support of its contention, Panera points to a comment in the Restatement that the general rule against modifying or terminating a unilateral-contract offer after the offeree begins performance "yields to a manifestation of intention which makes reliance unjustified," and so the offeror's "reservation of power to revoke [the offer] after performance has begun means that as yet there is no promise and no offer." See Restatement (Second) of Contracts § 45 cmt. b. We do not think that the reservation of power here accomplishes the goal that Panera hopes. Keeping in mind that the purpose of the rule precluding an offeror from modifying or terminating a unilateral-contract offer after the offeree begins performance is "to protect the offeree in justifiable reliance on the offeror's promise," see id., the alleged reservation of power here adds nothing beyond what the at-will relationship already provides, so we think this case in this respect is just like Cook. Panera tries to distinguish Cook by arguing that the offeree there had fully performed when the offeror attempted to modify the offer. But that fact is of no moment because the offer's terms were locked in before full performance, as is the case here. The crucial point is that the at-will employee in Cook had received a bonus offer from her employer, and the court held the employer to it. The at-will relationship did not render the bonus promise illusory even though the employer could have terminated the employee and thus made it impossible for her to satisfy the prerequisites to receiving the bonus. Likewise here, Panera could have terminated the managers if it chose and precluded them from receiving the bonus, but it did not. . . . Since the managers had begun performing the unilateral-contract offer, Panera was not entitled to move the goalposts on them by imposing a bonus cap, which was outside the contemplation of the unilateral-contract offer.

To protect the offeree's justifiable reliance on the offer, moreover, the language of a reservation of power to modify or terminate a unilateral-contract offer should be clear. The Restatement comment on which Panera relies draws from Spooner v. Reserve Life Insurance Co., 47 Wash.2d 454, 287 P.2d 735, 737 (1955), where an employer offered employees a bonus but also said that the "bonus is a voluntary contribution on the part of the Company. It is agreed by you and by us that it may be withheld, increased, decreased or discontinued, individually or collectively, with or without notice." No employee who read such a reservation could justifiably rely on actually receiving a bonus. Here, on the other hand, we have no such clear language, and employees are instead left to connect the alleged dots between their at-will status and a condition to payment. . . .

For these reasons, and given that we should construe a contract to avoid rendering terms meaningless or illusory, see Parker v. Pulitzer Publ'g Co., 882 S.W.2d 245, 250 (Mo. Ct. App. 1994), we reject Panera's contention that it reserved the power to modify or terminate its bonus offer . . .

Panera next argues that the district court erred in rejecting its novation, waiver, and estoppel defenses. A novation is the substitution of a new contract for an old one. Ponze v. Guirl, 794 S.W.2d 699, 702 (Mo. Ct. App. 1990). A waiver is the intentional relinquishment of a known right, and, to constitute a waiver, "conduct must be so manifestly consistent with and indicative of an intention to renounce a particular right or benefit that no other reasonable explanation of the conduct is possible." Acetylene Gas Co. v. Oliver, 939 S.W.2d 404, 409 (Mo. Ct. App. 1996). Equitable estoppel arises from the unfairness of allowing parties to assert their rights belatedly if they knew about those rights but did nothing to enforce them until the other party has, acting in good faith, been disadvantaged by changed conditions. Comens v. SSM St. Charles Clinic Med. Grp., Inc., 258 S.W.3d 491, 496 (Mo. Ct. App. 2008). Missouri courts do not favor equitable estoppel and do not allow it to be invoked lightly. Id.

Since continued at-will employment does not constitute consideration, Panera's novation defense fails as a matter of law because, when Panera imposed the cap, the only promises, if any, exchanged by Panera and the managers was continued at-will employment. The parties therefore did not form a new contract.

We also agree with the district court that Panera's imposition of the cap constituted a repudiation of the contract. A party's renunciation of a contractual duty before the time fixed for performance is a repudiation; but a repudiation ripens into a breach only if the promisee elects to treat it as such since the promisee can elect either to wait till the time for performance or to treat the repudiation as a breach and a final assertion by the promisor that he is no longer bound by the contract. Franconia Assocs. v. United States, 536 U.S. 129, 143, 122 S.Ct. 1993, 153 L.Ed.2d 132 (2002). By proceeding as they did, the managers cannot be said to have waived their claims or be equitably estopped from asserting them; they were allowed to perform their part of the agreement and wait and see if Panera followed through on its repudiation.

Panera also suggests that, by continuing to work, the managers accepted the cap. But silence is not automatically acceptance; something more than the employee's mere continuance of work is needed to show acceptance of a unilateral modification to employment terms. See Katz v. Anheuser–Busch, Inc., 347 S.W.3d 533, 545 (Mo. Ct. App. 2011). Panera insists that, if continuing to work is not enough to show acceptance, then the managers' mere continuing to work did not amount to an acceptance of their underlying employment agreements because such performance must be done with the intent to accept those agreements. See Monsanto Co. v. Garst Seed Co., 241 S.W.3d 401, 412–13 (Mo. Ct. App. 2007). That is true, but Panera forgets that the managers also signed their employment agreements, and "signatures remain a common, though not exclusive, method of demonstrating agreement." Morrow, 273 S.W.3d at 22–23.

AFFIRMED. ...

NOTES AND QUESTIONS:

A. Diversity jurisdiction. Federal courts have so-called diversity jurisdiction in cases where the matter in controversy exceeds $75,000 and is between citizens of different states.[6] However, under the *Erie* doctrine, the federal court will apply substantive state law.[7] If the case turns on an issue of state law that the state's highest court has not yet decided, the federal court must determine how the state's highest court would decide the issue.[8]

B. Acceptance by performance. According to section 62(1) of the Restatement (Second) of Contracts, if an offer allows acceptance by either promise or performance, and the offeree accepts by performance, the beginning of the offeree's performance constitutes acceptance.[9] Moreover, the beginning of

6. 28 U.S.C.A. § 1332 (West).

7. Erie R.R. Co. v. Tompkins, 304 U.S. 64, 80 (1938).

8. See Allstate Ins. Co. v. Thrifty Rent-A-Car Sys., Inc., 249 F.3d 450, 454 (6th Cir. 2001) ("If the state supreme court has not yet addressed the issue presented, we must predict how the court would rule by looking to all the available data.").

9. Restatement (Second) of Contracts § 62 (1). See, e.g., Smith v. 21st Cent. Nat. Fuels, LLC, No. CV 3:14-12507, 2016 WL 1465431, at *8 (S.D.W. Va. Apr. 14, 2016) (applying section 62(1) of the Restatement (Second) of Contracts); United Concrete Pipe Corp. v. Spin-Line Co., 430 S.W.2d 360, 364 (Tex. 1968) (applying section 62(1) of the Restatement (Second) of Contracts).

performance functions as a promise to render the entire performance.[10] At first glance, this set of rules seems odd. Why would the Restatement categorize the beginning of acceptance as an acceptance by performance, only to then state that said the beginning of performance operates as a promise on the part of the offeree to complete the offeree's performance? Does this seemingly contradictory approach yield reasonable outcomes?

C. Section 45 of the Restatement (Second) of Contracts. As a general rule, an offeror can revoke their offer at any time before acceptance takes effect, thereby terminating the offeree's power of acceptance.[11] This rule does not usually cause hardships for the offeree since the offeree can accept the offer before performing or preparing to perform. However, if an offer requires acceptance by performance, the offer is generally interpreted to mean that only full performance is sufficient to accept the offer. That puts the offeree in a potentially vulnerable position: what if the offeree has partially performed and the offeror then revokes the offer, thereby preventing the formation of a contract and depriving the offeree of his claim to compensation? To avert such a consequence, section 45(1) of the Restatement (Second) of Contracts provides that if an offer can only be accepted by performance, the beginning of performance creates an option contract that prevents the offeror from revoking their offer.[12] Does Mississippi law follow the Restatement in this regard?

D. Unilateral Contracts. Contracts formed via acceptance by performance are also referred to as *unilateral* contracts,[13] whereas contracts formed by

10. Restatement (Second) of Contracts § 62 (2). See, e.g., Smith v. 21st Cent. Nat. Fuels, LLC, No. CV 3:14-12507, 2016 WL 1465431, at *8 (S.D.W. Va. Apr. 14, 2016) (applying section 62(2) of the Restatement (Second) of Contracts); United Concrete Pipe Corp. v. Spin-Line Co., 430 S.W.2d 360, 364 (Tex. 1968) (applying section 62(2) of the Restatement (Second) of Contracts).

11. Restatement (Second) of Contracts § 42.

12. Restatement (Second) of Contracts § 45. Most courts confronting this issue have followed the rule expressed in section 42. See, e.g., Walker v. Am. Optical Corp., 509 P.2d 439, 441 (Or. 1973) (holding that a "bonus plan offered by [an] employer normally becomes binding as a unilateral contract when the employee begins performance of the terms of the proposed plan, in the sense that the plan cannot then be revoked by the employer"); Lucian v. All States Trucking Co., 171 Cal. Rptr. 262, 264 (Cal. App. 1st Dist. 1981) (holding that "a specific bonus plan normally becomes binding as a unilateral contract when the employee begins performance, in the sense that the plan then cannot be revoked by the employer").

13. See, e.g., Cornell v. Desert Fin. Credit Union, 524 P.3d 1133, 1136 (Ariz. 2023) (explaining that "unilateral contracts are formed upon the offeree's acceptance by performance"); Sateriale v. R.J. Reynolds Tobacco Co., 697 F.3d 777, 785 (9th Cir. 2012) ("In contrast to a bilateral contract, a unilateral contract involves the exchange of a promise for a performance."); Davis v. Jacoby, 34 P.2d 1026,

exchanging promises are also called *bilateral* contracts.[14] The Restatement (Second) of Contracts no longer uses this terminology, but many courts still do.[15]

E. Breach. There are two basic ways of breaching a contract. If a party's performance is due, and the party either does not perform or does not perform as required by the contract, the relevant party commits a breach by nonperformance.[16] Read section 235(2) of the Restatement (Second) of Contracts. If a party's performance is not yet due, but the party makes it clear in advance that the party has no intention of honoring the contract, the party breaches by (anticipatory) repudiation.[17] Read section 250(a) of the Restatement (Second) of Contracts.

F. Acceptance by Silence. As a general rule, a party's silence does not constitute acceptance. However, section 69 of the Restatement (Second) of Contracts recognizes several exceptions from this principle. Can any of these exceptions be applied in *Boswell*?

G. Argumentum a maiore ad minus. In *Boswell*, the plaintiffs were at-will employees, meaning Panera could let them go at any time without cause. As part of its defense, Panera essentially argues that since it could have fired the managers, it also had the power to change the terms of the bonus program. This type of reasoning is known as an "*argumentum a maiore ad minus*," an argument from the greater to the lesser. In some contexts, courts are receptive

---

1029 (Cal. 1934) ("'A unilateral contract is one in which no promisor receives a promise as consideration for his promise.") (internal citation omitted).

14. See, e.g., Cornell v. Desert Fin. Credit Union, 524 P.3d 1133, 1136 (Ariz. 2023) ("Bilateral contracts consist of an exchange of promises."); Davis v. Jacoby, 34 P.2d 1026, 1029 (Cal. 1934) ("'A bilateral contract is one in which there are mutual promises between two parties to the contract; each party being both a promisor and a promisee.'") (internal citation omitted).

15. E.g., Vanegas v. Am. Energy Services, 302 S.W.3d 299, 302 (Tex. 2009); SouthTrust Bank v. Williams, 775 So. 2d 184, 188 (Ala. 2000); Cornell v. Desert Fin. Credit Union, 524 P.3d 1133, 1136 (Ariz. 2023); Sateriale v. R.J. Reynolds Tobacco Co., 697 F.3d 777, 785 (9th Cir. 2012).

16. Cf. C. Valley Gen. Hosp. v. Smith, 75 Cal. Rptr. 3d 771, 781 (Cal. App. 5th Dist. 2008) ("We use the phrase 'breach by nonperformance' to mean an unjustified failure to perform a material contractual obligation when performance is due.").

17. Cf. C. Valley Gen. Hosp. v. Smith, 75 Cal. Rptr. 3d 771, 781 (Cal. App. 5th Dist. 2008) (holding that "[a]s a matter of definition, an anticipatory breach of contract occurs when the contract is repudiated by the promisor before the promisor's performance under the contract is due").

to this type of reasoning.[18] In the literature, however, "*a maiore ad minus*" arguments tend to be viewed with skepticism.[19]

---

18. See, e.g., Miller v. McClain, 249 U.S. 308, 312 (1919) (holding that the "greater power includes the lesser"). Andrews v. Warden, 958 F.3d 1072, 1076 (11th Cir. 2020) ("Because the greater power ordinarily includes the lesser power, the President's pardon power includes the authority to commute a sentence to a lesser punishment.").

19. See, e.g., Robert L. Hale, Unconstitutional Conditions and Constitutional Rights, 35 COLUM. L. REV. 321, 349 (1935) ("The proposition clearly does not hold, that the greater power necessarily includes the lesser."); Keith N. Hylton, A Theory of Minimum Contract Terms, with Implications for Labor Law, 74 TEX. L. REV. 1741, 1750 (1996) ("Though persuasive at first glance, the greater-includes-lesser power doctrine is unreliable as a theory of common-law rules.").

CHAPTER 6
PROTECTING THE OFFEREE

I. Introduction

As a general rule, the offeror can revoke their offer at any time.[1] A revocation can be an unwelcome surprise for offerees, especially those who have somehow relied on the offer before accepting it.

Example. On October 1, 2022, Biglaw, a national law firm, mails a signed letter to Alpha, a law student, offering to employ her for a minimum of one year starting on August 2, 2023, at an annual wage of $2,000,000. Alpha receives the letter the next day and is delighted. She does not accept the offer immediately. Instead, she rejects offers from competing law firms. The next day, one of Biglaw's partners calls Alpha and informs her that Biglaw revokes its offer. When Alpha replies that she accepts the offer of employment, the partner ends the phone call.

---

1. Restatement (Second) of Contracts §§ 36(1)(c), 42, 43. See, e.g., Angel, Tr. for Gobsmack Gift Tr. v. Tauch, 642 S.W.3d 481, 488 (Tex. 2022), reh'g denied (Apr. 22, 2022) (holding that "[a]lthough there are exceptions, most offers are revocable"); Normile v. Miller, 326 S.E.2d 11, 18 (N.C. 1985) (holding that "[i]t is a fundamental tenet of the common law that an offer is generally freely revocable"); Cook v. Coldwell Banker, 967 S.W.2d 654, 657 (Mo. App. E. Dist. 1998) ("Generally, an offeror may withdraw an offer at any time prior to acceptance unless the offer is supported by consideration.").

The question, then, is whether the law offers any protection to offerees or at least allows offerees to protect themselves. We have already discussed one mechanism that protects offerees against the revocation of offers: if an offer can only be accepted by performance, the beginning (or tender of the beginning) of performance will create an option contract that makes the offer irrevocable.[2] In this chapter, we discuss various other ways of making offers irrevocable.

II. The General Option Contract

First, under the general rules of contract law, the offeror can enter into a contract requiring him to abstain from revoking the offer. Such a contract is called an "option contract,"[3] but in the following, we will refer to it as a "general option contract" to distinguish it from other types of option contracts. Because the general option contract is formed under the general rules governing contract formation, it requires mutual assent and consideration.

Note that whenever the parties have formed an option contract, one must distinguish between the option contract, which requires the offeror to keep their offer open, and the main contract that results if the offeree exercises their option by accepting the offer (the "main contract").

> ***Example.*** On January 1, Alpha calls Beta and offers to paint Beta's house for $1,000. Beta replies: "I need some time to think about this, but how about the following: if you promise to keep your offer open for one week, I promise to pay you $10 just for keeping the offer open." Alpha replies: "Okay, deal." Two days later, Beta calls Alpha and tells him she accepts his offer to paint her house. In this case, the option contract is the contract whereby Alpha promises to keep his offer to paint the house open for the week in exchange for Beta's promise to pay $10. The main contract is the contract whereby Alpha promises to paint Beta's house in exchange for Beta's promise to pay Alpha $1,000.

Distinguishing between the general option contract and the main contract is essential, especially because each of these contracts requires mutual assent

2. Restatement (Second) of Contracts § 45.
3. Restatement (Second) of Contracts § 25.

and consideration. Just because the main contract is supported by consideration does not mean that the option contract is also supported by consideration and vice versa.

III. Section 87(1)(a) of the Rest. (2nd) of Contracts

Section 87(1) of the Restatement (Second) of Contracts provides for a simplified way of forming an option contract. Under this provision, a promise to keep an offer open is binding if the promise is in writing and signed, the promise specifies "purported consideration" for extending the offer, the duration for which the offer is extended is reasonable, and the contract created by accepting the offer is fair.[4]

Note that section 87(1) dispenses with both the mutual assent and the consideration requirements. Instead of mutual assent, section 87(1) requires only a unilateral promise. And in place of consideration, mere "purported consideration" is deemed sufficient. The "purported consideration requirement" is satisfied as long as the writing mentions some consideration for making the offer, regardless of whether the relevant consideration is ever paid or whether the parties even intended for the offeree to pay the consideration.[5] Thus, the "purported consideration" can be purely nominal.

However, the rule outlined in section 87(1) has garnered relatively little support among state courts.[6]

Question. On January 1, Beta receives a signed letter from Alpha in which Alpha offers to paint Beta's house for $1,000. The letter also states that "in exchange for having received $10 and other valuable consideration, this offer

4. Restatement (Second) of Contracts § 87(1).
5. Restatement (Second) of Contracts § 87 cmt. b.
6. See 1464-Eight, Ltd. v. Joppich, 154 S.W.3d 101, 110 (Tex. 2004) (noting that "[t]he position taken by section 87(1)(a) of the Restatement (Second) of Contracts is admittedly the minority position among the limited number of state supreme courts that have addressed the question"); see also Lewis v. Fletcher, 617 P.2d 834, 835 (Idaho 1980) (holding that mere purported consideration is insufficient to make a written and signed offer binding, so "the contract fails for want of consideration"); Am. Handkerchief Corp. v. Frannat Realty Co., 109 A.2d 793, 796 (N.J. 1954) (holding that purported consideration is insufficient to make a written and signed offer irrevocable). But see Real Est. Co. of Pittsburgh v. Rudolph, 153 A. 438, 439 (Pa. 1930) (holding that an offer can be made irrevocable via a merely purported consideration of $1); 1464-Eight, Ltd. v. Joppich, 154 S.W.3d 101, 110 (Tex. 2004) (explicitly following the principle set forth in section 87(1) of the Restatement (Second) of Contracts).

is irrevocable for ten days." Beta has not paid Alpha $10, and neither party intends for the $10 to be paid. Is Alpha's offer to paint Beta's house irrevocable for the specified duration? Assume that $1,000 is a fair price for painting the house and that the applicable state law corresponds precisely to the Restatement (Second) of Contracts.

Answer. As a general rule, the offeror can revoke his offer at any time.

The parties have not limited Alpha's ability to revoke his offer via an option contract under the general rules. The formation of an option contract requires mutual assent and consideration. Nothing suggests that Beta has assented to Alpha's promise to keep his offer open. Moreover, Alpha's promise to keep his offer open is not supported by consideration: the letter's reference to "$10 and other valuable consideration" is not consideration since both parties would agree that this wording does not impose any duty on Beta to pay the $10. Moreover, the $1,000 for painting the house is the consideration for the (potential future) contract to paint the house and therefore does not constitute consideration for the promise to keep the offer open.

However, Alpha's offer to paint the house is irrevocable under section 87(1)(a) of the Restatement (Second) of Contracts. Alpha's offer was in writing and signed. Furthermore, the exchange it proposed ($1,000 for painting the house) was fair, and the option's duration (ten days) was reasonable. Finally, the offer cited purported consideration for making the offer, meaning that the offer creates an option contract under section 87(1)(a). It follows that Alpha's offer is irrevocable for the stated period of ten days.

IV. Promissory Estoppel

A promise is binding under the doctrine of promissory estoppel if the promisor should reasonably have expected the promise to induce detrimental reasonable reliance by the promisee and the promise indeed induces such reliance.[7] Even if these conditions are satisfied, the promisor will only be held to this promise required to avoid injustice.[8]

7. Nelson v. Elway, 908 P.2d 102, 110 (Colo. 1995); Schoff v. Combined Ins. Co. of Am., 604 N.W.2d 43, 48 (Iowa 1999); Alaska Bussell Elec. Co. v. Vern Hickel Const. Co., 688 P.2d 576, 579 (Alaska 1984); Restatement (Second) of Contracts § 90.

8. Nelson v. Elway, 908 P.2d 102, 110 (Colo. 1995); Schoff v. Combined Ins. Co. of Am., 604 N.W.2d 43, 48 (Iowa 1999); Alaska Bussell Elec. Co. v. Vern Hickel Const. Co., 688 P.2d 576, 579 (Alaska 1984); Restatement (Second) of Contracts § 90.

In other words, if the offeror promises to keep their offer open and the other party relies on that promise by rejecting other offers, the promisor's offer may be irrevocable under promissory estoppel.

V. Section 87(2) of the Rest. (2nd) of Contracts

Under section 87(2) of the Restatement (Second) of Contracts, an offer can be binding as an option contract if the offer should reasonably expect their offer to induce substantial reliance and the offer in fact induces such reliance.[9] Even if these conditions are satisfied, the offer is only irrevocable to the extent required to prevent injustice.[10]

Question. Alpha is a painter. On January 1, he receives a letter from Beta stating: "Dear Alpha, I offer to pay you $10,000 in exchange for your promise to paint my portrait in oil. However, the portrait must be painted entirely in maroon." Immediately after receiving Beta's letter, Alpha purchases an ample supply of maroon oil colors for $500. On January 3, Beta calls Alpha and tells Alpha that he, Beta, revokes his offer. Does Alpha still have the power of acceptance? Assume that the applicable common law corresponds precisely to the Restatement (Second) of Contracts.

Answer. Alpha had the power of acceptance as a result of Beta's offer. The question is whether Alpha's power of acceptance was terminated by revocation. As a general rule, offers are freely revocable. Moreover, the parties have not formed an option contract under the general rules, given that Beta has not promised to keep his offer open. Similarly, Alpha cannot invoke promissory estoppel since Beta has not made a promise. Furthermore, Beta's offer is not irrevocable under § 87(1)(a) since it neither purports to be irrevocable nor recites any purported consideration. But what about section 87(2)? The critical requirements for an offer to be irrevocable under this section are that the offeror should reasonably have expected the offeree to rely on their offer and that the offer in fact induced such reliance. In the case at hand, it is difficult to view Alpha's reliance as reasonable since Alpha had to know that Beta could

9. Restatement (Second) of Contracts § 87(2). Some courts have explicitly embraced this rule. E.g., Cataldo Ambul. Serv., Inc. v. City of Chelsea, 688 N.E.2d 959, 961 (Mass. 1998); Rhode Island Hosp. Tr. Nat. Bank v. Varadian, 647 N.E.2d 1174, 1178 (Mass. 1995).
10. Restatement (Second) of Contracts § 87(2).

revoke the offer at any time and since Alpha could readily have accepted the offer before buying otherwise unusable oil colors.

VI. Section 45 of the Rest. (2nd) of Contracts

Under section 45 of the Restatement (Second) of Contracts, if an offer can only be accepted via performance, the beginning of such performance creates an option contract that makes the offer irrevocable.[11] In addition to the beginning of performance, the tender of the beginning of performance is also sufficient.[12] By contrast, actions of a merely preparatory nature are insufficient to create an option contract under this provision. Note, however, that according to some courts, substantial performance is required to make the offer irrevocable.[13]

> **Example.** Alpha offers to pay Beta $500 for painting Alpha's house while specifying that the offer can only be accepted by performance. Beta starts to paint Alpha's house the same day. However, when Beta has completed 2 % of his work, Alpha tries to revoke his offer. Assuming that the applicable common law corresponds to the Restatement (Second) of contracts, Alpha's attempt to revoke has no effect since the beginning of performance created an option contract under section 45.

VII. The Firm Offer Rule

Section 2-205 of the Uniform Commercial Code, also known as the "firm offer rule," allows merchants to make offers that are irrevocable for up to three months.[14] For the firm offer rule to apply, the offer's terms must provide assurance that the offer will be held open. If the offer only states that it is

---

11. Restatement (Second) of Contracts § 45. See, e.g., Strata Prod. Co. v. Mercury Expl. Co., 916 P.2d 822, 828 n.2 (N.M. 1996) (holding that "[t]he beginning of performance on an offer for a unilateral contract essentially creates a binding contract with the condition that the offeree complete performance"); Pavel Enterprises, Inc. v. A.S. Johnson Co., Inc., 674 A.2d 521, 530 (Md. 1996) (holding that part performance renders offer for a unilateral contract irrevocable); Boswell v. Panera Bread Co., 879 F.3d 296, 302 (8th Cir. 2018) (holding that "offeree must merely begin performance" to make offer for unilateral contract irrevocable).
12. Restatement (Second) of Contracts § 45.
13. E.g., Storti v. U. of Washington, 330 P.3d 159, 164 (Wash. 2014); Cook v. Coldwell Banker, 967 S.W.2d 654, 657 (Mo. App. E. Dist. 1998).
14. UCC § 2-205.

irrevocable, without stating a time, it is irrevocable for a reasonable time (though not exceeding three months). If the offer purports to be irrevocable for a time exceeding three months, it stops being irrevocable after three months unless it is irrevocable on some other basis. Importantly, revocable is not the same as revoked. Thus, even if an originally irrevocable offer becomes revocable, the offeree retains their power of acceptance unless the offer is actually revoked or the power of acceptance is terminated in some other way.

Berryman v. Kmoch

Supreme Court of Kansas, 221 Kan. 304 (1977)

FROMME, Justice:

Wade Berryman, a landowner, filed this declaratory judgment action to have an option contract declared null and void. Norbert H. Kmoch, the optionee, answered and counter-claimed seeking damages for Berryman's failure to convey the land. After depositions were taken and discovery proceedings completed both parties filed separate motions for summary judgment. The trial court entered a summary judgment for plaintiff and held the option was granted without consideration, was in effect an offer to sell subject to withdrawal at any time prior to acceptance and was withdrawn in July, 1973, prior to its being exercised by Kmoch. Kmoch has appealed.

The option agreement dated June 19, 1973, was signed by Wade Berryman of Meade, Kansas, and was addressed to Mr. Norbert H. Kmoch, 1155 Ash Street, Denver, Colorado. The granting clause provided:

'For $10.00 and other valuable consideration, I hereby grant unto you or your assigns an option for 120 days after date to purchase the following described real estate: (Then followed the legal description of 960 acres of land located in Stanton County, Kansas.)'

The balance of the option agreement sets forth the terms of purchase including the price for the land and the growing crops, the water rights and irrigation equipment included in the sale, the time possession was to be delivered to the purchaser, and other provisions not pertinent to the questions presented here on appeal.

Before examining the questions raised on appeal it will be helpful to set forth a few of the facts admitted and on which there is no dispute. Berryman was the owner of the land. Kmoch was a Colorado real estate broker. A third person, Samuel N. Goertz, was a Nebraska agricultural consultant. Goertz learned that Berryman was interested in selling the land and talked to Berryman about obtaining an option on the land for Kmoch. Goertz talked to Kmoch and Kmoch prepared the option contract dated June 19, 1973. Goertz and Kmoch flew to Johnson, Kansas, where a meeting with Berryman had been arranged. At this meeting the option agreement was signed by Berryman. Although the agreement recited the option was granted 'for $10.00 and other valuable consideration', the $10.00 was not paid.

The next conversation between Berryman and Kmoch occurred during the latter part of July, 1973. Berryman called Kmoch by telephone and asked to be released from the option agreement. Nothing definite was worked out between them. Berryman sold the land to another person. In August, Kmoch decided to exercise the option and went to the Federal Land Bank representative in Garden City, Kansas, to make arrangements to purchase the land. He was then informed by the bank representative that the land had been sold by Berryman. Kmoch then recorded the option agreement in Stanton County. After a telephone conversation with Berryman was unproductive, Kmoch sent a letter to Berryman in October, 1973, attempting to exercise his option on the land. Berryman responded by bringing the present action to have the option declared null and void.

Appellant, Kmoch, acknowledges that the $10.00 cash consideration recited in the option agreement was never paid. However, he points out the agreement included a provision for 'other valuable consideration' and that he should have been permitted to introduce evidence to establish time spent and expenses incurred in an effort to interest others in joining him in acquiring the land. He points to the deposition testimony of Goertz and another man by the name of Robert Harris, who had examined the land under option. Their services were sought by Kmoch to obtain a farm report on the land which might interest other investors. In addition appellant argues that promissory estoppel should have been applied by the trial court as a substitute for consideration.

An option contract to purchase land to be binding must be supported by consideration the same as any other contract. If no consideration was given in the present case the trial court correctly found there was no more than a continuing offer to sell. An option contract which is not supported by consideration is a mere offer to sell which may be withdrawn at any time prior to acceptance. (91 C.J.S. Vendor & Purchaser s 15, p. 868; 77 Am.Jur.2d, Vendor and Purchaser, s 34, p. 214; cf. Talbott v. Nibert, 167 Kan. 138, 144, 206 P.2d 131.) . .

.

We turn next to appellant's contention that the option contract should have been enforceable under the doctrine of promissory estoppel. This doctrine has been discussed in Marker v. Preferred Fire Ins. Co., 211 Kan. 427, 506 P.2d 1163, and in Kirkpatrick v. Seneca National Bank, 213 Kan. 61, 515 P.2d 781. In Marker it is held:

'In order for the doctrine of promissory estoppel to be invoked the evidence must show that the promise was made under circumstances where the promisor intended and reasonably expected that the promise would be relied upon by the promisee and further that the promisee acted reasonably in relying upon the promise. Furthermore, promissory estoppel should be applied only if a refusal to enforce it would be virtually to sanction the perpetration of fraud or would result in other injustice.' (211 Kan. 427, Syl. 4, 506 P.2d 1163.)

In Kirkpatrick it is held:

'Under the doctrine of promissory estoppel a promise is binding and will be enforced when it is a promise which the promisor should reasonably expect to induce action or forbearance of a definite and substantial character on the part of the promisee and which does induce such action or forbearance and if injustice can be avoided only by enforcement of the promise.' (213 Kan. 61, Syl. 1, 515 P.2d 781.)

In order for the doctrine of promissory estoppel to be invoked as a substitute for consideration the evidence must show (1) the promise was made under such circumstances that the promisor reasonably expected the promisee to act in reliance on the promise, (2) the promisee acted as could reasonably be expected in relying on the promise, and (3) a refusal by the court to enforce the promise must be virtually to sanction the perpetration of fraud or must result in other injustice.

The requirements are not met here. This was an option contract promising to sell the land to appellant. It was not a contract listing the real estate with Kmoch for sale to others. Kmoch was familiar with real estate contracts and personally drew up the present option. He knew no consideration was paid for the same and that it had the effect of a continuing offer subject to withdrawal at any time before acceptance. The acts which appellant urges as consideration conferred no special benefit on the promisor or on his land. The evidence which appellant desires to introduce in support of promissory estoppel does not relate to acts which could reasonably be expected as a result of extending the option promise. It relates to time, effort, and expense incurred in an attempt to interest other investors in this particular land. The appellant chose the form of the contract. It was not a contract listing the land for sale with one entrusted with duties and obligations to produce a buyer. The appellant was not obligated to do anything and no basis for promissory estoppel could be shown by the evidence proposed.

An option contract can be made binding and irrevocable by subsequent action in reliance upon it even though such action is neither requested nor given in exchange for the option promise. An option promise is no different from other promises in this respect but cases are rare in which an option holder will be reasonably induced to change his position in reliance upon an option promise that is neither under seal nor made binding by a consideration, or in which the option promisor has reason to expect such change of position. (1A Corbin on Contracts, s 263, pp. 502-504.)

When an option is conditioned upon a performance of certain acts, the performance of the acts may constitute a consideration to uphold a contract for option; but there is no such condition imposed if the acts were not intended to benefit nor were they incurred on behalf of the optionor.

The appellant argues that to assume Berryman gave the option without expecting something from him in return is to avoid the realities of the business world and that consideration was encompassed by a promise for a promise. The difficulty with that argument is apparent. Appellant did not promise to purchase the land. He was required to do nothing and any assertion that Berryman expected him to raise and pay money for the land as consideration for the option confuses motive with consideration.

In 17 Am.Jur.2d, Contracts, s 93, pp. 436, 437, it is said:

'The motive which prompts one to enter into a contract and the consideration for the contract are distinct and different things. . . . These inducements are not . . . either legal or equitable consideration, and actually compose no part of the contract. . . .'

In 1 Williston on Contracts, 3rd Ed., s 111, p. 439, it is stated:

'Though desire to obtain the consideration for a promise may be, and ordinarily is, the motive inducing the promisor to enter into a contract, yet this is not essential nor, on the other hand, can any motive serve in itself as consideration. . . .'

Appellant here confuses Berryman's possible motives-to sell the land-with consideration given. The fact Berryman expected appellant to expend time and money to find a buyer is really irrelevant because he was not bound to do so. He made no promise legally enforceable by Berryman to that effect. To be sufficient consideration, a promise must impose a legal obligation on the promisor. (17 Am.Jur.2d, Contracts, s 105, pp. 450-451.) As stated in 1A Corbin on Contracts, s 263, p. 505:

'. . . So, if the only consideration is an illusory promise, there is no contract and no binding option, although there may still be an operative offer and a power of acceptance.'

Time and money spent by a party in trying to sell property for which he holds an option cannot be construed as a consideration to the party from whom he has secured the option. (Comstock v. North, 88 Miss. 754, 41 So. 374; Axe v. Tolbert, 179 Mich. 556, 146 N.W. 418; Kelley v. Rouse, 188 Cal.App.2d 92, 10 Cal. Rptr. 235.) . . .

Now we turn to the question of revocation or withdrawal of the option-promise before acceptance.

Where an offer is for the sale of an interest in land or in other things, if the offeror, after making the offer, sells or contracts to sell the interest to another person, and the offeree acquires reliable information of that fact, before he has exercised his power of creating a contract by acceptance of the offer, the offer is revoked.

In Restatement of the Law, Second, Contracts, s 42, p. 96, it is said:

'An offeree's power of acceptance is terminated when the offeror takes definite action inconsistent with an intention to enter into the proposed contract and the offeree acquires reliable information to that effect.'

The appellant in his deposition admitted that he was advised in July, 1973, by telephone that Berryman no longer wanted to be obligated by the option. Appellant further admitted that he has advised in August, 1973, by a representative of the Federal Land Bank, which held a substantial mortgage on the land, that Berryman had disposed of this land. The appellant's power of acceptance was terminated thereby and any attempted exercise of the option in October came too late when you consider the appellant's own admissions.

Summary judgment was therefore proper and the judgment is affirmed.

. . .

NOTES AND QUESTIONS

*A. **Option contracts.*** An option contract is a contract by which a party promises to abstain from revoking their offer.[15] As a general rule, an option contract must satisfy the same formation requirements as any other contract, namely mutual assent and consideration.[16] However, under the common law, option contracts can also be formed in several other ways. Read sections 45, 87(1), 87(2), and 90(1) of the Restatement (Second) of Contracts.

*B. **Consideration.*** Assuming, hypothetically, that the parties' option agreement imposed a duty on Kmoch to pay $10 in exchange for Berryman's promise to keep the offer open. In that case, is the consideration requirement satisfied regardless of whether Kmoch actually pays the $10? How does the court justify its conclusion that Berryman's promise to keep his offer open was not supported by consideration?

*C. **Promissory estoppel.*** In the absence of consideration, a promise to keep an offer open can be binding under the doctrine of promissory estoppel.[17] For this doctrine to apply, the promisee must have detrimentally relied on the promise in a way that the promisor should have reasonably expected.[18] Moreover, enforcement of the promise must be necessary to prevent injustice.[19] In *Berryman*, the court dismisses the application of the promissory estoppel doctrine. What are the grounds for this rejection, and do you concur with the court's rationale?

*D. **Purported consideration.*** Section 87(1) of the Restatement (Second) of Contracts provides for a simplified way of forming an option contract. Under this provision, a promise to keep an offer open is binding if (1) the promise is in writing and signed, (2) the promise specifies purported consideration for extending the offer, (3) the duration for which the offer is extended is reasonable, and (4) the contract created by accepting the offer is fair.[20] Note that section 87(1) dispenses with both the mutual assent and the consideration requirements. Instead of mutual assent, section 87(1) requires only a unilateral promise. And in place of consideration, mere purported consideration is deemed sufficient. The purported consideration requirement is satisfied as

---

15. See Restatement (Second) of Contracts § 25 (defining option contract).
16. Restatement (Second) of Contracts § 17.
17. Restatement (Second) of Contracts § 90(1).
18. Restatement (Second) of Contracts § 90(1).
19. Restatement (Second) of Contracts § 90(1).
20. Restatement (Second) of Contracts § 87(1).

long as the writing mentions some consideration for making the offer, regardless of whether the relevant consideration was paid or whether the parties even intended for the offeree to pay the consideration.[21] Thus, the "purported consideration" can be purely nominal. However, the rule set forth in section 87(1) has garnered relatively little support among state courts.[22] How does the *Berryman* court deal with the rule in section 87(1)?

James Baird Co. v. Gimbel Bros. Inc

Circuit Court of Appeals, Second Circuit, 64 F.2d 344 (1933)

L. HAND, Circuit Judge.

The plaintiff sued the defendant for breach of a contract to deliver linoleum under a contract of sale; the defendant denied the making of the contract. . . .

The defendant, a New York merchant, knew that the Department of Highways in Pennsylvania had asked for bids for the construction of a public building. It sent an employee to the office of a contractor in Philadelphia, who had possession of the specifications, and the employee there computed the amount of the linoleum which would be required on the job, underestimating the total yardage by about one-half the proper amount. In ignorance of this mistake, on December twenty-fourth the defendant sent to some twenty or thirty contractors, likely to bid on the job, an offer to supply all the linoleum required by the specifications at two different lump sums, depending upon the quality used. These offers concluded as follows: 'If successful in being

21. Restatement (Second) of Contracts § 87 cmt. b.

22. See 1464-Eight, Ltd. v. Joppich, 154 S.W.3d 101, 110 (Tex. 2004) (noting that "[t]he position taken by section 87(1)(a) of the Restatement (Second) of Contracts is admittedly the minority position among the limited number of state supreme courts that have addressed the question"); see also Lewis v. Fletcher, 617 P.2d 834, 835 (Idaho 1980) (holding that mere purported consideration is insufficient to make a written and signed offer binding, so "the contract fails for want of consideration"); Am. Handkerchief Corp. v. Frannat Realty Co., 109 A.2d 793, 796 (N.J. 1954) (holding that purported consideration is insufficient to make a written and signed offer irrevocable); but see Real Est. Co. of Pittsburgh v. Rudolph, 153 A. 438, 439 (Pa. 1930) (holding that an offer can be made irrevocable via a merely purported consideration of $1); 1464-Eight, Ltd. v. Joppich, 154 S.W.3d 101, 110 (Tex. 2004) (explicitly following the principle set forth in section 87(1) of the Restatement (Second) of Contracts).

awarded this contract, it will be absolutely guaranteed, * * * and * * * we are offering these prices for reasonable' (sic), 'prompt acceptance after the general contract has been awarded.' The plaintiff, a contractor in Washington, got one of these on the twenty-eighth, and on the same day the defendant learned its mistake and telegraphed all the contractors to whom it had sent the offer, that it withdrew it and would substitute a new one at about double the amount of the old. This withdrawal reached the plaintiff at Washington on the afternoon of the same day, but not until after it had put in a bid at Harrisburg at a lump sum, based as to linoleum upon the prices quoted by the defendant. The public authorities accepted the plaintiff's bid on December thirtieth, the defendant having meanwhile written a letter of confirmation of its withdrawal, received on the thirty-first. The plaintiff formally accepted the offer on January second, and, as the defendant persisted in declining to recognize the existence of a contract, sued it for damages on a breach.

Unless there are circumstances to take it out of the ordinary doctrine, since the offer was withdrawn before it was accepted, the acceptance was too late. Restatement of Contracts, § 35. To meet this the plaintiff argues as follows: It was a reasonable implication from the defendant's offer that it should be irrevocable in case the plaintiff acted upon it, that is to say, used the prices quoted in making its bid, thus putting itself in a position from which it could not withdraw without great loss. While it might have withdrawn its bid after receiving the revocation, the time had passed to submit another, and as the item of linoleum was a very trifling part of the cost of the whole building, it would have been an unreasonable hardship to expect it to lose the contract on that account, and probably forfeit its deposit. While it is true that the plaintiff might in advance have secured a contract conditional upon the success of its bid, this was not what the defendant suggested. It understood that the contractors would use its offer in their bids, and would thus in fact commit themselves to supplying the linoleum at the proposed prices. The inevitable implication from all this was that when the contractors acted upon it, they accepted the offer and promised to pay for the linoleum, in case their bid were accepted.

It was of course possible for the parties to make such a contract, and the question is merely as to what they meant; that is, what is to be imputed to the words they used. Whatever plausibility there is in the argument, is in the fact that the defendant must have known the predicament in which the contractors would be put if it withdrew its offer after the bids went in. However, it seems entirely clear that the contractors did not suppose that they accepted the offer merely by putting in their bids. If, for example, the successful one had repudiated the contract with the public authorities after it had been awarded to him, certainly the defendant could not have sued him for a breach. If he had become bankrupt, the defendant could not prove against his estate. It seems plain therefore that there was no contract between them. And if there be any doubt as to this, the language of the offer sets it at rest. The phrase, 'if successful in being awarded this contract,' is scarcely met by the mere use of the prices in the bids. Surely such a use was not an 'award' of the contract to the defendant. Again, the phrase, 'we are offering these prices for * * * prompt acceptance after the general contract has been awarded,' looks to the usual communication of an acceptance, and precludes the idea that the use of the offer in the bidding shall be the equivalent. It may indeed be argued that this last language contemplated no more then an early notice that the offer had been accepted, the actual acceptance being the bid, but that would wrench its natural meaning too far, especially in the light of the preceding phrase. The contractors had a ready escape from their difficulty by insisting upon a contract before they used the figures; and in commercial transactions it does not in the end promote justice to seek strained interpretations in aid of those who do not protect themselves.

But the plaintiff says that even though no bilateral contract was made, the defendant should be held under the doctrine of 'promissory estoppel.' This is to be chiefly found in those cases where persons subscribe to a venture, usually charitable, and are held to their promises after it has been completed. It has been applied much more broadly, however, and has now been generalized in section 90, of the Restatement of Contracts. We may arguendo accept it as it there reads, for it does not apply to the case at bar. Offers are ordinarily made in exchange for a consideration, either a counter-promise or some other act which the promisor wishes to secure. In such cases they propose bargains; they presuppose that each promise or performance is an inducement to the other. . . . But a man may make a promise without expecting an equivalent; a donative promise, conditional or absolute. The common law provided for such by sealed instruments, and it is unfortunate that these are no longer generally available. The doctrine of 'promissory estoppel' is to avoid the harsh results of allowing the promisor in such a case to repudiate, when the promisee has acted in reliance upon the promise. Siegel v. Spear & Co., 234 N.

Y. 479, 138 N. E. 414, 26 A. L. R. 1205. Cf. Allegheny College v. National Bank, 246 N. Y. 369, 159 N. E. 173, 57 L. R. A. 980. But an offer for an exchange is not meant to become a promise until a consideration has been received, either a counter-promise or whatever else is stipulated. To extend it would be to hold the offeror regardless of the stipulated condition of his offer. In the case at bar the defendant offered to deliver the linoleum in exchange for the plaintiff's acceptance, not for its bid, which was a matter of indifference to it. That offer could become a promise to deliver only when the equivalent was received; that is, when the plaintiff promised to take and pay for it. There is no room in such a situation for the doctrine of 'promissory estoppel.'

Nor can the offer be regarded as of an option, giving the plaintiff the right seasonably to accept the linoleum at the quoted prices if its bid was accepted, but not binding it to take and pay, if it could get a better bargain elsewhere. There is not the least reason to suppose that the defendant meant to subject itself to such one-sided obligation. True, if so construed, the doctrine of 'promissory estoppel' might apply, the plaintiff having acted in reliance upon it, though, so far as we have found, the decisions are otherwise. Ganss v. Guffey Petroleum Co., 125 App. Div. 760, 110 N. Y. S. 176; Comstock v. North, 88 Miss. 754, 41 So. 374. As to that, however, we need not declare ourselves.

Judgment affirmed.

NOTES AND QUESTIONS

A. Restatement (First) of Contracts. *James Baird Co. v. Gimbel Bros. Inc.* predates the Restatement (Second) of Contracts (1981). Accordingly, the court cites the original Restatement of Contracts (1932) rather than the Restatement (Second) of Contracts However, the original Restatement of Contracts did not contain the provision explicitly governing reliance on offers, which can be found in section 87(2) of the Restatement (Second) of Contracts.

B. The firm offer rule. The so-called firm-offer rule in section 2-205 of the Uniform Commercial Code (UCC) allows merchants to make irrevocable offers with respect to the sale of goods. However, this rule was not available at the time of *Baird* either. Pennsylvania, incidentally the first state to adopt the UCC, did not enact the UCC until 1953, effective July 1, 1954.[23]

C. Promise to keep the offer open. The court rejects the argument that the

23. ACT OF APR. 6, 1953, 1953 PA. LAWS 3.

defendant promised to keep the offer open until after the bidding process. What legal rationale does the court invoke? Can you think of counterarguments?

D. The meaning of promise. The Restatement (Second) of Contracts defines the terms "contract," "promise," and "offer" in its sections 1, 2, and 24 respectively. How does the court in *Baird* conceptualize the relationship between an offer and a promise?

E. Section 87(2) of the Restatement. Section 87(2) of the Restatement (Second) of Contracts explicitly governs reliance on offers. Is this provision consistent or inconsistent with the court's view in *Baird*?

F. Protecting the offeree. How does the plaintiff fare in *Baird*? Is there anything that the plaintiff could or should have done to protect his interests?

G. Hypothetical variation. Assume that the facts of *Baird* occurred today in a state that has enacted Article 2 of the UCC and whose common law on contracts mirrors the Restatement (Second) of Contracts. How would this case be decided?

William A. Drennan v. Star Paving Company

Supreme Court of California, In Bank, 51 Cal.2d 409 (1958)

TRAYNOR, Justice

Defendant appeals from a judgment for plaintiff in an action to recover damages caused by defendant's refusal to perform certain paving work according to a bid it submitted to plaintiff.

On July 28, 1955, plaintiff, a licensed general contractor, was preparing a bid on the 'Monte Vista School Job' in the Lancaster school district. Bids had to be submitted before 8:00 p. m. Plaintiff testified that it was customary in that area for general contractors to receive the bids of subcontractors by telephone on the day set for bidding and to rely on them in computing their own bids. Thus on that day plaintiff's secretary, Mrs. Johnson, received by telephone between fifty and seventy-five subcontractors' bids for various parts of the school job. As each bid came in, she wrote it on a special form, which she brought into plaintiff's office. He then posted it on a master cost sheet setting forth the names and bids of all subcontractors. His own bid had to include the names of subcontractors who were to perform one-half of one per cent or more of the construction work, and he had also to provide a bidder's bond of ten per cent of his total bid of $317,385 as a guarantee that he would enter the contract if awarded the work.

Late in the afternoon, Mrs. Johnson had a telephone conversation with Kenneth R. Hoon, an estimator for defendant. He gave his name and telephone number and stated that he was bidding for defendant for the paving work at the Monte Vista School according to plans and specifications and that his bid was $7,131.60. At Mrs. Johnson's request he repeated his bid. Plaintiff listened to the bid over an extension telephone in his office and posted it on the master sheet after receiving the bid form from Mrs. Johnson. Defendant's was the lowest bid for the paving. Plaintiff computed his own bid accordingly and submitted it with the name of defendant as the subcontractor for the paving. When the bids were opened on July 28th, plaintiff's proved to be the lowest, and he was awarded the contract.

On his way to Los Angeles the next morning plaintiff stopped at defendant's office. The first person he met was defendant's construction engineer, Mr. Oppenheimer. Plaintiff testified: 'I introduced myself and he immediately told me that they had made a mistake in their bid to me the night before, they couldn't do it for the price they had bid, and I told him I would expect him to carry through with their original bid because I had used it in compiling my bid and the job was being awarded them. And I would have to go and do the job according to my bid and I would expect them to do the same.'

Defendant refused to do the paving work for less than $15,000. Plaintiff testified that he 'got figures from other people' and after trying for several months to get as low a bid as possible engaged L & H Paving Company, a firm in Lancaster, to do the work for $10,948.60.

The trial court found on substantial evidence that defendant made a definite offer to do the paving on the Monte Vista job according to the plans and specifications for $7,131.60, and that plaintiff relied on defendant's bid in computing his own bid for the school job and naming defendant therein as the subcontractor for the paving work. Accordingly, it entered judgment for plaintiff in the amount of $3,817.00 (the difference between defendant's bid and the cost of the paving to plaintiff) plus costs.

Defendant contends that there was no enforceable contract between the parties on the ground that it made a revocable offer and revoked it before plaintiff communicated his acceptance to defendant.

There is no evidence that defendant offered to make its bid irrevocable in exchange for plaintiff's use of its figures in computing his bid. Nor is there evidence that would warrant interpreting plaintiff's use of defendant's bid as the acceptance thereof, binding plaintiff, on condition he received the main contract, to award the subcontract to defendant. In sum, there was neither an option supported by consideration nor a bilateral contract binding on both parties.

Plaintiff contends, however, that he relied to his detriment on defendant's offer and that defendant must therefore answer in damages for its refusal to perform. Thus, the question is squarely presented: Did plaintiff's reliance make defendant's offer irrevocable?

Section 90 of the Restatement of Contracts states: 'A promise which the promisor should reasonably expect to induce action or forbearance of a definite and substantial character on the part of the promisee and which does induce such action or forbearance is binding if injustice can be avoided only by enforcement of the promise.' This rule applies in this state....

Defendant's offer constituted a promise to perform on such conditions as were stated expressly or by implication therein or annexed thereto by operation of law. (See 1 Williston, Contracts (3rd. ed.), s 24A, p. 56, s 61, p. 196.) Defendant had reason to expect that if its bid proved the lowest it would be used by plaintiff. It induced 'action * * * of a definite and substantial character on the part of the promisee.'

Had defendant's bid expressly stated or clearly implied that it was revocable at any time before acceptance we would treat it accordingly. It was silent on revocation, however, and we must therefore determine whether there are conditions to the right of revocation imposed by law or reasonably inferable in fact. In the analogous problem of an offer for a unilateral contract, the theory is now obsolete that the offer is revocable at any time before complete performance. Thus section 45 of the Restatement of Contracts provides: 'If an offer for a unilateral contract is made, and part of the consideration requested in the offer is given or tendered by the offeree in response thereto, the offeror is bound by a contract, the duty of immediate performance of which is conditional on the full consideration being given or tendered within the time stated in the offer, or, if no time is stated therein, within a reasonable time.' In explanation, comment b states that the 'main offer includes as a subsidiary promise, necessarily implied, that if part of the requested performance is given, the offeror will not revoke his offer, and that if tender is made it will be accepted.

Part performance or tender may thus furnish consideration for the subsidiary promise. Moreover, merely acting in justifiable reliance on an offer may in some cases serve as sufficient reason for making a promise binding (see s 90).'

Whether implied in fact or law, the subsidiary promise serves to preclude the injustice that would result if the offer could be revoked after the offeree had acted in detrimental reliance thereon. Reasonable reliance resulting in a foreseeable prejudicial change in position affords a compelling basis also for implying a subsidiary promise not to revoke an offer for a bilateral contract.

The absence of consideration is not fatal to the enforcement of such a promise. It is true that in the case of unilateral contracts the Restatement finds consideration for the implied subsidiary promise in the part performance of the bargained-for exchange, but its reference to section 90 makes clear that consideration for such a promise is not always necessary. The very purpose of section 90 is to make a promise binding even though there was no consideration 'in the sense of something that is bargained for and given in exchange.' (See 1 Corbin, Contracts 634 et seq.) Reasonable reliance serves to hold the offeror in lieu of the consideration ordinarily required to make the offer binding. In a case involving similar facts the Supreme Court of South Dakota stated that 'we believe that reason and justice demand that the doctrine (of section 90) be applied to the present facts. We cannot believe that by accepting this doctrine as controlling in the state of facts before us we will abolish the requirement of a consideration in contract cases, in any different sense than an ordinary estoppel abolishes some legal requirement in its application. We are of the opinion, therefore, that the defendants in executing the agreement (which was not supported by consideration) made a promise which they should have reasonably expected would induce the plaintiff to submit a bid based thereon to the Government, that such promise did induce this action, and that injustice can be avoided only by enforcement of the promise.' Northwestern Engineering Co. v. Ellerman, 69 S.D. 397, 408, 10 N.W.2d 879, 884; see also, Robert Gordon, Inc., v. Ingersoll-Rand Co., 7 Cir., 117 F.2d 654, 661; cf. James Baird Co. v. Gimbel Bros., 2 Cir., 64 F.2d 344.

When plaintiff used defendant's offer in computing his own bid, he bound himself to perform in reliance on defendant's terms. Though defendant did not bargain for this use of its bid neither did defendant make it idly, indifferent to whether it would be used or not. On the contrary it is reasonable to suppose that defendant submitted its bid to obtain the subcontract. It was bound to realize the substantial possibility that its bid would be the lowest, and that it would be included by plaintiff in his bid. It was to its own interest that the contractor be awarded the general contract; the lower the subcontract bid, the lower the general contractor's bid was likely to be and the greater its chance of acceptance and hence the greater defendant's chance of getting the paving subcontract. Defendant had reason not only to expect plaintiff to rely on its bid but to want him to. Clearly defendant had a stake in plaintiffs reliance on its bid. Given this interest and the fact that plaintiff is bound by his own bid, it is only fair that plaintiff should have at least an opportunity to accept defendant's bid after the general contract has been awarded to him.

It bears noting that a general contractor is not free to delay acceptance after he has been awarded the general contract in the hope of getting a better price. Nor can he reopen bargaining with the subcontractor and at the same time claim a continuing right to accept the original offer. See, R. J. Daum Const. Co. v. Child, Utah, 247 P.2d 817, 823. In the present case plaintiff promptly informed defendant that plaintiff was being awarded the job and that the subcontract was being awarded to defendant.

Defendant contends, however, that its bid was the result of mistake and that it was therefore entitled to revoke it. It relies on the rescission cases of M. F. Kemper Const. Co. v. City of Los Angeles, 37 Cal.2d 696, 235 P.2d 7, and Brunzell Const. Co. v. G. J. Weisbrod, Inc., 134 Cal.App.2d 278, 285 P.2d 989. . . . In those cases, however, the bidder's mistake was known or should have been known to the offeree, and the offeree could be placed in status quo. Of course, if plaintiff had reason to believe that defendant's bid was in error, he could not justifiably rely on it, and section 90 would afford no basis for enforcing it. Robert Gordon, Inc., v. Ingersoll-Rand, Inc., 7 Cir., 117 F.2d 654, 660. Plaintiff, however, had no reason to know that defendant had made a mistake in submitting its bid, since there was usually a variance of 160 per cent between the highest and lowest bids for paving in the desert around Lancaster. He committed himself to performing the main contract in reliance on defendant's figures. Under these circumstances defendant's mistake, far from relieving it of its obligation, constitutes an additional reason for enforcing it, for it misled plaintiff as to the cost of doing the paving. . . . As between the subcontractor who made the bid and the general contractor who reasonably relied on it, the loss resulting from the mistake should fall on the party who caused it. . . .

The judgment is affirmed.

GIBSON C. J., and SHENK, SCHAUER, SPENCE and MCCOMB, JJ., concur.

NOTES AND QUESTIONS

A. Promissory estoppel. How does the court justify the application of the promissory estoppel doctrine?

B. The Drennan rule. Section 87(2) of the Restatement (Second) of Contracts is generally known as the "*Drennan* rule" because it protects reliance on offers, thereby leading to the same outcome as the *Drennan* court's application of promissory estoppel. The *Drennan* rule is now widely followed.[24]

C. Hypothetical variation. Assume, hypothetically, that immediately after being awarded the bid, the plaintiff had called the defendant and left a voicemail on his answering machine stating, "Hi, this is Drennan. We were awarded the Monte Vista School project. I accept your offer to do the paving work for us." How would that have impacted the court's analysis?

D. Bid shopping and bid chopping. After having been awarded a building project, a general contractor will sometimes try to find a cheaper subcontractor ("bid shopping") or attempt to negotiate an even better deal with the original subcontractor ("bid chopping"). Either practice will prevent the general contractor from invoking section 87(2) of the Restatement (Second) of Contracts.[25]

E. Implied option contract offer. Eric Alden has suggested that the *Drennan* court should have taken a different approach.[26] According to Alden, the court should have interpreted the subcontractor's original communication as containing an implied offer to enter into an option contract and found that by

24. See, e.g., Seater Const. Co., Inc. v. Rawson Plumbing, Inc., 619 N.W.2d 293, 298 (Wis. App. 2000) (holding a subcontractor to his bid where the general contractor had relied on the bid in making a bid to the city); Alaska Bussell Elec. Co. v. Vern Hickel Const. Co., 688 P.2d 576, 580 (Alaska 1984) (following Drennan with respect to subcontractor's bid); Loranger Const. Corp. v. E. F. Hauserman Co., 374 N.E.2d 306, 309 (Mass. App. 1978), aff'd, 384 N.E.2d 176 (Mass. 1978) (following Drennan with respect to subcontractor's bid).

25. See, e.g., Complete Gen. Constr. Co. v. Kard Welding, Inc., 911 N.E.2d 959, 963 (Ohio App. 10th Dist. 2009) (declining to hold the subcontractor to this bid where the general contractor had attempted to get a better deal from the subcontractor); Foley Co. v. Warren Engr., Inc., 804 F. Supp. 1540, 1546–47 (N.D. Ga. 1992) (declining to hold the subcontractor to his bid where plaintiff had delayed acceptance in order to secure a better price).

26. Eric Alden, Reversing the Reliance Revolution in Contract, 93 WASH. L. REV. 1609, 1663 (2018).

submitting his bid to the city, the plaintiff accepted that option contract offer. What are your thoughts on this line of reasoning?

Cadillac Rubber & Plastics Inc. v. Tubular Metal Systems, LLC

Court of Appeals of Michigan, 952 N.W.2d 576 (Mich. App. 2020)

SAWYER, J.

Plaintiffs (collectively referred to as 'Avon') ... is a supplier of automotive parts. . . Motors. [Defendant Tubular is one of Plaintiff's customers. Defendant placed two purchase orders with plaintiff which provided that defendant would specify the amounts to be delivered each week. In this context, plaintiff had agreed to defendant's general terms of purchase. These terms of purchase contained, inter alia, the following text:]

"...[I]n consideration for ten US dollars (US$10.00), the payment of which shall be made by Buyer upon the termination or non-renewal of this Order, Seller grants to Buyer an irrevocable option during the term of this Order to purchase Supplies in such quantities as determined by Buyer. . . ." . . .

... Avon filed this action seeking declaratory judgment. . . . Avon . . . claimed that the "irrevocable option" ... "is . . . not binding on Avon because it is on Tubular's form and Avon did not separately sign the portion of the form that contains the alleged firm offer. MCL 440.2205." Avon requested a judgment declaring that . . . the alleged "irrevocable option" in Tubular's terms is invalid or unenforceable . . . . Following a hearing, the trial court issued a written opinion and granted summary disposition in favor of Tubular. Avon now appeals, and we affirm. . . . Avon . . . argues that the trial court erred by rejecting Avon's argument that the firm offer contained in Tubular's terms and conditions is not enforceable because Avon had not separately signed that document as required by MCL 440.2205. We disagree.

MCL 440.2205 provides:

An offer by a merchant to buy or sell goods in a signed writing which by its terms gives assurance that it will be held open is not revocable, for lack of consideration, during the time stated or if no time is stated for a reasonable time, but in no event may such period of irrevocability exceed 3 months; but any such term of assurance on a form supplied by the offeree must be separately signed by the offeror.

We agree with the trial court that the separate-signature requirement only applies when no consideration is given for the firm offer. The language clearly and unambiguously establishes a limitation on the length of time that an offer may be considered irrevocable if the firm offer is not supported by consideration—for the stated time, or a reasonable time if there is no stated time, but not for more than three months. In this case, the firm offer was supported by consideration, specifically $10. Therefore, this provision does not apply.

This interpretation of the statutory text is supported by the official comments to UCC § 2-205, upon which MCL 440.2205 is modeled.1 Comment 1 states, "This section is intended to modify the former rule which required that 'firm offers' be sustained by consideration in order to bind, and to require instead that they must merely be characterized as such and expressed in signed writings." MCL 440.2205, comment 1. Comment 3 provides:

This section is intended to apply to current "firm" offers and not to long term options, and an outside time limit of three months during which such offers remain irrevocable has been set. The three-month period during which firm offers remain irrevocable under this section need not be stated by days or by date. If the offer states that it is "guaranteed" or "firm" until the happening of a contingency which will occur within the three-month period, it will remain irrevocable until that event. A promise made for a longer period will operate under this section to bind the offeror only for the first three months of the period but may of course be renewed. If supported by consideration it may continue for as long as the parties specify. *This section deals only with the offer which is not supported by consideration.* [MCL 440.2205, comment 3 (emphasis added).]

In addition to the nonbinding comments, our conclusion is further supported by persuasive precedent from other jurisdictions. See, e.g., *In re Modern Dairy of Champaign, Inc.*, 171 F.3d 1106, 1110 (7th Cir. 1999); in *E. A. Coronis Assocs. v. M. Gordon Constr. Co.*, 90 N.J. Super. 69, 73, 216 A.2d 246 (App. Div., 1966) (UCC § 2-205 was designed to reverse the common-law rule that "an offer not supported by consideration could be revoked at any time prior to acceptance"); *Realty Dev., Inc. v. Kosydar*, 322 N.E.2d 328, 332 (Ohio App., 1974) ("In order to constitute a firm offer to sell, irrevocable and *unnecessary to be founded on consideration*, the quotation must be a 'signed writing' giving assurance that it will be held open for acceptance by the purchaser.") (emphasis added)....

In sum, the clear and unambiguous language of MCL 440.2205 supports the conclusion that that statute is simply inapplicable when a firm offer is supported by consideration. This interpretation is further supported by various persuasive authorities. And Avon makes no argument challenging the adequacy or existence of consideration in this case. Specifically, consideration of $10 was provided for in the agreement....

Affirmed....

FORT HOOD, P.J., concurred with SAWYER, J.

NOTES AND QUESTIONS

*A. **The Firm Offer Rule.*** Does the court's holding threaten to circumvent the limitations that UCC section 2-205 imposes on firm offers?

*B. **Berryman v. Kmoch.*** The court determines that the plaintiff's promise to keep its offer open was supported by consideration. Contrast this conclusion with *Berryman v. Kmoch*, where the court found no consideration for the promise to keep offer open. Why do the two cases differ on this issue?

*C. **Policy.*** What is the likely policy behind the separate-signature requirement in UCC section 2-205?

CHAPTER 7
BATTLE OF THE FORMS

I. Introduction

Under the common law matching principle, a contract is formed only if the acceptance matches the offer exactly. In practice, parties often rely on so-called "boilerplate terms," which are standardized clauses crafted in advance for recurring use across multiple contracts. If both the offer and the acceptance use boilerplate terms and the boilerplate terms diverge, we speak of a "battle of the forms."

II. The Common Law

How does the common law deal with diverging terms in offer and acceptance? For a contract to be formed, the acceptance must match the offer.[1] Therefore, if the offeree insists on different or additional terms, their reply does not constitute an acceptance of the offer.[2] Instead, their reply constitutes a counter-offer.[3] If the offeror then renders their performance, the offeror accepts the counteroffer by performance.

1. Restatement (Second) of Contracts §§ 50, 58.
2. Restatement (Second) of Contracts § 59.
3. Restatement (Second) of Contracts § 59.

Question. On January 1, Beta receives a letter from Alpha, in which Alpha offers to paint Beta's house for $10,000. On January 3, Alpha receives Beta's reply, which reads: "I accept but any disputes that arise out of our contract will be settled out of court by arbitrators." On January 5, Alpha starts painting Beta's house. Assume that the applicable common law corresponds exactly to the Restatement (Second) of Contracts. Have Alpha and Beta formed a contract? Is the arbitration clause part of the contract?

Answer. As a general rule, a contract requires mutual assent and consideration, and mutual assent is typically attained via offer and acceptance. Alpha's letter constituted an offer, but Beta did not accept that offer. Given that Beta insisted on an additional term, the arbitration clause, Beta's reply constituted a counteroffer. However, when Alpha began painting the house, Alpha thereby accepted Beta's counteroffer by performance, creating mutual assent. The consideration requirement is satisfied because each party gives so that the other gives. Therefore, the parties have formed a contract. Moreover, the arbitration clause is part of the contract because it was part of the counteroffer that Alpha accepted.

The offeree can accept the offer while at the same time requesting (rather than insisting upon) additional or different terms. As section 61 of the Restatement (Second) of Contracts clarifies, such requests, as long as they are mere suggestions, do not prevent a valid acceptance.[4] However, a mere suggestion in the sense of section 61, which does not prevent acceptance, also has a significant drawback. Specifically, such a suggestion has no effect and does not become part of the contract unless the original offeror assents to the suggestion. Doctrinally, this can best be explained as follows. An acceptance with a request for additional or different terms in the sense of section 61 constitutes both (a) an unconditional acceptance of the original offer made by the offeror and (b) an offer to amend the contract by including the additional or different terms suggested by the offeree. The unconditional acceptance creates a contract between the parties with the content that was intended by the offeror. The offeree's offer to amend the contract has no immediate effect. To have any legal effect, it needs to be accepted by the original offeror.

---

4. Restatement (Second) of Contracts § 61.

Question. On January 1, Beta receives a letter from Alpha, in which Alpha offers to paint Beta's house for $10,000. On January 3, Alpha receives Beta's reply, which reads: "I accept. Also, I would suggest that any disputes that arise out of our contract be settled out of court by arbitrators." On January 5, Alpha starts painting Beta's house. Assume that the applicable common law corresponds exactly to the Restatement (Second) of Contracts. Have Alpha and Beta formed a contract? Is the arbitration clause part of the contract?

Answer. As a general rule, a contract requires mutual assent and consideration, and mutual assent is typically attained via offer and acceptance. Alpha's letter constituted an offer. Beta accepted that offer via their letter because Beta's reference to an arbitration clause was a mere suggestion and thus did not prevent acceptance. It follows that the parties have reached mutual assent. The consideration requirement is met because Beta's promise serves as consideration for Alpha's promise and vice versa. The arbitration clause has not become part of the contract because Alpha's offer did not include an arbitration clause, and Beta accepted Alpha's offer as it was. A different outcome would occur if Alpha had assented to Beta's suggestion. However, we cannot read Alpha's performance as assenting to the arbitration clause. That is because a contract had already been formed by the time that Alpha rendered his performance, so Alpha was contractually obligated to paint the house.

Question. On January 1, Beta receives a letter from Alpha, in which Alpha offers to paint Beta's house for $10,000. On January 3, Alpha receives Beta's reply, which reads: "I accept. By the way, I would suggest that any disputes that arise out of our contract will be settled out of court by arbitrators." On January 5, Alpha calls Beta and tells them, "I love your idea regarding an arbitration clause. That works for me." Subsequently, Alpha starts painting Beta's house. Assume that the applicable common law corresponds exactly to the Restatement (Second) of Contracts. Have Alpha and Beta formed a contract? Is the arbitration clause part of the contract?

Answer. As explained in the answer to the previous question, a contract was formed when Beta accepted Alpha's offer, and, at that time, the contract did not contain the arbitration clause. However, when Alpha assented to Beta's suggestion in their phone call, the arbitration clause became part of the contract.

The above examples do not involve boilerplate terms. Still, they demonstrate the result of applying the matching principle to a situation in which the parties agree on the essential terms but disagree on ancillary terms. Where both parties are merchants using their own boilerplate terms, such disagreements are the norm. That is because it is unlikely that the offeree's boilerplate terms will exactly match the offeror's boilerplate terms.

Against this background, the practical consequences of applying the matching principle to transactions involving boilerplate terms can be rather frustrating. The last party to send their boilerplate terms before the other side begins performance prevails in the sense that their boilerplate terms become part of the contract. This outcome is problematic for two reasons. First, it seems arbitrary to let one party's boilerplate terms prevail based solely on the fact that that party was the last to send their boilerplate terms before the other party performed. Second, such a rule can incentivize parties to engage in a wasteful "war of attrition" by bombarding the other party with boilerplate terms.

II. Section 2-207 of the UCC

Regarding contracts for the sale of goods, section 2-207 of the Uniform Commercial Code seeks to avoid the drawbacks that accompany the application of the matching principle to the battle of the forms. Section 2-207 explicitly allows for the formation of contracts even when the acceptance diverges from the offer. Of course, as soon as one abandons the matching principle, two new questions arise. First, under what conditions is a contract formed even though the offer and acceptance don't match? We can refer to this issue as the "formation question." Second, given that the acceptance no longer needs to match the offer, which party's terms end up in the contract? We can refer to this problem as the "content question."

In analyzing cases or hypotheticals involving section 2-207, it is generally helpful to analyze the formation question before addressing the content question. This sequential approach is crucial because the legal principles governing the content question differ depending on how the contract was formed.

Before proceeding any further, you should read the text of section 2-207 if you have not already done so. To explain this provision in detail, we will analyze various hypothetical scenarios.

A. First Scenario

In the first scenario, both parties are merchants, the offeree's acceptance contains additional terms, and the offeree does not expressly condition their acceptance on the offeror's assent to the additional terms.

Question. Alpha, who runs a computer shop, writes the following letter to Beta, an attorney: "I offer to sell you an X5 Nixdorf computer for your office for $100." Beta writes back the next day: "I accept, but any disputes that arise out of our contract will be settled out of court by arbitrators." Alpha does not respond but delivers the computer. Beta accepts the delivery and pays the $100. Have the parties entered into a contract, and if so, is the arbitration clause part of the contract?

Answer. The parties have formed a contract. Alpha's letter constitutes an offer. Beta's reply did not match the offer because Beta insisted on an additional term, the arbitration clause. However, under section 2-207(1) of the Uniform Commercial Code, a definite and seasonable expression of acceptance creates a contract even if it contains different or additional terms, as long as the offeree did not expressly condition their acceptance on the offeror's assent to the additional or different terms. According to the widely prevailing view, an offeree who merely insists on additional or different terms does not thereby expressly condition their acceptance on the offeror's assent to the additional terms. Rather, the offeree has to state clearly that they do not want the contract unless the offeror assents to the additional or different terms. Since Beta made no such declaration, Beta did not condition their acceptance on assent to the arbitration clause. Therefore, Beta's acceptance created a contract under section 2-207(1).

The question remains whether the arbitration clause has become part of the contract. Since Alpha's offer was silent on how disputes should be settled, the arbitration clause constitutes an additional, rather than a different term. Where a contract has been formed under section 2-207(1) of the UCC, the question of whether additional terms become part of the contract is governed by section 2-207(2). Under sentence 2 of section 2-207(2), if both parties are merchants, any additional terms contained in the acceptance automatically become part of the contract unless one of three exceptions applies. The first exception applies where the offer has expressly limited the acceptance to the terms of the offer.[5] In the case at hand, Alpha's offer did not contain any such express limitation. The second exception applies where the additional term materially alters the offer.[6] Whether arbitration clauses materially alter the offer is controversial, with many courts deciding the issue based on the circumstances of the individual case. For simplicity, let us assume that Beta's arbitration clause does not amount to a material alteration. The third exception applies where the offeror has already objected to the additional clause or does so within a reasonable time.[7] Since Alpha has not objected to the arbitration clause, the arbitration clause becomes part of the contract.

B. Second Scenario

In the second scenario, either none or only one of the parties is a merchant, the offeree's acceptance contains additional terms, and the offeree does not expressly condition his acceptance on the offeror's assent to the additional terms.

Question. Same facts as in the previous question except that this time, Alpha offers to sell Beta a Nintendo Gameboy as a toy for Beta's child. Have the parties entered into a contract, and if so, is the arbitration clause part of the contract?

Answer. The only difference between the previous question and this one is that Beta is not a merchant because their purchase is for private purposes. This change has no impact on the contract formation question since section 2-207 (1) of the Uniform Commercial Code does not distinguish between merchants and non-merchants. Therefore, the answer to the contract formation question remains the same: the parties have formed a contract under section 2-207(1).

The question remains whether the arbitration clause has become part of the contract. Where a contract has been formed under section 2-207(1), the issue of whether additional terms become part of the contract is governed by section 2-207(2). However, because only one of the parties, Alpha, is a

5. UCC § 2-207(2) sentence 2 (a).
6. UCC § 2-207(2) sentence 2 (b).
7. UCC § 2-207(2) sentence 2 (c).

merchant, we cannot apply sentence 2 of section 2-207(2). Instead, we apply sentence 1 of section 2-207(2), which provides that the additional terms are merely proposals for addition to the contract. Accordingly, the fate of the arbitration clause depends on whether Alpha has assented to Beta's proposal to include the arbitration clause into the contract. Unfortunately for Beta, Alpha has done nothing that would signal such assent. In particular, we cannot argue that Alpha assented to the arbitration clause by delivering the Gameboy. That is because by the time that Alpha delivered the Gameboy, a contract had already been formed and Alpha was contractually obligated to perform. Hence, a reasonable observer had no reason to read Alpha's performance as signaling assent to the arbitration clause.

C. Third Scenario

In the second scenario, the offeree's acceptance contains additional or different terms, and the offeree expressly conditions their acceptance on the offeror's assent to the different or additional terms. In this scenario, it is immaterial whether one or both of the parties are merchants.

Question. Alpha, who runs a computer shop, writes the following letter to Beta, an attorney: "I offer to sell you an X5 Nixdorf computer for your office for $100." Beta writes back the next day: "I accept, but I only want the contract if you agree that any disputes that arise out of our contract will be settled out of court by arbitrators." Alpha does not respond but delivers the computer. Beta accepts the delivery and pays the $100. Have the parties entered into a contract, and if so, is the arbitration clause part of the contract?

Answer. The parties have not formed a contract under section 2-207(1) of the Uniform Commercial Code because Beta has expressly conditioned their acceptance on Alpha's assent to the additional term, the arbitration clause. However, where the parties' writings have failed to create a contract, a contract will be formed under sentence 1 of section 2-207(3), as long as both parties have taken actions that recognize the existence of a contract. Given that Alpha has delivered and Beta has paid for the computer, both parties' conduct recognizes the existence of a contract. Accordingly, the parties have formed a contract under sentence 1 of section 2-207(3).

The question remains whether the arbitration clause has become part of the contract. In cases where a contract is formed under sentence 1 of section 2-207(3), the issue of whether different or additional terms are part of the contract is governed by sentence 2 of section 2-207(3), a provision also known as the "knockout rule." Under the knockout rule, the contract includes only those terms that are included in both the offer and the acceptance plus any default provisions (gap fillers) provided by the Uniform Commercial Code. The arbitration clause is not a gap filler provision provided by the Uniform Commercial Code. Furthermore, the arbitration clause was only part of the acceptance and was not included in the offer. Accordingly, the arbitration clause has not become part of the contract.

D. **Fourth Scenario**

In this scenario, both parties are merchants, the offeree's acceptance contains a different term, and the offeree does not expressly condition their acceptance on the offeror's assent to the different term.

Question. Alpha, who runs a computer shop, writes the following letter to Beta, an attorney: "I offer to sell you an X5 Nixdorf computer for your office for $100. Any disputes arising under this contract shall be litigated in the courts of this state or in federal courts located in this state." Beta writes back the next day: "I accept, but any and all disputes are subject to arbitration." Alpha does not respond but delivers the computer. Beta accepts the delivery and pays the $100. Have the parties entered into a contract, and if so, is the arbitration clause part of the contract?

Answer. The parties have formed a contract under section 2-207(1) because Beta accepted Alpha's offer without expressly conditioning their acceptance on Alpha's assent to the arbitration clause. The question remains whether the arbitration clause has become part of the contract. Note that in this case, we are dealing with a different rather than with an additional term since the arbitration clause is inconsistent with a term in the offer. Unfortunately, where a contract has been formed under section 2-207(1) and the acceptance contains a different term, section 2-207 does not explicitly address which legal principles govern the question of whether the different term becomes part of the contract.

Scholars and courts have advanced three main views regarding this issue.

First, Professor Robert Summers, a professor at the Cornell Law School and famous scholar of commercial law, argued that because section 2-207 UCC does not address the fate of different terms, their inclusion is governed by the common law. This means that they do not become part of the contract unless the offeror assents to their inclusion. The key argument for this approach is that, as a general rule, gaps in the UCC are filled by application of the common law.[8] However, Professor Summers' view has garnered little support from courts, and it does not appear to be followed in any recent cases.[9] If one were to apply Professor Summers' approach to the case at hand, the arbitration clause would not become part of the contract because Alpha has not assented to the arbitration clause.

A second view holds that different terms must be treated like additional terms, so section 2-207(2) governs their inclusion in the contract.[10] The rationale underlying this view is that there are no obvious reasons for treating different terms differently from additional terms. Moreover, Comment 3 of the official comment explicitly states that section 2-207(2) governs the question of whether different terms become part of the contract. If one applied this approach to the case at hand, the fate of the arbitration clause would be

8. See UCC § 1-103.

9. Cf. Reilly Foam Corp. v. Rubbermaid Corp., 206 F. Supp. 2d 643, 653 (E.D. Pa. 2002) (noting, with a respect to the approach championed by Professor Summers, that "[t]his view has been widely discredited as a revival of the common law rule, and the Court is not aware of any jurisdiction in which it is currently in force.").

10. See, e.g., Aqua-Hot Heating Sys., Inc. v. Gorman-Rupp Co., No. 17-CV-01469-RBJ, 2018 WL 6249886, at *6 n.3 (D. Colo. Nov. 29, 2018) (applying CO law and holding that UCC § 2-207 (2) governs both different and additional terms); Wyman-Gordon Inv. Castings, Inc. v. Rutenberg, No. 8:19-CV-827-T-23CPT, 2020 WL 3266218, at *4 (M.D. Fla. Mar. 25, 2020), report and recommendation adopted, No. 8:19-CV-827-T-23CPT, 2020 WL 7408277 (M.D. Fla. July 24, 2020) ("If a contract is formed under section 2-207(1), then section 2-207(2) is used to determine if any additional or different terms become part of the contract."); Intl. Metal Sales, Inc. v. Glob. Steel Corp. and Glob. Steel Corp., No. 03-07-00172-CV, 2010 WL 1170218, at *8 (Tex. App.—Austin Mar. 24, 2010) (applying Texas law and holding that "different terms . . . become part of the contract unless (1) the offer explicitly limits acceptance to the terms of the offer, (2) they "materially alter" the contract, or (3) the party against whom the additional terms are asserted objects to the additional terms."). Under UCC section 2-20(2), the outcome may depend on whether the relevant terms materially alter the contract. The Daitom court seems to assume that different terms always materially alter the contract. However, those courts that apply section 2-207(2) of the UCC to different terms determine materiality on a case-by-case basis. See, e.g., Aqua-Hot Heating Sys., Inc. v. Gorman-Rupp Co., No. 17-CV-01469-RBJ, 2018 WL 6249886, at *6 n.3 (D. Colo. Nov. 29, 2018) (applying UCC § 2-207(2) to different and concluding that the different terms included in the acceptance "do attempt to materially alter the terms of the contract"); Gardner Zemke Co. v. Dunham Bush, Inc., 850 P.2d 319, 325 (N.M. 1993) (holding that section 2-207(2) governs the fate of different terms where the contract has been formed under section 2-207(1)).

governed by sentence 2 of section 2-207(2) because both parties are merchants. Moreover, given that Alpha's offer did not expressly limit acceptance to its terms and given that Alpha has not objected to the arbitration clause, the outcome would depend on whether the arbitration clause makes a material alteration. As previously noted, whether an arbitration clause constitutes a material alteration is controversial, with courts focusing on the circumstances of the individual case.

A third view applies 2-207(3) sentence 2, also known as the "knockout rule."[11] Courts justify the application of the knockout rule by pointing out that the knockout rule is widely thought to be a particularly fair and well-designed rule. If we apply the knockout rule to the case at hand, the arbitration clause does not become part of the contract because the arbitration clause is only contained in the acceptance and since arbitration is not the legal default.

III. Confirmation Letters

Following the parties' original exchange, it can be useful to memorialize the content of the agreement in a written confirmation. For that reason, section 2-207(1) of the UCC includes a rule about "a written confirmation which is sent within a reasonable time" after the parties' exchange. On its face, section 2-207(1) may imply that a written confirmation operates as acceptance, but that formulation is somewhat misleading. In fact, one has to distinguish two situations.

In the first scenario, no contract was formed prior to the confirmation letter, and the confirmation letter is the offeree's response to the offer. In that case, the confirmation letter, even though it purports to confirm rather than form a contract, forms the contract under section 2-207(1).[12]

In the second scenario, the confirmation letter was sent after the parties already reached an agreement, either orally or in writing. In that case, there is no need for an additional acceptance. Nonetheless, there is universal agree-

---

11. E.g., Daitom, Inc. v. Pennwalt Corp., 741 F.2d 1569, 1579 (10th Cir. 1984); Super. Boiler Works, Inc. v. R.J. Sanders, Inc., 711 A.2d 628, 635 (R.I. 1998).

12. See, e.g., Stand. Bent Glass Corp. v. Glassrobots Oy, 333 F.3d 440, 445 (3d Cir. 2003) (holding that "[u]nder UCC section 2–207(1), the offeree's expression of acceptance or transmission of a written confirmation generally results in the formation of a contract"); Step-Saver Data Sys., Inc. v. Wyse Tech., 939 F.2d 91, 101 (3d Cir. 1991) (treating "written confirmation" by offeree as acceptance within the meaning of section 2-207(1) where no contract had previously been formed).

that the confirmation letter rule in section 2-207(1) of the UCC applies.[13] Indeed, the official comments explicitly envision the confirmation letter rule applying to cases, where the parties have already reached an agreement "orally or by informal correspondence."[14] Thus, the confirmation letter becomes a mechanism for including additional or different terms into the already existing contract.

Daitom Inc. v. Pennwalt Corp

United States Court of Appeals, Tenth Circuit, 741 F.2d 1569 (1984)

WILLIAM E. DOYLE, Circuit Judge

. . . This is an appeal from the grant of summary judgment against Daitom, Inc. (Daitom), the plaintiff below. . . .

[Daitom Inc. ("Daitom") planned to build a plant to produce dextro calcium pantothenate. Kintech Services, Inc. ("Kintech") designed the plant for Daitom. Kintech determined that the production would require specialized automated drying equipment.] Kintech formulated specifications for the automated drying equipment. . . . On behalf of Daitom, Kintech invited various vendors to bid on the needed equipment.

Pennwalt, on September 7, 1976, submitted a proposal for the sale of two rotary vacuum dryers with dust filters and heating systems to dry dextro calcium pantothenate. The typewritten proposal specified the equipment to be sold, the . . . price, and delivery and payment terms. A pre-printed conditions of sale form was also attached to the proposal and explicitly made an integral part of the proposal by the typewritten sheet. . . . [One of the relevant terms " limited the warranties to repair and replacement of defective parts and limited the period of one year from the date of delivery for any action for breach of warranty.']

13. E.g., Dumont Tel. Co. v. Power & Tel. Supply Co., 962 F. Supp. 2d 1064, 1077 (N.D. Iowa 2013); Am. Parts Co., Inc. (Detroit Body Products Co. Div.) v. Am. Arb. Ass'n, 154 N.W.2d 5, 11 (Mich. App. 1967); Packgen v. Berry Plastics Corp., 973 F. Supp. 2d 48, 63 (D. Me. 2013); ICC Chem. Corp. v. Vitol, Inc., 425 Fed. Appx. 57, 59 (2d Cir. 2011); Aceros Prefabricados, S.A. v. TradeArbed, Inc., 282 F.3d 92, 98 (2d Cir. 2002).

14. UCC § 2-207 cmt. 1.

[O]n October 5, 1976, well within the thirty-day acceptance period specified in the proposal, Daitom issued a purchase order for the Pennwalt equipment. The purchase order consisted of a pre-printed form with the identification of the specific equipment and associated prices typewritten in the appropriate blank spaces on the front together with seventeen lengthy "boilerplate" or "standard" terms and conditions of sale on the back. In addition, on the front of the purchase order in the column marked for a description of the items purchased, Daitom typed the following:

"Rotary vacuum dryers in accordance with Kintech Services, Inc. specification 342 dated August 20, 1976, and in accordance with Stokes proposal dated September 7, 1976."

The two rotary vacuum dryers and the equipment that went along with them were manufactured by Pennwalt and delivered to Daitom's plant in early May 1977. For the reason that there had been no construction of Daitom's plant, the crated equipment was not immediately installed. Instead, it was stored outside in crates. On June 15, 1978, the dryers were finally installed and first operated by Daitom. Daitom notified Pennwalt of serious problems with the operation of the dryers on June 17, 1978.

Daitom's contention was that the dryers suffered from two . . . defects . . . . Pennwalt's repair personnel visited the Daitom plant to investigate . . . , but Daitom contends the dryers were not repaired and have never performed as required under the specifications and as represented by Pennwalt. This was the basis for the lawsuit.

This suit was brought in federal court on March 7, 1980, after Pennwalt's alleged failure to correct the difficulties with the dryers. On Pennwalt's motion, the district court granted summary judgment against Daitom on all . . . counts of its complaint. . . .

III. DISCUSSION

A. The Issues

. . . After considering the record in the instant case, it is apparent that the substantive law was not correctly applied and that summary judgment against Daitom . . . was improper. . . .

B. The Applicable Law

The district court found the dispute between Daitom and Pennwalt involved a "transaction in goods," between persons who are "merchants" and, therefore, was governed by Article 2 of the U.C.C. U.C.C. §§ 2–102, 2–104. The district court also stated that the dispute is a classic example of the "battle of the forms."

As previously noted, there has been agreement that the law of Pennsylvania governs these claims for breach of warranty and Pennsylvania has adopted the provisions of the U.C.C. Section 2–207 of the U.C.C. was specifically drafted to deal with the battle of the forms and related problems. U.C.C. § 2–207, Comment 1.

Section 2–207 has been commented on in one case as a "murky bit of prose," (Southwest Engineering Co., Inc. v. Martin Tractor Co., Inc., 205 Kan. 684, 473 P.2d 18, 25 (1970)), and as "one of the most important, subtle, and difficult in the entire code, and well it may be said that the product as it finally reads is not altogether satisfactory."... The Pennsylvania Supreme Court has not addressed the issues presented by this case. In the absence, therefore, of an authoritative pronouncement from the state's highest court, our task is to regard ourselves as sitting in diversity and predicting how the state's highest court would rule. Pennsylvania Glass Sand Corporation v. Caterpillar Tractor Company, 652 F.2d 1165, 1167 (3rd Cir.1981). This court must also follow any intermediate state court decision unless other authority convinces us that the state supreme court would decide otherwise.... Also, the policies underlying the applicable legal doctrines, the doctrinal trends indicated by these policies, and the decisions of other courts may also inform this court's analysis. Pennsylvania Glass Sand, supra, at 1167 (3rd Cir.1981). With these standards in mind, we proceed to consider and analyze the case.

C. The writings and the contract.

The trial court concluded that the parties' exchanged writings formed a contract. Thus, there was not a formal single document. Pennwalt's September 7, 1976 proposal constituted the offer and Daitom's October 5, 1976 purchase order constituted the acceptance.

It is essentially uncontested that Pennwalt's proposal constituted an offer. The proposal set forth in some detail the equipment to be sold to Daitom, the price, the terms of shipment, and specifically stated that the attached terms and conditions were an integral part of the proposal. One of those attached terms and conditions of sale limited the warranties to repair and replacement of defective parts and limited the period of one year from the date of delivery for any action for breach of warranty.

The proposal was sent to Kintech and forwarded to Daitom with a recommendation to accept the proposal. Daitom sent the October 5, 1976 purchase order to Pennwalt. This purchase order constituted an acceptance of Pennwalt's offer and formed a binding contract for the sale only pursuant to 2–207(1), despite the statement of terms additional to or different from those in the offer. But these terms were not without meaning or consequence. However, the acceptance was not expressly conditioned on Pennwalt accepting these additional or different terms. ... [For an acceptance to quality as expressly conditioned] the offeree must explicitly communicate his or her unwillingness to proceed with the transaction unless the additional or different terms in its response are accepted by the offeror. . . . Here the additional or different terms in Daitom's purchase order were, to be sure, boilerplate terms. And though important in themselves, they do not come out and state an unwillingness to proceed with the purchase of the rotary dryers if the terms were not assented to by Pennwalt. . . .

Having found an offer and an acceptance which was not made expressly conditional on assent to additional or different terms, we must now decide the effect of those additional or different terms on the resulting contract and what terms became part of it. The district court simply resolved this dispute by focusing solely on the period of limitations specified in Pennwalt's offer of September 7, 1976. Thus, the court held that while the offer explicitly specified a one-year period of limitations in accordance with § 2–725(1) allowing such a reduction, Daitom's acceptance of October 5, 1976 was silent as to the limitations period. Consequently, the court held that § 2–207(2) was inapplicable and the one-year limitations period controlled, effectively barring Daitom's action for breach of warranties.

While the district court's analysis undertook to resolve the issue without considering the question of the application of § 2–207(2) to additional or different terms, we cannot accept its approach or its conclusion. We are unable to ignore the plain implication of Daitom's reservation in its boilerplate warranties provision of all its rights and remedies available at law. Such an explicit reservation impliedly reserves the statutory period of limitations; without such a reservation, all other reservations of actions and remedies are without effect.

The statutory period of limitations under the U.C.C. is four years after the cause of action has accrued. U.C.C. § 2–725(1). Were we to determine that this four-year period became a part of the contract rather than the shorter one-year period, Daitom's actions on breach of warranties were timely brought and summary judgment against Daitom was error.

We realize that our conclusion requires an inference to be drawn from a construction of Daitom's terms; however, such an inference and construction are consistent with the judicial reluctance to grant summary judgment where there is some reasonable doubt over the existence of a genuine material fact. See Williams v. Borden, Inc., 637 F.2d 731, 738 (10th Cir.1980). When taking into account the circumstances surrounding the application of the one-year limitations period, we have little hesitation in adopting the U.C.C.'s four-year limitations reservation, the application of which permits a trial on the merits. Thus, this court must recognize that certain terms in Daitom's acceptance differed from terms in Pennwalt's offer and decide which become part of the contract. The district court certainly erred in refusing to recognize such a conflict.6

The difficulty in determining the effect of different terms in the acceptance is the imprecision of drafting evident in § 2–207. The language of the provision is silent on how different terms in the acceptance are to be treated once a contract is formed pursuant to § 2–207(1). That section provides that a contract may be formed by exchanged writings despite the existence of additional or different terms in the acceptance. Therefore, an offeree's response is treated as an acceptance while it may differ substantially from the offer. This section of the provision, then, reformed the mirror-image rule; that common law legal formality that prohibited the formation of a contract if the exchanged writings of offer and acceptance differed in any term.

Once a contract is recognized pursuant to § 2–207(1), 2–207(2) provides the standard for determining if the additional terms stated in the acceptance become a part of the contract. Between merchants, such additional terms become part of the resulting contract unless 1) the offer expressly limited acceptance to its terms, 2) the additional terms materially alter the contract obligations, or 3) the offeror gives notice of his or her objection to the additional terms within a reasonable time. Should any one of these three possibilities occur, the additional terms are treated merely as proposals for incorporation in the contract and absent assent by the offeror the terms of the offer control. In any event, the existence of the additional terms does not prevent a contract from being formed.

Section 2–207(2) is silent on the treatment of terms stated in the acceptance that are different, rather than merely additional, from those stated in the offer. It is unclear whether "different" terms in the acceptance are intended to be included under the aegis of "additional" terms in § 2–

207(2) and, therefore, fail to become part of the agreement if they materially alter the contract. Comment 3 suggests just such an inclusion However, Comment 6 suggests that different terms in exchanged writings must be assumed to constitute mutual objections by each party to the other's conflicting terms and result in a mutual "knockout" of both parties' conflicting terms; the missing terms to be supplied by the U.C.C.'s "gap-filler" provisions. At least one commentator, in support of this view, has suggested that the drafting history of the provision indicates that the word "different" was intentionally deleted from the final draft of § 2–207(2) to preclude its treatment under that subsection. The plain language, comments, and drafting history of the provision, therefore, provide little helpful guidance in resolving the disagreement over the treatment of different terms pursuant to § 2–207.

Despite all this, the cases and commentators have suggested three possible approaches. The first of these is to treat "different" terms as included under the aegis of "additional" terms in § 2–207(2). Consequently, different terms in the acceptance would never become part of the contract, because, by definition, they would materially alter the contract (i.e., the offeror's terms). Several courts have adopted this approach. E.g., Mead Corporation v. McNally-Pittsburg Manufacturing Corporation, 654 F.2d 1197 (6th Cir.1981) . . . [Editor: Do you agree with the court's summary of the consequences that would arise from an application of § 2–207(2) to different terms?]

The second approach, which leads to the same result as the first, is that the offeror's terms control because the offeree's different terms merely fall out; § 2–207(2) cannot rescue the different terms since that subsection applies only to additional terms. Under this approach, Comment 6 (apparently supporting a mutual rather than a single term knockout) is not applicable because it refers only to conflicting terms in confirmation forms following oral agreement, not conflicting terms in the writings that form the agreement. This approach is supported by Professor Summers. J.J. White & R.S. Summers, Uniform Commercial Code, § 1–2, at 29 (2d ed. 1980).

The third, and preferable approach, which is commonly called the "knock-out" rule, is that the conflicting terms cancel one another. Under this view the offeree's form is treated only as an acceptance of the terms in the offeror's form which did not conflict. The ultimate contract, then, includes those non-conflicting terms and any other terms supplied by the U.C.C., including terms incorporated by course of performance (§ 2–208), course of dealing (§ 1–205), usage of trade (§ 1–205), and other "gap fillers" or "off-the-rack" terms (e.g., implied warranty of fitness for particular purpose, § 2–315). As stated previously, this approach finds some support in Comment 6. Professor White supports this approach as the most fair and consistent with the purposes of § 2–207. White & Summers, supra, at 29. Further, several courts have adopted or recognized the approach. E.g., Idaho Power Company v. Westinghouse Electric Corporation, 596 F.2d 924 (9th Cir.1979)...

We are of the opinion that this is the more reasonable approach, particularly when dealing with a case such as this where from the beginning the offeror's specified period of limitations would expire before the equipment was even installed. The approaches other than the "knock-out" approach would be inequitable and unjust because they invited the very kind of treatment which the defendant attempted to provide.

Thus, we are of the conclusion that if faced with this issue the Pennsylvania Supreme Court would adopt the "knock-out" rule and hold here that the conflicting terms in Pennwalt's offer and Daitom's acceptance regarding the period of limitations and applicable warranties cancel one another out. Consequently, the other provisions of the U.C.C. must be used to provide the missing terms.

This particular approach and result are supported persuasively by the underlying rationale and purpose behind the adoption of § 2–207. As stated previously, that provision was drafted to reform the infamous common law mirror-image rule and associated last-shot doctrine that enshrined the fortuitous positions of senders of forms and accorded undue advantages based on such fortuitous positions. White & Summers, supra at 25. To refuse to adopt the "knock-out" rule and instead adopt one of the remaining two approaches would serve to re-enshrine the undue advantages derived solely from the fortuitous positions of when a party sent a form. Cf., 3 Duesenberg & King at 93 (1983 Supp.). This is because either approach other than the knock-out rule for different terms results in the offeror and his or her terms always prevailing solely because he or she sent the first form. Professor Summers argues that this advantage is not wholly unearned, because the offeree has an opportunity to review the offer, identify the conflicting terms and make his or her acceptance conditional. But this joinder misses the fundamental purpose of the U.C.C. in general and § 2–207 in particular, which is to preserve a contract and fill in any gaps if the parties intended to make a contract and there is a reasonable basis for giving an appropriate remedy. U.C.C. §§ 2–204(3); § 2–207(1); § 2–207(3). Thus, this approach gives the offeree some protection. While it is laudable for business persons to read the fine print and boilerplate provisions in exchanged forms, there is nothing in § 2–207 mandating such careful consideration. The provision seems drafted with a recognition of the reality that merchants seldom review exchanged forms with the scrutiny of lawyers. The "knock-out" rule is therefore the best approach. Even if a term eliminated by operation of the "knock-out" rule is reintroduced by operation of the U.C.C.'s gap-filler provisions, such a result does not indicate a weakness of the approach. On the contrary, at least the reintroduced term has the merit of being a term that the U.C.C. draftpersons regarded as fair. . . . Consequently, the ruling of the district court . . . must be reversed and the matter remanded for trial consistent with this court's ruling.

NOTES AND QUESTIONS

A. Contract formation. In determining whether the parties have reached mutual assent regarding a contract for the sale of goods, one can distinguish three main scenarios. In the first scenario, the acceptance matches the offer. In that case, there is no need to invoke section 2-207 of the Uniform Commercial Code regarding the contract's formation. In the second scenario, the acceptance contains different or additional terms, but the offeree has not expressly conditioned their acceptance on the offeree's assent to the additional or different terms. The contract is then formed under section 2-207(1) of the Uniform Commercial Code. In the third scenario, the parties have not reached mutual assent through their writings, but both parties behave as though a contract had been formed. In that case, a contract is formed under sentence 1 of section 2-207(3). Which, if any, of these scenarios is present in *Daitom*?

B. Conditional acceptance. Under section 2-207(1) of the UCC, the formation of a contract requires that the offeree does not expressly condition their acceptance on the offeror's assent to the additional or different terms.[15] The question then arises: when is an acceptance "expressly made conditional" per section 2-207(1)? In *Daitom*, the court holds that acceptance is conditional under section 2-207(1) of the UCC if "the offeree . . . explicitly communicate[s] his or her unwillingness to proceed with the transaction unless the additional or different terms in its response are accepted by the offeror." In other words,

15. UCC § 2-207(3) sentence 1.

it is insufficient for the offeree to merely state that they "insist" on the inclusion of different or additional terms. Rather, for the acceptance to be conditional, the offeree has to make it clear that they are not interested in a contract unless the offeror assents to the different or additional terms. This approach has gained widespread acceptance over time.[16]

C. Boilerplate language and conditional acceptance. Can an acceptance be made expressly conditional through language in the offeree's boilerplate terms? Courts have generally answered this question in the affirmative.[17] However, does this approach defeat the purpose of section 2-207(1)?

D. The consequences of a conditional acceptance. Suppose the offeree has expressly conditioned their acceptance on the offeror's assent to additional or different terms in the offer. If the offeror subsequently assents to the additional or different terms, the contract is formed under the matching principle

---

16. See, e.g., Aqua-Hot Heating Sys., Inc. v. Gorman-Rupp Co., No. 17-CV-01469-RBJ, 2018 WL 6249886, at *5 (D. Colo. Nov. 29, 2018) (holding that for an acceptance to be conditional within the meaning of UCC § 2-207(1), the offeree must "explicitly communicate [its] unwillingness to proceed with the transaction unless the additional or different terms in its response [were] accepted by the offeror"); Reilly Foam Corp. v. Rubbermaid Corp., 206 F. Supp. 2d 643, 651 n. 3 (E.D. Pa. 2002) (holding that for a conditional acceptance, the offeree's reply "must demonstrate an unwillingness to proceed with the transaction unless its conditions are met."); Commun. Supply Corp. v. Iron Bow Techs., LLC, 529 F. Supp. 3d 423, 435 (W.D. Pa. 2021) (holding that defendant's reply to the offer would only have been a conditional acceptance if defendant "had responded with different or additional terms and 'explicitly communicate[d] [its] unwillingness to proceed with the transaction' unless [offeror accepted those terms"); Foamade Industries v. Visteon Corp., No. 271949, 2008 WL 582566, at *8 (Mich. App. Mar. 4, 2008) (holding that defendant's reply does not constitute a conditional acceptance because it does not "contain language suggesting that [offeree] was unwilling to proceed absent an assurance of [offeror's] assent."); Cosden Oil & Chem. Co. v. Karl O. Helm Aktiengesellschaft, 736 F.2d 1064, 1075 (5th Cir. 1984) (noting that "[s]ection 2.207(a) 'was intended to apply only to an acceptance which clearly reveals that the offeree is unwilling to proceed with the transaction unless he is assured of the offeror's assent to the additional or different terms therein.'") (internal citation omitted).

17. See, e.g., PCS Nitrogen Fertilizer, L.P. v. Christy Refractories, L.L.C., 225 F.3d 974, 979 (8th Cir. 2000) ("Although an acceptance containing additional or different terms (such as an arbitration clause) will typically not preclude § 2–207(1) contract formation, the creation of a contract is prevented where "acceptance is expressly made conditional on assent to the additional or different terms."); White Consol. Industries, Inc. v. McGill Mfg. Co., Inc., 165 F.3d 1185, 1191 (8th Cir. 1999) (applying Minnesota law and categorizing an acceptance as a conditional acceptance where boilerplate language in the acceptance "The purchase order was "an acceptance of [the Seller's] offer subject to the express condition that the Seller assent that this [p]urchase [o]rder constitutes the entire agreement between Buyer and Seller."); Dresser Industries, Inc., Waukesha Engine Div. v. Gradall Co., 965 F.2d 1442, 1449 (7th Cir. 1992) ("When a party sends a written offer that makes acceptance of the agreement subject to its terms, and the offeree responds with a form making its acceptance expressly conditional on assent to its new or different terms, no contract is formed unless the offeror accepts the offeree's terms.").

and includes the different or additional terms. If the offeror does not assent to the different or additional terms, a contract may still be formed under sentence 1 of section 2-207(3) as long as both parties have engaged in conduct recognizing the existence of a contract.

In applying these principles, one scenario is particularly worth noting. Assume that the offeree has expressly conditioned their acceptance on the offeror's assent to additional or different terms in the offer. Furthermore, assume that the offeror delivers the goods, and the offeree completes the payment. In this scenario, no contract is formed under section 2-207(1) because the acceptance is expressly conditional. But can we argue that a contract has been formed under the matching principle because the offeror assents to the additional or different terms by delivering the goods? The answer is no. In order for a contract to be formed under the matching principle by the offeror's assent to the different or additional term, the offeror's assent must be "express."[18] This means that the offeror's conduct must demonstrate not only assent to the contract but also willingness to accept the different or additional terms. Mere performance does not qualify as express assent. Otherwise, section 2-207(3) sentence 1 would become irrelevant.

E. The contract's content. If a contract has been formed under section 2-207 of the Uniform Commercial Code, the question arises whether the different or additional terms have become part of the contract. The rules that govern this question depend on how the contract was formed. If the contract was formed under section 2-207(1), the fate of additional terms is explicitly governed by section 2-207(2). If the contract was formed under sentence 1 of section 2-207(3), the fate of additional and different terms is governed by the so-called knockout rule in sentence 2 of section 2-207(3). However, section 2-207 does not explicitly address what happens to *different* terms if the contract was formed under section 2-207(1). How does the court in *Daitom* resolve this issue? Do you agree with the court's reasoning?

F. Scholarly works. Section 2-207 has inspired a considerable body of scholarly work. Particularly instructive are Victor P. Goldberg's The "Battle of the Forms": Fairness, Efficiency, and the Best-Shot Rule,[19] which explores both fairness and efficiency considerations, and Giesela Rühl's The Battle of the

---

18. E.g., Rich Products Corp. v. Kemutec, Inc., 66 F. Supp. 2d 937, 962 (E.D. Wis. 1999), aff'd, 241 F.3d 915 (7th Cir. 2001); TE Connectivity Corp. v. Sumitomo Elec. Wiring Sys., Inc., 644 F. Supp. 3d 393, 399 (E.D. Mich. 2022); Deere & Co. v. Ohio Gear, 462 F.3d 701, 707 (7th Cir. 2006).
19. 76 OR. L. REV. 155 (1997).

Forms: Cultural and Economic Observations,[20] which analyzes how the battle of the forms varies across legal regimes in different countries.

Brown Machine, Division of John Brown, Inc. v. Hercules

Missouri Court of Appeals, Eastern District, 770 S.W.2d 416 (1989)

STEPHAN, Judge

Hercules Inc. ("Hercules") appeals from the judgment of the trial court awarding respondent Brown Machine $157,911.55 plus interest after a jury verdict in favor of Brown Machine in its action against Hercules for indemnification. We reverse.

In early 1976 Brown Machine had sold appellant Hercules a T–100 trim press. The trim press was a piece of equipment apparently used in manufacturing Cool Whip bowls. The initial sales negotiations between the two companies for the trim press began in October 1975. Bruce Boardman, an engineer at Hercules, asked Jim Ryan, Brown Machine's district sales manager, to send Hercules a quote for a trim press. On November 7, 1975, Brown Machine submitted its original proposal No. 51054 for the model T–100 trim press to Hercules. The proposal set out sixteen numbered paragraphs describing the machine to be sold. Attached to the proposal was a printed form of fifteen paragraphs in boilerplate style captioned "TERMS AND CONDITIONS OF SALE". The eighth paragraph provided as follows:

8. LIABILITY: The purchaser agrees to pay in behalf of BROWN all sums which BROWN becomes legally obligated to pay because of bodily injury or property damage caused by or resulting from the use or misuse of the IOS [item of sale], including reasonable attorneys fees and legal expenses. The purchaser agrees to indemnify and hold BROWN harmless from all actions, claims, or demands arising out of or in any way connected with the IOS, its operation, use or misuse, or the design construction or composition of any product made or handled by the IOS, including all such actions, claims, or demands based in whole or in part on the default or negligence of BROWN.

Tim Wilson, Hercules' purchasing agent, reviewed the proposal submitted

20. 24 U. PA. J. INT'L ECON. L. 189 (2003).

by Brown Machine. On January 7, 1976, he telephoned Jim Ryan at Brown Machine. Mr. Ryan's call report reflected that Hercules had prepared its purchase order No. 03361 in response to Brown Machine's proposal but that Hercules had objected to the payment term requiring a twenty percent deposit be paid with the order. After talking with Mr. Fassett, Brown Machine's product manager, Mr. Ryan told Mr. Wilson that Brown Machine could not waive the deposit and that an invoice for payment would be forwarded to Hercules.

Mr. Fassett issued a work order that day giving the shop instructions concerning the trim press equipment, followed by a written order the next day. The written order noted that "customer gave verbal P.O. [purchase order] for this stock machine. Will issue revision when formal purchase order received."

On January 19, 1976, Brown Machine received Hercules' written purchase order No. 03361 dated January 6, 1976. The order was for a "Brown T–100 Trim-press in accordance with Brown Machine quote # 51054. All specifications cited within quote except item # 6.1.1 which should read: 'Reverse trim' instead of 'Standard regular forward trim.' " In a blue box on the bottom left of the purchase order form in bold print appeared "THIS ORDER EXPRESSLY LIMITS ACCEPTANCE TO THE TERMS STATED HEREIN INCLUDING THOSE PRINTED ON THE REVERSE SIDE. ANY ADDITIONAL OR DIFFERENT TERMS PROPOSED BY THE SELLER ARE REJECTED UNLESS EXPRESSLY AGREED TO IN WRITING." The reverse side of Hercules' purchase order, captioned "TERMS AND CONDITIONS" contained sixteen boilerplate paragraphs, the last of which provided:

16. OTHER TERMS: No oral agreement or other understanding shall in any way modify this order, or the terms or the conditions hereof. Seller's action in (a) accepting this order, (b) delivering material; or (c) performing services called for hereunder shall constitute an acceptance of the above terms and conditions.

The purchase order contained no indemnity provision.

Brown Machine received two copies of the purchase order. One had been stamped "Vendor's Copy" at the bottom; the other was marked "ACKNOWLEDGMENT", with a space labeled "accepted by" for signature by Brown Machine. Brown Machine did not return this prepared acknowledgment to Hercules.

The next day, on January 20, 1976, Mr. Fassett issued his second machine order to the shop revising his description to reflect that Brown Machine had received Hercules' formal purchase order and that the machine was no longer inventoried as a Brown stock item. On January 21, 1976, Brown Machine sent Hercules an invoice requesting payment of $4,882.00, the twenty percent deposit for the trim press.

Rather than returning the acknowledgment of the purchase order prepared by Hercules, Mr. Fassett of Brown Machine sent Hercules an "ORDER ACKNOWLEDGEMENT" dated February 5, 1976. This letter stated as follows:

Below in detail are the specifications covering the equipment ordered, and the equipment will be manufactured to meet these specifications. If these specifications and terms and conditions of Sale are not in accordance with your understanding, please ADVISE US WITHIN SEVEN (7) DAYS OF RECEIPT OF THIS ACKNOWLEDGEMENT. If we do not hear from you within this period of time, we are proceeding with the construction of the equipment as per these specifications and terms as being agreed; and any changes occurring later may result in additional charges.

ONE T—100 TRIM PRESS AS FOLLOWS ...

The paragraphs following set out the same sixteen specifications contained in Brown Machine's original proposal. Paragraph 6.1.1 of the specifications again provided for "Standard-regular forward trim". Page four of the acknowledgment contained the same "TERMS AND CONDITIONS OF SALE" which had accompanied Brown Machine's earlier proposal of November 7, 1975, including paragraph eight on liability and indemnity. Only two minor changes had been penned in on page four, neither of which has any bearing on the issues presented for appeal.

Hercules responded with a letter on February 9, 1976, to Mr. Fassett that "This is to advise you that Provision 6.1 of your order acknowledgement dated 2/5/76 should read 'Reverse Trim' instead of 'Standard-regular forward trim.' All other specifications are correct." On February 16, 1976, Mr. Fassett confirmed the change in provision 6.1.1 and informed the shop that same day of the requested modification to be made.

Hercules never paid the twenty percent deposit. Brown Machine sent Hercules an invoice dated April 14, 1976, requesting final payment of the total purchase price. Brown eventually shipped the trim press to Hercules and Hercules paid the agreed-upon purchase price.

Sometime later, James Miller, an employee of Hercules, and his wife sued

Brown Machine because of injuries he sustained while operating the trim press at Hercules' plant in Union, Missouri. Brown Machine demanded that Hercules defend the Miller lawsuit, but Hercules refused. Brown Machine eventually settled the Millers' lawsuit. Brown Machine later initiated this action against Hercules for indemnification of the settlement amount paid the Millers. Brown Machine claimed a condition of the original sales contract for the trim press required Hercules to indemnify Brown Machine for any claims arising from operation or misuse of the trim press.

Hercules' four points on appeal challenge the submissibility of Brown Machine's case, the verdict director given by Brown Machine, admission of certain allegedly prejudicial testimony and, finally, an instructional error. The dispositive issue on appeal is whether the parties had agreed to an indemnification provision in their contract for the sale of the T–100 trim press.

Hercules' first point disputes Brown Machine's contention that its initial proposal on November 7, 1975, constitutes the offer and that Hercules verbally accepted the offer by the telephone call on January 7, 1976, followed by its written purchase order dated January 6, 1976, which Brown Machine received January 19, 1976.

Article two of the Uniform Commercial Code governs transactions involving the sale of goods. U.C.C. § 2–102 (1977). Because the term "offer" is not defined in the code, the common law definition remains relevant. U.C.C. § 1–103. An offer is made when the offer leads the offeree to reasonably believe that an offer has been made. . . . Restatement (Second) of Contracts § 24 (1981) defines "offer" as "the manifestation of willingness to enter into a bargain, so made as to justify another person in understanding that his assent to that bargain is invited and will conclude it."

The general rule is that a price quotation is not an offer, but rather is an invitation to enter into negotiations or a mere suggestion to induce offers by others. . . . However, price quotes, if detailed enough, can amount to an offer creating the power of acceptance; to do so, it must reasonably appear from the price quote that assent to the quote is all that is needed to ripen the offer into a contract. . . . .

In this case Hercules could not have reasonably believed that Brown Machine's quotation was intended to be an offer, but rather an offer to enter into negotiations for the trim press. The cover letter accompanying the proposal mentioned that Brown Machine's sales representative would contact Hercules "to discuss this quote" and that the quotation was submitted for

Hercules "approval." The sale price as quoted also included the notation "We have included a mechanical ejector (item 9.1.2) because we understand this unit may be used for development of many items that would require this option. However, if you decide this is not necessary $2,575.00 could be deducted from the above price for a total of $21,835.00." Most importantly, paragraph three of the terms and conditions of sale attached to the proposal expressly provided: "No order, sale, agreement for sale, accepted proposal, offer to sell and/or contract of sale shall be binding upon BROWN unless accepted by BROWN ... on BROWN standard 'Order Acknowlegment' [sic] form." Thus, because the quotation reasonably appeared to be an offer to enter into negotiations for the sale of a trim press with a mechanical ejector for $24,410.00 with acceptance conditioned upon Brown's order acknowledgment form, no firm offer existed. . . . Brown's price quote was merely a proposal, not an offer, because of its provision that Hercules' acceptance was not binding upon Brown until Brown acknowledged the acceptance.

Even if we were to accept Brown Machine's characterization of its proposal as an offer, the quotation by its own terms and conditions expired thirty days after its issuance ("All quoted prices are subject to change without notice except those written proposals which shall expire without notice ... thirty (30) calendar days from date issued ..."). Hercules' written purchase order was dated January 6, 1976, and their telephone conversation of January 7, 1976, were both well beyond the expiration of the quote. Thus, even if the quotation were construed as an offer, there was no timely acceptance. . . .

If the acceptance of a price quotation, sufficiently detailed to constitute an offer, is not binding on the seller because the time within which it could have been accepted has lapsed, the purchase order, not the price quotation, is treated as the offer since the purchase order did not create an enforceable contract. . . . Thus, we believe Hercules' purchase order constitutes the offer. As a general rule, orders are considered as offers to purchase. . . .

The question then arises whether Brown Machine's acknowledgment containing the indemnity provision constitutes a counter offer or an acceptance of Hercules' offer with additional or different terms. Section 400.2–207, RSMo 1986, which mirrors § 2–207 of the Uniform Commercial Code provides the workable rule of law addressing the problem of the discrepancies in the independently drafted documents exchanged between the two parties.1 Section 400.2–207 provides as follows:

(1) A definite and seasonable expression of acceptance or a written confir-

mation which is sent within a reasonable time operates as an acceptance even though it states terms additional to or different from those offered or agreed upon, unless acceptance is expressly made conditional on assent to the additional or different terms.

(2) The additional terms are to be construed as proposals for addition to the contract. Between merchants such terms become part of the contract unless:

(a) the offer expressly limits acceptance to the terms of the offer;

(b) they materially alter it; or

(c) notification of objection to them has already been given or is given within a reasonable time after notice of them is received.

(3) Conduct by both parties which recognizes the existence of a contract is sufficient to establish a contract for sale although the writings of the parties do not otherwise establish a contract. In such cases the terms of the particular contract consist of those terms on which the writings of the parties agree, together with any supplementary terms incorporated under any other provision of this act.

Under subsection (1) an offeree's response to an offer operates as a valid acceptance of the offer even though it contains terms additional to, or different from, the terms of the offer unless the "acceptance is expressly made conditional" on the offeror's assent to the additional or different terms. Where the offeree's acceptance is made "expressly conditional" on the offeror's assent, the response operates not as an acceptance but as a counter offer which must be accepted by the original offeror. . . . Restatement (Second) of Contracts § 59 (1981) expresses it succinctly: "[A]n offeree's reply which purports to accept an offer but makes acceptance conditional on the offeror's assent to terms not contained in the original offer is effective as a counteroffer rather than acceptance."

The general view held by the majority of states is that, to convert an acceptance to a counter offer under UCC § 2–207(1), the conditional nature of the acceptance must be clearly expressed in a manner sufficient to notify the offeror that the offeree is unwilling to proceed with the transaction unless the additional or different terms are included in the contract. . . . The conditional assent provision has been construed narrowly to apply only to an acceptance which clearly shows that the offeree is unwilling to proceed absent assent to the additional or different terms. . . .

We find nothing in Brown Machine's acknowledgment of February 5, 1976, which reflects its unwillingness to proceed unless it obtained Hercules' assent to the additional and different terms in Brown Machine's acknowledgment, that is, page four of the acknowledgment styled "TERMS AND CONDITIONS OF SALE" which contained the indemnity provision. Brown Machine's acknowledgment was not "expressly made conditional" on Hercules' assent to the additional or different terms as provided for under § 2–207(1). Acceptance will be considered a counteroffer only if the acceptance is expressly made conditional on assent to the additional terms. . . . We conclude Brown Machine's acknowledgment did not operate as a counter offer within the scope of § 2–207(1).

Having determined that Brown Machine's order acknowledgment is not a counter offer, we believe that Brown Machine's acknowledgment operates as acceptance with additional or different terms from the offer, since the purchase order contained no indemnity provision. Under § 2–207(2), additional terms become a part of the contract between merchants unless (a) the offer expressly limits acceptance to the terms of the offer; (b) they materially alter it; or (c) notification of objection to them has already been given or is given within a reasonable time after notice of them is given. Hercules' purchase order here expressly limited acceptance to the terms of its offer. Given such an express limitation, the additional terms, including the indemnification provision, failed to become part of the contract between the parties.

We can conclude Hercules intended the indemnity provision to become a part of the parties' contract only if Hercules, as offeror, expressly assented to the additional terms, and, thus, effectively waived its condition that acceptance be limited to the terms of its offer, the purchase order. While the text of § 2–207 does not incorporate such a provision, Official Comment 3 to § 2–207 states: "Whether or not additional or different terms will become part of the agreement depends upon the provisions of subsection (2). If they are such as materially to alter the original bargain, they will not be included unless expressly agreed to by the other party." The indemnification provision was clearly a material alteration to the parties' agreement.

The evidence does not establish that Hercules expressly assented to the additional terms contained in Brown Machine's order acknowledgment. Brown Machine's order acknowledgment of February 5, 1976, indicated that "[i]f these specifications and terms and conditions of Sale are not in accordance with your understanding, please ADVISE US WITHIN SEVEN (7) DAYS OF RECEIPT OF THIS ACKNOWLEDGEMENT." Hercules replied by letter four days later advising Brown Machine that provision 6.1.1 should provide for reverse trim instead of standard regular forward trim, followed by "all other specifications are correct." Hercules' use of the term "specifications" is unambiguous and clearly refers only to the protocol for the machine's manufacture. Nothing in its response can be construed as express assent to Brown Machine's additional "terms and conditions of sale." Express assent under § 2–207(2) cannot be presumed by silence or mere failure to object. . . .

We believe it is clear as a matter of law that the indemnification clause cannot be held to be part of the contract agreed upon by the parties. The judgment of the trial court is reversed. We need not address the remaining points raised by Hercules.

Reversed.

SMITH, P.J., and SATZ, J., concur.

NOTES AND QUESTIONS

A. Price Quote. In *Brown Machine*, the court concludes that Hercules's purchase order constitutes an offer, rather than Brown Machine's price quote. What arguments does the court adduce in support of this interpretation? What would have been the outcome of the case if the court had concluded that Brown Machine's price quote was an offer?

B. UCC v. common law. *Brown Machine* was governed by Article 2 of the UCC. What would have been the outcome of the case if the contract had been governed by the common law?

C. Acceptance v. confirmation. Section 2-207(1) of the UCC governs both acceptances and confirmation letters. In which of these two categories, if any, does Brown Machine's February 5 letter fall?

D. Acceptance under Section 2-207(1). One of the questions arising under section 2-207(1) of the UCC is which combination of written and/or oral communications can trigger the application of this provision. It is uncontroversial that section 2-207(1) can apply if a written offer is accepted in writing.[21]

---

21. See, e.g., Album Graphics, Inc. v. Beatrice Foods Co., 408 N.E.2d 1041, 1047 (Ill. App. 1st Dist. 1980) (noting that the "[g]eneral purpose of section 2-207 is to allow parties to enforce their agreement . . . despite discrepancies between a written offer and a written acceptance"); Leighton Industries, Inc. v. Callier Steel Pipe & Tube, Inc., No. 89 C 8235, 1991 WL 18413, at *3 (N.D. Ill. Feb. 6, 1991) ("Section 2–207 concerns transactions between merchants[9] and allows parties to enforce their agreement despite discrepancies between the written offer and the written acceptance.")

By contrast, courts disagree on whether section 2-207(1) applies to the written acceptance of an oral bid.[22] Similarly, it is controversial whether section 2-207(1) governs the oral acceptance of a written bid.[23] Can you imagine why these cases are controversial?

E. Written confirmations. Section 2-207(1) of the UCC also applies to "written confirmation[s]." The official comments explain that this alternative was meant to cover situations where a contract was initially formed either orally or by informal correspondence, and one of the parties then followed up with a written confirmation.[24] These are precisely the situations where courts have applied section 2-207(1).[25] By contrast, section 2-207(1) does not apply if a written confirmation is used to introduce different or additional terms if the original agreement was in writing and signed by both parties.[26]

(footnote omitted). Note that some courts decline to apply section 2-207(1) if each contractual term was individually negotiated. See Columbia Hyundai, Inc. v. Carl Hyundai, Inc., 484 S.E.2d 468, 470 (S.C. 1997) (arguing that if each term of the contract was negotiated, the contract does not involve a battle of forms, thereby precluding the application of section 2-207).

22. Compare Dorton v. Collins & Aikman Corp., 453 F.2d 1161, 1169 (6th Cir. 1972) with ProCD, Inc. v. Zeidenberg, 86 F.3d 1447, 1452 (7th Cir. 1996) (limiting the application of section 2–207 to cases where both parties use form contracts).

23. Compare Northrop Corp. v. Litronic Industries, 29 F.3d 1173, 1177 (7th Cir. 1994) (applying section 2-207(1) to oral acceptance) with Calhoun v. Cullum's Lumber Mill, Inc., 545 S.E.2d 41, 44 (Ga. App. 2001) (holding that section 2-207(1) is inapplicable to "oral acceptance of a written timber bid").

24. UCC § 2-207 Off. Cmt. 1

25. Am. Parts Co., Inc. (Detroit Body Products Co. Div.) v. Am. Arb. Ass'n, 154 N.W.2d 5, 11 (Mich. App. 1967) (holding that 2-207(1) applies to a "written confirmation, where an agreement has been reached either orally or by informal correspondence between the parties").

26. Pritts v. J. I. Case Co., 310 N.W.2d 261, 267 (Mich. App. 1981) (holding that section 2-207(1) "does not permit one party to send a written confirmation (or purchase order form) which varies the terms of an original written agreement which has been signed by both parties.").

CHAPTER 8
ELECTRONIC CONTRACTING

ProCD, Inc. v. Zeidenberg

United States Court of Appeals, Seventh Circuit, 86 F.3d 1447 (1996)

Editor: Plaintiff ProCD produced a CD-ROM that contained information compiled from telephone directories. ProCD sought to limit purchasers' use of the product by subjecting them to a license agreement. At the time, a so-called "shrink-wrap license" would typically accompany CD-ROM software bought in brick-and-mortar stores. The CD-ROM was packaged in shrink-wrap, and CD-ROM's exterior packaging would contain a warning stating that the customer agreed to the terms of a license agreement by opening the plastic shrink-wrap. Crucially, the terms of that license agreement were not usually displayed on the outside of the box. ProCD took a slightly different approach. Its CD-ROMs were not shrink-wrapped. However, the data on the CD-ROM was encrypted and could be accessed via only a program included on the CD-ROM. When starting that program, customers would be prompted to agree to the plaintiff's licensing agreement. A statement on the outside of the box would warn customers that the software on the CD-ROM came with a licensing agreement. Even though this approach did not constitute a shrink-wrap license in the literal sense, the court reasoned that it was equivalent to a shrink-wrap license.

EASTERBROOK, Circuit Judge

Must buyers of computer software obey the terms of shrinkwrap licenses?

. . .

ProCD, the plaintiff, has compiled information from more than 3,000 telephone directories into a computer database. We may assume that this database cannot be copyrighted . . . . ProCD sells a version of the database . . . on CD–ROM discs.

The database in SelectPhone (trademark) cost more than $10 million to compile and is expensive to keep current. It is much more valuable to some users than to others. The combination of names, addresses, and SIC codes enables manufacturers to compile lists of potential customers. Manufacturers and retailers pay high prices to specialized information intermediaries for such mailing lists; ProCD offers a potentially cheaper alternative. People with nothing to sell could use the database as a substitute for calling long distance information, or as a way to look up old friends who have moved to unknown towns, or just as an electronic substitute for the local phone book. ProCD decided to engage in price discrimination, selling its database to the general public for personal use at a low price (approximately $150 for the set of five discs) while selling information to the trade for a higher price. . . .

If ProCD had to recover all of its costs and make a profit by charging a single price—that is, if it could not charge more to commercial users than to the general public—it would have to raise the price substantially over $150. The ensuing reduction in sales would harm consumers who value the information at, say, $200. They get consumer surplus of $50 under the current arrangement but would cease to buy if the price rose substantially. If because of high elasticity of demand in the consumer segment of the market the only way to make a profit turned out to be a price attractive to commercial users alone, then all consumers would lose out—and so would the commercial clients, who would have to pay more for the listings because ProCD could not obtain any contribution toward costs from the consumer market.

To make price discrimination work, however, the seller must be able to control arbitrage. An air carrier sells tickets for less to vacationers than to business travelers, using advance purchase and Saturday-night-stay requirements to distinguish the categories. A producer of movies segments the market by time, releasing first to theaters, then to pay-per-view services, next to the videotape and laserdisc market, and finally to cable and commercial tv. Vendors of computer software have a harder task. Anyone can walk into a retail store and buy a box. Customers do not wear tags saying "commercial user" or "consumer user." Anyway, even a commercial-user-detector at the door would not work, because a consumer could buy the software and resell to a commercial user. That arbitrage would break down the price discrimination and drive up the minimum price at which ProCD would sell to anyone.

Instead of tinkering with the product and letting users sort themselves—for example, furnishing current data at a high price that would be attractive only to commercial customers, and two-year-old data at a low price—ProCD turned to the institution of contract. Every box containing its consumer product declares that the software comes with restrictions stated in an enclosed license. This license, which is encoded on the CD–ROM disks as well as printed in the manual, and which appears on a user's screen every time the software runs, limits use of the application program and listings to non-commercial purposes.

Matthew Zeidenberg bought a consumer package of SelectPhone (trademark) in 1994 from a retail outlet in Madison, Wisconsin, but decided to ignore the license. He formed Silken Mountain Web Services, Inc., to resell the information in the SelectPhone (trademark) database. The corporation makes the database available on the Internet to anyone willing to pay its price—which, needless to say, is less than ProCD charges its commercial customers. Zeidenberg has purchased two additional SelectPhone (trademark) packages, each with an updated version of the database, and made the latest information available over the World Wide Web, for a price, through his corporation. ProCD filed this suit seeking an injunction against further dissemination that exceeds the rights specified in the licenses (identical in each of the three packages Zeidenberg purchased). The district court held the licenses ineffectual because their terms do not appear on the outside of the packages. The court added that the second and third licenses stand no different from the first, even though they are identical, because they *might* have been different, and a purchaser does not agree to—and cannot be bound by—terms that were secret at the time of purchase. . . .

Following the district court, we treat the licenses as ordinary contracts accompanying the sale of products, and therefore as governed by the common law of contracts and the Uniform Commercial Code. . . . [T]he district court held, that placing the package of software on the shelf is an "offer," which the customer "accepts" by paying the asking price and leaving the store with the goods. *Peeters v. State,* 154 Wis. 111, 142 N.W. 181 (1913). In Wisconsin, as elsewhere, a contract includes only the terms on which the parties have agreed. One cannot agree to hidden terms, the judge concluded. So far, so good—but one of the terms to which Zeidenberg agreed by purchasing the software is that the transaction was subject to a license. Zeidenberg's position therefore must be that the printed terms on the outside of a box are the parties' contract—except for printed terms that refer to or incorporate other terms. But why would Wisconsin fetter the parties' choice in this way? Vendors can put the entire terms of a contract on the outside of a box only by using microscopic type, removing other information that buyers might find more useful (such as what the software does, and on which computers it works), or both. The "Read Me" file included with most software, describing system requirements and potential incompatibilities, may be equivalent to ten pages of type; warranties and license restrictions take still more space. Notice on the outside, terms on the inside, and a right to return the software for a refund if the terms are unacceptable (a right that the license expressly extends), may be a means of doing business valuable to buyers and sellers alike. See E. Allan Farnsworth, 1 *Farnsworth on Contracts* § 4.26 (1990); *Restatement (2d) of Contracts* § 211 comment a (1981) ("Standardization of agreements serves many of the same functions as standardization of goods and services; both are essential to a system of mass production and distribution. Scarce and costly time and skill can be devoted to a class of transactions rather than the details of individual transactions.")....

Transactions in which the exchange of money precedes the communication of detailed terms are common. Consider the purchase of insurance. The buyer goes to an agent, who explains the essentials (amount of coverage, number of years) and remits the premium to the home office, which sends back a policy. On the district judge's understanding, the terms of the policy are irrelevant because the insured paid before receiving them. Yet the device of payment, often with a "binder" (so that the insurance takes effect immediately even though the home office reserves the right to withdraw coverage later), in advance of the policy, serves buyers' interests by accelerating effectiveness and reducing transactions costs. Or consider the purchase of an airline ticket. The traveler calls the carrier or an agent, is quoted a price, reserves a seat, pays, and gets a ticket, in that order. The ticket contains elaborate terms, which the traveler can reject by canceling the reservation. To use the ticket is to accept the terms, even terms that in retrospect are disadvantageous. See *Carnival Cruise Lines, Inc. v. Shute,* 499 U.S. 585 . . . (1991) . . . . Just so with a ticket to a concert. The back of the ticket states that the patron promises not to record the concert; to attend is to agree. A theater that detects a violation will confiscate the tape and escort the violator to the exit. One *could* arrange things so that every concertgoer signs this promise before forking over the money, but that cumbersome way of doing things not only would lengthen queues and raise prices but also would scotch the sale of tickets by phone or electronic data service.

Consumer goods work the same way. Someone who wants to buy a radio set visits a store, pays, and walks out with a box. Inside the box is a leaflet containing some terms, the most important of which usually is the warranty, read for the first time in the comfort of home. By Zeidenberg's lights, the warranty in the box is irrelevant; every consumer gets the standard warranty implied by the UCC in the event the contract is silent; yet so far as we are aware no state disregards warranties furnished with consumer products. Drugs come with a list of ingredients on the outside and an elaborate package insert on the inside. The package insert describes drug interactions, contraindications, and other vital information—but, if Zeidenberg is right, the purchaser need not read the package insert, because it is not part of the contract.

Next consider the software industry itself. Only a minority of sales take place over the counter, where there are boxes to peruse. A customer may place an order by phone in response to a line item in a catalog or a review in a magazine. Much software is ordered over the Internet by purchasers who have never seen a box. Increasingly software arrives by wire. . . . The user purchases a serial number, which activates the software's features. On Zeidenberg's arguments, these unboxed sales are unfettered by terms—so the seller has made a broad warranty and must pay consequential damages for any shortfalls in performance, two "promises" that if taken seriously would drive prices through the ceiling or return transactions to the horse-and-buggy age.

According to the district court, the UCC does not countenance the sequence of money now, terms later. New words may be designed to fortify the current rule with a more precise text that curtails uncertainty. . . . Our case has only one form; UCC § 2–207 is irrelevant. . . .

What then does the current version of the UCC have to say? We think that the place to start is § 2–204(1): "A contract for sale of goods may be made in any manner sufficient to show agreement, including conduct by both parties which recognizes the existence of such a contract." A vendor, as master of the offer, may invite acceptance by conduct, and may propose limitations on the kind of conduct that constitutes acceptance. A buyer may accept by performing the acts the vendor proposes to treat as acceptance. And that is what happened. ProCD proposed a contract that a buyer would accept by *using* the software after having an opportunity to read the license at leisure. This Zeidenberg did. He had no choice, because the software splashed the license on the screen and would not let him proceed without indicating acceptance. So although the district judge was right to say that a contract can be, and often is, formed simply by paying the price and walking out of the store, the UCC permits contracts to be formed in other ways. ProCD proposed such a different way, and without protest Zeidenberg agreed. Ours is not a case in which a consumer opens a package to find an insert saying "you owe us an extra $10,000" and the seller files suit to collect. Any buyer finding such a demand can prevent formation of the contract by returning the package, as can any consumer who concludes that the terms of the license make the software worth less than the purchase price. Nothing in the UCC requires a seller to maximize the buyer's net gains. . . .

Some portions of the UCC impose additional requirements on the way parties agree on terms. A disclaimer of the implied warranty of merchantability must be "conspicuous." UCC § 2–316(2), incorporating UCC § 1–201(10). Promises to make firm offers, or to negate oral modifications, must be "separately signed." UCC §§ 2–205, 2–209(2). These special provisos reinforce the impression that, so far as the UCC is concerned, other terms may be as inconspicuous as the forum-selection clause on the back of the cruise ship ticket in *Carnival Lines*. Zeidenberg has not located any Wisconsin case—for that matter, any case in any state—holding that under the UCC the ordinary terms found in shrinkwrap licenses require any special prominence, or otherwise are to be undercut rather than enforced. In the end, the terms of the license are conceptually identical to the contents of the package. Just as no court would dream of saying that SelectPhone (trademark) must contain 3,100 phone books rather than 3,000, or must have data no more than 30 days old, or must sell for $100 rather than $150—although any of these changes would be welcomed by the customer, if all other things were held constant—so, we believe, Wisconsin would not let the buyer pick and choose among terms. Terms of use are no less a part of "the product" than are the size of the database and the speed with which the software compiles listings. Competition among vendors, not judicial revision of a package's contents, is how consumers are protected in a market economy. *Digital Equipment Corp. v. Uniq*

Digital Technologies, Inc., 73 F.3d 756 (7th Cir.1996). ProCD has rivals, which may elect to compete by offering superior software, monthly updates, improved terms of use, lower price, or a better compromise among these elements. As we stressed above, adjusting terms in buyers' favor might help Matthew Zeidenberg today (he already has the software) but would lead to a response, such as a higher price, that might make consumers as a whole worse off....

Reversed and remanded.

NOTES AND QUESTIONS

*A. **The legal significance of shrink-wraps.*** The approach pioneered in *ProCD* has become the prevailing view regarding shrink-wrap terms.[1] Nevertheless, some courts diverge from this approach and argue that, depending on the circumstances, the shrink-wrap terms may either signify acceptance under section 2-207(1) of the UCC or serve as a written confirmation falling under the same provision.[2] How would *ProCD* have been decided if the court had embraced this alternative viewpoint?

*B. **Hill v. Gateway.*** In *ProCD*, a notice on the exterior of the software's box alerted customers to the necessity to enter into a license agreement. In a later case decided by Judge Easterbrook, *Hill v. Gateway 2000, Inc.*, the buyer ordered a computer over the phone and paid via credit card.[3] The seller subsequently sent the box containing the computer. On the outside, the box did not display any notice of additional terms. However, inside the box, the customer found a list of legal terms advising him that they would be binding unless he returned the computer within 30 days.[4] Citing its earlier decision in *ProCD*, the court held that the customer accepted the terms by keeping the computer for more than 30 days.[5]

---

1. E.g., M.A. Mortenson Co., Inc. v. Timberline Software Corp., 998 P.2d 305, 313 (Wash. 2000); DeFontes v. Dell, Inc., 984 A.2d 1061, 1071 (R.I. 2009); O'Quinn v. Verizon Wireless, 256 F. Supp. 2d 512, 516 (M.D. La. 2003).
2. See, e.g., Step-Saver Data Sys., Inc. v. Wyse Tech., 939 F.2d 91, 101-103 (3d Cir. 1991) (concluding that the shrink-wrap terms constitute an acceptance within the meaning of UCC § 2-207); Klocek v. Gateway, Inc., 104 F. Supp. 2d 1332, 1340 (D. Kan. 2000) ("Under § 2–207, the Standard Terms constitute either an expression of acceptance or written confirmation."); Rogers v. Dell Computer Corp., 138 P.3d 826, 832 (Okla. 2005), as corrected (Nov. 16, 2005), as corrected (Nov. 29, 2005) (arguing that under section 2-206(1) of the UCC, the contract was formed were shipped).
3. Hill v. Gateway 2000, Inc., 105 F.3d 1147, 1148 (7th Cir. 1997)
4. Hill v. Gateway 2000, Inc., 105 F.3d 1147, 1148 (7th Cir. 1997)
5. Hill v. Gateway 2000, Inc., 105 F.3d 1147, 1150 (7th Cir. 1997)

C. Later case law. Even courts following *ProCD* have emphasized the need to provide the customer with effective notice. Thus, in *DeFontes v. Dell*, the Rhode Island Supreme Court follows *ProCD* in principle but stresses that the shrink-wrap terms become part of the contract only if the consumer had a reasonable opportunity to reject them: "[T]he crucial question in this case is whether defendants reasonably invited acceptance by making clear in the terms and conditions agreement that (1) by accepting defendants' product the consumer was accepting the terms and conditions contained within and (2) the consumer could reject the terms and conditions by returning the product."[6]

D. Click-wraps and browse-wraps. The rise of online shopping has caused merchants to devise novel ways for incorporating their boilerplate terms into contracts. Courts commonly distinguish between "click-wrap" contracts and "browse-wrap" contracts. In the case of "click-wraps," the customer assents to contractual terms by clicking on a button or checking a box, thereby explicitly signaling his approval.[7] As long as the customer is provided with adequate notice of the terms before he assents, click-wrap contracts fit squarely within the traditional paradigm of mutual assent and are therefore routinely enforced.[8] The term "browse-wrap" refers to contract terms that the consumer supposedly assents to simply by using a website.[9] In other words, browse-wraps purport to be binding even though the user has not clicked on a special button or otherwise made his agreement explicit.[10] Courts typically hold that such browse-wraps become part of the contract if the consumer had

---

6. DeFontes v. Dell, Inc., 984 A.2d 1061, 1071 (R.I. 2009).

7. E.g., TruLogic, Inc. v. Gen. Electric Co., 2021-Ohio-2860, ¶ 38, appeal not allowed, 177 N.E.3d 1001 (Ohio 2021); Hancock v. Am. Tel. and Tel. Co., Inc., 701 F.3d 1248, 1255 (10th Cir. 2012); Feldman v. Google, Inc., 513 F. Supp. 2d 229, 236 (E.D. Pa. 2007).

8. E.g., Hancock v. Am. Tel. and Tel. Co., Inc., 701 F.3d 1248, 1258 (10th Cir. 2012); i.Lan Sys., Inc. v. Netscout Serv. Level Corp., 183 F. Supp. 2d 328, 338 (D. Mass. 2002); One Beacon Ins. Co. v. Crowley Marine Services, Inc., 648 F.3d 258, 270 (5th Cir. 2011); but see Specht v. Netscape Commun. Corp., 306 F.3d 17, 32 (2d Cir. 2002) (finding no mutual assent where customer clicked a download button to obtain free software without having been given effective notice that he was consenting to boilerplate terms).

9. E.g., Southwest Airlines Co. v. BoardFirst, L.L.C., No. 3:06–CV–0891–B, 2007 WL 4823761, at *4 (N.D. Tex. Sept. 12, 2007); StubHub, Inc. v. Ball, 676 S.W.3d 193, 200 (Tex. App.—Hous. [14th Dist.] 2023)

10. See, e.g., Southwest Airlines Co. v. BoardFirst, L.L.C., No. 3:06–CV–0891–B, 2007 WL 4823761, at *4 (N.D. Tex. Sept. 12, 2007) ("Unlike a clickwrap agreement, a browsewrap agreement "does not require the user to manifest assent to the terms and conditions expressly. [...] A party instead gives his assent simply by using the website.").

adequate notice of the terms and used the website with such notice.[11] Conversely, courts have refused to enforce browse-wrap terms that they deemed too inconspicuous to be noticed.[12]

E. The downsides of ProCD. What risks, if any, does the *ProCD* approach create for customers?

F. Is Software a Good?

Whether Article 2 of the Uniform Commercial Code applies to software transactions turns on whether software qualifies as a "good" under UCC § 2-105(1). In the era when software was commonly delivered in tangible form—via floppy disks, CD-ROMs, or similar media—courts had little difficulty characterizing software as a good.

For software that is downloaded or transmitted electronically, the classification is less intuitive. Nonetheless, the prevailing view remains that generic, mass-marketed software constitutes a good within the meaning of Article 2, even when delivered electronically.[13]

By contrast, transactions involving software that is custom-developed for a particular client are generally treated as service contracts, regardless of whether the software is ultimately delivered in tangible or intangible form. In such cases, the dominant purpose of the transaction is deemed to be the provision of services rather than the sale of a movable item.[14]

---

11. E.g., Major v. McCallister, 302 S.W.3d 227, 230 (Mo. App. S. Dist. 2009). Cf. Vitacost.com, Inc. v. McCants, 210 So. 3d 761, 762 (Fla. 4th Dist. App. 2017) ("'Browsewrap' agreements have only been enforced when the purchaser has actual knowledge of the terms and conditions, or when the hyperlink to the terms and conditions is conspicuous enough to put a reasonably prudent person on inquiry notice.").

12. E.g., Long v. Provide Com., Inc., 200 Cal. Rptr. 3d 117, 125–26 (Cal. App. 2d Dist. 2016); Vitacost.-com, Inc. v. McCants, 210 So. 3d 761, 765-66 (Fla. 4th Dist. App. 2017).

13. *See, e.g.*, Pain Ctr. of SE Indiana LLC v. Origin Healthcare Sols. LLC, 893 F.3d 454, 459 (7th Cir. 2018)(noting that Indiana courts treat the purchase of generic software as a sale of goods); Olcott Intern. & Co., Inc. v. Micro Data Base Sys., Inc., 793 N.E.2d 1063, 1071 (Ind. App. 2003) (holding that Article 2 of the UCC applies to the sale of "pre-existing, standardized software modules").

14. *See, e.g.*, Conwell v. Gray Loon Outdoor Mktg. Group, Inc., 906 N.E.2d 805, 812 (Ind. 2009) (holding that a contract to fashion, program, and host a website constitutes a service contract and stressing that "[i]t would be a mistake . . . to treat software as a good simply because it was contained in a tangible medium"); Wharton Mgt. Group v. Sigma Consultants, Inc., No. C.A. 89C-JA-165, 1990 WL 18360, at *3 (Del. Super. Jan. 29, 1990), aff'd, 582 A.2d 936 (Del. 1990)(categorizing a software contract as a service contract even though it involved "a tangible end product" since the service element predominated); Pearl Investments, LLC v. Stand. I/O, Inc., 257 F. Supp. 2d 326, 353 (D. Me. 2003)(holding that a contract to develop software from scratch constitutes a service contract). *But see* D.P. Tech. Corp. v. Sherwood Tool, Inc., 751 F. Supp. 1038, 1040 (D. Conn. 1990) (applying CT law and a software contract as a sale of goods, even though the software was specifically designed for the purchaser); Micro Data Base Sys., Inc. v. Dharma Sys., Inc., 148 F.3d 649, 655

(7th Cir. 1998)(applying Article 2 of the UCC to a contract that called for software to be developed from existing software). Some courts treat software as a good without explicitly discussing whether an exception applies to specifically designed software. See Wachter Mgt. Co. v. Dexter & Chaney, Inc., 144 P.3d 747, 750 (Kan. 2006)(holding that "[c]omputer software is considered to be goods subject to the UCC even though incidental services are provided along with the sale of the software").

CHAPTER 9
CONSIDERATION

I. Introduction

As a general rule, forming a contract requires mutual assent and consideration.[1] What is consideration? Simply put, consideration is what is given in return for a promise. It is not sufficient that both sides give something. Instead, each side must give so that the other side gives.[2]

In other words, there must be a bargain, a quid pro quo.[3]

---

1. Cuppy v. Gen. Acc. Fire & Life Assur. Corp., 378 S.W.2d 629, 632 (Ky. 1964); Reichert v. Keefe Commissary Network, L.L.C., No. C17-5848RBL, 2018 WL 2018452, at *1 (W.D. Wash. May 1, 2018); Drummond v. Akselrad, No. 23-CV-179 (LJL), 2023 WL 3173780, at *4 (S.D.N.Y. May 1, 2023); Restatement (Second) of Contracts § 17.
2. Read Restatement (Second) of Contracts §§ 17, 71(2). See, e.g., Belanger v. Yorke, 226 A.3d 215, 223 (Me. 2020)(holding that a "return promise is bargained for if it is sought by the promisor in exchange for his promise and is given by the promisee in exchange for that promise.")(citing section 71(2) of the Restatement (Second) of Contracts). There are exceptions to this rule. As we will see in later chapters, there are some cases in which a one-sided promise is binding even though it is not supported by consideration. See Restatement (Second) of Contracts §§ 82-94.
3. Id. § 71(1). See, e.g., Belanger v. Yorke, 226 A.3d 215, 224 (Me. 2020)(requiring a quid-pro-quo for the consideration requirement to be met); Stelmack v. Glen Alden Coal Co., 14 A.2d 127, 128–29 (Pa. 1940)(holding that "[t]he detriment incurred must be the 'quid pro quo', or the 'price' of the promise, and the inducement for which it was made"); Drummond v. Akselrad, No. 23-CV-179 (LJL), 2023 WL 3173780, at *4 (S.D.N.Y. May 1, 2023)("For consideration to be valid, it must be "bargained for," meaning that the promisor must seek it in exchange for his promise, and the promisee must give it in exchange for that promise."). But see Hovas v. O'Brien, 654 S.W.2d 801, 803 (Tex. App.--Hous. [14th Dist.] 1983), writ refused NRE (Oct. 5, 1983)(" A quid pro quo is not required to create a valid consideration.")

Question. Alpha calls Beta and says: "I want to do a good deed today, so I promise to drive you to school each morning for the rest of the school year." Beta responds: "I also aspire to do a good deed. Therefore, I promise to buy you lunch every day for the rest of the school year." Is Alpha's promise supported by consideration?

Answer. Alpha's promise is not supported by consideration. Admittedly, each side gives something: Alpha promises to drive Beta to school, and Beta promises to buy lunch for Alpha. However, both promises are given independently. Neither side gives to induce the other to give.

Question. Alpha calls Beta and says: "If you promise to buy me lunch every day for the rest of the school year, then I promise to drive you to school each morning for the rest of the school year." Beta replies: "You have a deal." Is Alpha's promise to drive Beta to school supported by consideration?

Answer. In this case, Alpha's promise serves as consideration for Beta's promise and vice versa. Each party's promise is given to induce the other party's promise.

To determine whether the bargain requirement is satisfied, we apply general principles of interpretation. Accordingly, in case of a misunderstanding between the parties, we ask how a reasonable observer would have understood the situation.[4]

Question. Alpha calls Beta and says: "If you promise to buy me lunch every day for the rest of the school year, then I promise to drive you to school each morning for the rest of the school year." Beta replies: "Deal!" However, unknown to Beta, Alpha has a crush on Beta. Alpha could not care less about whether or not Beta buys lunch. Instead, Alpha only promises to drive Beta to school every morning to spend time with Beta. Is Alpha's promise supported by consideration?

Answer. Alpha's promise is supported by consideration. To determine whether a promise is supported by consideration, we apply general principles

4. See Restatement (Second) of Contracts § 71 cmt. b.

of interpretation. In other words, unless Beta was aware of Alpha's intended meaning, we ask how a reasonable observer in Beta's shoes would have understood Alpha's statement.[5] A reasonable observer in Beta's shoes would have assumed that Alpha promised to drive Beta to school to obtain Beta's promise to buy lunch. Therefore, the consideration requirement is satisfied.

II. Unpacking the Consideration Requirement

Consideration requires that each side gives so that the other side gives.[6] This seemingly straightforward requirement has given rise to numerous rules and exceptions that we will discuss in detail below. To understand the logic inherent in these rules, it is helpful to unpack the consideration requirement further.[7] It has two elements. First, something must be given. And second, that something must be given in order to induce the other side to give.

Let us focus more closely on the first of these two elements. There is general agreement that the category of things the promisee can give to satisfy the consideration requirement is exceedingly broad, including, for example, a promise, a performance, a forbearance, the creation of a legal relationship, the termination of a legal relationship, or the modification of legal relationship.[8] But will *anything* suffice for the first element of the consideration requirement? According to the traditional view, what is given must either involve a benefit to the promisee or a legal detriment to the promisor.[9] By

5. See Restatement (Second) of Contracts § 71 cmt. b.

6. See Restatement (Second) of Contracts § 71. See also Belanger v. Yorke, 226 A.3d 215, 223 (Me. 2020)(holding that a "return promise is bargained for if it is sought by the promisor in exchange for his promise and is given by the promisee in exchange for that promise.")(citing section 71(2) of the Restatement (Second) of Contracts).

7. But see Sugarhouse Fin. Co. v. Anderson, 610 P.2d 1369, 1372 (Utah 1980)(pointing out that "[n]o completely satisfactory and comprehensive definition of 'consideration' has ever been devised") (citation omitted).

8. Restatement (Second) of Contracts § 71. See Martindale v. Sandvik, Inc., 800 A.2d 872, 878 (N.J. 2002)(holding that consideration can consist of "an act, a forbearance, or the creation, modification, or destruction of a legal relation")(internal citation omitted); Block v. Seneca Mortg. Servicing, 221 F. Supp. 3d 559, 572 (D.N.J. 2016)(holding that "[c]onsideration is a bargained-for exchange of promises or performance that may consist of an act, a forbearance, or the creation, modification, or destruction of a legal relation")(internal citation omitted).

9. But see, e.g., Manwill v. Oyler, 361 P.2d 177, 178 (Utah 1961) (holding that "[t]he principle that in order for a contract to be valid and binding, each party must be bound to give some legal consideration to the other by conferring a benefit upon him or suffering a legal detriment at his request is firmly implanted in the roots of our law"); Carlisle v. T & R Excavating, Inc., 704 N.E.2d 39, 43 (Ohio App. 9th Dist. 1997)(holding that "[u]nder Ohio law, consideration consists of either a

contrast, the modern view endorsed by the Restatement (Second) of Contracts explicitly dispenses with the need for a benefit or legal detriment.[10] According to this view, as long as the bargain requirement is met, there is no need to additionally focus on whether the consideration involves a benefit for the promisee or a legal detriment for the promisor.[11] Of course, even under this modern view, the existence of a legal detriment or benefit can help explain why, in a given case, the bargain requirement is satisfied.[12] But again, under the modern view, neither a benefit nor a legal detriment are necessary elements of a bargain.[13]

The law's generosity concerning the first element of the consideration requirement is compensated by its rigor regarding the second element, namely the requirement that what is given must be given as part of an exchange ("quid pro quo").

Question. Alpha and Beta enter into an agreement whereby Alpha promises to pay Beta $100,000,000 for a peppercorn. Is Alpha's promise to pay the $100,000,000 supported by consideration?

Answer. Recall that in determining whether the consideration requirement is satisfied, we apply the general rules of interpretation. If the two parties shared an understanding that Alpha's promise to pay was indeed made to induce Beta to give the peppercorn, then the consideration requirement would be met. However, if the parties understood the arrangement as a mere pretext or sham,

---

benefit to the promisor or a detriment to the promisee"); Cox Commun., Inc. v. T-Mobile US, Inc., 273 A.3d 752, 764 (Del. 2022), reargument denied (Mar. 22, 2022)("Consideration requires that each party to a contract convey a benefit or incur a legal detriment, such that the exchange is "bargained for.").

10. E.g., Block v. Seneca Mortg. Servicing, 221 F. Supp. 3d 559, 572 (D.N.J. 2016); Sipko v. Koger, Inc., 70 A.3d 512, 522 (N.J. 2013); Shebar v. Sanyo Bus. Sys. Corp., 544 A.2d 377, 383 (N.J. 1988); Restatement (Second) of Contracts § 79(a).

11. Restatement (Second) of Contracts § 79(a).

12. See, e.g., Thrash v. Deason, 435 So. 2d 69, 70 (Ala. 1983)(holding that "detriment to a promisor, and benefit to a promisee, constitutes sufficient consideration in support of ... release" from a legal obligation); Storti v. U. of Washington, 330 P.3d 159, 164 (Wash. 2014)(holding that "[a]s long as [an] employees incur some legal detriment—by continuing to work, for example—the requirement of consideration is met"); Lloyd's Credit Corp. v. Marlin Mgt. Services, Inc., 614 A.2d 812, 814 (Vt. 1992)(" Either a benefit to the promisor or a detriment to the promisee is sufficient consideration for a contract.").

13. Block v. Seneca Mortg. Servicing, 221 F. Supp. 3d 559, 572 (D.N.J. 2016); Sipko v. Koger, Inc., 70 A.3d 512, 522 (N.J. 2013); Shebar v. Sanyo Bus. Sys. Corp., 544 A.2d 377, 383 (N.J. 1988); Restatement (Second) of Contracts § 79(a); Restatement (Second) of Contracts § 79(a).

> merely to justify the arrangement in the eyes of the law, then the situation changes. Under this shared understanding, the payment was not truly promised to induce Beta to give. Consequently, the consideration requirement is not satisfied. Similarly, without a shared understanding, we rely on a reasonable (objective) interpretation of the agreement, and a reasonable observer would not believe that the payment promise was given to induce Beta to give the peppercorn. In sum, unless the parties shared an understanding that Alpha made their promise to induce Beta to give the peppercorn, the consideration requirement is not met.

What if the consideration is worth less than the promise? That does not matter.[14] Section 79 (b) of the Restatement (Second) of Contracts explicitly clarifies that once the bargain requirement is met, the court will not inquire into whether the exchange involves equivalent values. Even so-called "mixed gifts"—promises made in part to obtain the consideration and in part as a gift —are deemed to be supported by consideration.[15]

III. Settlement of Claims

There is no doubt that relinquishing a valid legal claim can constitute consideration. For example, assume that Alpha owes Beta $100. If Beta relinquishes that claim in exchange for Alpha promising to mow Beta's lawn, the consideration requirement is satisfied. The more interesting question is whether relinquishing an unfounded legal claim can constitute consideration.

---

14. E.g., Baker v. Bristol Care, Inc., 450 S.W.3d 770, 782 (Mo. 2014)("Accordingly, any bargained-for exchange will supply the consideration needed to form a contract, regardless of whether a court believes (with the benefit of hindsight) that the promisor gave a promise that was worth more—even far more—than the benefit or detriment received in the exchange."): Apfel v. Prudential-Bache Securities Inc., 616 N.E.2d 1095, 1097 (N.Y. 1993)("Under the traditional principles of contract law, the parties to a contract are free to make their bargain, even if the consideration exchanged is grossly unequal or of dubious value.")(citation omitted); Drummond v. Akselrad, No. 23-CV-179 (LJL), 2023 WL 3173780, at *4 (S.D.N.Y. May 1, 2023)(holding that the court will not scrutinize the "adequacy of consideration); Carter v. SSC Odin Operating Co., LLC, 976 N.E.2d 344, 352 (Ill. 2012) ("Principles of contract law do not require that the values Gott and defendant exchanged be equivalent."); King Cnty. v. Taxpayers of King Cnty., 949 P.2d 1260, 1267 (Wash. 1997)(holding that court will not examine adequacy of consideration).

15. Restatement (Contracts) § 71 cmt. c. See Arthur T. von Mehren, Civil-Law Analogues to Consideration: An Exercise in Comparative Analysis, 72 Harv. L. Rev. 1009, 1031 (1959) (pointing out that "[t]he common law tends to classify all mixed gifts as enforceable under the rule that the court will not investigate the adequacy of the consideration").

Example. In the famous case of *Fiege v. Boehm,* a lady relinquished claims against the purported father of her child in exchange for his promise to pay birth expenses and support.[16] Assume that the lady's claims were unfounded because the gentleman was not the father. In that case, is the gentleman's promise nonetheless supported by consideration?

It is undisputed that relinquishing a contentious claim can constitute consideration if the contentious claim was *objectively* uncertain at the time of the settlement.[17] Such uncertainty can exist because the law is unclear or because the facts are unclear.

But what if any reasonable person would have known there was no claim? In such a scenario, the views diverge on whether consideration can be found. According to the Restatement and the prevailing view among courts, it is sufficient that the party relinquishing the claim honestly believed that the claim was valid, even if that belief was unreasonable.[18] By contrast, the court in *Fiege* took the opposite view, asserting that the relevant claim "must have a reasonable basis of support."[19]

IV. Past Performance

What if the promisee has rendered a service even *before* the promisor has made his promise? Can we then find consideration for the promise? Usually, the answer is no. This outcome follows directly from the general definition of the consideration requirement that each party must give to induce the other party to give. If one party's performance lies in the past, the other party cannot possibly give their promise to induce that (already past) performance.

Question. Alpha paints Beta's house while Beta is at work. When Beta returns and sees that Alpha has painted Beta's house, Beta tells Alpha: "Great job. I

---

16. Fiege v. Boehm, 123 A.2d 316, 321 (Md. 1956).
17. E.g. Fiege v. Boehm, 123 A.2d 316, 322 (Md. 1956); Cohen v. Sabin, 307 A.2d 845, 849 (Pa. 1973).
18. Restatement (Second) § 74. See Wahl v. Barnum, 22 N.E. 280, 282 (N.Y. 1889)(holding that "[i]n the absence of fraud or duress, a settlement of a disputed claim, preferred in good faith by a promisee against a promisor, is a legal consideration for a promise; and the fact that the promisor had a legal defense to the claim settled is no defense to an action on the new promise"); Denburg v. Parker Chapin Flattau & Klimpl, 624 N.E.2d 995, 1000 (N.Y. 1993)(holding that "[t]o constitute sufficient consideration, for example, a party need only have a good-faith belief in the merit of its position").
19. Fiege v. Boehm, 123 A.2d 316, 322 (Md. 1956).

promise to pay you $1,000 in consideration of your work." Alpha replies that they accept Beta's offer. Have the parties entered into a binding contract?

Answer. The parties have not formed a contract. Whereas Alpha and Beta have reached mutual assent, Beta's promise to pay Alpha is not supported by consideration. Since Alpha had already completed their work by the time Beta made the promise, Beta could not possibly have made their own promise in order to induce Alpha to paint the house.

However, the past performance doctrine does not apply if the performance was not complete when the promise was made, and the promise was made at least in part to induce the completion of the relevant services.

V. Illusory Promises

"Illusory" promises are statements that sound like promises but fail to commit the purported promisor. In other words, illusory promises are nothing but empty rhetoric. Due to the absence of a genuine commitment on the promisor's part, these promises cannot be regarded as valid consideration for promises made by the other party.[20] However, one should not be too quick to classify a promise as illusory. In determining whether a party has undertaken a meaningful commitment, we have to keep in mind that each party is required to fulfill their duties in good faith.[21]

Example. Alpha promises to mow Beta's lawn, and, in exchange, Beta promises to pay Alpha $100 if Beta wants to. In this case, Beta has made no commitment, and thus Beta's promise is illusory and cannot serve as consideration.

---

20. E.g., Hill v. Peoplesoft USA, Inc., 412 F.3d 540, 543 (4th Cir. 2005); Donna S. v. Travis S., 874 S.E.2d 746, 754 (W. Va. 2022); Maze v. Bd. of Directors for Cmmw. Postsecondary Educ. Prepaid Tuition Tr. Fund, 559 S.W.3d 354, 367 (Ky. 2018); RAM Engr. & Const., Inc. v. U. of Louisville, 127 S.W.3d 579, 586 (Ky. 2003); Restatement (Second) of Contracts § 77 cmt. a.

21. E.g., RAM Engr. & Const., Inc. v. U. of Louisville, 127 S.W.3d 579, 585 (Ky. 2003); Blank v. Chelmsford Ob/Gyn, P.C., 649 N.E.2d 1102, 1105 (Mass. 1995); Vander Veur v. Groove Ent. Techs., 452 P.3d 1173, 1177 (Utah 2019); Restatement (Second) of Contracts § 205.

Example. Alpha promises to paint a portrait of Beta, and, in exchange, Beta promises to pay Alpha $10,000 if Beta likes the portrait. In this case, Beta has committed because they are under a duty to determine in good faith whether they like the portrait, and if they do, they must pay Alpha whether they want to or not.

VI. Preexisting Duties

What if a party promises something that the party is under a duty to do anyway? Does the preexisting duty prevent the relevant promise from serving as consideration for the other party's promise?

Example. Alpha still has not paid back $100 that they borrowed from Beta two weeks ago. Beta promises to mow Alpha's lawn if, in exchange, Alpha finally pays back the $100 they owe. Is Beta's promise to mow Alpha's lawn supported by consideration?

Under the so-called preexisting duty doctrine, the promise to fulfill a prior duty cannot serve as consideration unless (i) the duty was owed to a different person, (ii) the new obligation somehow differs from the preexisting one, or (iii) the requirements of the settlement doctrine are met.[22]

Question. Alpha enters into a contract with Beta under which Alpha has to pay Beta $100, and Beta promises to paint Alpha's house. Subsequently, Alpha pays the money, but Beta fails to paint Alpha's house. Exasperated, Alpha calls Beta, and the two agree that Alpha will pay Beta another $50, and, in exchange, Beta will finally make good on Beta's promise to paint the house. Is Alpha's promise to pay the additional $50 supported by consideration?

Answer. Alpha's promise to pay another $50 is not supported by consideration. Beta's promise to finally paint the house does not constitute consideration for the promise to pay the additional $50. Beta already owed Alpha a duty to paint Alpha's house, and the requirements of the settlement doctrine are

22. See Restatement (Second) of Contracts § 73. The principle that performance of pre-existing duty cannot serve cannot serve as consideration for a promise is generally accepted. E.g. Anderson v. Soap Lake Sch. Dist., 423 P.3d 197, 215–16 (Wash. 2018); Hanna v. Landsman, 945 N.W.2d 534, 547 (S.D. 2020); James v. James, 493 P.3d 1258, 1270 (Wyo. 2021).

not met. Neither was Beta's duty objectively uncertain nor is there any indication that Beta believed in good faith that he had no duty to paint Alpha's house.

Under Restatement § 73, the consideration requirement is satisfied if a newly incurred obligation differs from an already existing one and that difference is not just a pretense.

Example. Alpha owes Beta $100. Beta's brother Gamma calls Alpha and tells them, "If you pay Beta the $100 you owe them, I promise to pay you $10." The next day, Alpha pays the $100 to Beta. Does Gamma have a contractual obligation to pay Alpha $10? The answer is yes. Alpha and Gamma have reached mutual assent, given that Gamma accepted Alpha's offer by performance. The issue is whether Gamma's promise is supported by consideration. Alpha paid $100 in exchange for Gamma's promise to pay $10, so there was a quid pro quo. However, the question remains whether a preexisting duty precludes the finding of consideration. Usually, the fulfillment of a preexisting duty is not considered sufficient consideration. However, in the case at hand, the promisor (Gamma) was not the person to whom the preexisting debt was owed. Therefore, we have no trouble finding consideration.

This exception from the preexisting duty doctrine makes sense both on a formal doctrinal level and as a matter of legal policy. Having a duty towards one person—Beta—is different from having a duty towards another person—Gamma. Therefore, if Alpha had promised Gamma to pay the $100 to Beta, Alpha would have created a new duty. Moreover, if incurring a duty to Gamma suffices as consideration, then the same must be true for the actual payment of $100.

Hamer v. Sidway

Court of Appeals of New York, 27 N.E. 256 (1891)

. . . Appeal from order of the General Term of the Supreme Court in the fourth judicial department, made July 1, 1890, which reversed a judgment in favor of plaintiff entered upon a decision of the court on trial at Special Term and granted a new trial. This action was brought upon an alleged contract.

The plaintiff presented a claim to the executor of William E. Story, Sr., for $5,000 and interest from the 6th day of February, 1875. She acquired it through several mesne assignments from William E. Story, 2d. The claim being rejected by the executor, this action was brought. It appears that William E. Story, Sr., was the uncle of William E. Story, 2d; that at the celebration of the golden wedding of Samuel Story and wife, father and mother of William E. Story, Sr., on the 20th day of March, 1869, in the presence of the family and invited guests he promised his nephew that if he would refrain from drinking, using tobacco, swearing and playing cards or billiards for money until he became twenty-one years of age he would pay him a sum of $5,000. The nephew assented thereto and fully performed the conditions inducing the promise. When the nephew arrived at the age of twenty-one years and on the 31st day of January, 1875, he wrote to his uncle informing him that he had performed his part of the agreement and had thereby become entitled to the sum of $5,000. The uncle received the letter and a few days later and on the sixth of February, he wrote and mailed to his nephew the following letter:

'Buffalo, Feb. 6, 1875.

'W. E. Story, Jr.:

'Dear Nephew--Your letter of the 31st ult. came to hand all right, saying that you had lived up to the promise made to me several years ago. I have no doubt but you have, for which you shall have five thousand dollars as I promised you. I had the money in the bank the day you was 21 years old that I intend for you, and you shall have the money certain. Now, Willie I do not intend to interfere with this money in any way till I think you are capable of taking care of it and the sooner that time comes the better it will please me. I would hate very much to have you start out in some adventure that you thought all right and lose this money in one year. The first five thousand dollars that I got together cost me a heap of hard work. You would hardly believe me when I tell you that to obtain this I shoved a jackplane many a day, butchered three or four years, then came to this city, and after three months' perseverance I obtained a situation in a grocery store. I opened this store early, closed late, slept in the fourth story of the building in a room 30 by 40 feet and not a human being in the building but myself. All this I done to live as cheap as I could to save something. I don't want you to take up with this kind of fare. I was here in the cholera season '49 and '52 and the deaths averaged 80 to 125 daily and plenty of small-pox. I wanted to go home, but Mr. Fisk, the gentleman I was working for, told me if I left then, after it got healthy he probably would not want me. I stayed. All the money I have saved I know just how I got it. It did not come to me in any mysterious way, and the reason I speak of this is that money got in this way stops longer with a fellow that gets it with hard knocks than it does when he finds it. Willie, you are 21 and you have many a thing to learn yet. This money you have earned much easier than I did besides acquiring good habits at the same time and you are quite welcome to the money; hope you will make good use of it. I was ten long years getting this together after I was your age. Now, hoping this will be satisfactory, I stop. One thing more. Twenty-one years ago, I bought you 15 sheep. These sheep were put out to double every four years. I kept track of them the first eight years; I have not heard much about them since. Your father and grandfather promised me that they would look after them till you were of age. Have they done so? I hope they have. By this time you have between five and six hundred sheep, worth a nice little income this spring. Willie, I have said much more than I expected to; hope you can make out what I have written. To-day is the seventeenth day that I have not been out of my room, and have had the doctor as many days. Am a little better to-day; think I will get out next week. You need not mention to father, as he always worries about small matters.

Truly Yours,

'W. E. Story.

'P. S.--You can consider this money on interest.'

The nephew received the letter and thereafter consented that the money should remain with his uncle in accordance with the terms and conditions of the letters. The uncle died on the 29th day of January, 1887, without having paid over to his nephew any portion of the said $5,000 and interest....

PARKER, J.

The question which provoked the most discussion by counsel on this appeal, and which lies at the foundation of plaintiff's asserted right of recovery, is whether by virtue of a contract defendant's testator William E. Story became indebted to his nephew William E. Story, 2d, on his twenty-first birthday in the sum of five thousand dollars.... The defendant contends that the contract was without consideration to support it, and, therefore, invalid. He asserts that the promisee by refraining from the use of liquor and tobacco was not harmed but benefited; that that which he did was best for him to do independently of his uncle's promise, and insists that it follows that unless the promisor was benefited, the contract was without consideration. A contention, which if well founded, would seem to leave open for controversy in many cases whether that which the promisee did or omitted to do was, in fact, of such benefit to him as to leave no consideration to support the enforcement of the promisor's agreement. Such a rule could not be tolerated, and is without foundation in the law. The Exchequer Chamber, in 1875, defined consideration as follows: 'A valuable consideration in the sense of the law may consist either in some right, interest, profit or benefit accruing to the one party, or some forbearance, detriment, loss or responsibility given, suffered or undertaken by the other.' Courts 'will not ask whether the thing which forms the consideration does in fact benefit the promisee or a third party, or is of any substantial value to anyone. It is enough that something is promised, done, forborne or suffered by the party to whom the promise is made as consideration for the promise made to him.' (Anson's Prin. of Con. 63.)

'In general a waiver of any legal right at the request of another party is a sufficient consideration for a promise.' (Parsons on Contracts, 444.)

'Any damage, or suspension, or forbearance of a right will be sufficient to sustain a promise.' (Kent, vol. 2, 465, 12th ed.)

Pollock, in his work on contracts, page 166, after citing the definition given by the Exchequer Chamber already quoted, says: 'The second branch of this judicial description is really the most important one. Consideration means not so much that one party is profiting as that the other abandons some legal right in the present or limits his legal freedom of action in the future as an inducement for the promise of the first.'

Now, applying this rule to the facts before us, the promisee used tobacco, occasionally drank liquor, and he had a legal right to do so. That right he abandoned for a period of years upon the strength of the promise of the testator that for such forbearance he would give him $5,000. We need not speculate on the effort which may have been required to give up the use of those stimulants. It is sufficient that he restricted his lawful freedom of action within certain prescribed limits upon the faith of his uncle's agreement, and now having fully performed the conditions imposed, it is of no moment whether such performance actually proved a benefit to the promisor, and the court will not inquire into it, but were it a proper subject of inquiry, we see nothing in this record that would permit a determination that the uncle was not benefited in a legal sense. Few cases have been found which may be said to be precisely in point, but such as have been support the position we have taken. . . .

All concur.

ORDER REVERSED AND JUDGMENT OF SPECIAL TERM AFFIRMED.

NOTES AND QUESTIONS

A. Consideration. Section 72 of Restatement (Second) of Contracts provides that, in principle, any bargained-for performance constitutes consideration. Section 71(2) defines when a performance or a promise is bargained for. If the bargain requirement is satisfied, no legal detriment or legal benefit is required.[23] How does the Restatement differ from the court's approach in *Hamer v. Sidway*?

B. Hypothetical variation. What would have been the outcome of the case if the uncle had contacted the nephew a few weeks after the initial promise and told him that he no longer wants to adhere to the bargain?

C. Social obligation. Would it be reasonable to argue the uncle's promise to pay the $5,000 should be interpreted as an attempt to induce a mere social obligation?

D. Hypothetical. Consider the following hypothetical: On January 1, 2020, Alpha learns that his 30-year-old nephew Beta habitually uses heroin. On January 2, 2020, Alpha calls Beta and tells him: "If you abstain from using heroin from January 5, 2020, to December 1, 2022, I will pay you $10,000." On January 3, 2020, Beta leaves a message on Alpha's answering machine saying: "You have a deal." In fact, Beta completely abstains from using heroin between January 2, 2020 and January 1, 2023. On January 2, 2023, Beta immediately starts using heroin again. On January 2, 2023, Beta contacts Alpha and demands payment of the $10,000, but Beta refuses. Can Beta demand damages for breach of contract?

---

23. Restatement (Second) of Contracts § 79.

Plowman et al. v. Indian Refining Co

District Court, E.D. Illinois, 20 F. Supp. 1 (1937)

LINDLEY, District Judge

Thirteen persons and the administrators of five deceased persons brought this suit, alleging that defendant, in 1930, made separate contracts to pay each of the individual plaintiffs and each of the deceased persons whose administrators sued, monthly sums equal to one-half of the wages formerly earned by such parties as employees of the defendant for life. Each of the claimants had been employed for some years at a fixed rate of wages, usually upon an hourly basis but payable monthly or semimonthly.

The theory of plaintiffs is that on July 28, 1930, (with two exceptions), the vice president and general manager of the refinery plant called the employees, who had rendered long years of service separately into his office and made with each a contract, to pay him, for the rest of his natural life, a sum equal to one-half of the wages he was then being paid. The consideration for the contracts, it is said, arose out of the relationship then existing, the desire to provide for the future welfare of these comparatively aged employees and the provision in the alleged contracts that the employees would call at the office for their several checks each pay-day.

Most of the employees were participants in group insurance, the premiums for which had been paid approximately one-half by the employee and one-half by the company, and, according to plaintiffs, their parts of the premiums were to be deducted from their payments as formerly. This procedure was followed.

The employees were retained on the payroll, but, according to their testimony, they were not to render any further services, their only obligation being to call at the office for their remittances. Most of them testified that it was agreed that the payments were to continue throughout the remainder of their lives. But two testified that nothing was said as to the time during which the payments were to continue. As to still others the record is silent as to direct testimony in this respect.

The payments were made regularly until June 1, 1931, when they were cut off and each of the employees previously receiving the same was advised by defendant's personnel officer that the arrangement was terminated.

Defendant does not controvert many of these facts, but insists that the whole arrangement was included in a letter sent to each of the employees as follows:

'Confirming our conversation of today, it is necessary with conditions as they are throughout the petroleum industry, to effect substantial economies throughout the plant operation. This necessitates the reducing of the working force to a minimum necessary to maintain operation. In view of your many years of faithful service, the management is desirous of shielding you as far as possible from the effect of reduced plant operation and has, therefore, placed you upon a retirement list which has just been established for this purpose.

'Effective August 1, 1930, you will be carried on our payroll at a rate of $--- per month. You will be relieved of all duties except that of reporting to Mr. T. E. Sullivan at the main office for the purpose of picking up your semi-monthly checks. Your group insurance will be maintained on the same basis as at present, unless you desire to have it cancelled.' (Signed by the vice-president.)

It contends and offered evidence that nothing was said to any employee about continuing the payments for his natural life; that the payments were gratuitous, continuing at the pleasure and will of defendant . . . ; that there was no consideration for the promise to make the payments . . . . Defendant admits the payments as charged and the termination of the arrangement on June 1, 1931.

. . . Plaintiff Kogan, an employee aged 72, testified that for some years prior to July 28, 1930, he had been employed as a drill pressman and in general repair work in the machine shops; that on July 28, 1930, he talked to Mr. Anglin, the vice-president and general manager, in the latter's private office; that Anglin said then that the oil industry was in a deplorable condition; that the management found it necessary to cut down expenses, and therefore, to lay off certain employees; that the witness was to be relieved of his duties, but that he would receive one-half of his salary and would be retained upon the pay roll; that this was being done because of the witness' many years of services; that the company did not desire to discharge him without further compensation; that he would be excused from all labor and required only to report to the main office to get his checks; that the company would carry his insurance in accord with previous practice; and that he would have all the privileges of hospitalization and in other respects of regular employees. The witness said he expressed his preference to work, but was told that that was impossible. He says that he was told that the arrangement was permanent, that is, for as long as he lived; that he would receive a letter confirming this conversation, which he should keep; that his labor would end on July 31, 1930; that he received the letter within a day or two; that thereafter he reported regularly at the office and obtained the checks until May 29, 1931, when he was told by the personnel department that the check then received would be the last one. This action, he said he was then told, was taken because of the necessity for further retrenchment. He testified that he sought no other employment; that nothing was said to him about working or not working for other parties, and that when he received the letter he kept it without comment or objection.

Other claimants testified substantially the same. Beanblossom said that he was told that the layoff was by the direction of the president; that he was still on the pay roll but that he would have no work to do; that the arrangement would last all his life; and that if conditions improved he would probably get his job back. Gibson testified that nothing was said about the time during which the payments would continue but that he inferred that they were for life. Teufel testified that nothing was said about how long the payments would continue.

Stout, Robb, Ploman, McClure, Smith, and Courter testified substantially as did Kogan. Reeves testified that he was told he was given a pension for life; Kendall that he was in the hospital when he heard about the arrangement with other men and sent his nurse to ask for his payments and that thereafter he received checks until June 1, 1931. Mrs. Burrell testified that her husband was deceased; that he received the letter previously mentioned and the payments, until June 1, 1931. Mrs. Hoth and Mrs. Baker testified similarly concerning their husbands. Plaintiffs offered no testimony as to any conversations between any of the deceased men and the manager. Mr. and Mrs. Hooks, son-in-law and daughter of Davenport, one of the deceased employees, testified that Wells, the plant superintendent, came to their house and said that he preferred to talk to them rather than to Davenport because the latter was not then well; that the company was desirous of making a 'settlement' with him for half salary for the remainder of his life. They directed him to talk to Davenport.

In behalf of defendant, the assistant secretary testified that there were no minutes showing any corporate action with regard to the arrangement and that there was nothing in the records of the corporation, in bylaws, resolution or minutes authorizing, directing, or ratifying the payments or giving anybody authority to make the same. Anglin, vice-president and general manager in charge of manufacturing at the Lawrenceville Refinery where these men were employed, testified that he said to Kogan that, due to depressed conditions the company found it necessary to reduce expenses and lay off certain men; that it had no pension plan; that in an effort to be perfectly fair the company would keep him on the pay roll but relieve him of all duties except to pick up his check; that he said that the arrangement was voluntary with the company, and terminable at its pleasure, and that he hoped it would last during Kogan's lifetime, but that there might be a change in the policy of the company. His testimony as to the other employees was the same. He denied promising any of them that the payments would persist so long as they lived. He sent the letters as he promised confirming the arrangement.

He testified that the letters were in compliance with what he had said; that no complaint or demand for any additional provisions was thereafter made; that he himself was employed orally; that he had no written contract; that he had no authority from the directors to make the arrangement; that he hired and fired men in Lawrenceville upon recommendation of the foreman; that a change in the management occurred when the Indian Refining Company was purchased by the Texas Company between October, 1930, and January, 1931; and that after the latter date he was not general manager at Lawrenceville.

Wells testified that he was plant superintendent; that he had no authority to make any contracts such as are alleged in the bill of complaint; that he sent some of the complainants in to see the manager; that he talked to the daughter and son-in-law of Davenport because the latter was ill, but later, on their suggestion, talked to Davenport. He testified that he said nothing about a settlement but did say that one-half of Mr. Davenport's salary would be paid to him. He said that he recalled no conversation with Courter and that he never told any of the claimants that the arrangement was permanent.

The present vice-president and general manager testified that he came into office January, 1931; and that no complaint was received by him by any plaintiff until suit was started.

Thus, it is undisputed that a separate arrangement was made by the local office with each of the claimants, most of them on July 28, 1930, to continue them upon the pay roll, deliver to them semimonthly a check, upon their calling for same, for one-half of the former wages; that this was done until June 1, 1931. It is also undisputed that the letters sent out said nothing about how long the payments should continue but were wholly silent in that respect. It is also undisputed that insurance payments were deducted from the checks that were delivered; that the employees were retained on the pay roll; that they did no active work after August 1, 1931; that they received their checks as mentioned; that the payments terminated on June 1, 1931; that most of them called at the office for their checks and received same; and that in at least two instances the checks were mailed. The controverted question of fact arises upon the testimony of most of the plaintiffs that each of them was told that the payments would continue until their death. This is denied.

Let us assume, without so deciding, for the purpose of disposition of this case, that each of the employees was told that the payments would continue for his lifetime. Then the questions remaining are legal in character. . . . Presented . . . is the . . . question of whether, admitting the facts as alleged by plaintiffs, there was any consideration for a contract to pay a pension for life. However strongly a man may be bound in conscience to fulfill his engagements, the law does not recognize their sanctity or supply any means to compel their performance, except when founded upon a sufficient consideration. . . .

The long and faithful services of the employees are relied upon as consideration; but past or executed consideration is a self-contradictory term. Consideration is something given in exchange for a promise or in a reliance upon the promise. Something which has been delivered before the promise is executed, and, therefore, made without reference to it, cannot properly be legal consideration. . . .

It is further contended that there was a moral consideration for the alleged contracts. The doctrine of validity of moral consideration has received approval in some courts, but quite generally it is condemned because it is contrary in character to actual consideration. Early Illinois cases, (Spear v. Griffith, 86 Ill. 552; Lawrence v. Oglesby, 178 Ill. 122, 52 N.E. 945) recognize its validity. But their doctrine has been modified and no longer prevails in Illinois. See Hart v. Strong, 183 Ill. 349, 55 N.E. 629; Hobbs v. Greifenhagen, 91 Ill.App. 400. . . . Thus in Hart v. Strong, 183 Ill. 349, 55 N.E. 629, 631, the court said: 'The agreement to receive less than the amount due on the note was made upon the purely moral consideration that John W. Hart, believing himself about to die, thought he ought not to have exacted so large a consideration for the reconveyance. But such an obligation does not form a valid consideration unless the moral duty were once a legal one. 'But the morality of the promise, however certain or however urgent the duty, does not, of itself, suffice for a consideration.' 1 Pars. Cont. 434.'

Upon the same ground, appreciation of past services or pleasure afforded the employer thereby is not a sufficient consideration. Schwerdt v. Schwerdt, 141 Ill.App. 386; ... Williams v. Forbes, (Contracts, vol. 1, p. 230): '... if there be no legal consideration, no motive, such as love and respect, or affection for another or a desire to do justice, or fear of trouble, or a desire to equalize the shares in an estate, or to provide for a child, or regret for having advised an unfortunate investment, will support a promise.'

Plaintiffs have proved that they were ready, willing, and able to travel to and report semimonthly to the main office. But this does not furnish a legal consideration. The act was simply a condition imposed upon them in obtaining gratuitous pensions and not a consideration. The employees went to the office to obtain their checks. Such acts were benefits to them and not detriments. They were detriments to defendant and not benefits. This is not consideration. Williston on Contracts, vol. 1, pp. 231-235, and cases cited; Restatement of Contracts, par. 75, illus. 2.

In the absence of valid agreement to make payments for the rest of their natural lives, clearly the arrangement was one revocable at the pleasure of defendant. If defendant agreed to make the payments for life, then, fatal to plaintiffs' cases is the lack of consideration. We have merely a gratuitous arrangement without consideration, and therefore, void as a contract.

In this enlightened day, I am sure, no one controverts the wisdom, justice, and desirability of a policy, whether promoted and fostered by industry voluntarily or by state or federal government, looking to the promotion and assurance of financial protection of deserving employees in their old age. We have come to realize that the industry wherein the diligent worker labors for many years should bear the cost of his living in some degree of comfort through his declining years until the end of his life. To impose this expense upon the industry, to the creation of whose product he has contributed, is not unfair or unreasonable, for, eventually, obviously, under wise budgeting and cost accounting systems, this element of cost is passed on to the consumer of the product. The public bears the burden- as, indeed, it does eventually of all governmental expenditures and corporate costs, either in taxes or price of products purchased. Surely no one would have the temerity to urge that such a policy is not more fair and reasonable, more humane and beneficent, than the poorhouse system of our earlier days. The recognition of the soundness of this proposition is justified by the resulting contribution to the advance of standards of living, hygienic and sanitary environment, and, in some degree at least, of culture and civilization.

But, in the absence of statute creating it, such a policy does not enter into the relationship of employer or employee, except when so provided by contract of the parties. The court is endowed with no power of legislation; nor may it read into contracts provisions upon which the parties' minds have not met.

Viewing the testimony most favorably for the plaintiffs, despite the desirability of the practice of liberality between employer and employee, the court must decide a purely legal question- whether under plaintiffs' theory there were valid contracts. The obvious answer is in the negative. Consequently, there will be a decree in favor of defendant dismissing plaintiffs' bill for want of equity.

The foregoing includes my findings of fact and conclusions of law.

NOTES AND QUESTIONS

*A. **Moral Consideration.*** The court's assertion that the law does not acknowledge "moral consideration" is generally accepted as accurate.[24] What arguments does the court make against the sufficiency of moral consideration? What other arguments can you think of?

*B. **Consideration Substitutes.*** The law recognizes various "consideration substitutes" that render promises binding even though they are unsupported by consideration.[25] Can any of these consideration substitutes be applied to the case at hand?

*C. **The timing of the pension promise.*** Assume, hypothetically, that the promise to pay the pension had been made before the employees were instructed to cease working. Would that have altered the outcome of the case?

*D. **Statutes of frauds.*** According to the plaintiffs, the defendant promised to pay them half of their salaries for the rest of their lives. As a general rule, contracts that cannot be performed within one year have to be in writing to be enforceable.[26] However, courts have not applied this principle to contracts

---

24. See, e.g., Shepard v. Rhodes, 7 R.I. 470, 470 (1863) (holding that "[n]o action can be maintained on a promise founded upon a mere moral consideration").
25. See Restatement (Second) of Contracts, §§ 82 et seq.
26. Restatement (Second) of Contracts § 110.

that last for the remainder of a person's life.[27] The formal reason is that the person might die before the year is over which means that the contract can potentially be performed in less than a year.[28] But can you think of other, more substantive arguments?

E. Historical Context. The defendant stopped making pension payments in 1931, and the case was decided in 1937. Both occurred during the Great Depression (1929-1939). Could this historical context have influenced the decision? And should it have?

27. Collection & Investigation Bureau of Maryland, Inc. v. Linsley, 375 A.2d 47, 49 (Md. Spec. App. 1977) (holding that "[w]hen the promise is for an indefinite period such as for the life of the promisor, it is not within the ambit of the Statute of Frauds because, life being itself indefinite and uncertain, the promisor may die within the space of one year"); Hampton v. Caldwell & Hall, 129 S.W. 816, 817 (Ark. 1910) (rejecting the application of the statute of frauds where the obligor's death would have brought the contract to an end).

28. Hampton v. Caldwell & Hall, 129 S.W. 816, 817 (Ark. 1910); Collection & Investigation Bureau of Maryland, Inc. v. Linsley, 375 A.2d 47, 49 (Md. Spec. App. 1977).

CHAPTER 10
CONSIDERATION SUBSTITUTES

Webb v. McGowin

Court of Appeals of Alabama, 168 So. 196 (Ala. Ct. App. 1935)

BRICKEN, Presiding Judge

This action is in assumpsit. The complaint as originally filed was amended. The demurrers to the complaint as amended were sustained, and because of this adverse ruling by the court the plaintiff took a non-suit, and the assignment of errors on this appeal are predicated upon said action or ruling of the court.

A fair statement of the case presenting the questions for decision is set out in appellant's brief, which we adopt.

"On the 3d day of August, 1925, appellant while in the employ of the W.T. Smith Lumber Company, a corporation, and acting within the scope of his employment, was engaged in clearing the upper floor of mill No. 2 of the company. While so engaged he was in the act of dropping a pine block from the upper floor of the mill to the ground below; this being the usual and ordinary way of clearing the floor, and it being the duty of the plaintiff in the course of his employment to so drop it. The block weighed about 75 pounds.

"As appellant was in the act of dropping the block to the ground below, he was on the edge of the upper floor of the mill. As he started to turn the block loose so that it would drop to the ground, he saw J. Greeley McGowin, testator of the defendants, on the ground below and directly under where the block would have fallen had appellant turned it loose. Had he turned it loose it would have struck McGowin with such force as to have caused him serious bodily harm or death. Appellant could have remained safely on the upper floor of the mill by turning the block loose and allowing it to drop, but had he done this the block would have fallen on McGowin and caused him serious injuries or death. The only safe and reasonable way to prevent this was for appellant to hold to the block and divert its direction in falling from the place where McGowin was standing and the only safe way to divert it so as to prevent its coming into contact with McGowin was for appellant to fall with it to the ground below. Appellant did this, and by holding to the block and falling with it to the ground below, he diverted the course of its fall in such way that McGowin was not injured. In thus preventing the injuries to McGowin appellant himself received serious bodily injuries, resulting in his right leg being broken, the heel of his right foot torn off and his right arm broken. He was badly crippled for life and rendered unable to do physical or mental labor.

"On September 1, 1925, in consideration of appellant having prevented him from sustaining death or serious bodily harm and in consideration of the injuries appellant had received, McGowin agreed with him to care for and maintain him for the remainder of appellant's life at the rate of $15 every two weeks from the time he sustained his injuries to and during the remainder of appellant's life; it being agreed that McGowin would pay this sum to appellant for his maintenance. Under the agreement McGowin paid or caused to be paid to appellant the sum so agreed on up until McGowin's death on January 1, 1934. After his death the payments were continued to and including January 27, 1934, at which time they were discontinued. Thereupon plaintiff brought suit to recover the unpaid installments accruing up to the time of the bringing of the suit.

"The material averments of the different counts of the original complaint and the amended complaint are predicated upon the foregoing statement of facts."

In other words, the complaint as amended averred in substance: (1) That on August 3, 1925, appellant saved J. Greeley McGowin, appellee's testator, from death or grievous bodily harm; (2) that in doing so appellant sustained bodily injury crippling him for life; (3) that in consideration of the services rendered and the injuries received by appellant, McGowin agreed to care for him the remainder of appellant's life, the amount to be paid being $15 every two weeks; (4) that McGowin complied with this agreement until he died on January 1, 1934, and the payments were kept up to January 27, 1934, after which they were discontinued.

The action was for the unpaid installments accruing after January 27, 1934, to the time of the suit. The principal grounds of demurrer to the original and amended complaint are: (1) It states no cause of action; (2) its averments show the contract was without consideration; (3) it fails to allege that McGowin had, at or before the services were rendered, agreed to pay appellant for them; (4) the contract declared on is void under the statute of frauds.

1. The averments of the complaint show that appellant saved McGowin from death or grievous bodily harm. This was a material benefit to him of infinitely more value than any financial aid he could have received. Receiving this benefit, McGowin became morally bound to compensate appellant for the services rendered. Recognizing his moral obligation, he expressly agreed to pay appellant as alleged in the complaint and complied with this agreement up to the time of his death; a period of more than 8 years.

Had McGowin been accidentally poisoned and a physician, without his knowledge or request, had administered an antidote, thus saving his life, a subsequent promise by McGowin to pay the physician would have been valid. Likewise, McGowin's agreement as disclosed by the complaint to compensate appellant for saving him from death or grievous bodily injury is valid and enforceable.

Where the promisee cares for, improves, and preserves the property of the promisor, though done without his request, it is sufficient consideration for the promisor's subsequent agreement to pay for the service, because of the material benefit received. . . . In Boothe v. Fitzpatrick, 36 Vt. 681, the court held that a promise by defendant to pay for the past keeping of a bull which had escaped from defendant's premises and been cared for by plaintiff was valid, although there was no previous request, because the subsequent promise obviated that objection; it being equivalent to a previous request. On the same principle, had the promisee saved the promisor's life or his body from grievous harm, his subsequent promise to pay for the services rendered would have been valid. Such service would have been far more material than caring for his bull. Any holding that saving a man from death or grievous bodily harm is not a material benefit sufficient to uphold a subsequent promise to pay for the service, necessarily rests on the assumption that saving life and preservation of the body from harm have only a sentimental value. The converse of this is true. Life and preservation of the body have material, pecuniary values, measurable in dollars and cents. Because of this, physicians practice their profession charging for services rendered in saving life and curing the body of its ills, and surgeons perform operations. The same is true as to the law of negligence, authorizing the assessment of damages in personal injury cases based upon the extent of the injuries, earnings, and life expectancies of those injured.

In the business of life insurance, the value of a man's life is measured in dollars and cents according to his expectancy, the soundness of his body, and his ability to pay premiums. The same is true as to health and accident insurance.

It follows that if, as alleged in the complaint, appellant saved J. Greeley McGowin from death or grievous bodily harm, and McGowin subsequently agreed to pay him for the service rendered, it became a valid and enforceable contract.

2 2. It is well settled that a moral obligation is a sufficient consideration to support a subsequent promise to pay where the promisor has received a material benefit, although there was no original duty or liability resting on the promisor. . . . In the case of State ex rel. Bayer v. Funk, supra, the court held that a moral obligation is a sufficient consideration to support an executory promise where the promisor has received an actual pecuniary or material benefit for which he subsequently expressly promised to pay.

The case at bar is clearly distinguishable from that class of cases where the consideration is a mere moral obligation or conscientious duty unconnected with receipt by promisor of benefits of a material or pecuniary nature. Park Falls State Bank v. Fordyce, supra. Here the promisor received a material benefit constituting a valid consideration for his promise.

3. Some authorities hold that, for a moral obligation to support a subsequent promise to pay, there must have existed a prior legal or equitable obligation, which for some reason had become unenforceable, but for which the promisor was still morally bound. This rule, however, is subject to qualification in those cases where the promisor, having received a material benefit from the promisee, is morally bound to compensate him for the services rendered and in consideration of this obligation promises to pay. In such cases the subsequent promise to pay is an affirmance or ratification of the

services rendered carrying with it the presumption that a previous request for the service was made. . . .

Under the decisions above cited, McGowin's express promise to pay appellant for the services rendered was an affirmance or ratification of what appellant had done raising the presumption that the services had been rendered at McGowin's request.

4. The averments of the complaint show that in saving McGowin from death or grievous bodily harm, appellant was crippled for life. This was part of the consideration of the contract declared on. McGowin was benefited. Appellant was injured. Benefit to the promisor or injury to the promisee is a sufficient legal consideration for the promisor's agreement to pay. Fisher v. Bartlett, 8 Greenl. (Me.) 122, 22 Am.Dec. 225; State ex rel. Bayer v. Funk, supra.

5. Under the averments of the complaint the services rendered by appellant were not gratuitous. The agreement of McGowin to pay and the acceptance of payment by appellant conclusively shows the contrary.

6. The contract declared on was not void under the statute of frauds (Code 1923, § 8034). The demurrer on this ground was not well taken. 25 R.C.L. 456, 457 and 470, § 49.

The cases of Shaw v. Boyd, 1 Stew. & P. 83, and Duncan v. Hall, 9 Ala. 128, are not in conflict with the principles here announced. In those cases the lands were owned by the United States at the time the alleged improvements were made, for which subsequent purchasers from the government agreed to pay. These subsequent purchasers were not the owners of the lands at the time the improvements were made. Consequently, they could not have been made for their benefit.

From what has been said, we are of the opinion that the court below erred in the ruling complained of; that is to say, in sustaining the demurrer, and for this error the case is reversed and remanded.

Reversed and remanded.

SAMFORD, Judge (concurring).

The questions involved in this case are not free from doubt, and perhaps the strict letter of the rule, as stated by judges, though not always in accord, would bar a recovery by plaintiff, but following the principle announced by Chief Justice Marshall in Hoffman v. Porter, Fed.Cas. No. 6,577, 2 Brock. 156, 159, where he says, "I do not think that law ought to be separated from justice, where it is at most doubtful," I concur in the conclusions reached by the court.

. . .

NOTES AND QUESTIONS:

A. Section 86 of the Restatement (Second) of Contracts. The court's holding in *Webb v. McGowin* is now enshrined in section 86 of the Restatement (Second) of Contracts. Under this norm, a promise is binding without consideration if (1) the promise was given in recognition of a benefit that the promisor previously received (2) the promisor is unjustly enriched by the benefit previously received, the (3) the promise is not out of proportion to the value of the benefit previously received, and (4) enforcing the promise is necessary to prevent injustice. If we apply section 86 of the Restatement to the facts in *Webb v. McGowin*, should we reject Webb's claim on the ground that McGowin was not unjustly enriched by Webb's actions since Webb was already being paid for his work in the lumber mill?

B. Quid pro quo. Could one have argued that Webb's actions in saving McGowin were the quid pro quo for McGowin's promise to pay Webb?

C. Emergency Services. Even in the absence of a promise to pay, rescuers can sometimes demand compensation for their services under a body of law known as unjust enrichment law. Unjust enrichment law and contract law are based on fundamentally different logics. In contract law, remedies are granted because a legally binding promise was broken. In the law of unjust enrichment, a remedy is granted because one party is enriched at another party's expense and there is no justification for that enrichment. Section 20 of the Restatement (Third) of Restitution summarizes the law on unjust enrichment, including emergency services. Anyone who performs necessary professional services to save another person's life or health can demand restitution to the extent required to avoid unjust enrichment, provided that intervening without prior request was justified in the circumstances.[1] The value of the unjust enrichment is equal to what can reasonably be charged for the services provided.[2]

Note that unlike contract law in general or section 86 of the Restatement (Second) of Contracts in particular, section 20(1) of the Restatement (Third) of Restitution does not require any promise at all. This reflects the distinguishing characteristic of unjust enrichment: a claim is granted because the

---

1. Restatement (Third) of Restitution § 20(1).
2. Restatement (Third) of Restitution § 20(2),

defendant is unjustly enriched at the plaintiff's expense, not because of a promise. If the facts in *Webb v. McGowin* had occurred today, could Webb have successfully invoked section 20(2) of the Restatement (Third) of Restitution?

*D. **Mills v. Wyman.*** Recall the facts in *Mills v. Wyman*. If those facts had occurred today, could the plaintiff have successfully invoked section 20(2) of the Restatement (Third) of Restitution?

Mills v. Wyman

Supreme Judicial Court of Massachusetts, 3 Pick. 207 (1825)

PARKER C. J.

General rules of law established for the protection and security of honest and fair-minded men, who may inconsiderately make promises without any equivalent, will sometimes screen men of a different character from engagements which they are bound in *foro conscientiae* to perform. This is a defect inherent in all human systems of legislation. The rule that a mere verbal promise, without any consideration, cannot be enforced by action, is universal in its application, and cannot be departed from to suit particular cases in which a refusal to perform such a promise may be disgraceful.

The promise declared on in this case appears to have been made without any legal consideration. The kindness and services towards the sick son of the defendant were not bestowed at his request. The son was in no respect under the care of the defendant. He was twenty-five years old, and had long left his father's family. On his return from a foreign country, he fell sick among strangers, and the plaintiff acted the part of the good Samaritan, giving him shelter and comfort until he died. The defendant, his father, on being informed of this event, influenced by a transient feeling of gratitude, promises in writing to pay the plaintiff for the expenses he had incurred. But he has determined to break this promise, and is willing to have his case appear on record as a strong example of particular injustice sometimes necessarily resulting from the operation of general rules.

It is said a moral obligation is a sufficient consideration to support an express promise; and some authorities lay down the rule thus broadly; but upon examination of the cases, we are satisfied that the universality of the rule cannot be supported, and that there must have been some preexisting obligation, which has become inoperative by positive law, to form a basis for an effective promise. The cases of debts barred by the statute of limitations, of debts incurred by infants, of debts of bankrupts, are generally put for illustration of the rule. Express promises founded on such preexisting equitable obligations may be enforced; there is a good consideration for them; they merely remove an impediment created by law to the recovery of debts honestly due, but which public policy protects the debtors from being compelled to pay. In all these cases there was originally a *quid pro quo;* and according to the principles of natural justice the party receiving ought to pay; but the legislature has said he shall not be coerced; then comes the promise to pay the debt that is barred, the promise of the man to pay the debt of the infant, of the discharged bankrupt to restore to his creditor what by the law he had lost. In all these cases there is a moral obligation founded upon an antecedent valuable consideration. These promises therefore have a sound legal basis. They are not promises to pay something for nothing; not naked pacts; but the voluntary revival or creation of obligation which before existed in natural law, but which had been dispensed with, not for the benefit of the party obliged solely, but principally for the public convenience If moral obligation, in its fullest sense, is a good substratum for an express promise, it is not easy to perceive why it is not equally good to support an implied promise. What a man ought to do, generally he ought to be made to do, whether he promise or refuse. But the law of society has left most of such obligations to the *interior* forum, as the tribunal of conscience has been aptly called. Is there not a moral obligation upon every son who has become affluent by means of the education and advantages bestowed upon him by his father, to relieve that father from pecuniary embarrassment, to promote his comfort and happiness, and even to share with him his riches, if thereby he will be made happy? And yet such a son may, with impunity, leave such a father in any degree of penury above that which will expose the community in which he dwells, to the danger of being obliged to preserve him from absolute want. Is not a wealthy father under strong moral obligation to advance the interest of an obedient, well-disposed son, to furnish him with the means of acquiring and maintaining a becoming rank in life, to rescue him from the horrors of debt incurred by misfortune? Yet the law will uphold him in any degree of parsimony, short of that which would reduce his son to the necessity of seeking public charity. Without doubt there are great interests of society which justify withholding the coercive arm of the law from these duties of imperfect obligation, as they are called; imperfect, not because they are less binding upon the conscience than those which are called perfect, but because the wisdom of the social law does not impose sanctions upon them.

A deliberate promise, in writing, made freely and without any mistake, one which may lead the party to whom it is made into contracts and expenses, cannot be broken without a violation of moral duty. But if there was nothing paid or promised for it, the law, perhaps wisely, leaves the execution of it to the conscience of him who makes it. It is only when the party making the promise gains something, or he to whom it is made loses something, that the law gives the promise validity. And in the case of the promise of the adult to pay the debt of the infant, of the debtor discharged by the statute of limitations or bankruptcy, the principle is preserved by looking back to the origin of the transaction, where an equivalent is to be found. An exact equivalent is not required by the law; for there being a consideration, the parties are left to estimate its value: though here the courts of equity will step in to relieve from gross inadequacy between the consideration and the promise.

These principles are deduced from the general current of decided cases upon the subject, as well as from the known maxims of the common law. The general position, that moral obligation is a sufficient consideration for an express promise, is to be limited in its application, to cases where at some time or other a good or valuable consideration has existed.

A legal obligation is always a sufficient consideration to support either an express or an implied promise; such as an infant's debt for necessaries, or a father's promise to pay for the support and education of his minor children. But when the child shall have attained to manhood, and shall have become his own agent in the world's business, the debts he in curs, whatever may be their nature, create no obligation upon the father; and it seems to follow, that his promise founded upon such a debt has no legally binding force. The cases of instruments under seal and certain mercantile contracts, in which considerations need not be proved, do not contradict the principles above suggested. The first import a consideration in themselves, and the second belong to a branch of the mercantile law, which has found it necessary to disregard the point of consideration in respect to instruments negotiable in their nature and essential to the interests of commerce.

Instead of citing a multiplicity of cases to support the positions I have taken, I will only refer to a very able review of all the cases in the note in 3

Bos. & Pul. 249. The opinions of the judges had been variant for a long course of years upon this subject, but there seems to be no case in which it was nakedly decided, that a promise to pay the debt of a son of full age, not living with his father, though the debt were incurred by sickness which ended in the death of the son, without a previous request by the father proved or presumed, could be enforced by action.

It has been attempted to show a legal obligation on the part of the defendant by virtue of our statute, which compels lineal kindred in the ascending or descending line to support such of their poor relations as are likely to become chargeable to the town where they have their settlement. But it is a sufficient answer to this position, that such legal obligation does not exist except in the very cases provided for in the statute, and never until the party charged has been adjudged to be of sufficient ability thereto. We do not know from the report any of the facts which are necessary to create such an obligation. Whether the deceased had a legal settlement in this commonwealth at the time of his death, whether he was likely to become chargeable had he lived, whether the defendant was of sufficient ability, are essential facts to be adjudicated by the court to which is given jurisdiction on this subject. The legal liability does not arise until these facts have all been ascertained by judgment, after hearing the party intended to be charged.

For the foregoing reasons we are all of opinion that the nonsuit directed by the Court of Common Pleas was right, and that judgment be entered thereon for costs for the defendant.

NOTES AND QUESTIONS

A. Moral Consideration. The court's holding in *Mills v. Wyman* reflects modern contract law which does not view "moral consideration" to be an adequate substitute for consideration. However, modern contract law also recognizes a variety of consideration substitutes. Notably, some of these alternatives seem rooted, at least partially, in the notion that the promisor carries a moral obligation to honor their commitment in certain contexts. Read sections 82 et seq. of the Restatement (Second) of Contracts!

B. Protecting Excessively Generous Promisors. The consideration requirement helps protect altruistic promisors against the effects of their generosity. In the spur of the moment, well-meaning promisors may overextend themselves and suffer subsequent remorse. In other words, the consideration requirement serves a cautionary function.[3] It may also serve an evidentiary function because the presence of consideration lends greater credence to the assertion that a promise was indeed made.[4] Can you argue that one or both of these functions help explain the outcome of *Mills v. Wyman*?

*C. **Promises Made in Recognition for Benefits Received.*** According to section 86 of the Restatement (Second) of Contracts, a promise is binding without consideration if (1) the promisor made the promise in recognition of a previously received benefit, (2) the promisor is unjustly enriched by the relevant benefit, the (3) the promise is not out of proportion to the value of the benefit, and (4) enforcing the promise is necessary to prevent injustice. Would applying this principle to *Mills v. Wyman*'s facts lead to a different outcome?

*D. **Comparative Law.*** Civil law countries such Germany do not require consideration to form a contract.[5] However, these legal systems protect promisors in other ways.[6] For example, under German law, gratuitous promises must be notarized to be enforceable.[7] How does the notarization requirement compare to the consideration requirement in terms of the warning and evidentiary effects? Can you think of any disadvantages of a notarization requirement?

---

3. See Lon Fuller, Consideration and Form, 41 COLUM. L. REV. 799, 800 (1941).
4. Cf. Lon Fuller, Consideration and Form, 41 COLUM. L. REV. 799, 800 (1941) (listing the evidentiary function as one of the purposes of legal formalities).
5. See, e.g., Arthur T. von Mehren, Civil-Law Analogues to Consideration: An Exercise in Comparative Analysis, 72 Harv. L. Rev. 1009, 1018 (1959) (mentioning that neither French nor German law impose a consideration requirement)
6. For a general discussion of this issue see Arthur T. von Mehren, Civil-Law Analogues to Consideration: An Exercise in Comparative Analysis, 72 Harv. L. Rev. 1009 (1959).
7. Bürgerliches Gesetzbuch [BGB][Civil Code], § 518(2) (Ger.).

CHAPTER 11
STATUTE OF FRAUDS

I. Introduction

As a general rule, a contract does not need to be in writing.[1] Oral agreements are usually sufficient. However, all states have enacted so-called statutes of frauds, which require certain types of contracts to be in writing and signed. Failure to comply with a statute of frauds does not prevent the contract's formation but renders the contract unenforceable.[2]

The statutes of frauds are inspired by the English statute of frauds that the English Parliament enacted in 1677.[3] Ironically, the English Statute of Frauds was, for the most part, repealed in 1954.[4] As the name "statute of frauds" suggests, a key motivation behind the original English statute of frauds was to prevent fraud. However, the potential benefits of requiring contracts to be in writing extend well beyond this purpose. In his seminal 1941 article, Lon Fuller delineates three different functions served by writing requirements: the evidentiary function, the cautionary function, and the channeling function.[5]

1. See, e.g., Bergal v. Bergal, 153 N.E.3d 243, 251 (Ind. App. 2020)("Generally, oral agreements are enforceable"); Petit-Clair v. Atty. Gen. for New Jersey, 730 Fed. Appx. 120, 125 (3d Cir. 2018) (unpublished) (noting that "generally speaking, oral agreements are enforceable even if they are not fixed in writing").
2. Restatement (Second) of Contracts § 138.
3. See AN Act for the Prevention of Frauds and Perjuries, Stat. 29 Car. 2, c. 3, § 5 (1677) (Eng.).
4. Law Reform (Enforcement of Contracts) Act, June 4, 1954, Stat. 2 and 3 Eliz. 2, c. 34 (1954).
5. Lon Fuller, Consideration and Form, 41 Colum. L. Rev. 799, 800-01 (1941).

Writing requirements serve an evidentiary function in that they ensure the existence of a written document as evidence and, at the same time, make it more difficult to raise fraudulent claims unsupported by written evidence. Writing requirements serve a cautionary function because the creation of a signed writing puts parties on notice that they are incurring a potentially significant obligation. The channeling function is based on the idea that legal formalities such as the writing requirements "channel" the parties' objectives into a form that is easy for courts and third parties to understand, thereby providing, in Fuller's words, "a simple test ... of enforceability."[6]

To apply the statute of frauds, one must analyze three questions. First, does a contract trigger a writing requirement? Second, is the writing requirement satisfied? Third, if the writing requirement is not satisfied, can the contract nonetheless be enforced due to reliance or part performance? Incidentally, if both parties have fully performed their duties under the contract, the Statute of Frauds becomes irrelevant.[7]

II. Does the Contract Have to Be in Writing?

For common law contracts, states' statutes of frauds are the most significant sources of writing requirements.[8] However, writing requirements can be found across many other statutes as well. Of particular practical importance is section 2-201 of the Uniform Commercial Code. This provision imposes a writing requirement for the sale of goods for $500 or more.[9] Still, the following explanations will focus on states' statutes of frauds, leaving a discussion of section 2-201 of the Uniform Commercial Code for a later time. For simplicity, the pertinent provisions of the Restatement (Second) of

---

6. Lon Fuller, Consideration and Form, 41 COLUM. L. REV. 799, 801 (1941).

7. Restatement (Second) of Contracts § 145. This principle is generally accepted. E.g., Caulkins v. Petrillo, 513 A.2d 43, 45 (Conn. 1986); Miller v. Sire, 224 F. 424, 425 (2d Cir. 1915); Newkirk v. C.C. Bradley & Son, 67 N.Y.S.2d 459, 462 (N.Y. App. Div. 4th Dept. 1947); Winkel v. Fam. Health Care, P.C., 668 P.2d 208, 210 (Mont. 1983).

8. E.g. Ala. Code § 8-9-2 (West); Alaska Stat. Ann. § 09.25.010 (West); Cal. Civ. Code Ann. § 1624 (West); Colo. Rev. Stat. Ann. § 38-10-112 (West); Ky. Rev. Stat. Ann. § 371.010 (West); Mich. Comp. Laws Ann. § 566.132 (West); Minn. Stat. Ann. § 513.01 (West); Miss. Code Ann. § 15-3-1 (West); Mo. Rev. Stat. Ann. § 432.010 (West); Neb. Rev. Stat. Ann. § 36-202; Nev. Rev. Stat. Ann. § 111.220 (West); N.Y. Gen. Oblig. Law § 5-701 (McKinney); Ohio Rev. Code Ann. § 1335.05 (West); Okla. Stat. Ann. tit. 15, § 136 (West); Tex. Bus. & Com. Code Ann. § 26.01 (Vernon); Utah Code Ann. § 25-5-4; Va. Code Ann. § 11-2 (West); Wash. Rev. Code Ann. § 19.36.010; Wis. Stat. Ann. § 241.02 (West).

9. Uniform Commercial Code § 2-201 (1).

Contracts are used as a baseline. References to pertinent state legislation are provided in the footnotes.

A. The Promise to Answer for the Duty of Another

Section 110(1)(b) of the Restatement (Second) of Contracts imposes a writing requirement for contracts requiring one of the parties to answer for another person's duty or duties.[10] However, this so-called suretyship provision comes with an important exception. The writing requirement does not apply if the promisor's primary goal is to further their own interests.[11]

Question. Alpha offers to pay Beta $10,000 if Beta promises to paint Alpha's house. However, Beta is concerned that Alpha may lack the money to pay. Therefore, Beta calls Alpha's wealthy friend Gamma, explains the situation, and asks if Gamma is willing to pay Alpha's debt if Alpha cannot or will not pay. Gamma tells Beta that if Beta accepts Alpha's offer to paint their house, Gamma promises to pay Beta if Alpha fails to pay. Beta gladly acquiesces and subsequently enters into the contract with Alpha. After Beta has painted Alpha's house, Alpha is unable to pay Beta. Assume that the applicable state law corresponds exactly to the Restatement (Second) of Contracts. Does the contract between Beta and Gamma trigger the statute of frauds?

Answer. The answer is yes. Section 110(1)(b) of the Restatement (Second) of Contracts requires contracts to answer for the debt of another to be in writing.

---

10. Restatement (Second) of Contracts § 110 (1) (b). States' statutes of frauds also include this provision. E.g., Ala. Code § 8-9-2 (West); Alaska Stat. Ann. § 09.25.010 (West); Cal. Civ. Code Ann. § 1624 (West); Colo. Rev. Stat. Ann. § 38-10-112 (West); Ga. Code Ann. § 13-5-30 (West); Ind. Code Ann. § 32-21-1-1 (West); Ky. Rev. Stat. Ann. § 371.010 (West); Ohio Rev. Code Ann. § 1335.05 (West); Mich. Comp. Laws Ann. § 566.132 (West); Minn. Stat. Ann. § 513.01 (West); Miss. Code Ann. § 15-3-1 (West); Mo. Rev. Stat. Ann. § 432.010 (West); Neb. Rev. Stat. Ann. § 36-202; Nev. Rev. Stat. Ann. § 111.220 (West); N.Y. Gen. Oblig. Law § 5-701 (McKinney); Okla. Stat. Ann. tit. 15, § 136 (West); Tex. Bus. & Com. Code Ann. § 26.01 (b)(2) (Vernon); Utah Code Ann. § 25-5-4; Va. Code Ann. § 11-2 (West); Wis. Stat. Ann. § 241.02 (West).

11. Restatement (Second) of Contracts § 116; Tex. Bus. & Com. Code Ann. § 26.01 (b)(3) (Vernon). States whose statutory law does not explicitly include this provision have embraced it via their common law. E.g., Otto Contracting Co., Inc. v. S. Schinella & Son, Inc., 427 A.2d 856, 858 (Conn. 1980); Rosewood Care Ctr., Inc. v. Caterpillar, Inc., 877 N.E.2d 1091, 1099 (Ill. 2007); Trans-Gear, Inc. v. Lichtenberger, 715 N.E.2d 608, 611 (Ohio App. 11th Dist. 1998); UCSF-Stanford Health Care v. Hawaii Mgt. All. Benefits & Services, Inc., 58 F. Supp. 2d 1162, 1167 (D. Haw. 1999).

Question. Alpha enters into a contract with Beta, a general contractor, under which Beta is to build a house on Alpha's property in exchange for $1,000,000. Unfortunately, Beta cannot purchase the necessary bricks because his supplier, Gamma, fears that Beta will be unable to pay. To prevent Beta's liquidity problems from delaying the house's construction, Alpha calls Gamma and promises, in exchange for Gamma entering into a contract with Beta, that Alpha will pay for the bricks if Beta cannot or will not pay. Gamma gladly acquiesces and sells Beta the bricks. Once the house has been built, Beta fails to pay Gamma for the bricks. Assume that the applicable state law corresponds exactly to the Restatement (Second) of Contracts. Can Gamma demand payment from Alpha?

Answer. Gamma has an enforceable claim against Alpha. Alpha and Gamma reached mutual assent, and the consideration requirement is satisfied because Alpha gave their promise in exchange for Gamma's promise to extend credit to Beta. Section 110(1)(b) of the Restatement (Second) of Contracts requires contracts to answer for the debt of another to be in writing. However, section 116 of the Restatement makes an exception from the writing requirement if the promisor's primary purpose is to advance their own interests. Alpha's key objective was to ensure the construction of their home. Therefore, Alpha chiefly acted in their own interest. Accordingly, the contract did not have to be in writing, and Alpha's promise to Gamma is enforceable.

B. An Agreement Made on Consideration of Marriage

Section 110(1)(c) of the Restatement (Second) of Contracts imposes a writing requirement for promises that are made in exchange for marriage or in exchange for the promise to marry.[12] However, this writing requirement does not cover mutual promises to marry.[13]

12. Restatement (Second) of Contracts §§ 110 (1) (c), 124.

13. Restatement (Second) of Contracts § 124. States' statutes of frauds often include this exception as well. E.g., Ala. Code § 8-9-2 (West); Alaska Stat. Ann. § 09.25.010 (West); Colo. Rev. Stat. Ann. § 38-10-112 (West); Ky. Rev. Stat. Ann. § 371.010 (West);Minn. Stat. Ann. § 513.01 (West); Mich. Comp. Laws Ann. § 566.132 (West); Miss. Code Ann. § 15-3-1 (West); Nev. Rev. Stat. Ann. § 111.220 (West); N.Y. Gen. Oblig. Law § 5-701 (McKinney); Okla. Stat. Ann. tit. 15, § 136 (West); Utah Code Ann. § 25-5-4; Wash. Rev. Code Ann. § 19.36.010; Wis. Stat. Ann. § 241.02 (West). Some states have case law making it clear that the writing requirement for promises on consideration of marriage does not

Question. Beta is Alpha's child. One day, Alpha calls Gamma and tells Gamma that they offer to pay Gamma $1,000,000 if, in return, Gamma promises to marry Beta. Gamma gladly accepts. Two weeks later, Gamma marries Beta. Subsequently, Gamma calls Alpha and demands payment of the $1,000,000. Assume that the applicable common law corresponds exactly to the Restatement (Second) of Contracts. Does the contract between Alpha and Gamma fall within the statute of frauds?

Answer. Alpha's promise to pay was made in exchange for a promise to marry. Therefore, it falls within the statute of frauds and is not enforceable because it was not in writing.

C. Sale of an Interest in Land

Section 110(1)(d) of the Restatement (Second) of Contracts subjects contracts for the sale of an interest in land to the statute of frauds.[14] All U.S. states have adopted some version of this rule.[15]

D. An Agreement Not to Be Performed Within One Year

Perhaps most importantly, section 110(1)(e) of the Restatement extends the statute of frauds to contracts that cannot be performed within one year.[16]

---

extend to mutual promises to marry. E.g., Derby v. Phelps, 2 N.H. 515, 516 (1823); Coggins v. Cannon, 99 S.E. 823, 824 (S.C. 1919); Short v. Stotts, 58 Ind. 29, 37 (1877).

14. Restatement (Second) of Contracts §§ 110 (1) (d), 125.

15. E.g., Ala. Code § 8-9-2 (West); Alaska Stat. Ann. § 09.25.010 (West); Colo. Rev. Stat. Ann. § 38-10-112 (West); Ariz. Rev. Stat. Ann. § 33-413; Conn. Gen. Stat. Ann. § 52-550 (West); Ga. Code Ann. § 13-5-30 (a)(3)(West); Iowa Code Ann. § 622.32 (West); Ky. Rev. Stat. Ann. § 371.010 (West); Mich. Comp. Laws Ann. § 566.132 (West); Mo. Rev. Stat. Ann. § 432.010 (West); Miss. Code Ann. § 15-3-1 (West); Neb. Rev. Stat. Ann. § 36-202; Nev. Rev. Stat. Ann. § 111.220 (West); N.H. Rev. Stat. Ann. § 506:2; N.Y. Gen. Oblig. Law § 5-701 (McKinney); Ohio Rev. Code Ann. § 1335.05 (West); Okla. Stat. Ann. tit. 15, § 136 (West); Utah Code Ann. § 25-5-4; Va. Code Ann. § 11-2 (West); Minn. Stat. Ann. § 513.01 (West); Wash. Rev. Code Ann. § 19.36.010; Wis. Stat. Ann. § 241.02 (West). See also Black v. Powers, 628 S.E.2d 546, 558 (Va. App. 2006)(holding that, as a matter of common law, contracts on consideration of marriage have to be signed and in writing under the law of the Virgin Islands).

16. Restatement (Second) of Contracts §§ 110(1)(e), 130. All states have enacted this provision. E.g., Ala. Code § 8-9-2 (West); Alaska Stat. Ann. § 09.25.010 (West); Cal. Civ. Code Ann. § 1624 (West); Colo. Rev. Stat. Ann. § 38-10-112 (West); Conn. Gen. Stat. Ann. § 52-550 (West); Ga. Code Ann. § 13-5-30 (a)(5)(West); Ind. Code Ann. § 32-21-1-1 (West); Ky. Rev. Stat. Ann. § 371.010 (West); Mich. Comp. Laws Ann. § 566.132 (West); Minn. Stat. Ann. § 513.01 (West); Miss. Code Ann. § 15-3-1 (West); Mo. Rev. Stat. Ann. § 432.010 (West); Neb. Rev. Stat. Ann. § 36-202; Nev. Rev. Stat. Ann. §

Contracts not to be performed within a year excludes all contracts that may legally be performed within one year. Thus, if the contract allows the parties to render their performance within one year, the contract does not trigger the one-year provision, even if the performance can and does take more than a year.[17]

> **Question.** Alpha promises to pay Beta $100,000 in return for a promise by Beta to renovate Alpha's house "within two years." Does the contract have to be in writing?
>
> **Answer.** The answer is no. The one-year provision does not apply because Beta does not breach the contract if he renovates the house within one year. The contract only prohibits Beta from taking more than two years to renovate Alpha's house.

Most courts do not apply the one-year provision to contracts that last for the remainder of a person's life.[18] That is because the person might die before the year ends, which means the contract can potentially be performed in less than a year.[19]

How do contractual termination rights impact the applicability of the one-year provision? Suppose a contract stipulates a two-year duration but provides that the contract can be terminated every six months. Does such a contract need to be in writing under the one-year provision or not? Courts are divided on this issue. Some have held that the one-year provision is inapplic-

---

111.220 (West); N.H. Rev. Stat. Ann. § 506:2; N.Y. Gen. Oblig. Law § 5-701 (McKinney); Ohio Rev. Code Ann. § 1335.05 (West); Okla. Stat. Ann. tit. 15, § 136 (West); Tex. Bus. & Com. Code Ann. § 26.01 (b)(6) (Vernon); Utah Code Ann. § 25-5-4; Va. Code Ann. § 11-2 (West); Wash. Rev. Code Ann. § 19.36.010; Wis. Stat. Ann. § 241.02 (West).

17. See Durham v. Hiatt, 26 N.E. 401, 402 (Ind. 1891) (noting that the one-year provision "has no application to a contract which may or may not be performed within a year").

18. Collection & Investigation Bureau of Maryland, Inc. v. Linsley, 375 A.2d 47, 49 (Md. Spec. App. 1977) (holding that "[w]hen the promise is for an indefinite period such as for the life of the promisor, it is not within the ambit of the Statute of Frauds because, life being itself indefinite and uncertain, the promisor may die within the space of one year"); Hampton v. Caldwell & Hall, 129 S.W. 816, 817 (Ark. 1910) (rejecting the application of the statute of frauds where the obligor's death would have brought the contract to an end). But see Gilliam v. Kouchoucos, 340 S.W.2d 27, 30 (Tex. 1960)(holding that contracts for more than one year are not exempt from the statute of frauds because of the possibility that they might be terminated by death).

19. Hampton v. Caldwell & Hall, 129 S.W. 816, 817 (Ark. 1910); Collection & Investigation Bureau of Maryland, Inc. v. Linsley, 375 A.2d 47, 49 (Md. Spec. App. 1977).

if the contract can be terminated within a year.[20] Others have held that termination rights prevent the application of the one-year provision only if both parties have an equal right to terminate the contract within a year.[21] Yet others have taken the position that termination rights are irrelevant to the application of the one-year provision since termination by one party excuses nonperformance rather than constituting performance.[22] Finally, some courts differentiate based on the type of termination right. According to this approach, contractual provisions that allow a party to terminate the contract in case of a breach do not take the contract out of the statute of frauds.[23]

III. Satisfying the Writing Requirement

If a contract falls within the statute of frauds, the next question is whether the writing requirement is satisfied. A writing must meet several requirements to satisfy the statute of frauds. First, it must be signed by the party to be charged (*i.e.*, the person against whom the contract is being enforced) or by an agent acting on their behalf. Second, it must indicate that a contract was formed or that the party to be charged made an offer. Third, it must identify the contract's subject matter. Fourth, it must include the central terms of any unperformed obligations.[24]

Note that for the contract to be enforceable, it is not necessary that both parties have signed the contract. Instead, the decisive question is whether the writing is signed by the party to be charged or by an agent acting on their behalf.[25] Moreover, it is noteworthy that the writing has to contain the

---

20. E.g., Marini v. D'Apolito, 557 N.Y.S.2d 45, 46 (N.Y. App. Div. 1st Dept. 1990)("When one of the parties reserves the right to terminate the agreement, however, which right may be exercised within one year, the agreement is taken outside the statute of frauds.").

21. E.g., Foley v. Interactive Data Corp., 765 P.2d 373, 381 (Cal. 1988); Littlejohn v. Nalco Chem. Co., No. CV-F-84-630 REC, 1985 WL 56769, at *3 (E.D. Cal. Feb. 11, 1985).

22. E.g., Sullivan v. Leor Energy, LLC, 600 F.3d 542, 547 (5th Cir. 2010).

23. Celi v. Canadian Occidental Petroleum Ltd., 804 F. Supp. 465, 469 (E.D.N.Y. 1992)(holding that "termination of an agreement as a result of its breach is not performance thereof"); Toussaint v. Blue Cross & Blue Shield of Michigan, 292 N.W.2d 880, 891 (Mich. 1980), disapproved of by Cotran v. Rollins Hudig Hall Intern., Inc., 948 P.2d 412 (Cal. 1998)(holding that right to terminate for good cause does not take contract out of the statute of frauds).

24. Restatement (Second) of Contracts § 131.

25. Ala. Code § 8-9-2 (West); Cal. Civ. Code Ann. § 1624 (West); Colo. Rev. Stat. Ann. § 38-10-112 (West); Ind. Code Ann. § 32-21-1-1 (West); Ky. Rev. Stat. Ann. § 371.010 (West); Mich. Comp. Laws Ann. § 566.132 (West); Minn. Stat. Ann. § 513.01 (West); Mo. Rev. Stat. Ann. § 432.010 (West); Neb. Rev. Stat. Ann. § 36-202; Nev. Rev. Stat. Ann. § 111.220 (West); Wis. Stat. Ann. § 241.02 (West).

contract's essential terms, but only to the extent that the promises have not yet been performed.[26] Also, the writing need not have been created at the time when the contract was formed.[27]

The signature requirement is satisfied by any symbol meant to authenticate the writing. The "symbol" does not have to be created with a pen. It can be made by typing with a keyboard or using a rubber stamp.

IV. Substitutes

In practice, failure to comply with the writing requirement often proves irrelevant because a so-called writing substitute is present. Once both parties have fully performed their duties under the contract, the statute of frauds no longer applies. [28]

Moreover, even full or partial performance by only one of the parties may suffice to make the contract enforceable despite the lack of a writing. The relevant rules differ across the various writing requirements. Contracts for the sale of an interest in land no longer trigger the statute of frauds once the interest in land has been transferred.[29] By contrast, mere payment of the price is insufficient to take the contract out of the statute of frauds.[30] Contracts that cannot be performed within one year are taken out of the statute of frauds if at least one party has fully performed.[31] By contrast, the fact that one or both parties have partly performed will not take this type of contract out of the statute of frauds.[32] Regarding agreements made on consideration of marriage, the subsequent marriage does not make such agreements enforceable.[33]

---

26. Restatement (Second) of Contracts § 131.

27. Restatement (Second) of Contracts § 131 cmt. d.

28. Restatement (Second) of Contracts § 145. This principle is generally accepted. E.g., Caulkins v. Petrillo, 513 A.2d 43, 45 (Conn. 1986); Miller v. Sire, 224 F. 424, 425 (2d Cir. 1915); Newkirk v. C.C. Bradley & Son, 67 N.Y.S.2d 459, 462 (N.Y. App. Div. 4th Dept. 1947); Winkel v. Fam. Health Care, P.C., 668 P.2d 208, 210 (Mont. 1983).

29. Wiggins v. Barrett & Associates, Inc., 669 P.2d 1132, 1137 (Or. 1983); Restatement (Second) of Contracts § 125(3).

30. Restatement (Second) of Contracts § 125 cmt. e.

31. E.g., Yates v. Ball, 181 So. 341, 345 (Fla. 1937), Restatement (Second) of Contracts § 130(2).

32. E.g., Pollmann v. Belle Plaine Livestock Auction, Inc., 567 N.W.2d 405, 409 (Iowa 1997); McBride v. City of McCook, 321 N.W.2d 905, 906 (Neb. 1982); Kusper v. Poll Farms, Inc., 649 F. Supp. 2d 917, 920 (N.D. Ind. 2009); French v. Sabey Corp., 951 P.2d 260, 264 (Wash. 1998).

33. Restatement (Second) of Contracts § 145 cmt. d. See Rossiter v. Rossiter, 666 P.2d 617, 621 (Haw. App. 1983)(holding that marriage is insufficient to make the contract enforceable without writing and noting that "[t]he mere act of marriage is almost universally held to be insufficient part

According to the Restatement (Second) of Contracts and a substantial number of courts, parties can sometimes invoke estoppel to overcome the lack of a writing.[34] Read section 139 of the Restatement (Second) of Contracts. However, this approach remains controversial. Some courts have held that estoppel cannot overcome a failure to comply with the statute of frauds.[35] Others allow the application of the estoppel doctrine but limit it to narrowly defined circumstances. These include cases where the party to be charged had previously announced that they would not invoke the statute of frauds,[36] had promised to execute in writing and then gone back on that promise,[37] or had falsely claimed that the statute of frauds was complied with.[38] Some courts have held, more broadly, that the estoppel principle must be limited to cases where enforcement of the writing requirement would lead to "manifest injustice."[39]

---

performance" to take the contract out of the statute of frauds"); Kersey v. Kersey, 802 So. 2d 523, 525 (Fla. 1st Dist. App. 2001)(holding that marriage will not take antenuptial agreement out of statute of frauds). But see Hodges v. Ettinger, 189 N.E. 113, 115 (Ohio 1934)(holding that marriage will take the contract out of the statute of frauds).

34. Restatement (Second) of Contracts § 139. See, e.g., Alaska Democratic Party v. Rice, 934 P.2d 1313, 1316 (Alaska 1997)(adopting section 139 of the Restatement (Second) of Contracts with respect to employment contracts); Brown v. Branch, 758 N.E.2d 48, 51 (Ind. 2001)(holding that the doctrine of promissory estoppel can overcome a failure to comply with the statute of frauds); Kolkman v. Roth, 656 N.W.2d 148, 153 (Iowa 2003)(holding that "part performance and promissory estoppel to be compatible doctrines as exceptions to the statute of frauds"); Davis v. Harmony Dev., LLC, 460 P.3d 230, 236 (Wyo. 2020)(holding that the promissory estoppel doctrine constitutes an exception to the statute of frauds).

35. See, e.g., DK Arena, Inc. v. EB Acquisitions I, LLC, 112 So. 3d 85, 95 (Fla. 2013)(holding that a failure to comply with the statute of frauds cannot be overcome through the estoppel doctrine). See also Sawyer v. Mills, 295 S.W.3d 79, 89 (Ky. 2009), as modified (Nov. 2, 2009)(holding that "it is not clear that under Kentucky law promissory estoppel can defeat the Statute of Frauds")

36. See, e.g., Fericks v. Lucy Ann Soffe Tr., 100 P.3d 1200, 1204 (Utah 2004)(holding that "in order to establish the promissory estoppel exception to the statute of frauds, '[t]he acts and conduct of the promissor must so clearly manifest an intention that he will not assert the statute that to permit him to do so would be to work a fraud upon the other party.'")(internal citation omitted).

37. Moore Burger, Inc. v. Phillips Petroleum Co., 492 S.W.2d 934, 938 (Tex. 1972); Nagle v. Nagle, 633 S.W.2d 796, 800 (Tex. 1982).

38. 21 Turtle Creek Square, Ltd. v. New York State Teachers' Ret. System, 432 F.2d 64, 65 (5th Cir. 1970); Tiffany Inc. v. W. M. K. Transit Mix, Inc., 493 P.2d 1220, 1226 (Ariz. App. 1st Div. 1972).

39. E.g., Au v. Republic State Mortg. Co., No. CIV. 11-00251 JMS, 2013 WL 1339738, at *5 (D. Haw. Mar. 29, 2013). For a similar view see In re Est. of Hennel, 80 N.E.3d 1017, 1022 (N.Y. 2017)(holding that "where the elements of promissory estoppel are established, and the injury to the party who acted in reliance on the oral promise is so great that enforcement of the statute of frauds would be unconscionable, the promisor should be estopped from reliance on the statute of frauds")

Crabtree v. Elizabeth Arden Sales Corp

Court of Appeals of New York, 110 N.E.2d 551 (1953)

FULD, JUDGE.

In September of 1947, Nate Crabtree entered into preliminary negotiations with Elizabeth Arden Sales Corporation, manufacturers and sellers of cosmetics, looking toward his employment as sales manager. Interviewed on September 26th, by Robert P. Johns, executive vice-president and general manager of the corporation, who had apprised him of the possible opening, Crabtree requested a three-year contract at $25,000 a year. Explaining that he would be giving up a secure well-paying job to take a position in an entirely new field of endeavor which he believed would take him some years to master he insisted upon an agreement for a definite term. And he repeated his desire for a contract for three years to Miss Elizabeth Arden, the corporation's president. When Miss Arden finally indicated that she was prepared to offer a two-year contract, based on an annual salary of $20,000 for the first six months, $25,000 for the second six months and $30,000 for the second year, plus expenses of $5,000 a year for each of those years, Crabtree replied that that offer was 'interesting'. Miss Arden thereupon had her personal secretary make this memorandum on a telephone order blank that happened to be at hand:

"EMPLOYMENT AGREEMENT WITH NATE CRABTREE

Date Sept. 26-1947 6: PM
At 681-5th Ave . . .
Begin 20000.
6 months 25000.
6 months 30000.
5000 per year
Expense money
(2 years to make good)
Arrangement with
Mr Crabtree
By Miss Arden
Present Miss Arden
Mr John

Mr Crabtree
Miss O'Leary"

A few days later, Crabtree 'phoned Mr. Johns and telegraphed Miss Arden; he accepted the 'invitation to join the Arden organization', and Miss Arden wired back her 'welcome'. When he reported for work, a 'pay-roll change' card was made up and initialed by Mr. Johns, and then forwarded to the payroll department. Reciting that it was prepared on September 30, 1947, and was to be effective as of October 22d, it specified the names of the parties, Crabtree's 'Job Classification' and, in addition, contained the notation that 'This employee is to be paid as follows:

"First six months of employment $20,000. per annum
Next six months of employment 25,000. per annum
After one year of employment 30,000. per annum
Approved by RPJ (initialed)"

After six months of employment, Crabtree received the scheduled increase from $ 20,000 to $ 25,000, but the further specified increase at the end of the year was not paid. Both Mr. Johns and the comptroller of the corporation, Mr. Carstens, told Crabtree that they would attempt to straighten out the matter with Miss Arden, and, with that in mind, the comptroller prepared another 'pay-roll change' card, to which his signature is appended, noting that there was to be a 'Salary increase' from $ 25,000 to $ 30,000 a year, 'per contractual arrangements with Miss Arden'. The latter, however, refused to approve the increase and, after further fruitless discussion, plaintiff left defendant's employ and commenced this action for breach of contract.

At the ensuing trial, defendant denied the existence of any agreement to employ plaintiff for two years, and further contended that, even if one had been made, the statute of frauds barred its enforcement. The trial court found against defendant on both issues and awarded plaintiff damages of about $ 14,000, and the Appellate Division, two justices dissenting, affirmed. Since the contract relied upon was not to be performed within a year, the primary question for decision is whether there was a memorandum of its terms, subscribed by defendant, to satisfy the statute of frauds, Personal Property Law, s 31.

Each of the two payroll cards the one initialed by defendant's general manager, the other signed by its comptroller unquestionably constitutes a memorandum under the statute. That they were not prepared or signed with the intention of evidencing the contract, or that they came into existence subsequent to its execution, is of no consequence . . . ; it is enough, to meet the statute's demands, that they were signed with intent to authenticate the information contained therein and that such information does evidence the terms of the contract . . . . Those two writings contain all of the essential terms of the contract the parties to it, the position that plaintiff was to assume, the salary that he was to receive except that relating to the duration of plaintiff's employment. Accordingly, we must consider whether that item, the length of the contract, may be supplied by reference to the earlier unsigned office memorandum, and, if so, whether its notation, '2 years to make good', sufficiently designates a period of employment.

The statute of frauds does not require the 'memorandum . . . to be in one document. It may be pieced together out of separate writings, connected with one another either expressly or by the internal evidence of subject-matter and occasion.' Marks v. Cowdin, supra, 226 N.Y. 138, 145, 123 N.E. 139, 141, see, also, 2 Williston, op cit., p. 1671; Restatement, Contracts, s 208, subd. (a). Where each of the separate writings has been subscribed by the party to be charged, little if any difficulty is encountered. See, e. g., Marks v. Cowdin, supra, 226 N.Y. 138, 144-145, 123 N.E. 139, 141. Where, however, some writings have been signed, and others have not as in the case before us there is basic disagreement as to what constitutes a sufficient connection permitting the unsigned papers to be considered as part of the statutory memorandum. The courts of some jurisdictions insist that there be a reference, of varying degrees of specificity, in the signed writing to that unsigned, and, if there is no such reference, they refuse to permit consideration of the latter in determining whether the memorandum satisfies the statute. See, e. g., Osborn v. Phelps, 19 Conn. 63; Hewett Grain & Provision Co. v. Spear, 222 Mich. 608, 193 N.W. 291. That conclusion is based upon a construction of the statute which requires that the connection between the writings and defendant's acknowledgment of the one not subscribed, appear from examination of the papers alone, without the aid of parol evidence. The other position which has gained increasing support over the years is that a sufficient connection between the papers is established simply by a reference in them to the same subject matter or transaction. . . . The statute is not pressed 'to the extreme of a literal and rigid logic', Marks v. Cowdin, supra, 226 N.Y. 138, 144, 123 N.E. 139, 141, and oral testimony is admitted to show the connection between the documents and to establish the acquiescence, of the party to be charged, to the contents of the one unsigned.. . .

The view last expressed impresses us as the more sound, and, indeed although several of our cases appear to have gone the other way, see, e. g., Newbery v. Wall, 65 N.Y. 484; Wilson v. Lewiston Mill Co., 150 N.Y. 314, 44 N.E. 959 this court has on a number of occasions approved the rule, and we now definitively adopt it, permitting the signed and unsigned writings to be read together, provided that they clearly refer to the same subject matter or transaction....

The language of the statute 'Every agreement . . . is void, unless . . . some note or memorandum thereof be in writing, and subscribed by the party to be charged', Personal Property Law, s 31-does not impose the requirement that the signed acknowledgment of the contract must appear from the writings alone, unaided by oral testimony. The danger of fraud and perjury, generally attendant upon the admission of parol evidence, is at a minimum in a case such as this. None of the terms of the contract are supplied by parol. All of them must be set out in the various writings presented to the court, and at least one writing, the one establishing a contractual relationship between the parties, must bear the signature of the party to be charged, while the unsigned document must on its face refer to the same transaction as that set forth in the one that was signed. Parol evidence to portray the circumstances surrounding the making of the memorandum serves only to connect the separate documents and to show that there was assent, by the party to be charged, to the contents of the one unsigned. If that testimony does not convincingly connect the papers, or does not show assent to the unsigned paper, it is within the province of the judge to conclude, as a matter of law, that the statute has not been satisfied. True, the possibility still remains that, by fraud or perjury, an agreement never in fact made may occasionally be enforced under the subject matter or transaction test. It is better to run that risk, though, than to deny enforcement to all agreements, merely because the signed document made no specific mention of the unsigned writing. As the United States Supreme Court declared, in sanctioning the admission of parol evidence to establish the connection between the signed and unsigned writings. 'There may be cases in which it would be a violation of reason and common sense to ignore a reference which derives its significance from such (parol) proof. If there is ground for any doubt in the matter, the general rule should be enforced. But where there is no ground for doubt, its enforcement would aid, instead of discouraging, fraud.' Beckwith v. Talbot, supra, 95 U.S. 289, 292 . . . .

Turning to the writings in the case before us the unsigned office memo, the payroll change form initialed by the general manager Johns, and the paper signed by the comptroller Carstens it is apparent, and most patently, that all three refer on their face to the same transaction. The parties, the position to be filled by plaintiff, the salary to be paid him, are all identically set forth; it is hardly possible that such detailed information could refer to another or a different agreement. Even more, the card signed by Carstens notes that it was prepared for the purpose of a 'Salary increase per contractual arrangements with Miss Arden'. That certainly constitutes a reference of sorts to a more comprehensive 'arrangement,' and parol is permissible to furnish the explanation.

The corroborative evidence of defendant's assent to the contends of the unsigned office memorandum is also convincing. Prepared by defendant's agent, Miss Arden's personal secretary, there is little likelihood that that paper was fraudulently manufactured or that defendant had not assented to its contents. Furthermore, the evidence as to the conduct of the parties at the time it was prepared persuasively demonstrates defendant's assent to its terms. Under such circumstances, the courts below were fully justified in finding that the three papers constituted the 'memorandum' of their agreement within the meaning of the statute.

Nor can there be any doubt that the memorandum contains all of the essential terms of the contract. . . . Only one term, the length of the employment, is in dispute. The September 26th office memorandum contains the notation, '2 years to make good'. What purpose, other than to denote the length of the contract term, such a notation could have, is hard to imagine. Without it, the employment would be at will, see Martin v. New York Life Ins. Co., 148 N.Y. 117, 121, 42 N.E. 416, 417, and its inclusion may not be treated as meaningless or purposeless. Quite obviously, as the courts below decided, the phrase signifies that the parties agreed to a term, a certain and definite term, of two years, after which, if plaintiff did not 'make good', he would be subject to discharge. And examination of other parts of the memorandum supports that construction. Throughout the writings, a scale of wages, increasing plaintiff's salary periodically, is set out; that type of arrangement is hardly consistent with the hypothesis that the employment was meant to be at will. The most that may be argued from defendant's standpoint is that '2 years to make good', is a cryptic and ambiguous statement. But, in such a case, parol evidence is admissible to explain its meaning. . . . Having in mind the relations of the parties, the course of the negotiations and plaintiff's insistence upon security of employment, the purpose of the phrase or so the trier of the facts was warranted in finding was to grant plaintiff the tenure he desired.

The judgment should be affirmed, with costs.

LOUGHRAN, C. J., and LEWIS, CONWAY, DESMOND, DYE and FROESSEL, JJ., concur.

NOTES AND QUESTIONS

A. Elizabeth Arden and Nate Crabtree. Elizabeth Arden (1881-1966) was a remarkable entrepreneur. Born in Canada, she founded her eponymous company in New York in 1910, rapidly transforming it into a global powerhouse.[40] In 1962, the French government recognized her contribution to the field of cosmetics by awarding her France's highest order of merit, the National Order of the Legion of Honor. However, Elizabeth Arden did not limit her interests to the world of business. A passionate suffragette, she marched for women's right to vote. She also owned a racing horse stable that produced a Kentucky Derby winner ("Jet Pilot," 1947). Meanwhile, little is known about Nate Crabtree. It is worth noting, though, that he was being quite well compensated. Accounting for inflation, an annual salary of $25,000 in 1947 corresponds to an annual salary of $344,923 in 2023.

B. The Statute(s) of Frauds. Statutes of frauds require certain types of contracts to be in writing in order to be enforceable. These statutes are inspired by the English statute of frauds that the English Parliament enacted in 1677.[41] Ironically, the English Statute of Frauds was, for the most part, repealed in 1954.[42] Importantly, the failure to comply with a statute of frauds impacts only the enforceability of a contract, not its formation.[43]

C. The purpose of writing requirements. As the name "statute of frauds"

---

40. In 1970, four years after Ms. Arden's death, the pharmaceutical corporation Eli Lilly bought her company.

41. See AN ACT FOR THE PREVENTION OF FRAUDS AND PERJURIES, Stat. 29 Car. 2, c. 3, § 5 (1677) (Eng.).

42. Law Reform (Enforcement of Contracts) Act, June 4, 1954, Stat. 2 and 3 Eliz. 2, c. 34 (1954).

43. Restatement (Second) of Contracts § 138.

suggests, a key motivation behind the original statute of frauds was to prevent fraudulent claims. However, the potential benefits of writing requirements extend well beyond this purpose. In his seminal 1941 article, Lon Fuller delineates three different functions served by writing requirements: the evidentiary function, the cautionary function, and the channeling function.[44] Whereas the former two are self-explanatory, the channeling function requires further explanation. The channeling function is based on the idea that legal formalities such as the writing requirements "channel" the parties' objectives into a form that is easy for courts and third parties to understand, thereby providing, in Fuller's words, "a simple test ... of enforceability."[45]

D. Applying the statute of frauds. To apply the statute of frauds, one must address three questions. First, does a contract trigger a writing requirement?[46] Second, is the writing requirement satisfied?[47] Third, if the writing requirement is not satisfied, can the contract nonetheless be enforced due to reliance or part performance?[48] If both parties have fully performed their duties under the contract, the Statute of Frauds becomes irrelevant.[49]

E. The one-year provision. Under section 130 of the Restatement (Second) of Contracts, one category of contracts that must be in writing includes contracts that cannot be performed within one year.[50] This provision excludes all contracts that may be performed within one year. Thus, if the contract allows the parties to render their performance within one year, the contract does not trigger the one-year-provision, even if the performance can take more than a year.[51] Why did the employment contract in *Crabtree* trigger the one-year provision?

F. The writing. A writing satisfies the statute of frauds if it is signed by the party to be charged, identifies the contract's subject matter, indicates that the formation of a contract or at least the making of an offer by the party to be charged, and includes the central terms of any unperformed obligations.[52]

---

44. Lon Fuller, Consideration and Form, 41 COLUM. L. REV. 799, 800-01 (1941).
45. Id. at 801.
46. See Restatement (Second) of Contracts §§ 110 et seq.
47. See id. §§ 131 et seq.
48. Id. §§ 125(3), 129, 130(2).
49. Id. § 145.
50. Id. § 110(1)(e).
51. See Durham v. Hiatt, 26 N.E. 401, 402 (Ind. 1891) (noting that the one-year provision "has no application to a contract which may or may not be performed within a year").
52. Restatement (Second) of Contracts § 131.

Importantly, the writing need not have been created at the time of the contract.[53] Why was the protocol created by Elizabeth Arden's secretary (alone) insufficient to satisfy the writing requirement? Why were the pay stubs alone insufficient to satisfy the writing requirement?

G. Combining several writings. At times, no single document satisfies all the criteria mandated by the statute of frauds. However, there are a few scenarios in which several writings can cumulatively satisfy the writing requirement. The first and most straightforward scenario arises when the party to be charged has signed several different writings that, together, have the necessary content to satisfy the statute of frauds.[54] The second scenario occurs where at least one of the writings is signed, the writings are physically connected, such as being stapled together, and the party to be charged acquiesced in the creation of this physical connection.[55] In the third scenario, the signed writing implicitly or explicitly references the unsigned writings.[56] The *Crabtree* court goes even further and introduces a fourth scenario. According to the court, several writings, at least one of which is signed, may collectively satisfy the statute of frauds if the writings refer, on their face, to the same transaction. Section 132 of the Restatement (Second) of Contracts embraces this holding, and all modern cases that raise the issue appear to follow the same rule.[57] Do you believe that the court's holding in *Crabtree* consistent is with the functions that Lon Fuller ascribed to writing requirements?

H. Performance by one party. Full performance by both parties always renders the Statute of Frauds irrelevant.[58] However, for some writing requirements, performance by one party is also sufficient to make the contract enforceable. In particular, the one-year provision ceases to apply if either of the two parties has fully performed.[59] Does this rule align with the functions served by the one-year provision?

I. Electronic communications. In recent years, courts have frequently considered the extent to which electronic communications such as emails or

53. Id. cmt. d.
54. Id. § 132 cmt. b.
55. Id. cmt. c.
56. Id. cmt. c.
57. E.g., Walsh v. Coyle, No. S-4561, 1992 WL 12549793, at *1 (Alaska 1992); U. of Kentucky v. Regard, 670 S.W.3d 903, 913 (Ky. 2023); Crossroads Estates Homeowners Assn. v. Landwehr, No. 1 CA-CV 21-0378, 2022 WL 1180096, at *2 (Ariz. App. 2022).
58. Restatement (Second) of Contracts § 145.
59. Id. § 110 (2)

text messages constitute writings for the purpose of state statutes of frauds. In general, courts have treated electronic writings the same way as traditional documents.[60] Consequently, an email that does not contain the sender's name, either as part of a signature block or simply typed below the message, cannot be qualified as a signed writing.[61] The same principles have also applied to text messages.[62]

60. See, e.g., Agosta v. Fast Sys. Corp., 26 N.Y.S.3d 534, 537 (N.Y. App. 2016) (holding that an email under which the sender's name is typed can constitute a signed writing); Newmark & Co. Real Estate Inc. v. 2615 E. 17 St. Realty LLC, 80 A.D.3d 476, 477.

61. See, e.g., Preston v. Nichols, 189 N.Y.S.3d 837, 838 (N.Y. App. Div. 4th Dept. 2023) (holding that "an email without a typed name or signature block cannot satisfy the statute of frauds").

62. See St. John's Holdings, LLC v. Two Elecs., LLC, No. 16 MISC 000090 RBF, 2016 WL 1460477, at *9 (Mass. Land Ct. 2016) (holding that a text message at the end of which the sender had added his first name constituted a signed writing for statute of fraud purposes); see also Heffernan v. Keith, 127 So. 2d 903, 904 (Fla. DCA 1961) (holding that a telegram satisfied the Statute of Frauds).

CHAPTER 12
INFANCY

Dodson v. Shrader

Supreme Court of Tennessee, 824 S.W.2d 545 (1992)

O'BRIEN, Justice

This is an action to disaffirm the contract of a minor for the purchase of a pick-up truck and for a refund of the purchase price. The issue is whether the minor is entitled to a full refund of the money he paid or whether the seller is entitled to a setoff for the decrease in value of the pick-up truck while it was in the possession of the minor.

In early April of 1987, Joseph Eugene Dodson, then 16 years of age, purchased a used 1984 pick-up truck from Burns and Mary Shrader. The Shraders owned and operated Shrader's Auto Sales in Columbia, Tennessee. Dodson paid $4,900 in cash for the truck, using money he borrowed from his girlfriend's grandmother. At the time of the purchase there was no inquiry by the Shraders, and no misrepresentation by Mr. Dodson, concerning his minority. However, Mr. Shrader did testify that at the time he believed Mr. Dodson to be 18 or 19 years of age.

In December 1987, nine (9) months after the date of purchase, the truck began to develop mechanical problems. A mechanic diagnosed the problem as a burnt valve, but could not be certain without inspecting the valves inside the engine. Mr. Dodson did not want, or did not have the money, to effect these repairs. He continued to drive the truck despite the mechanical problems. One month later, in January, the truck's engine "blew up" and the truck became inoperable.

Mr. Dodson parked the vehicle in the front yard at his parents' home where he lived. He contacted the Shraders to rescind the purchase of the truck and requested a full refund. The Shraders refused to accept the tender of the truck or to give Mr. Dodson the refund requested.

Mr. Dodson then filed an action in general sessions court seeking to rescind the contract and recover the amount paid for the truck. The general sessions court dismissed the warrant and Mr. Dodson perfected a de novo appeal to the circuit court. At the time the appeal was filed in the circuit court Mr. Shrader, through counsel, declined to accept the tender of the truck without compensation for its depreciation. Before the circuit court could hear the case, the truck, while parked in Dodson's front yard, was struck on the left front fender by a hit-and-run driver. At the time of the circuit court trial, according to Shrader, the truck was worth only $500 due to the damage to the engine and the left front fender.

The case was heard in the circuit court in November 1988. The trial judge, based on previous common-law decisions and, under the doctrine of stare decisis reluctantly granted the rescission. The Shraders were ordered, upon tender and delivery of the truck, to reimburse the $4,900 purchase price to Mr. Dodson. The Shraders appealed.

The Court of Appeals, per Todd, J., affirmed; Cantrell, J., concurring separately, Koch, J., dissenting.

The earliest recorded case in this State, on the issue involved, appears to be in Wheaton v. East, 13 Tenn. 35 (5 Yeager 41) (1833). In pronouncing the rule to apply governing infant's contracts, the court said:

We do not perceive that any general rule, as to contracts which are void and voidable, can be stated with more precision that is done by Lord Ch. J. Eyre in Keane v. Boycott, 2 H. Black, 511, and quoted with approbation by Judge Story, 1 Mason's Rep. 82, and by Chancellor Kent, 2 Com. 193, which is this: "that when the court can pronounce the contract to be to the infant's prejudice, it is void, and when to his benefit, as for necessaries, it is good; and when the contract is of any uncertain nature, as to benefit or prejudice, it is voidable only, at the election of the infant." ...

The law on the subject of the protection of infant's rights has been slow to evolve. However, in Human v. Hartsell, 24 Tenn.App. 678, 148 S.W.2d 634, 636 (1940) the Court of Appeals noted:

The last case in Tennessee holding a minor's contract void and adopting as the criterion for determining whether a given contract is void or only voidable [based upon] the prejudicial, uncertain or beneficial effect upon the rights and interests of the minor, appears to be the case of Robinson v. Coulter, supra, [90 Tenn. 705, 18 S.W. 250] decided November 12, 1891. In Tuck v. Payne, 159 Tenn. 192, 17 S.W.2d 8, in an opinion by Mr. Justice McKinney, the modern rule that contracts of infants are not void but only voidable and subject to be disaffirmed by the minor either before or after attaining majority appears to have been favored.

Under this rule the efforts of early authorities to classify contracts as beneficial or harmful and determine whether they are void or only voidable upon the basis of such classification are abandoned in favor of permitting the infant himself when he has become of age to determine what contracts are and what are not to his interest and liking. He is thus permitted to assume the burden of a contract, clearly disadvantageous to him, if he deems himself under a moral obligation to do so.

The adoption of this rule does not lead to any retrenchment of the infant's rights but gives him the option of invoking contracts found to be advantageous but which, if held void, could not be enforced against the other party to the contract. Thus the minor can secure the advantage of contracts advantageous to himself and be relieved of the effect of an injudicious contract.

In Tuck, supra, 17 S.W.2d at p. 9, the court applied the rule based upon the maxims that he who seeks equity must do equity, that he who comes into equity must come with clean hands, that no one can take advantage of his own wrong, that he that has committed inequity shall not have equity, and that minors will not be permitted to use the shield of infancy as a cover, or turn it into a sword with which to injure others dealing with them in good faith.

As noted by the Court of Appeals, the rule in Tennessee, as modified, is in accord with the majority rule on the issue among our sister states. This rule is based upon the underlying purpose of the "infancy doctrine" which is to protect minors from their lack of judgment and "from squandering their wealth through improvident contracts with crafty adults who would take advantage of them in the marketplace." Halbman v. Lemke, 99 Wis.2d 241, 245, 298 N.W.2d 562, 564 (1980).

There is, however, a modern trend among the states, either by judicial action or by statute, in the approach to the problem of balancing the rights of minors against those of innocent merchants. As a result, two (2) minority rules have developed which allow the other party to a contract with a minor to refund less than the full consideration paid in the event of rescission.

The first of these minority rules is called the "Benefit Rule." E.g., Hall v. Butterfield, 59 N.H. 354 (1879); Johnson v. Northwestern Mut. Life Insurance Co., 56 Minn. 365, 59 N.W. 992 (1894); Berglund v. American Multigraph Sales Co., 135 Minn. 67, 160 N.W. 191 (1916); Porter v. Wilson, 106 N.H. 270, 209 A.2d 730 (1965); Valencia v. White, 134 Ariz. 139, 654 P.2d 287 (Ariz.App.1982). The rule holds that, upon rescission, recovery of the full purchase price is subject to a deduction for the minor's use of the merchandise. This rule recognizes that the traditional rule in regard to necessaries has been extended so far as to hold an infant bound by his contracts, where he failed to restore what he has received under them to the extent of the benefit actually derived by him from what he has received from the other party to the transaction. See Porter v. Wilson, 106 N.H. 270, 209 A.2d 730, 13 A.L.R.3d 1247 (1965); Valencia v. White, supra, 2 Williston on Contracts, § 238, p. 43 (3rd Ed. Jaeger 1959). Berglund v. American Multigraph Sales Co., supra.

The other minority rule holds that the minor's recovery of the full purchase price is subject to a deduction for the minor's "use" of the consideration he or she received under the contract, or for the "depreciation" or "deterioration" of the consideration in his or her possession. See Carter v. Jays Motors, 3 N.J.Super. 82, 65 A.2d 628 (N.J.S.Ct., App.Div.1949); Creer v. Active Automobile Exch., 99 Conn. 266, 121 A. 888 (Conn.1923); Rodriguez v. Northern Auto Auction, 225 N.Y.S.2d 107 (N.Y.App.Div.1962); Pettit v. Liston, 97 Or. 464, 191 P. 660 (1920).

We are impressed by the statement made by the Arizona Appeals Court in Valencia v. White, supra, citing the Court of Appeals of Ohio in Haydocy Pontiac Inc. v. Lee, 19 Ohio App.2d 217, 250 N.E.2d 898 (1969):

At a time when we see young persons between 18 and 21 years of age demanding and assuming more responsibilities in their daily lives; when we see such persons emancipated, married, and raising families; when we see such persons charged with the responsibility for committing crimes; when we see such persons being sued in tort claims for acts of negligence; when we see such persons subject to military service; when we see such persons engaged in business and acting in almost all other respects as an adult, it seems timely to re-examine the case law pertaining to contractual rights and responsibilities of infants to see if the law as pronounced and applied by the courts should be redefined.

In Pettit v. Liston, supra, the Oregon court, endeavoring to resolve issues similar to those at hand in this case noted that in dealing with the right of the minor to rescind his contract and the conditions under which he may do so, the decisions of the courts in the different states have not only conflicted upon the main question involved, but many of the decisions of the same court in the same state seem to be inconsistent with each other; and often times one court has made its decision turn upon a distinction or difference not recognized by the courts of other states as a distinguishing feature. As a result, rules have been promulgated which are considered to be suitable and appropriate upon considerations of principal and public policy.

Upon serious reflection we are convinced that a modified form of the Oregon rule should be adopted in this State concerning the rights and responsibilities of minors in their business dealings.

This is no quantum leap in the evolution of the common law. As early as 1842, in the case of Jacob v. The State, 22 Tenn. 372, 388, 3 Humphreys 514 (1842), Justice Turley delivered a profound dissertation on the policy and principles of the common law:

The common law has been aptly called the "lex non scripta," because it is a rule prescribed by the common consent and agreement of the community as one applicable to its different relations, and capable of preserving the peace, good order, and harmony of society, and rendering unto every one that which of right belongs to him. Its sources are to be found in the usages, habits, manners, and customs of a people. Its seat is in the breast of the judges who are its expositors and expounders. Every nation must of necessity have its common law, let it be called by what name it may, and it will be simple or complicated in its details, as society is simple or complicated in its relations. A few plain and practical rules will do for a wandering horde of savages, but they must and will be much more extensively ramified when civilization has polished, and commerce and arts and agriculture enriched, a nation. The common law of a country will, therefore, never be entirely stationary, but will be modified, and extended by analogy, construction and custom, so as to embrace new relations, springing up from time to time, from an amelioration or change of society. The present common law of England is as dissimilar from that of Edward III. as is the present state of society. And we apprehend that no one could be found to contend that hundreds of principles, which have in more modern times been examined, argued, and determined by the judges, are not principles of the common law, because not found in the books of that period. They are held to be great and immutable principles, which have slumbered in their repositories, because the occasion called for their exposition had not arisen. The common law, then, is not like the statute law, fixed, and immutable but by positive enactment, except where a principle has been adjudged as the rule of action.

If, then, one generation be not so hedged in by the principles of the common law, established by another, as to be prohibited from extending them, by analogy and construction, to new relations and modifications of society, by what principle shall a sovereign state, which has adopted the common law of another as one of its rule of action, be so prohibited?

Such, then, is the common law, that though principles once established by judicial determination can only be changed by legislative enactment, yet such is its malleability (if we may use the expression) that new principles may be developed, and old ones extended, by analogy, so as to embrace newly-created relations and changes produced by time and circumstances....

The late Justice Joseph W. Henry, past member and former Chief Justice of this Court stated the message of the flexibility of the common law in more modern language in Dunn v. Palermo, 522 S.W.2d 679, 688 (Tenn.1975), as follows:

This Court in the past has not hesitated to depart from the rigid common law where "the reason for the common law rule does not exist." Brown v. Shelby, 206 Tenn. 71, 332 S.W.2d 166 (1960).

The common law does not have the force of Holy Writ; it is not a last will and testament, nor is it a cadaver embalmed in perpetuity, nor is it to be treated like the sin of Judah—"written with a pen of iron and with the point of a diamond." Jeremiah 17:1.

Former Chief Justice Frantz of Colorado, in his dissenting opinion in Tesone v. School Dist. No. Re–2, In County of Boulder, 152 Colo. 596, 384 P.2d 82 (1963), made this erudite observation on the common law:

"The common law of America is evolutionary; it is not static and immutable. It is in constant growth, going through mutations in adapting itself to changing conditions and in improving and refining doctrine. By its very nature, it seeks perfection in the achievement of justice."

This is an eloquent description of the greatness and the glory of the common law.

We state the rule to be followed hereafter, in reference to a contract of a minor, to be where the minor has not been overreached in any way, and there has been no undue influence, and the contract is a fair and reasonable one, and the minor has actually paid money on the purchase price, and taken and used the article purchased, that he ought not to be permitted to recover the amount actually paid, without allowing the vender of the goods reasonable compensation for the use of, depreciation, and willful or negligent damage to the article purchased, while in his hands. If there has been any fraud or imposition on the part of the seller or if the contract is unfair, or any unfair advantage has been taken of the minor inducing him to make the purchase, then the rule does not apply. Whether there has been such an overreaching on the part of the seller, and the fair market value of the property returned, would always, in any case, be a question for the trier of fact. This rule will fully and fairly protect the minor against injustice or imposition, and at the same time it will be fair to a business person who has dealt with such minor in good faith.

This rule is best adapted to modern conditions under which minors are permitted to, and do in fact, transact a great deal of business for themselves, long before they have reached the age of legal majority. Many young people work and earn money and collect it and spend it oftentimes without any oversight or restriction. The law does not question their right to buy if they have the money to pay for their purchases. It seems intolerably burdensome for everyone concerned if merchants and business people cannot deal with them safely, in a fair and reasonable way. Further, it does not appear consistent with practice of proper moral influence upon young people, tend to encourage honesty and integrity, or lead them to a good and useful business future, if they are taught that they can make purchases with their own money, for their own benefit, and after paying for them, and using them until they are worn out and destroyed, go back and compel the vendor to return to them what they have paid upon the purchase price. Such a doctrine can only lead to the corruption of principles and encourage young people in habits of trickery and dishonesty.

In view of the foregoing considerations, we conclude that the rule, as we have indicated, and which we have paraphrased from that adopted in the State of Oregon, will henceforth be the rule to be utilized in this State.

We note that in this case, some nine (9) months after the date of purchase, the truck purchased by the plaintiff began to develop mechanical problems. Plaintiff was informed of the probable nature of the difficulty which apparently involved internal problems in the engine. He continued to drive the vehicle until the engine "blew up" and the truck became inoperable. Whether or not this involved gross negligence or intentional conduct on his part is a matter for determination at the trial level. It is not possible to determine from this record whether a counterclaim for tortious damage to the vehicle was asserted. After the first tender of the vehicle was made by plaintiff, and refused by the defendant, the truck was damaged by a hit-and-run driver while parked on plaintiff's property. The amount of that damage and the liability for that amount between the purchaser and the vendor, as well as the fair market value of the vehicle at the time of tender, is also an issue for the trier of fact.

The case is remanded to the trial court for further proceedings in accordance with this judgment. The costs on appellate review are assessed equally between the parties.

REID, C.J. and DROWOTA, DAUGHTREY, AND ANDERSON, JJ., concur.

NOTES AND QUESTIONS:

A. Age of majority. The age of majority varies across U.S. states. In forty-eight states and the District of Columbia, the age of majority is eighteen. Alabama and Nebraska stand out with an age of majority set at nineteen.[1]

B. Emancipation by marriage. Historically, a person's minority would end upon marriage, and many states still adhere to this rule.[2] This principle is grounded in the belief that a married minor assumes responsibility for their own family and therefore cannot be subjected to their parents' authority.[3] However, the modern trend, however, is to reject emancipation by marriage.

---

1. ALA. CODE § 26-1-1, NEB. REV. ST. § 43-2101.
2. See, e.g., NEB. REV. ST. § 43-2101(1); LA. CIV. CODE ANN. ART. 367; N.H. Rev. Stat. Ann. § 21-B:3; CAL. FAM. CODE ANN. § 7002 (West); HAW. REV. STAT. ANN. § 577-25 (Lexis); N.C. GEN. STAT. ANN. § 7B-3509 (West); Wyo. Stat. Ann. § 14-1-201 (West); KAN. STAT. ANN. § 38-101 (West).
3. See Delaware, L. & W.R. Co. v. Petrowsky, 250 F. 554, 559 (2d Cir. 1918) ("[T]he marriage of a minor . . . works an emancipation [because] marriage gives rise to a new relation inconsistent with subjection to the control and care of the parent. The husband is the head of a new family and as such is subject to obligations and duties to his wife and children which require him to be the master of himself, his time, his labor, earnings, and conduct.").

In particular, the desire to protect minors has led some states to prohibit any marriage involving a minor or allow such a marriage only if the minor is already fully emancipated.[4]

*C. **Child marriage.*** Even with judicial or parental approval, many states now mandate that minors must be at least sixteen or seventeen years old to marry. [5] Moreover, over the last few years, ten states have enacted legislation prohibiting marriage with minors under all circumstances.[6] Other states have recently introduced a minimum age for marriage but have stopped short of prohibiting all marriages involving minors.[7] However, some states such as California impose no minimum age requirement for marriages that receive judicial approval.[8] Child marriage very much remains a reality in the United States. A study from 2021 examined marriages occurring between 2000 and 2018 involving at least one minor, and the study identified 1,223 marriages where one party was fourteen years old—and even a few cases involving marriage with a ten- or eleven-year-old spouse.[9]

D. Emancipation by military service. In some states, minors are emancipated once they serve in the military.[10]

E. The necessaries doctrine. A traditional exception to the infancy doctrine is the so-called "necessaries" or "necessities" doctrine under which minors

---

4. See, e.g., TEX. FAM. CODE ANN. § 6.205 (Vernon) ("A marriage is void if either party to the marriage is younger than 18 years of age, unless a court order removing the disabilities of minority of the party for general purposes has been obtained in this state or in another state.").
5. See Marie Johnson-Dahl, Sixteen Candles on My Wedding Cake: Implications of Banning Child Marriage in America, 2020 U. ILL. L. REV. 1045, 1053 (2020) (listing the various state rules).
6. See MICH. COMP. LAWS ANN. § 551.103 (West) (eff. Sept. 19, 2023); CONN. GEN. STAT. ANN. § 46b-20a (West) (eff. July 1, 2023); MASS. GEN. LAWS ANN. ch. 207, § 7 (West) (eff. July 1, 2022); DEL. CODE ANN. tit. 13, § 123 (West) (eff. May 9, 2018); VT. STAT. ANN. TIT. 18, § 5142 (West) (eff. July 1, 2023); N.J. STAT. ANN. § 37:1-6 (West) (eff. June 22, 2018); MINN. STAT. ANN. § 517.02 (West) (eff. Aug. 1, 2020); 23 PA. STAT. AND CONSOL. STAT. ANN. § 1304 (West) (eff. July 7, 2020); N.Y. DOM. REL. LAW § 15-a (McKinney) (eff. Aug. 21, 2021); 15 R.I. GEN. LAWS ANN. § 15-2-14 (West) (June 7, 2021).
7. See, e.g., NEV. REV. STAT. ANN. § 122.020 (West) (eff. Oct. 1, 2019) (generally limiting marriage to adults but allowing marriage by seventeen-year-olds in "extraordinary circumstances"); W. VA. CODE ANN. § 48-2-301 (West) (eff. June 9, 2023) (generally requiring a minimum age of eighteen but allowing exceptions for minors who are at least sixteen years old).
8. CAL. FAM. CODE ANN. §§ 302, 304 (West)
9. See Unchained at Last, United States' Child Marriage Problem 4 (2021).
10. See, e.g., WYO. STAT. ANN. § 14-1-201 (West) (providing for emancipation by military service); CAL. FAM. CODE ANN. § 7002 (West) (providing for emancipation of minors who are "on active duty" with the U.S. Armed Forces).

can enter into enforceable contracts to secure necessaries such as food and shelter.[11] What might be the policy justification for this doctrine?

F. Necessaries defined. In determining which purposes count as necessaries, courts consider the circumstances of each individual case.[12] For example, leasing an apartment was held not be a necessary where minor had the opportunity to live with her parents.[13]

G. Statutory exemptions. Many states have enacted statutory rules exempting certain types of contracts from the infancy doctrine. Examples include statutes governing employment contracts with minors,[14] statutes allowing minors to take on loans for educational purposes,[15] and statutes governing the liability of minors for the costs of housing and utilities.[16]

8. Lack of uniformity. As *Dodson* and the explanations in the above notes show, the level of protection granted to minors varies substantially across states. What do you think explains this lack of uniformity?

---

11. E.g., Douglass v. Pflueger Hawaii, Inc., 135 P.3d 129, 135 (Haw. 2006), as corrected (May 30, 2006); Creech ex rel. Creech v. Melnik, 556 S.E.2d 587, 591 (N.C. App. 2001); Yale Diagnostic Radiology v. Est. of Harun Fountain, 838 A.2d 179, 182 (Conn. 2004); Young v. Weaver, 883 So. 2d 234, 239 (Ala. Civ. App. 2003).

12. See, e.g., Yale Diagnostic Radiology v. Est. of Harun Fountain, 838 A.2d 179, 182 (Conn. 2004) (holding that medical services are necessaries); Adamowski v. Curtiss-Wright Flying Serv., 15 N.E.2d 467, 468 (Mass. 1938) (holding that aviation instruction is not covered by the necessaries doctrine); Ex parte Odem, 537 So. 2d 919, 920 (Ala. 1988) (holding that under Alabama law, hospital cannot invoke necessaries doctrine to recover attorneys' fees incurred to enforce minor's hospital bill); Zelnick v. Adams, 561 S.E.2d 711, 716 (Va. 2002) (holding that attorneys' services provided to an infant can be covered by the necessaries doctrine if there was a need for them).

13. Young v. Weaver, 883 So. 2d 234, 239 (Ala. Civ. App. 2003).

14. HAW. REV. STAT. ANN. § 390-2 (Lexis) (governing the conditions under which minors can be employed).

15. See, e.g., A.R.S. § 44-140.01 (allowing minors of at least sixteen years of age to take on educational loans).

16. E.g., OR. REV. STAT. ANN. § 109.697 (West) (governing the conditions under which minors can be held liable for housing and utility costs).

CHAPTER 13
MISTAKE

I. Introduction

A party to a contract may try to get out of the contract by arguing that she was mistaken regarding some fact or other. However, in the absence of fraud, such mistakes rarely allow a party to avoid the contract. In the following sections, we will discuss the relevant rules. First, we will define some of the relevant legal terms.

II. Mistake

A mistake is a "belief that is not in accord with the facts."[1] To invoke the mistake doctrine, the party must have held the mistaken belief at the time the contract was formed.[2]

> **Example.** Alpha enters into a contract under which she has to paint Beta's house in exchange for $1000. At the time that the parties enter into the

---

1. E.g., Pet. of Barney, 710 A.2d 408, 411 (N.H. 1998); Har-Mar Collisions, Inc. v. Scottsdale Ins. Co., 212 So. 3d 892, 901 (Ala. 2016); Midland Mut. Life Ins. v. Robison, No. 185868, 1997 WL 33353689, at *2 (Mich. App. Feb. 21, 1997); Restatement (Second) of Contracts § 151.
2. E.g., Associated Petroleum Products, Inc. v. N.W. Cascade, Inc., 203 P.3d 1077, 1082 n.5 (Wash. App. Div. 2 2009); Consol. Rail Corp. v. Ferro Corp., No. CV 03-717, 2005 WL 8176015, at *4 (D.N.J. Apr. 14, 2005); Denaxas v. Sandstone Ct. of Bellevue, L.L.C., 63 P.3d 125, 131 (Wash. 2003).

contract, Alpha believes that Beta's house has an area of 1900 square feet. However, the house has 5000 square feet. In this case, Alpha is mistaken within the meaning of the mistake doctrine.

Moreover, the mistake must be based on facts that existed at the time of contract formation.[3] In other words, if, at the time the contract is formed, a party believes that a particular event will occur in the future, and if that belief turns out to be wrong, the party is not mistaken within the meaning of the mistake doctrine. In this scenario, the party's belief does not relate to facts in existence when the contract was formed but rather to events that occurred or did not occur after the contract's formation.

Example. On January 1, Alpha enters into a contract with Beta, under which Alpha has to paint Beta's house between June 1 and June 30 in exchange for $1000. At the time of contract formation, Alpha believes that it will not rain in June. However, it rains without interruption from June 1 to June 30. Alpha's erroneous belief regarding the weather does not constitute a mistake within the meaning of the mistake doctrine since it relates to a future fact rather than a fact existing when the contract was made.

III. Bilateral v. Unilateral Mistakes

The rules governing the relevance of mistakes depend, in part, on whether the mistake was mutual or unilateral. "Mutual" mistakes, or "bilateral" mistakes, are mistakes shared by both parties, whereas mistakes are "unilateral" if only one party held the relevant erroneous belief at the time of the making of the contract.

A. Bilateral Mistakes

Mutual mistakes are also known as "bilateral mistakes." Bilateral mistakes allow the parties to avoid the contract if a substantial number of requirements are met.

---

3. E.g., Midland Mut. Life Ins. v. Robison, No. 185868, 1997 WL 33353689, at *2 (Mich. App. Feb. 21, 1997); U.S. v. Heatley, 39 F. Supp. 2d 287, 309 (S.D.N.Y. 1998); Hicks v. Sparks, 89 A.3d 476 (Del. 2014); Ryan v. Ryan, 640 S.E.2d 64, 69 (W. Va. 2006).

First, the bilateral mistake must relate to a basic assumption on which the contract was made.[4] This requirement is important because it excludes various common erroneous beliefs that we do not think should allow a party to escape their contractual obligations. For example, mistakes regarding the parties' financial situation do not constitute mistakes regarding a basic assumption.[5] The same is true for mistakes about market conditions.[6]

Second, the mistake must have a material impact on the parties' bargain.[7] Minor burdens will not suffice.

Third, only the party whom the mistake affects adversely can avoid the contract.[8]

> **Example.** Alpha sells Beta a parcel of land, which both parties believed to have a size of 1.2 acres, while, in fact, it only measured 0.9 acres. In this case, both parties are mistaken regarding a fact existing at the time of the contract (the property's size). However, only Beta is adversely affected by the mistake, and therefore only Beta would be able to avoid the contract.

Fourth, even the adversely affected party cannot avoid the contract if she bears the risk of the mistake.[9]

If these four requirements are met, the contract can generally be avoid-

---

4. Nichols v. City Of Evansdale, 687 N.W.2d 562, 571 (Iowa 2004); Denaxas v. Sandstone Ct. of Bellevue, L.L.C., 63 P.3d 125, 131 (Wash. 2003); Restatement (Second) of Contracts § 152.
5. Step Plan Services, Inc. v. Koresko, 12 A.3d 401, 412 (Pa. Super. 2010); Homeland Energy Sols., LLC v. Retterath, 938 N.W.2d 664, 703 (Iowa 2020); Restatement (Second) of Contracts § 152 cmt. b.
6. Homeland Energy Sols., LLC v. Retterath, 938 N.W.2d 664, 703 (Iowa 2020); Restatement (Second) of Contracts § 152 cmt. b. See Ryan v. Ryan, 640 S.E.2d 64, 69 (W. Va. 2006) (holding that basic assumption "does not include the continuation of existing market conditions").
7. Nichols v. City Of Evansdale, 687 N.W.2d 562, 571 (Iowa 2004); State v. Robinson, 638 N.W.2d 564, 574 (Wis. 2002), abrogated by State v. Kelty, 716 N.W.2d 886 (Wis. 2006); Denaxas v. Sandstone Ct. of Bellevue, L.L.C., 63 P.3d 125, 131 (Wash. 2003); Duclersaint v. Fed. Nat. Mortg. Ass'n, 696 N.E.2d 536, 539 n.4 (Mass. 1998); Restatement (Second) of Contracts § 152.
8. Nichols v. City Of Evansdale, 687 N.W.2d 562, 571 (Iowa 2004); State v. Robinson, 638 N.W.2d 564, 574 (Wis. 2002), abrogated by State v. Kelty, 716 N.W.2d 886 (Wis. 2006); State, Dept. of Human Services ex rel. Palmer v. Unisys Corp., 637 N.W.2d 142, 150 (Iowa 2001); EBSCO Industries, Inc. v. Royal Ins. Co. of Am., 775 So. 2d 128, 131 (Ala. 2000); Duclersaint v. Fed. Nat. Mortg. Ass'n, 696 N.E.2d 536, 539 n.4 (Mass. 1998); Restatement (Second) of Contracts § 152.
9. Nichols v. City Of Evansdale, 687 N.W.2d 562, 571 (Iowa 2004); State v. Robinson, 638 N.W.2d 564, 574 (Wis. 2002), abrogated by State v. Kelty, 716 N.W.2d 886 (Wis. 2006); Denaxas v. Sandstone Ct. of Bellevue, L.L.C., 63 P.3d 125, 131 (Wash. 2003); Land Baron Inv. v. Bonnie Springs Fam. LP, 356 P.3d 511, 517 (Nev. 2015); State, Dept. of Human Services ex rel. Palmer v. Unisys Corp., 637 N.W.2d 142, 150 (Iowa 2001); Duclersaint v. Fed. Nat. Mortg. Ass'n, 696 N.E.2d 536, 539 n.4 (Mass. 1998); Restatement (Second) of Contracts § 152.

[10] There is no requirement that the other party is to blame for the mistake or that the contract's enforcement would be unconscionable.

B. Unilateral Mistakes

For a unilateral mistake to allow the mistaken party to avoid the contract, all the elements required for the mutual mistake doctrine must be satisfied.[11] In addition, though, one of two additional requirements must be satisfied.

First, a unilateral mistake will allow the mistaken party to avoid the contract if, in light of the mistake, it would be unconscionable to enforce the contract.[12]

Second, and alternatively, a unilateral mistake will allow the mistaken party to avoid the contract if the other party caused or should have recognized the mistake.[13]

IV. Risk Allocation

Neither unilateral nor bilateral mistakes allow the mistaken party to avoid the contract if that party bears the risk of the mistake. As a general rule, the appropriate allocation of risk depends on what is reasonable given the circumstances of the individual case.[14] However, two particular risk allocation scenarios are, at least in principle, generally recognized.

---

10. Nichols v. City Of Evansdale, 687 N.W.2d 562, 571 (Iowa 2004); State v. Robinson, 638 N.W.2d 564, 574 (Wis. 2002), abrogated by State v. Kelty, 716 N.W.2d 886 (Wis. 2006); State, Dept. of Human Services ex rel. Palmer v. Unisys Corp., 637 N.W.2d 142, 150 (Iowa 2001); Duclersaint v. Fed. Nat. Mortg. Ass'n, 696 N.E.2d 536, 539 n.4 (Mass. 1998); Restatement (Second) of Contracts § 152.

11. DSP Venture Group, Inc. v. Allen, 830 A.2d 850, 853 (D.C. App. 2003) (listing the various requirements); Flippo Const. Co., Inc. v. Mike Parks Diving Corp., 531 A.2d 263, 272 (D.C. App. 1987) (listing the relevant factors); Restatement (Second) of Contracts § 152 (listing the various requirements); AIG Hawaii Ins. Co., Inc. v. Bateman, 923 P.2d 395, 399 (Haw. 1996), amended on reconsideration in part sub nom. AIG Hawai'i Ins. Co., Inc. v. Bateman, 925 P.2d 373 (Haw. 1996)

12. Flippo Const. Co., Inc. v. Mike Parks Diving Corp., 531 A.2d 263, 272 (D.C. App. 1987); AIG Hawaii Ins. Co., Inc. v. Bateman, 923 P.2d 395, 399 (Haw. 1996), amended on reconsideration in part sub nom. AIG Hawai'i Ins. Co., Inc. v. Bateman, 925 P.2d 373 (Haw. 1996); Restatement (Second) of Contracts § 153.

13. Flippo Const. Co., Inc. v. Mike Parks Diving Corp., 531 A.2d 263, 272 (D.C. App. 1987); AIG Hawaii Ins. Co., Inc. v. Bateman, 923 P.2d 395, 399 (Haw. 1996), amended on reconsideration in part sub nom. AIG Hawai'i Ins. Co., Inc. v. Bateman, 925 P.2d 373 (Haw. 1996); Restatement (Second) of Contracts § 153.

14. Flippo Const. Co., Inc. v. Mike Parks Diving Corp., 531 A.2d 263, 272 (D.C. App. 1987); AIG

First, the contract itself may allocate the risk to one of the parties.[15]

Second, a party bears the risk of the mistake if they were aware of their limited knowledge regarding the pertinent facts but chose to enter into the contract anyway. This scenario is often referred to as conscious ignorance.[16]

ACA Galleries Inc. v. Kinney

United States District Court, S.D. New York, 928 F.Supp.2d 699 (2013)

CEDARBAUM, DISTRICT JUDGE

ACA Galleries, Inc. ("ACA"), a New York corporation, sues Joseph Kinney, a citizen of North Carolina, for selling it a forged Milton Avery painting. . . . ACA seeks to recover the $200,000 that it paid for the painting. . . . [Both parties have moved for summary judgment.]. For the reasons that follow, ACA's motion is denied, and Kinney's motion is granted.

FACTS

The following facts are undisputed. In March of 2007, Kinney contacted ACA via email and informed it that he was selling a Milton Avery oil painting, entitled "Summer Table, Gloucester." After some negotiation, Kinney shipped the painting from North Carolina to a warehouse in New York to exhibit the work and allow ACA, and any other prospective buyer, to inspect it. Jeffrey Bergen, the president and chief operating officer of ACA, did inspect the

---

Hawaii Ins. Co., Inc. v. Bateman, 923 P.2d 395, 399 (Haw. 1996), amended on reconsideration in part sub nom. AIG Hawai'i Ins. Co., Inc. v. Bateman, 925 P.2d 373 (Haw. 1996); Restatement (Second) of Contracts § 154. Cf. Handle Const. Co., Inc. v. Norcon, Inc., 264 P.3d 367, 372 (Alaska 2011) (holding that "a court has 'broad discretion in determining when to deny relief to a mistaken contracting party under the theory that a party bore the risk of the mistake.'") (internal citation omitted).

15. Wasser & Winters Co. v. Ritchie Bros. Auctioneers (Am.), Inc., 185 P.3d 73, 78 (Alaska 2008); Flippo Const. Co., Inc. v. Mike Parks Diving Corp., 531 A.2d 263, 272 (D.C. App. 1987); Land Baron Inv. v. Bonnie Springs Fam. LP, 356 P.3d 511, 517 (Nev. 2015); Kentera v. Fremont Inv. & Loan, No. CV-10-8259-PCT-SMM, 2014 WL 2884143, at *2 (D. Ariz. June 25, 2014); Restatement (Second) of Contracts § 154.

16. DSP Venture Group, Inc. v. Allen, 830 A.2d 850, 853 (D.C. App. 2003); Kendrick v. Barker, 15 P.3d 734, 740 (Wyo. 2001); Handle Const. Co., Inc. v. Norcon, Inc., 264 P.3d 367, 372 (Alaska 2011); Wasser & Winters Co. v. Ritchie Bros. Auctioneers (Am.), Inc., 185 P.3d 73, 78 (Alaska 2008); Flippo Const. Co., Inc. v. Mike Parks Diving Corp., 531 A.2d 263, 272 (D.C. App. 1987); Knudsen v. Jensen, 521 N.W.2d 415, 419 (S.D. 1994); Kentera v. Fremont Inv. & Loan, No. CV-10-8259-PCT-SMM, 2014 WL 2884143, at *2 (D. Ariz. June 25, 2014); Restatement (Second) of Contracts § 154.

painting and determined it was a genuine Milton Avery work. The parties agreed on a purchase price of $200,000. The bill of sale describes the painting as "Milton Avery Oil on Canvas."

Shortly after ACA wired the purchase price to Kinney and Kinney released the painting to ACA, ACA had the painting examined by the Milton and Sally Avery Arts Foundation (the "Avery Foundation"). The Avery Foundation determined that the painting was not authentic. Bergen informed Kinney of this determination and demanded return of the purchase price. Kinney initially promised that he would refund ACA's money, but never did.

DISCUSSION

Summary judgment should be granted "if the movant shows that there is no genuine dispute as to any material fact and the movant is entitled to judgment as a matter of law." Fed.R.Civ.P. 56(a). A genuine dispute as to a material fact exists when the evidence is such that a reasonable finder of fact could return a verdict for the non-moving party. Anderson v. Liberty Lobby, Inc., 477 U.S. 242, 248, 106 S.Ct. 2505, 2510, 91 L.Ed.2d 202 (1986). In deciding whether a genuine dispute exists, a court must "construe the facts in the light most favorable to the non-moving party and must resolve all ambiguities and draw all reasonable inferences against the movant." Dallas Aerospace, Inc. v. CIS Air Corp., 352 F.3d 775, 780 (2d Cir.2003).

I. Contract Claim

ACA argues that it is entitled to rescission of the contract under the doctrine of mutual mistake, namely that both parties were mistaken as to the authenticity of the painting. There are disputed issues of fact regarding Kinney's knowledge of the Avery painting's authenticity, but in order to pursue rescission by mutual mistake, ACA states that it assumes Kinney was unaware that the painting was inauthentic. Whether or not an issue of fact exists with respect to Kinney's knowledge, summary judgment must be granted for Kinney and against ACA on the contract claim because the doctrine of mutual mistake cannot be invoked by ACA to avoid the consequences of its negligent behavior in failing to authenticate the painting, a risk that ACA bore.

A mutual mistake under New York law means that both parties "shared the same erroneous belief as to a material fact, and their acts did not in fact accomplish their mutual intent." Allen v. WestPoint–Pepperell, Inc., 945 F.2d 40, 46 (2d Cir.1991). . . . In order to obtain rescission based on mutual mistake, ACA must show "that the mistake in question is mutual, substantial, material and exists at the time the contract is entered." Rodriguez v. Mower, 56 A.D.3d 857, 858, 866 N.Y.S.2d 815 (3d Dep't 2008).

However, the doctrine of mutual mistake "may not be invoked by a party to avoid the consequences of its own negligence." P.K. Dev., Inc. v. Elvem Dev. Corp., 226 A.D.2d 200, 201, 640 N.Y.S.2d 558 (1st Dep't 1996). Mutual mistake is further limited if the party wishing to invoke the doctrine bears the risk of the mistake because he was aware of his limited knowledge but acted anyway. Under § 154 of the Restatement (Second) of Contracts, a party bears the risk of a mistake when "he is aware, at the time the contract is made, that he has only limited knowledge with respect to the facts to which the mistake relates but treats his limited knowledge as sufficient." Koam Produce, Inc. v. DiMare Homestead, Inc., 329 F.3d 123, 127–28 (2d Cir.2003) (quoting Restatement (Second) of Contracts § 154 (1981)). "Contract avoidance on the grounds of mutual mistake is not permitted just because one party is disappointed in the hope that the facts accord with his wishes." In re Schenck Tours, Inc., 69 B.R. 906, 914 (Bankr.E.D.N.Y.1987). . . . In such situations, it is sometimes said that in a sense there is no mistake at all, but rather "conscious ignorance." Restatement (Second) of Contracts § 154 cmt. c (1981).

Courts have found that the failure to investigate constitutes negligence sufficient to bar the application of the mutual mistake doctrine. For example, in P.K. Development, the First Department denied rescission based on mutual mistake where the corporate seller of a residential cooperative unit failed to investigate its own property before sale and thus failed to discover that the unit had been unoccupied, which made it more valuable. 226 A.D.2d at 201–02, 640 N.Y.S.2d 558. The uniqueness of the subject of the transaction is considered when assessing the risk a party bears. For example, when a civil engineering company turned out not to have the earning potential that it had been presumed to have before the defendant agreed to purchase it, the Second Circuit found no mutual mistake. See Leasco Corp. v. Taussig, 473 F.2d 777, 781 (2d Cir.1972). The court reasoned that a civil engineering business is "personalized, highly technical, and extremely risky" and that "neither party could safely assume that the projected earnings would be realized." Id.

It is undisputed that Kinney gave ACA access to the painting at a New York City storage facility before the purchase. It is also undisputed that Bergen inspected the painting and believed it to be authentic, but ACA waited until after the purchase to have the painting examined by the Avery Foundation. ACA's failure to take advantage of its opportunity to consult the Avery

Foundation before buying the painting precludes it from claiming mutual mistake.

II. FRAUD CLAIMS

Although ACA moves for summary judgment only on its contract claim, Kinney moves for summary judgment dismissing all of ACA's claims, including those sounding in fraud. There are fiercely disputed issues of fact as to whether Kinney knew that the Avery painting was a forgery. However, Kinney's motion for summary judgment on ACA's fraud claims must be granted because, as a matter of New York law, ACA's reliance on any representations made by Kinney was unreasonable and thus ACA's fraud claims fail. Even if a genuine dispute of fact exists regarding some fraud elements, plaintiff cannot establish reasonable reliance on the authenticity of the painting. Reasonable reliance is an essential element of fraud. . . .

Fraud under New York law requires "(1) defendant's knowing misrepresentation of a material fact, (2) made with intent to deceive, (3) plaintiff's reasonable reliance, and (4) damages." Perrin & Nissen Ltd. v. SAS Group Inc., No. 06 Civ. 13089(MGC), 2009 WL 855693, at *6 (S.D.N.Y. Mar. 27, 2009) . . . .

The oft-quoted definition of reasonable or justifiable reliance is that "if the facts represented are not matters peculiarly within the party's knowledge, and the other party has the means available to him of knowing, by the exercise of ordinary intelligence, the truth or the real quality of the subject of the representation, he must make use of those means, or he will not be heard to complain that he was induced to enter into the transaction by misrepresentations." Danann Realty Corp. v. Harris, 5 N.Y.2d 317, 322, 184 N.Y.S.2d 599, 157 N.E.2d 597 (1959) (internal quotations omitted). As a matter of law, "a sophisticated plaintiff cannot establish that it entered into an arm's length transaction in justifiable reliance on alleged misrepresentations if that plaintiff failed to make use of the means of verification that were available to it." HSH Nordbank AG v. UBS AG, 95 A.D.3d 185, 194–95, 941 N.Y.S.2d 59 (1st Dep't 2012) (internal quotations omitted).

ACA cannot establish justifiable reliance because it had the opportunity to fully investigate the authenticity of the painting but failed to do so. Although Bergen's sworn affidavit states that Kinney advised him that the painting could not be removed from storage before purchase, there is no allegation or evidence that Kinney did not permit inspection by the Avery Foundation, or any other expert, at the warehouse. Kinney has submitted a copy of an email from an employee at the Avery Foundation sent to him on April 3,

2007—the day before ACA was sent a proposed bill of sale for the painting—confirming that Sean Avery Cavanaugh, vice president of the Avery Foundation, was available to see the painting for authentication. ACA argues that this email indicates Kinney had concerns about the painting's authenticity. But summary judgment can nonetheless be granted because ACA's reliance was not justifiable. It remains undisputed that ACA itself did not have the painting authenticated prior to purchase, while the email submitted by Kinney indicates that doing so would have been feasible.

That ACA failed to avail itself of the opportunity to have the painting inspected by the Avery Foundation or another expert prior to purchase, and instead relied only on Bergen's inspection, was not reasonable. ACA is in the business of buying and selling art. Such a business must be cognizant of forgery of the works of well-known artists like Avery.

Courts have found that failure to investigate bars a finding of reasonable reliance. For example, in Stuart Silver, plaintiffs with real estate investment experience invested in a condominium project that ultimately failed. 245 A.D.2d at 96–97, 665 N.Y.S.2d 415. They alleged fraud based on misrepresentations in the offering materials and oral promises that they would double their investment and receive a guaranteed return. Id. at 98, 665 N.Y.S.2d 415. The court held that whether or not the promises had been made, plaintiffs were "relatively sophisticated investors who should have understood the risks of investing in a real estate venture" without conducting their own due diligence investigation or consulting lawyers and accountants. Id. at 99, 665 N.Y.S.2d 415. It was unreasonable, the court found, to rely on the alleged oral promises by defendants without conducting further investigation. The plaintiffs never visited the site, investigated defendant's investment history, or requested supporting documentation for financial projections. Id. at 97, 99, 665 N.Y.S.2d 415.

Even if some level of investigation is done, a failure to investigate fully can bar a finding of reasonable reliance. For example, in Peach Parking Corp. v. 346 W. 40th St., LLC, Hertz Corp., and Kinney System Inc., Hertz, a car rental company, was aware of potential structural issues in a parking lot but did not undertake a detailed study; instead, it retained an architectural firm to perform only a "cursory observation" of the property. 42 A.D.3d 82, 84–85, 835 N.Y.S.2d 172 (1st Dep't 2007). The court refused to allow Hertz to amend its pleadings to add fraud claims because Hertz had not justifiably relied on any promises about the building's condition; rather, Hertz declined to have structural engineers inspect the property when, had it undergone this "more rigorous inspection, it would have discovered the full extent of the problems." Id. at 87, 835 N.Y.S.2d 172.

When an art gallery has access to information regarding a painting's authenticity, but fails to pursue the information, it cannot reasonably rely on defendant's representations or omissions regarding the painting. In a federal case applying New York law, plaintiff's fraud claim was dismissed because, inter alia, the allegations failed to establish that the plaintiff had justifiably relied on defendant Sotheby's representation that a painting, later found to be inauthentic, would be accompanied at sale by a letter from an expert "discussing" the painting. Foxley v. Sotheby's Inc., 893 F.Supp. 1224, 1229 (S.D.N.Y.1995). The court held that plaintiff's access—his ability to request the letter himself and see what it said about the painting's authenticity—negated justifiable reliance. Id. Although the plaintiff alleged that he lacked sophistication and familiarity with the particular artistic style of the painting, the court reasoned that plaintiff was "a sophisticated purchaser of art at auction. He certainly knew how to demand a letter described in an auction catalog," as he successfully did several years after he had already purchased the painting. Id. It was only then, years later, that plaintiff discovered that the expert's letter was based not on the original art but instead on a photograph of the piece, and thus the expert's letter did not properly authenticate his purchase. The letter's contents were "readily available," and thus neither Sotheby's failure to deliver the letter nor Sotheby's representations about the letter itself could be actionable. Id.

The very fact that ACA felt the need to seek authentication by the Avery Foundation after the purchase indicates that it knew how to do so prior to the purchase. ACA's decision to wait is not protected under New York law.

For the foregoing reasons, ACA's motion for partial summary judgment is denied. Kinney's motion for summary judgment dismissing all of ACA's claims is granted.

SO ORDERED.

NOTES AND QUESTIONS

A. Pacta sunt servanda. Parties are bound to the contract that they have formed. This principle is encapsulated in the Latin maxim "pacta sunt servanda," or "agreements must be kept." An exception to this norm is the mistake doctrine, which, on occasion, permits a party to avoid a contract.

B. Conscious ignorance. If a party knows that they have limited knowledge regarding pertinent facts but enters into the contract anyway, that party bears the risk of their mistake.[17] Some courts have even embraced the more far-reaching principle that a party cannot avoid a contract based on mistake if the mistake is due to their own negligence.[18] Other courts have taken the more limited position that only gross negligence regarding the mistake is per se enough to exclude the invocation of the mistake doctrine.[19] How would you describe the court's approach in *ACA Galleries Inc. v. Kinney*?

C. Misrepresentation. The Restatement (Second) of Contracts deals with questions of fraudulent and non-fraudulent misrepresentation in sections 159 et seq. Section 164 of the Restatement (Second) of Contracts states that a fraudulent misrepresentation will allow the victim to avoid the contract only if victim was justified in relying on the misrepresentation. However, section 172 of the Restatement (Second) of Contracts clarifies that the victim's failure to know or discover the pertinent facts does not make the victim's reliance unjustified unless the victim's behavior demonstrates a lack of good faith. The official comments to section 172 differentiate further. On the one hand, the victim is generally allowed to rely on the other party's assertions, and even the failure to make a reasonable investigation does not make their reliance unjustified.[20] On the other hand, the victim is not protected if a cursory investigation would have revealed the truth.[21] Would an application of these criteria have led to a different outcome in the case at hand?

---

17. Restatement (Second) of Contracts § 154(b).
18. See, e.g., Webb v. Webb, 301 S.E.2d 570, 576 (W. Va. 1983) (holding that "a party may not avoid the legal consequences on the ground of mistake, even a mistake of fact, where such mistake is the result of the negligence of the complaining party"); Motorists Mut. Ins. Co. v. Columbus Fin., Inc., 861 N.E.2d 605, 610 (Ohio App. 10th Dist. 2006) (noting that "the Ohio Supreme Court has recognized the doctrine of mutual mistake as a ground for rescission only where the complainant is not negligent in failing to discover the mistake").
19. See, e.g., Kutsche v. Ford, 192 N.W. 714, 716 (Mich. 1923) (holding that gross negligence precludes invocation of the mistake doctrine).
20. Restatement (Second) of Contracts § 172 ct. b.
21. Id.

CHAPTER 14
DURESS

Coburn v. Rhodig

Court of Appeals of Arizona, Division 1, 2019 WL 1530298 (2019)

MORSE, JUDGE

Michael Rhodig ("Husband") appeals from the spousal maintenance arrearage order in favor of Laurin Coburn ("Wife"). For the reasons stated below, we affirm the order.

FACTUAL AND PROCEDURAL HISTORY

The parties divorced in 2010. The consent decree required Husband to pay non-modifiable spousal maintenance of $ 3000 per month for 60 months starting December 2009. Husband stopped paying Wife in August 2010. After exchanging several emails in late 2010 in which Husband threatened to leave the state or commit suicide if Wife enforced the decree in court, the parties agreed that Husband would pay Wife a $ 5000 lump sum payment plus $ 1000 per month for twelve months, with the "final payment" due December 15, 2011. Wife agreed to "waive any other unpaid support owed her by [Husband]."

Husband made all payments due under the agreement. In December 2014, Wife filed a petition to enforce the spousal maintenance arrearages she claimed were due under the consent decree. According to Wife, she signed the agreement under duress. Husband argued the agreement was enforceable and supported the equitable defenses of wavier, estoppel, and laches.

... [T]he superior court found the agreement invalid because Wife signed it under duress. The court also rejected Husband's equitable defenses and reinstated the prior judgment against Husband for $ 136,000 in spousal maintenance arrearages plus $ 37,259.39 in interest. Husband filed a timely notice of appeal from the judgment....

DISCUSSION

... To constitute duress, an act or threat must be wrongful and preclude a party from exercising his or her free will and judgment.... This definition is based on the Restatement of Contracts § 492 (1932).... The Restatement (Second) of Contracts § 175 (1981) updated this definition due to its "vagueness and impracticability," providing that a contract is voidable if a party's "assent is induced by an improper threat by the other party that leaves the victim no reasonable alternative." See Restatement (Second) of Contracts § 175 cmt. b and § 175(1). The Restatement (Second) of Contracts § 176 details what constitutes an improper threat.

Under either definition of duress, the evidence supports the conclusion that Wife entered into the agreement under duress. The superior court found economic duress because Husband's failure to make the support payments created Wife's financial distress. The court relied on Inter-Tel, 195 Ariz. at 117-18, ¶¶ 37-40, which held that "duress does not exist merely because one party takes advantage of the financial difficulty of the other," but the court may find duress where one party contributed to or caused the financial difficulty of the other. The conduct that caused Wife's financial distress must have been improper or unfair. See USLife Title Co., 152 Ariz. at 357 ("Unless wrongful, unlawful or unconscionable pressure is applied there is no business compulsion amounting to duress ....") (quoting Frank Culver Elec., Inc. v. Jorgenson, 136 Ariz. 76, 78 (App. 1983)). This is consistent with Restatement (Second) of Contracts § 176(2)(b), which provides, "A threat is improper if the resulting exchange is not on fair terms, and ... the effectiveness of the threat in inducing the manifestations of assent is significantly increased by prior unfair dealing by the party making the threat." This section addresses "cases in which the party making the threat has by unfair dealing achieved an advantage over the recipient that makes his threat unusually effective." See Restatement (Second) of Contracts § 176 cmt. f (emphasis added).

Wife acknowledged that Husband was unable to pay the amounts owed under the consent decree. Thus, the evidence does not support the conclusion that Husband improperly or unfairly caused Wife's financial distress. Husband's failure to pay support was due to his own financial difficulties, not an improper motive. As such, it does not constitute a wrongful or improper threat.

In contrast, Husband's threats to leave the state or commit suicide if Wife enforced the decree in court were wrongful and improper. A threat to commit suicide, while not a crime, is a wrongful threat of physical violence. See Restatement (Second) of Contracts § 176(1)(a) and cmt. b (stating threat of physical violence need not be directed at the recipient of the threat or his relative "if the threat in fact induces the recipient to manifest his assent"). Additionally, Husband's threat to ensure Wife would not receive any support payments if she went to court was improper because it violated his court-ordered obligation to pay support. See Restatement (Second) of Contracts § 176(1)(a) and cmt. b; see also A.R.S. § 12-864 (defining contempt of court as the failure to obey court order or judgment). Such threats constitute highly "manipulative conduct during the bargaining stage" and are, therefore, improper. See Restatement (Second) of Contracts § 176 cmt. f.

The record also supports the conclusion that Husband's threats induced Wife to forego the substantial amount of spousal maintenance to which she was otherwise entitled, resulting in an unfair exchange. See Restatement (Second) of Contracts § 176(2)(b) and cmt. f. Wife signed the agreement because she feared Husband would harm himself based on his threats. Although Husband claimed his suicide threats were not serious, Wife believed him. Wife also signed the agreement because Husband told her he was not going to pay her anything unless she signed. In fact, Husband did not pay Wife anything until after she agreed to the modification.

Husband contends that Wife's assent was not a result of his threats because two months passed between his threats in October and the date Wife signed the agreement in December. We disagree. Less than three weeks passed between when Husband last threatened to leave the state "or worse" and when Wife signed the agreement. Wife's response to the threats was to try and reach an agreement, thus supporting her claim that she took his threats seriously.

In addition to an improper threat, duress requires the absence of a reasonable alternative. See Inter-Tel, 195 Ariz. at 118-19, ¶ 42 (concluding no reasonable alternative available where plaintiff could not find another lender due to defendant bank's conduct); Sharp v. Sharp, 179 Ariz. 205, 209 (App. 1994) (rejecting claim that wife signed agreement under duress because she could have called her attorney a second time or mailed a letter when her attorney did not accept her collect call), superseded by rule on other grounds as recognized in Hutki v. Hutki, 244 Ariz. 39, 43, ¶ 18 (App. 2018); Pleasants v. Home Fed. Sav. & Loan Ass'n, 116 Ariz. 319, 321 (App. 1977) (finding no duress where reasonable alternative was available to plaintiffs); see also Restatement (Second) of Contracts § 175.

Wife contends that she had no reasonable alternative in light of Husband's threats to leave the state or commit suicide. The superior court did not expressly state that Wife had no reasonable alternative, but by finding duress, we presume the court made this finding. See Rinegar v. Rinegar, 231 Ariz. 85, 90, ¶ 20 (App. 2012) (presuming superior court found every fact necessary to support its ruling because parties did not request written findings of fact or conclusions of law).

Husband argues that Wife could have sought relief in the courts, as she did in 2014. Wife contends this was not a reasonable alternative because Husband threatened to leave the state or commit suicide if she took him to court. Asserting one's rights in court is generally a reasonable alternative. See generally, Republic Nat'l Life Ins. Co., 137 Ariz. at 65. "This alternative may not, however, be reasonable if the threat involves, for instance ... the use of oppressive tactics, or the possibility of emotional consequences." Restatement (Second) of Contracts § 175 cmt. b. "The standard is a practical one under which account must be taken of the exigencies in which victim finds himself ...." Id.

Husband's threats constitute "oppressive tactics" with "emotional consequences" to Wife if he followed through. Wife believed Husband's threats were serious: she contacted Husband's son after receiving Husband's threats; both she and Husband's son attempted to contact Husband for several days after the threat was made; and, after Wife contacted security services, security services performed a wellness check at Husband's home. Although Husband claimed he was not serious, nothing in the record suggests that Wife's belief and response were unreasonable. Husband cannot make improper threats, then claim he was not serious after Wife acceded to his threats. See generally Ray v. Mangum, 163 Ariz. 329, 333 (1989) (holding that where conflicting testimony exists, one party's unspoken assumptions and beliefs are not clear evidence that other party agreed). In light of these facts, we cannot find the court erred by finding the agreement was a result of duress and, therefore, not enforceable under Rule 69.3. . . .

We affirm the arrearage judgment. Wife is awarded her costs on appeal upon compliance with Arizona Rule of Civil Appellate Procedure 21.

NOTES AND QUESTIONS

*A. **Duress.*** The law distinguishes two types of duress: duress by physical compulsion and duress by threat.[1] In the case of duress by physical compulsion, there is no manifestation of assent in the legal sense.[2] For example, if the offeror puts a pen in the offeree's hand and then forcibly moves the offeree's hand across the paper to create the appearance of a signature, the offeree has not manifested his assent, and the offer has not been accepted. By contrast, in the case of duress by threat, a contract is created, but the victim has the power to avoid the contract.[3]

B. Duress by threat. According to section 175 of the Restatement (Second) of Contracts, duress by threat comprises three pivotal elements. The first is an improper threat. The second is a causal relationship between the improper threat and the victim's manifestation of assent. The third is the lack of a reasonable alternative for the victim.[4] By contrast, section 492 of the first Restatement of Contracts (1932) focused on whether the threat was wrongful and prevented the victim from exercising their free will. Since the promulgation of the Restatement (Second) of Contracts, courts have tended to favor the improper threat test.[5] However, the free will test also remains in use,[6] and it is

1. Restatement (Second) of Contracts §§ 174, 175.
2. Restatement (Second) of Contracts § 174.
3. Restatement (Second) of Contracts § 175.
4. Restatement (Second) of Contracts § 175.
5. See, e.g. Andreini v. Hultgren, 860 P.2d 916, 921 (Utah 1993) ("We . . . explicitly adopt the legal standards of duress set forth in sections 175 and 176 of the Restatement (Second) of Contracts."); Richards v. Allianz Life Ins. Co. of N.A., 62 P.3d 320, 328 (N.M. App. 2002) (applying the principles set forth in sections 175 and 176 of the Restatement (Second) of Contracts); Osborne v. Howard U. Physicians, Inc., 904 A.2d 335, 339 (D.C. App. 2006) (applying the improper-threat test); Balogh v. Balogh, 332 P.3d 631, 646 (Haw. 2014) ("It is well established that an agreement is voidable due to duress when "a party's manifestation of assent is induced by an improper threat by the other party that leaves the victim no reasonable alternative.").
6. See, e.g., Mullins v. Oates, 179 P.3d 930, 937 (Alaska 2008) (holding that duress requires the threat to preclude the victim from exercising their free will.); Vail/Arrowhead, Inc. v. Dist. Ct. for the Fifth Jud. Dist., Eagle Cnty., 954 P.2d 608, 612 (Colo. 1998) ("A contract is voidable on the grounds of duress if a party's manifestation of assent is induced by an improper threat that leaves

unclear whether the two tests yield divergent outcomes in practice. The essential advantage of the Restatement (Second)'s approach does not lie in superior results but in greater clarity.[7]

*C. **Legitimate and illegitimate threats.*** Many threats are within the bounds of acceptable conduct. For example, an employee is within his rights to threaten to quit unless the employer agrees to a raise. A buyer may threaten to find another seller for future transactions unless the seller improves the quality of their goods. Therefore, not every threat is sufficient for duress. Instead, the threat must be "improper" or "wrongful"—the terminology used in the Restatement (Second) of Contracts and the first Restatement of Contracts respectively.[8]

D. The impropriety of threats. Section 176 of the Restatement (Second) helps determine when a threat is improper. To begin, it is always improper to threaten a person with a crime, tort, or criminal prosecution.[9] Moreover, threatening a party with civil litigation constitutes an improper threat if the threatening party acts in bad faith.[10] Threatening a party with a breach of contract is improper if the threat amounts to a breach of the duty of good faith and fair dealing.[11] Also, a threat is improper if the threatened conduct harms the victim without substantially benefiting the threatening party, and the contract induced by the threat is unfair to the victim.[12] Additionally, threatening another party is improper if the threat relies on prior unfair behavior and the contract induced by the threat is unfair.[13] Finally, any threat is improper if the threatened conduct constitutes "a use of power for illegitimate ends" and if the resulting contract is unfair to the victim.[14]

E. Threats in Coburn. In *Coburn,* the court draws a distinction between the threat not to make divorce payments and the threat of committing suicide.

---

no reasonable alternative"); EverBank v. Marini, 134 A.3d 189, 197 (Vt. 2015) (holding that "[d]uress generally requires a threat that arouses such a fear as to preclude a party from exercising free will and judgment") (internal citation omitted).

7. Indeed, this appears to be its raison d'être. See Restatement (Second) of Contracts § 175 ct. b (justifying the rejection of the free-will test because of its vagueness).

8. Restatement (Second) of Contracts § 175 (focusing on impropriety), Restatement of Contracts (1923) § 492 (focusing on wrongfulness).

9. Restatement (Second) of Contracts § 176 (1) (a) & (b).

10. Restatement (Second) of Contracts § 176 (1) (c).

11. Restatement (Second) of Contracts § 176 (1) (d).

12. Restatement (Second) of Contracts § 176 (2) (a).

13. Restatement (Second) of Contracts § 176 (2) (b).

14. Restatement (Second) of Contracts § 176 (2) (c).

Which, if any, of these threats did the court deem improper, and if so, what were the underlying reasons? Do you concur with the court's assessment?

F. Threats by third parties. The threat need not be made by one of the contracting parties. A threat issued by a third party makes the contract voidable except if the party benefiting from the threat (1) had no reason to know of the threat, (2) acted in good faith, and (3) either gave value or relied on the transaction.[15]

G. Economic duress. The duress doctrine's application is particularly challenging when the victim's distress is financial, a scenario that courts and scholars refer to as "economic duress." According to the prevailing view, for a contract to be voidable based on so-called economic duress, the victim's financial difficulties must have been caused by the threatening party. By contrast, the duress doctrine does not apply if the threatening party merely exploited pre-existing financial difficulties to drive a hard bargain.[16] Even if the victim has shown that the threatening party caused the financial distress, the victim still needs to demonstrate the lack of a reasonable alternative.[17] Generally, if one party threatens to withhold payment, the victim is expected to pursue legal remedies, such as litigation, rather than give in to the threatening party's demand.[18] Moreover, a victim threatened with non-payment may be able to

---

15. Restatement (Second) of Contracts § 175(2).

16. See, e.g., Oregon Bank v. Nautilus Crane & Equip. Corp., 683 P.2d 95, 103 (Or. App. 1984) (holding that a party invoking economic duress must show "financial distress caused by the wrongful acts or threats"); Orix Credit All., Inc. v. Bell Realty, Inc., No. 93 CIV. 4949 (LAP), 1995 WL 505891, at *6 (S.D.N.Y. Aug. 23, 1995) (rejecting the application of the economic duress doctrine under NY law where plaintiff had not caused defendant's financial difficulties); Akbarieh v. Bluestone, No. CIV.A. 93-0451 (JHG), 1994 WL 72406, at *4 (D.D.C. Feb. 15, 1994), aff'd, No. 94-7057, 1994 WL 475005 (D.C. Cir. July 1, 1994) (rejecting economic duress under DC law because financial difficulties were not caused by plaintiff); First Texas Sav. Ass'n of Dallas v. Dicker Ctr., Inc., 631 S.W.2d 179, 185-86 (Tex. App.—Tyler 1982) ("It seems to be a settled principle of law that economic duress may be claimed only when the party against whom it is claimed was responsible for claimant's financial distress."); Ponder v. Lincoln Nat. Sales Corp., 612 So. 2d 1169, 1171 (Ala. 1992) (holding that "merely taking advantage of another's financial difficulty is not duress").

17. E.g., Oregon Bank v. Nautilus Crane & Equip. Corp., 683 P.2d 95, 103 (Or. App. 1984).

18. Cf. Totem Marine Tug & Barge, Inc. v. Alyeska Pipeline Serv. Co., 584 P.2d 15, 22 (Alaska 1978) (noting that "[a]n available legal remedy, such as an action for breach of contract, may provide such an alternative"); Nelson v. Stanley Blacker, Inc., 713 F. Supp. 107, 110 (S.D.N.Y. 1989) ("In order to prevail on a claim of duress, plaintiff must show, inter alia, that he had available no legal remedies to avoid the duress") (internal citation omitted); Davis & Associates, Inc. v. Health Mgt. Services, Inc., 168 F. Supp. 2d 109, 117 (S.D.N.Y. 2001) (rejecting the application of the economic duress doctrine where plaintiff had failed to demonstrate that he was unable to escape his financial distress by bringing a breach of contract action).

secure financing from alternative sources.[19] Consequently, the relevance of the economic duress doctrine is confined to cases where, for various reasons, the victim could not reasonably be expected to seek legal remedies and was unable to secure financing elsewhere, such as due to an imminent threat of insolvency.[20]

H. Unfair Persuasion. Certain individuals are particularly vulnerable to coercion. For example, an elderly or sick person may be so utterly dependent on their caretaker that the latter does not find it difficult to bend the former to their will, even without resorting to threats that meet the threshold for duress. Recognizing this vulnerability, section 177 of the Restatement (Second) of Contracts identifies specific circumstances where unfair persuasion can render a contract voidable.[21]

---

19. Totem Marine Tug & Barge, Inc. v. Alyeska Pipeline Serv. Co., 584 P.2d 15, 22 (Alaska 1978) (noting that "other sources of funds may provide an alternative to succumbing to the coercing party's demands").

20. See, e.g., Totem Marine Tug & Barge, Inc. v. Alyeska Pipeline Serv. Co., 584 P.2d 15, 24 (Alaska 1978) (holding that no reasonable alternative exists where the victim is "faced with impending bankruptcy" and is "unable to meet its pressing debts other than by" succumbing to the threatening party's demands).

21. Restatement (Second) of Contracts § 177.

CHAPTER 15
THE PAROL EVIDENCE RULE

I. Background: Contractual Amendments

After a contract has been formed, the parties are free to amend the contract.[1] An agreement amending a contract is itself a contract. Accordingly, it has to meet the general requirements of mutual assent and consideration.[2]

Question. Alpha and Beta enter into a contract whereby Alpha promises to build a two-story mansion for Beta in exchange for $1,000,000. One week later, Beta decides they would prefer a three-story mansion. The parties, therefore, agree that the mansion will have three stories, and Beta will pay $1,500,000 instead of the originally agreed-upon $1,000,000. Did the original agreement constitute an enforceable contract? How about the amendment?

Answer. The original agreement was an enforceable contract. The parties had reached mutual assent, and Beta's promise to pay $1,000,000 served as consid-

---

1. E.g., Archambo v. Lawyers Title Ins. Corp., 646 N.W.2d 170, 176 (Mich. 2002); Schildkamp v. Feed Commodities Intl., LLC, No. 2016-205, 2016 WL 7369034, at *3 (Vt. Dec. 16, 2016); Foti Fuels, Inc. v. Kurrle Corp., 90 A.3d 885, 895 (Vt. 2013).
2. E.g., Patterson v. Metro. Life Ins. Co., No. 3:16-CV-01189-AKK, 2017 WL 6508581, at *4 (N.D. Ala. Dec. 20, 2017); Sadri v. Realty Exchangers, Inc., 119 Wash. App. 1039 (Wash. App. Div. 2 2003); Foti Fuels, Inc. v. Kurrle Corp., 90 A.3d 885, 895 (Vt. 2013).

for Alpha's promise to build the two-story mansion and vice versa. The amendment also constitutes a contract and, therefore, has to meet the requirements of mutual assent and consideration. Here, the parties reached an agreement. Moreover, the consideration requirement is satisfied since Alpha's obligation was changed from building a two-story mansion to building a three-story mansion, and in exchange, the price to be paid by Beta was changed from $1,000,000 to $1,500,000.

As a general rule, contractual amendments that only change one party's duties are not binding because the consideration requirement is not satisfied. However, as summarized in section 89 of the Restatement (Second) of Contracts, the law recognizes an important exception from this principle. A one-sided promise amending a contract is binding without consideration if neither party has fully performed, the amendment is fair, and the amendment adjusts the contract to unanticipated circumstances.[3]

Question. Alpha and Beta enter into a contract whereby Alpha promises to build a two-story mansion for Beta in exchange for $1,000,000. One week later, Alpha urges Beta to raise the price from $1,000,000 to $1,500,000, and Beta reluctantly agrees. Assume that the applicable common law corresponds exactly to the Restatement (Second) of Contracts. Is the amendment binding?

Answer. For the contractual amendment to be binding, it has to meet the general contract formation requirements of mutual assent and consideration. The parties reached mutual assent. However, Beta's promise to pay an additional $500,000 is not supported by consideration since there was no quid pro quo for this promise. Moreover, section 89 of the Restatement (Second) of Contracts does not apply since Alpha's demand for a price increase was not justified by unanticipated circumstances.

---

3. Restatement (Second) of Contracts Section 89(b). See Zhang v. Eighth Jud. Dist. Ct. of State ex rel. Cnty. of Clark, 103 P.3d 20, 23–24 (Nev. 2004), abrogated by Buzz Stew, LLC v. City of N. Las Vegas, 181 P.3d 670 (Nev. 2008)(embracing the rule in section 89(b) of the Restatement (Second) of Contracts); Roussalis v. Wyoming Med. Ctr., Inc., 4 P.3d 209, 240 (Wyo. 2000)(holding that section 89(b) of the Restatement (Second) of Contracts constitutes "an appropriate and applicable exception to the "pre-existing duty rule"); Wilder v. Cody Country Chamber of Com., 868 P.2d 211, 219 (Wyo. 1994)(holding section 89 of the Restatement (Second) of Contracts to be applicable); Angel v. Murray, 322 A.2d 630, 636 (R.I. 1974)(holding the rule now contained in section 89 (b) of the Restatement (Second) of Contracts to be the "proper" and "applicable" rule of law).

Question. Alpha and Beta enter into a contract whereby Alpha promises to build a two-story mansion for Beta in exchange for $1,000,000. A few weeks later, a hurricane destroys numerous houses in the area, and, as a result, the prices for labor and building materials rise steeply, a development that neither Alpha nor Beta had anticipated at the time of the contract. Alpha, therefore, urges Beta to raise the price from $1,000,000 to $1,500,000, and Beta reluctantly agrees. The change in the contract price reflects the rise in Alpha's construction costs. Assume that the applicable common law corresponds exactly to the Restatement (Second) of Contracts. Is the amendment binding?

Answer. For the contractual amendment to be binding, it has to meet the general contract formation requirements of mutual assent and consideration. The parties reached mutual assent. Beta's promise to pay an additional $500,000 is not supported by consideration since there was no quid-pro-quo for this promise. However, for contractual amendments, section 89 of the Restatement (Second) of Contracts dispenses with the consideration requirement if neither party has fully performed, the amendment adjusts the contract to unanticipated circumstances, and the adjustment is fair. Given the changed prices for labor and construction material, which neither party had anticipated, raising the contract price by $500,000 was fair. Therefore, the amendment is binding despite the lack of consideration.

II. Introduction to the Parol Evidence Rule

Instead of amending a contract, the parties may also decide to commit an existing contractual agreement to writing. There can be many good reasons for putting a contract into writing. For example, a written document can serve as evidence in case of future disagreements. Moreover, if an agreement was reached orally or by correspondence, the parties may want to ensure that they are genuinely on the same page regarding the various aspects of their agreement. However, creating a writing also raises a new problem: what happens if the writing deviates from the original agreement? Can the original agreement still be invoked, or should the court look only to the writing? The so-called parol evidence rule answers this question and related ones. In very simple terms, under the parol evidence rule, once the parties commit their agreement to one or more writings that they intend as the final expression of their agreement, these writings may discharge earlier oral or written versions of their agreement.

A. Integration

The parol evidence rule governs the impact of so-called integrations. An integration consists of one or more writings that the parties intend as a final expression of some or all of their agreement.[4] It is crucial to distinguish an integration from a contractual amendment. In case of a contractual amendment, the parties intend to change an existing contract. In other words, the parties seek to replace an existing contract with a different one. By contrast, an integration aims to commit an existing agreement to writing. This difference is of fundamental significance because integrations and contractual amendments are subject to very different rules. For example, a contractual amendment is a new contract that requires mutual assent and consideration.[5] By contrast, the integration does not create a new contract; it merely documents an existing one. Therefore, in the case of an integration, as long as the promises committed to paper are supported by consideration, the creation of the integration does not require any additional consideration.

> **Example.** Alpha and Beta enter into an oral contract whereby Alpha promises to build a two-story mansion for Beta in exchange for $1,000,000. A week later, Alpha and Beta commit their agreement to writing in order to have a final version of their deal on paper. The writing constitutes an integration, and its creation does not require additional consideration.

> **Example.** Alpha and Beta enter into an oral contract whereby Alpha promises to build a two-story mansion for Beta by January 31 in exchange for $1,000,000. The oral agreement includes a term under which "time is of the essence" regarding Beta's performance. A week later, Alpha and Beta commit

---

4. E.g., J.H. Moneymaker Const., Inc. v. Thurman, No. S-787, 1989 WL 1598336, at *2 (Alaska Feb. 22, 1989); Mitford v. de Lasala, 666 P.2d 1000, 1004 (Alaska 1983); Leo A. Daly Co. v. Omaha-Douglas Pub. Bldg. Commn., 324 N.W.2d 252, 257 (Neb. 1982); Restatement (Second) of Contracts § 209.

5. E.g., Patterson v. Metro. Life Ins. Co., No. 3:16-CV-01189-AKK, 2017 WL 6508581, at *4 (N.D. Ala. Dec. 20, 2017); Sadri v. Realty Exchangers, Inc., 119 Wash. App. 1039 (Wash. App. Div. 2 2003); Foti Fuels, Inc. v. Kurrle Corp., 90 A.3d 885, 895 (Vt. 2013).

their agreement to writing in order to have a final version of their deal on paper. The writing does not mention that time is of the essence. The writing constitutes an integration, and its creation does not require additional consideration. This is true even though the writing diverges from the earlier oral agreement. What distinguishes the integration from a contractual amendment is that the writing was intended as the final expression of the original agreement, not as a new agreement changing the original agreement.

The parties do not have to sign the writing for the writing to qualify as an integration. Instead, it is sufficient that both parties intended the writing to be a final expression as part or all of their agreement.[6]

An integration can either be complete or partial. It is complete if it constitutes a complete and exclusive statement of the parties' agreement. [7] By contrast, any integration that does not amount to a complete and exclusive statement of the parties' agreement is a partial integration.[8]

Example. Alpha and Beta orally agree that Alpha will paint Beta's house for $5,000. The oral agreement includes stipulations regarding the deadline for Alpha's work, the paint type, and the color. Alpha and Beta both sign a document that reads, "Final agreement regarding price: the price that Beta will pay Alpha for painting Beta's house is $5,000, other matters as orally agreed." In this case, the writing is meant as a final expression of part of their deal but not as a complete statement of their agreement. Accordingly, the writing constitutes a partial integration.

B. The Impact of an Integration

An integration, whether partial or complete, discharges prior oral or

6. Restatement (Second) of Contracts § 209 cmt. b. See Conn Acoustics, Inc. v. Xhema Const., Inc., 870 A.2d 1178, 1183 (Conn. App. 2005)(holding that unsigned agreement constituted integration only if it could be shown that the parties intended it as a final expression as part or all of their agreement.). But see Rosenfeld v. Brooks, 895 S.W.2d 132, 135 (Mo. App. E. Dist. 1995)(holding that a written letter "together with the signatures . . . constitutes a wholly integrated agreement").

7. Whalen v. Connelly, 545 N.W.2d 284, 290 (Iowa 1996); Ozerol v. Howard U., 545 A.2d 638, 641 (D.C. App. 1988), on reh'g, 555 A.2d 1033 (D.C. App. 1989); Restatement (Second) of Contracts § 210(1)

8. Segal Wholesale, Inc. v. United Drug Serv., 933 A.2d 780, 784 (D.C. App. 2007); DePhillips v. Zolt Const. Co., Inc., 959 P.2d 1104, 1108 n.2 (Wash. 1998); Abercrombie v. Hayden Corp., 883 P.2d 845, 851 (Or. 1994); Restatement (Second) of Contracts § 210(1).

written agreements to the extent that they are inconsistent with the integration.[9] If the integration is complete, it also discharges consistent additional terms in prior agreements if they are within the integration's scope.[10]

Example. On January 1, Alpha and Beta enter into an oral contract, according to which Alpha will paint Beta's house for $10,000 by March 31. The oral agreement includes the stipulation that Alpha will use biodegradable paint. On January 2, Alpha and Beta set up a writing that they intend to be the complete and final expression of their agreement. The writing states that Alpha will paint Beta's house for $10,000 by March 31 but does not mention the type of paint to be used. Is Alpha contractually obligated to use biodegradable paint?

Answer. The original oral contract between Alpha and Beta included an obligation to use biodegradable paint. However, that obligation was discharged under the parol evidence rule. The parties intended the writing as a final and complete expression of their agreement, meaning it constituted a complete integration. Given that the duty to use biodegradable paint fell within the scope of the complete integration, it was discharged.

Question. On January 1, Alpha and Beta agree that Alpha will paint Beta's house for $5,000. On January 2, Alpha and Beta enter into an oral agreement that Beta will repair Alpha's car for $500. On January 3, Alpha and Beta sign a writing stating: "Alpha will paint Beta's house for $5,000. This document is a final and complete expression of our agreement." Has the writing discharged the January 2 agreement?

---

9. E.g., Individual Healthcare Specialists, Inc. v. BlueCross BlueShield of Tennessee, Inc., 566 S.W.3d 671, 696–97 (Tenn. 2019); Calomiris v. Woods, 727 A.2d 358, 361–62 (Md. 1999)Abercrombie v. Hayden Corp., 883 P.2d 845, 850 (Or. 1994); Loe v. Town of Thomaston, 600 A.2d 1090, 1092 (Me. 1991); Darner Motor Sales, Inc. v. Universal Underwriters Ins. Co., 682 P.2d 388, 397 (Ariz. 1984); Interstate Indus. Unif. Rental Serv., Inc. v. F. R. Lepage Bakery, Inc., 413 A.2d 516, 519 (Me. 1980); Restatement (Second) of Contracts § 213(1).

10. E.g., Individual Healthcare Specialists, Inc. v. BlueCross BlueShield of Tennessee, Inc., 566 S.W.3d 671, 696 (Tenn. 2019); Abercrombie v. Hayden Corp., 883 P.2d 845, 850 (Or. 1994); Interstate Indus. Unif. Rental Serv., Inc. v. F. R. Lepage Bakery, Inc., 413 A.2d 516, 519 (Me. 1980); Restatement (Second) of Contracts § 213(2).

Answer. The writing has not discharged the January 2 agreement. While the writing constitutes a complete integration, the January 2 agreement is an entirely different contract and not within the scope of the integration.

Incidentally, the rule that a complete integration discharges both inconsistent and consistent prior agreements within its scope follows directly from the first rule according to which any integration will discharge prior inconsistent terms. That becomes clear if one considers the following. By definition, the complete integration is adopted as a complete and exclusive statement of the parties' agreement. That means that a complete integration, explicitly or by implication, makes two claims. First, the complete integration claims that the terms in the complete integration are part of the parties' agreement. Second, the complete integration, because it claims to be complete and exclusive, makes the explicit or implicit claim that there are no other terms outside the documents that are part of the parties' agreement. It follows that any prior additional terms not included in the complete integration are, strictly speaking, inconsistent with the complete integration because the integrated agreement claims that there *are no additional or different terms.*

Despite its somewhat misleading name, the parol evidence rule is a substantive law rule, not an evidentiary rule:[11] it governs the discharge of prior agreements as a result of certain later agreements. This substantive law rule—like all substantive law rules—may indirectly affect the question of what evidence the jury gets to look at.[12] After all, irrelevant evidence may not be presented to the jury.

III. Looking Beyond the Document

A critical controversy arising in the context of the parol evidence rule

11. E.g., Weiss v. Smulders, 96 A.3d 1175, 1189 (Conn. 2014); Conway v. 287 Corp. Ctr. Associates, 901 A.2d 341, 346 (N.J. 2006); First Nat. Bank in Durant v. Honey Creek Ent. Corp., 54 P.3d 100, 103 (Okla. 2002); HLO Land Ownership Associates Ltd. Partn. v. City of Hartford, 727 A.2d 1260, 1265 (Conn. 1999); Heyman Associates No. 1 v. Ins. Co. of State of Pa., 653 A.2d 122, 135 (Conn. 1995); TIE Commun., Inc. v. Kopp, 589 A.2d 329, 332 (Conn. 1991); 1010 Potomac Associates v. Grocery Manufacturers of Am., Inc., 485 A.2d 199, 210 (D.C. App. 1984).

12. Cf. Fram Corp. v. Davis, 401 A.2d 1269, 1272 (R.I. 1979)(noting that "[t]he parol evidence rule does not exclude evidence because it is untrustworthy or an undesirable means of establishing a fact" but rather "declares that certain kinds of facts are not to be considered as a matter of substantive law").

concerns the question of what evidence can be considered in ascertaining whether a writing constitutes an integration as well as in determining whether an integration is complete or partial. More specifically, courts in different jurisdictions disagree regarding the extent to which evidence outside of the document—so-called extrinsic evidence—can be considered in answering these questions. Extrinsic evidence includes, for example, any evidence regarding the circumstances surrounding the oral negotiations that preceded the document's creation. Regarding extrinsic evidence, courts fall into roughly two camps: the so-called "four-corner" jurisdictions and those following the Restatement (Second) of Contracts.

The four-corner approach holds that determining whether a writing constitutes an integration has to start with the writing. If the writing, on its face, looks like a final expression of part or all of the agreement, then, as a matter of law, it is an integration.[13] The court will not look beyond the four corners of the document, meaning that extrinsic evidence will not be considered. Only if the writing is ambiguous on its face will extrinsic evidence be considered to determine whether it constitutes an integration.

The four-corners approach to determining whether an integration is partial or complete follows the same pattern. If an integrated agreement looks complete on its face, then the writing will be deemed a complete integration. No extrinsic evidence will be considered. Only if the writing is ambiguous on its face regarding its completeness will extrinsic evidence be considered to determine whether the integration is partial or complete.[14]

The Restatement (Second) of Contracts and many jurisdictions take a more generous approach regarding extrinsic evidence. Even if a writing, on its face, looks like a final expression of the parties' agreement, extrinsic evidence can be used to refute this conclusion.[15] Similarly, even if an integrated agree-

---

13. E.g., Cooper Realty Co. v. U.S., 36 Fed. Cl. 284, 289 (1996); PNC Bank, N.A. v. Springboro Med. Arts, Inc., 41 N.E.3d 145, 151 (Ohio App. 2d Dist. 2015).

14. E.g., Town Bank v. City Real Est. Dev., LLC, 793 N.W.2d 476, 488 (Wis. 2010); In re Integrated Agri, Inc., No. 01-84536, 2005 WL 3088612, at *5 (Bankr. C.D. Ill. Nov. 17, 2005); Vanhook Enterprises, Inc. v. Kay & Kay Contracting, LLC, 543 S.W.3d 569, 572 (Ky. 2018); Town Bank v. City Real Est. Dev., LLC, 793 N.W.2d 476, 488 (Wis. 2010).

15. E.g., Ozerol v. Howard U., 545 A.2d 638, 641 (D.C. App. 1988), on reh'g, 555 A.2d 1033 (D.C. App. 1989); Darner Motor Sales, Inc. v. Universal Underwriters Ins. Co., 682 P.2d 388, 398 (Ariz. 1984); Interstate Indus. Unif. Rental Serv., Inc. v. F. R. Lepage Bakery, Inc., 413 A.2d 516, 519 (Me. 1980); Restatement (Second) of Contracts § 214(a).

looks complete on its face, extrinsic evidence can refute this conclusion.[16]

The clash between Restatement and four-corners jurisdictions becomes particularly relevant if the writing explicitly states that it is a final and complete expression of the contract. Such a provision is called an "integration clause" or "merger clause." [17] Four-corners jurisdictions generally view merger clauses as conclusive evidence that the writing constitutes a complete integration.[18] By contrast, Restatement jurisdictions view merger clauses only as one, albeit important, piece of evidence that can be refuted by other extrinsic evidence.[19] In some jurisdictions, courts only view merger clauses as conclusive if the parties are sophisticated businesspersons with equal bargaining strengths and access to legal counsel.[20]

IV. The Parol Evidence Rule's Limits

The parol evidence rule has various essential limitations.

A. Later Agreements

Most importantly, the parol evidence rule does not affect agreements that the parties have entered into *after* the partial or complete integration was made.[21]

---

16. E.g., Howard U. v. Good Food Services, Inc., 608 A.2d 116, 126–27 (D.C. App. 1992); Interstate Indus. Unif. Rental Serv., Inc. v. F. R. Lepage Bakery, Inc., 413 A.2d 516, 519 (Me. 1980); In re Sabertooth, LLC, 443 B.R. 671, 694 (Bankr. E.D. Pa. 2011), aff'd sub nom. In re Green Goblin, Inc., No. CIV.A. 12-4076, 2014 WL 5800601 (E.D. Pa. Nov. 6, 2014); Rempel v. Nationwide Life Ins. Co., Inc., 471 Pa. 404, 370 A.2d 366, 371 (Pa.1977); § 214(b).

17. Tangren Fam. Tr. v. Tangren, 182 P.3d 326, 330 (Utah 2008)(noting that integration clauses 'are routinely incorporated in agreements in order to signal to the courts that the parties agree that the contract is to be considered completely integrated.'")

18. E.g., Weiss v. Smulders, 96 A.3d 1175, 1189 (Conn. 2014); Tempo Shain Corp. v. Bertek, Inc., 120 F.3d 16, 21 (2d Cir. 1997); Tangren Fam. Tr. v. Tangren, 182 P.3d 326, 331 (Utah 2008); Kentucky Fried Chicken Corp. v. Collectramatic, Inc., 547 A.2d 245, 247 (N.H. 1988); Air Safety, Inc. v. Teachers Realty Corp., 706 N.E.2d 882, 886 (Ill. 1999).

19. Restatement (Second) of Contracts § 209(3). See, e.g., Howard U. v. Good Food Services, Inc., 608 A.2d 116, 127 (D.C. App. 1992)(holding that a merger clause "may be a significant, though not conclusive, factor in ascertaining the parties' intent")

20. Whalen v. Connelly, 545 N.W.2d 284, 291 (Iowa 1996); Franklin v. White, 493 N.E.2d 161, 166 (Ind. 1986).

21. Smidt v. Porter, 695 N.W.2d 9, 21 (Iowa 2005); Whalen v. Connelly, 545 N.W.2d 284, 291 (Iowa 1996); First Bank v. Brumitt, 519 S.W.3d 95, 111 (Tex. 2017).

C. Oral Conditions

The parties to a contract are free to stipulate that one or more contractual duties shall be subject to one or more conditions.[22] Alternatively, instead of subjecting individual duties to conditions, they can also make the entire contract subject to a condition. In this case, the non-occurrence of a condition renders the contract non-existent.[23] But what happens if the parties subject an otherwise completely integrated agreement to an oral condition? In that case, the agreement is not integrated concerning the condition,[24] which means that the integrated agreement does not discharge the condition. However, the agreement is deemed a complete integration once the condition occurs.[25]

C. Interpretation

Can extrinsic evidence be used to interpret an integrated agreement? Predictably, four-corners states and states following the restatement approach come to different conclusions.

According to the four corners approach, extrinsic evidence cannot be considered if a writing is unambiguous on its face.[26] Only if the writing is

22. See, e.g., Massachusetts Mun. Wholesale Elec. Co. v. Town of Danvers, 577 N.E.2d 283, 288 (Mass. 1991) ("Parties to a contract, of course, are free to create whatever conditions precedent they choose.").

23. See e.g., Davidson v. Barstad, 435 P.3d 640, 646 (Mont. 2019) ("The failure or non-satisfaction of a condition precedent to contract formation renders the contemplated contract non-existent as never formed and thus non-binding and unenforceable. . . ."); Sharifi v. Steen Automotive, LLC, 370 S.W.3d 126, 143–44 (Tex. App.—Dallas 2012) ("A condition precedent may be either a condition to the formation of a contract or a condition to an obligation to perform an existing agreement. . . . Thus, conditions precedent may relate to either the formation of contracts or to the liability under them. Id. If there is a condition precedent to the formation of a contract, then no binding contract will arise until the specified condition has occurred or been performed.").

24. E.g., Rogers v. Jackson, 804 A.2d 379, 381 (Me. 2002); Restatement (Second) of Contracts § 217. See Fram Corp. v. Davis, 401 A.2d 1269, 1273 (R.I. 1979)(holding that extrinsic evidence can be used to show existence of oral condition).

25. The Cantamar, L.L.C. v. Champagne, 142 P.3d 140, 148 (Utah App. 2006); Restatement (Second) of Contracts § 217 cmt. b.

26. E.g., Kentucky Fried Chicken Corp. v. Collectramatic, Inc., 547 A.2d 245, 247 (N.H. 1988); Air Safety, Inc. v. Teachers Realty Corp., 706 N.E.2d 882, 884 (Ill. 1999); Rakowski v. Lucente, 104 Ill.2d 317, 323, 84 Ill.Dec. 654, 472 N.E.2d 791 (1984); Sowerwine v. Keith, 997 P.2d 1018, 1020 (Wyo. 2000); Air Safety, Inc. v. Teachers Realty Corp., 706 N.E.2d 882, 884 (Ill. 1999); TRINOVA Corp. v. Pilkington Bros., P.L.C., 638 N.E.2d 572, 575 (Ohio 1994), order clarified, 640 N.E.2d 1144 (Ohio 1994); HLO Land Ownership Associates Ltd. Partn. v. City of Hartford, 727 A.2d 1260, 1265 (Conn. 1999);

ambiguous on its face will extrinsic evidence be considered.[27] By contrast, states that follow the Restatement generally allow extrinsic evidence to be considered.[28]

However, even in Restatement jurisdictions, extrinsic evidence is used only to interpret, not contradict, the integrated agreement.[29] Not all jurisdictions fall clearly into one camp or the other; instead, some states follow intermediate approaches.[30]

Thus, one can distinguish three scenarios. In the first one, the integrated agreement is ambiguous on its face. In this scenario, both four-corners states and states following the Restatement allow the use of extrinsic evidence to interpret the writing.

In the second scenario, the meaning suggested by the extrinsic evidence cannot be reconciled with the clear meaning of the writing. In that case, both

---

Heyman Associates No. 1 v. Ins. Co. of State of Pa., 653 A.2d 122, 135 (Conn. 1995); Farm Credit Bank v. Whitlock, 144 Ill.2d 440, 447, 163 Ill.Dec. 510, 581 N.E.2d 664 (1991); In re Claims Against Pierce Elevator, 868 N.W.2d 781, 801 (Neb. 2015)(holding that extrinsic evidence cannot be used to "explain the terms of a contract that is not ambiguous")(internal citation omitted).

27. Sowerwine v. Keith, 997 P.2d 1018, 1020 (Wyo. 2000); Air Safety, Inc. v. Teachers Realty Corp., 706 N.E.2d 882, 884 (Ill. 1999); HLO Land Ownership Associates Ltd. Partn. v. City of Hartford, 727 A.2d 1260, 1265 (Conn. 1999); Heyman Associates No. 1 v. Ins. Co. of State of Pa., 653 A.2d 122, 135 (Conn. 1995); Farm Credit Bank v. Whitlock, 144 Ill.2d 440, 447, 163 Ill.Dec. 510, 581 N.E.2d 664 (1991).

28. Restatement (Second) of Contracts § 214(c). See, e.g., McMahon Food Corp. v. Burger Dairy Co., 103 F.3d 1307, 1314 (7th Cir. 1996) (noting that "Illinois follows the more liberal standard of the Restatement (Second) of Contracts § 214, that parol evidence is admissible . . . to explain the meaning of even a fully integrated agreement); Harris v. Ski Park Farms, Inc., 844 P.2d 1006, 1014 (Wash. 1993)(explicitly rejecting the idea that extrinsic evidence is only admissible if the contract's language is ambiguous).

29. Restatement (Second) of Contracts § 215. See, e.g., Weiss v. Smulders, 96 A.3d 1175, 1189–90 (Conn. 2014)(holding that the parol evidence rule does not forbid the presentation of evidence outside the four corners of the document but simply prohibits "the use of such evidence to vary or contradict the terms of such a contract"); Individual Healthcare Specialists, Inc. v. BlueCross BlueShield of Tennessee, Inc., 566 S.W.3d 671, 697 (Tenn. 2019)(holding that where a contract is completely integrated, "general extrinsic evidence of context may be used to interpret the contractual language in line with the parties' intent, but the parol evidence rule prohibits the use of evidence of pre-contract negotiations in order to vary, contradict, or supplement the contractual terms of a fully integrated agreement"); Houston Expl. Co. v. Wellington Underwriting Agencies, Ltd., 352 S.W.3d 462, 469 (Tex. 2011)(holding that the parol evidence rule "does not prohibit consideration of surrounding circumstances that inform, rather than vary from or contradict, the contract text")

30. For example, Arizona follows the Restatement approach in principle, but with a twist: "the judge first considers the offered evidence and, if he or she finds that the contract language is "reasonably susceptible" to the interpretation asserted by its proponent, the evidence is admissible to determine the meaning intended by the parties." Taylor v. State Farm Mut. Auto. Ins. Co., 854 P.2d 1134, 1140 (Ariz. 1993).

four-corners states and states following the Restatement conclude that the writing prevails.

In the third scenario, the writing is clear and unambiguous on its face. However, once one considers the extrinsic evidence, the writing no longer appears unambiguous but instead becomes susceptible to different interpretations. In this scenario, the four-corners approach and the Restatement approach may yield different outcomes. Whereas the four-corners approach rejects the use of extrinsic evidence in this scenario, the Restatement approach will allow the use of extrinsic evidence.

D. Fraud, Duress, Illegality, Mistake, Lack of Consideration, etc.

The parol evidence rule does not bar the use of extrinsic evidence to show that the agreement is void or voidable based on duress, mistake, lack of consideration, illegality, or other reasons.[31] However, courts are divided on whether, in certain situations, the parol evidence limits the use of extrinsic evidence to show fraud. According to some courts, a party cannot use extrinsic evidence to show fraud in the inducement where the alleged fraudulent statement directly contradicts the written agreement.[32] By contrast, the Restatement and the majority of courts take the view that extrinsic evidence can always be used to establish fraud.[33]

31. Restatement (Second) of Contracts § 214(d). See, e.g., Tangren Fam. Tr. v. Tangren, 182 P.3d 326, 330–31 (Utah 2008)(holding that extrinsic evince can be used "where the contract is alleged to be a forgery, a joke, a sham, lacking in consideration, or where a contract is voidable for fraud, duress, mistake, or illegality").

32. Toy v. Metro. Life Ins. Co., 928 A.2d 186, 204–05 (Pa. 2007); Deschamps v. Treasure State Trailer Ct., Ltd., 230 P.3d 800, 806 (Mont. 2010); Sherrodd, Inc. v. Morrison-Knudsen Co., 815 P.2d 1135, 1137 (Mont. 1991); Dahmes v. Indus. Credit Co., 110 N.W.2d 484, 490 (Minn. 1961); One-O-One Enterprises, Inc. v. Caruso, 848 F.2d 1283, 1287 (D.C. Cir. 1988); Tyler v. Eq. Life Assur. Soc. of U.S., 512 So. 2d 55, 57 (Ala. 1987). For an intermediate view see S. Exposition Mgt. Co. v. U. Auto Sales, Inc., 740 So. 2d 992, 997 (Ala. 1998)(holding that extrinsic evidence of fraud can be used to show that agreement is void but not to demonstrate a breach of contract).

33. Restatement (Second) of Contracts § 214(d); Tangren Fam. Tr. v. Tangren, 182 P.3d 326, 330–31 (Utah 2008); Ozerol v. Howard U., 545 A.2d 638, 643 (D.C. App. 1988), on reh'g, 555 A.2d 1033 (D.C. App. 1989); First Nat. Bank in Durant v. Honey Creek Ent. Corp., 54 P.3d 100, 104 (Okla. 2002); Heyman Associates No. 1 v. Ins. Co. of State of Pa., 653 A.2d 122, 135 (Conn. 1995); Oxton v. Rudland, 897 N.W.2d 356, 360 (S.D. 2017); Poeppel v. Lester, 827 N.W.2d 580, 584 (S.D. 2013); C & J Vantage Leasing Co. v. Wolfe, 795 N.W.2d 65, 85 (Iowa 2011); Aspiazu v. Mortimer, 82 P.3d 830, 833 (Idaho 2003); Dixon v. SouthTrust Bank of Dothan, N.A., 574 So. 2d 706, 708 (Ala. 1990).

Question. Alpha persuades Beta to promise to paint Alpha's house for $10,000. Beta agrees only because Alpha assures them that the house measures no more than 2,000 square feet. In reality, Alpha's house measures 3,000 square feet. The parties subsequently sign a completely integrated agreement, which states, among other things, that Beta will paint Alpha's house for $10,000 and that "Alpha has made no representation regarding the size of the house." Can Beta use extrinsic evidence to show that the writing was induced by fraud?

Answer. According to the Restatement and most courts, extrinsic evidence can always be used to show fraud. However, some courts will bar the use of extrinsic evidence since the fraudulent statement—namely, Alpha's claim that the house measured no more than 2,000 square feet—directly contradicts the content of the integration. The intuition behind this approach is that Beta could have protected themselves had they read the document.

E. Remedies

Sometimes, a party wants the court to rescind (=unmake) or reform (=change the content of) the written contract. In these cases, the parol evidence rule does not bar the party from bringing in prior agreements or negotiations as evidence of the grounds that justify rescission or reformation.[34] More generally, the parol evidence rule does not bar the party from using prior agreements or negotiations as evidence regarding equitable remedies.

F. Collateral Agreements

The most complex limitation to the parol evidence rule pertains to so-called "collateral agreements." In simple terms, collateral agreements are agreements that, for some reason or other, you would not expect to be mentioned in the written agreement.

If it is reasonable for the parties to omit a particular prior agreement from their integration, it would be patently unfair if the integration discharged the relevant agreement. After all, if it is reasonable to omit the relevant agreement

---

34. Restatement (Second) of Contracts § 214 (e).

from the writing, then the mere fact that it was omitted from the writing does not show that the parties wanted to discharge the omitted agreement.

When dealing with entirely different contracts between the same parties —e.g., one contract concerning violin lessons and another contract regarding the construction of a house—no special legal rule is necessary to conclude that a complete integration regarding one of the contracts will not discharge the other one. That is because even complete integrations only discharge prior agreements within their scope.

However, sometimes, even related agreements cannot necessarily be expected to be reflected in the same written document. In this case, courts also avoid the conclusion that the written agreement discharges the separate, albeit related agreement.[35] However, the case law on this matter is not always coherent, and the terminology used varies widely.

The Restatement (Second) of Contracts treats the collateral agreements issue as part of the distinction between completely and partially integrated agreements. According to section 216(2), of the Restatement, an integration is partial rather than complete if it omits a term that a party agreed to for separate consideration. Moreover, the integration is partial rather than complete if it omits a term the parties might naturally omit from their writing.[36] The consequence of treating the integration as a partial one is that the collateral agreement will not be discharged except to the extent that it conflicts with the writing.

Many courts reject the view that the existence of a collateral agreement stands in the way of finding an integration to be complete. Instead, these courts treat collateral agreements as an exception from the parol evidence rule.[37] However, the criteria for finding a collateral agreement remain the

35. HLO Land Ownership Associates Ltd. Partn. v. City of Hartford, 727 A.2d 1260, 1265 (Conn. 1999)(holding that extrinsic evidence is admissible "to prove a collateral oral agreement which does not vary the terms of the writing"); Heyman Associates No. 1 v. Ins. Co. of State of Pa., 653 A.2d 122, 135 (Conn. 1995)("By implication, such evidence may still be admissible if relevant '(1) to explain an ambiguity appearing in the instrument; (2) to prove a collateral oral agreement which does not vary the terms of the writing; (3) to add a missing term in a writing which indicates on its face that it does not set forth the complete agreement; or (4) to show mistake or fraud.'").

36. Restatement (Second) of Contracts § 216. Some courts have embraced this rule. E.g., Abercrombie v. Hayden Corp., 883 P.2d 845, 851 (Or. 1994); n re Sabertooth, LLC, 443 B.R. 671, 694 (Bankr. E.D. Pa. 2011), aff'd sub nom. In re Green Goblin, Inc., No. CIV.A. 12-4076, 2014 WL 5800601 (E.D. Pa. Nov. 6, 2014); Felco, Inc. v. Doug's N. Hill Bottle Shop, Inc., 579 N.W.2d 576, 581 (N.D. 1998);

37. Genevieve J. Parmely Revocable Tr. v. Magness, 996 N.W.2d 362, 367 (S.D. 2023) (holding that "the parol evidence rule does not prohibit a party from using oral extrinsic evidence to prove a

same. Courts ask whether the parties might naturally have omitted the agreement from their integration[38] and also tend to recognize a collateral agreement where a term was agreed to for separate consideration.[39]

V. Contemporaneous Agreements

Courts in four-corners jurisdictions routinely hold that the parol evidence rule discharges not only prior agreements but also contemporaneous ones to the extent that they are inconsistent with the integration or, in the case of complete integration, fall within its scope.[40] Under the Restatement, contemporaneous agreements can be used as evidence to show that the integration was not complete, with the consequence that the integration only discharges the contemporaneous oral agreement to the extent that it is inconsistent with the integration.[41]

---

collateral oral agreement"); West v. Quintanilla, 573 S.W.3d 237, 245 (Tex. 2019)(holding that the parol evidence rule "does not preclude enforcement of an agreement that is 'collateral' to and not inconsistent with" the integrated agreement); Boy Scouts of Am. v. Responsive Terminal Sys., Inc., 790 S.W.2d 738, 745 (Tex. App.--Dallas 1990), writ granted (Nov. 14, 1990), writ denied (Jan. 16, 1991), writ withdrawn (Jan. 16, 1991)(holding that "the parol evidence rule does not preclude enforcement of . . . agreements which are collateral to, are not inconsistent with, and do not vary or contradict the express or implied terms or obligations" of the integration); Patrick v. Ressler, 2005-Ohio-4971, ¶ 28 (holding that "[a]n exception to [the parol evidence rule] is the 'collateral agreement' rule," which allows extrinsic evidence to be used to show the existence of collateral agreements); ERI Consulting Engineers, Inc. v. Swinnea, 318 S.W.3d 867, 875 (Tex. 2010)(holding that the collateral evidence rule is an exception to the parol evidence rule).

38. See Redland v. Redland, 346 P.3d 857, 869 (Wyo. 2015)(holding that the parol evidence rue does not apply to agreements that "reasonable parties . . . would naturally or obviously or normally" omit from the writing); West v. Quintanilla, 573 S.W.3d 237, 245 (Tex. 2019)(holding that "[a] collateral agreement is one that is supported by separate consideration and that the parties 'might naturally' make separately under the circumstances"); Lee v. Joseph E. Seagram & Sons, Inc., 413 F. Supp. 693, 701 (S.D.N.Y. 1976), aff'd, 552 F.2d 447 (2d Cir. 1977)(holding that the collateral agreement "must be one that parties would not ordinarily be expected to embody in the writing").

39. See Rowe v. Allely, 507 N.W.2d 293, 296 (Neb. 1993)(holding "that the parol evidence rule does not apply to a separate and distinct agreement supported by separate consideration").

40. E.g., In re Claims Against Pierce Elevator, 868 N.W.2d 781, 801–02 (Neb. 2015); Lay v. Destafino, No. 1210383, 2023 WL 2053907, at *4 (Ala. Feb. 17, 2023); Whalen v. Connelly, 545 N.W.2d 284, 291 (Iowa 1996); Ozerol v. Howard U., 545 A.2d 638, 642 (D.C. App. 1988), on reh'g, 555 A.2d 1033 (D.C. App. 1989).

41. Cf. Restatement (Second) of Contracts § 215.

Lower Kuskokwim School District v. Alaska Diversified Contractors, Inc.

Supreme Court of Alaska, 734 P.2d 62 (1987)

MATTHEWS, Justice

The Lower Kuskokwim School District (the School District) appeals a jury's decision that it breached contracts with Alaska Diversified Contractors and Fischbach & Moore (ADF). The relevant contracts called for ADF to build several schools for the School District. At trial, the central dispute was over when completion was required.

The contracts state on their face that completion was required by August 31, 1980. ADF, however, presented evidence that the School District told ADF during a pre-bid conference it could actually complete construction up to eleven months later and that this was the purpose behind a contract provision which imposes only nominal liquidated damages for the first eleven months after August 31.

After work began, the School District pressured ADF to complete the schools by August 31, 1980. ADF employees testified that they did accelerate the work pace in response to this pressure. ADF seeks compensation for its costs resulting from what it perceives as this unwarranted acceleration.

The jury found that the contracts entitled ADF to complete work later than the stated date. The jury found the School District liable for $6,447,000.00, although this amount was reduced by the School District's counterclaims. The School District has appealed on a number of issues.

The School District argues that the parol evidence rule bars the court or the jury from using its pre-bid statements to contradict or vary the written contracts.

The parol evidence rule bars evidence of prior negotiations or agreements to vary or contradict the terms of an integrated written contract. *Johnson v. Curran,* 633 P.2d 994, 995 n. 1 (Alaska 1981); *Kupka v. Morley,* 541 P.2d 740, 747–48 n. 9 (Alaska 1975). An integrated agreement is an agreement which is "adopted by the parties as a complete and exclusive statement of the terms of the agreement." Restatement (Second) of Contracts § 210(1) (1981).

Although the court below did not rule on whether the contracts were integrated, we can make that ruling because the question of integration is one for the court. *Mitford v. de Lasala,* 666 P.2d 1000, 1004 (Alaska 1983); . . . Restatement, *supra* § 209(2), and comment c.

First, we must determine whether the agreements are integrated. According to the Restatement: "Where the parties reduce an agreement to a writing which in view of its completeness and specificity reasonably appears to be a complete agreement, it is taken to be an integrated agreement unless it is established by other evidence that the writing did not constitute a final expression." Restatement, *supra* § 209(3).

Here, we have no doubt that the agreements were integrated. They contain thirty-six pages (plus supplementary provisions), of sixty specific articles, including detailed provisions on every subject from definitions to payment of taxes to cleanup responsibilities. In our view, it would be unreasonable to hold that the parties did not intend these provisions to embody their complete agreement. Or, put another way, the oral statements made at the pre-bid conference do not negate the lengthy and detailed written agreements which the parties signed subsequently.

The next question is whether the evidence offered by ADF contradicts or varies the writings. In our view it does. The contracts state that completion was due on August 31, 1980. They also state that if the contractor, i.e., ADF, fails to complete the contracts by the deadline, the School District could terminate the contracts. ADF's evidence, however, indicates that ADF could complete construction eleven months after the deadline without breaching the contracts. That is, the School District could not use the threat of termination to force ADF to complete the project by August 31, 1980. Thus, since ADF's evidence contradicts the written agreements, the parol evidence rule bars the court or the jury from using this evidence.

Given our conclusion that the written agreements were the complete and final agreements and that these agreements required completion by August 31, it follows that the School District did not modify or breach the agreements by requesting compliance with the deadline. Hence, we do not need to reach the remaining issues raised by the School District. The judgment below is REVERSED and the case REMANDED for disposition consistent with this opinion

NOTES AND QUESTIONS

A. Partial or Complete Integration. In *Lower Kuskokwim School District*, does the court address the question of whether the contracts were completely or partially integrated? Is this question relevant to the outcome of the case?

B. Collateral Agreement. Should the court have applied the collateral agreements doctrine?

C. Policy. What goals does the parol evidence rule likely serve?

D. Efficiency. Is the parol evidence rule (likely to be) Kaldor-Hicks efficient?

CHAPTER 16
INTERPRETATION

White City Shopping Center L.P. v. PR Restaurants, LLC
Superior Court of Massachusetts, Worcester County, 21 Mass. L. Rptr. 565 (2006)

JEFFREY A. LOCKE, Justice.

INTRODUCTION

Plaintiff White City Shopping Center, LP ("White City") brought this declaratory judgment action against defendant PR Restaurants, LLC ("PR") seeking a declaration that it is not in breach of its commercial lease with PR. PR counterclaimed against White City for breach of contract, breach of implied covenant of good faith and fair dealing, and violation of G.L.c. 93A. PR now moves for a preliminary injunction, seeking to enjoin White City, its partners, employees or agents, from taking any action which would violate the exclusive use provision of its commercial lease with White City. Such actions include White City taking any action that would permit Chair 5 Restaurants, ("Chair 5"), the intervening party, from operating a Qdoba restaurant at the White City Shopping Center ("Shopping Center"). For the following reasons, the defendant's motion is *Denied.*

BACKGROUND

Defendant, PR, is a Massachusetts limited liability company that operates 22 Panera Bread ("Panera") restaurants in the New England area. Panera is a café-style restaurant chain that sells sandwiches, coffee, and soup. Mitchell J.

Roberts is the manager of PR. PR is a tenant under a commercial lease for approximately 4,469 square feet of retail space in the Shopping Center located on Route 9, in Shrewsbury. White City, a limited partnership, is the landlord of the Shopping Center. Chair 5, the intervening party, is a Delaware limited liability company and franchisee of Qdoba, a Mexican-style restaurant chain that sells burritos, quesadillas, and tacos. Both Panera and Qdoba compete in the same "fast-casual" restaurant market.

On March 14, 2001, White City entered into a ten-year lease ("the Lease") with PR for retail space to operate a Panera restaurant in the Shopping Center. Lease negotiations lasted several months partly because of PR's request to include an exclusivity clause in the Lease. PR authored the clause which underwent three revisions prior to the Lease's execution. The exclusivity clause that both parties initially agreed to restricted White City from entering into new leases with businesses that primarily sell sandwiches. In its first iteration, Section 4.07 of the Lease states, in relevant part:

Landlord agrees not to enter into a lease, occupancy agreement or license affecting space in the Shopping Center or consent to an amendment to an existing lease permitting use ... for a bakery or restaurant reasonably expected to have annual sales of sandwiches greater than ten percent (10%) of its total sales or primarily for the sale of high-quality coffees or teas, such as, but not limited to, Starbucks, Tea-Luxe, Pete's Coffee and Tea, and Finagle a Bagle ... The foregoing shall not apply to (i) the use of the existing, vacant freestanding building in the Shopping Center for a Dunkin Donuts-type business, or for a business serving near-Eastern food and related products, (ii) restaurants primarily for sit-down table service, (iii) a Jewish delicatessen or (iv) a KFC restaurant operating in a new building following the demolition of the existing, freestanding building. No new building shall violate the no-build provision of this Lease.

Lease § 4.07 (emphasis supplied).

The Lease contained no definition of "sandwiches" or "near-Eastern" food.2 During lease negotiations, PR and White City did not discuss the definition of "sandwiches" or the type of food products they intended the term to cover. Furthermore, the parties never indicated, specified, or agreed that the term "sandwiches" included tacos, burritos, and quesadillas.

Following the Lease's execution in March, the parties amended the exclusivity clause to include additional restrictions. On December 30, 2005, Section 4.07 of the Lease was amended, as follows:

The foregoing restriction shall also apply (without limitation) to a Dunkin Donuts location and to a Jewish-style delicatessen within the Shopping Center, but shall not apply to (i) use of the existing, freestanding building in the Shopping Center partially occupied by Strawberries and recently expanded for a business serving near-eastern food and related products, (ii) restaurants for primarily for sit down table service or (iii) a Papa Gino's restaurant (provided the same continues to operate with substantially the same categories of menu items as now apply to its stores and franchisees generally).

Lease § 4.07.

Sometime after the amendment, PR learned that White City had entered into discussions with Chair 5 to lease commercial space. Chair 5 planned to develop and construct a Qdoba restaurant in the same Shopping Center as Panera. After learning of the parties' plans, PR had its attorney contact White City to express concern and seek an assurance that White City would not enter into a lease with Chair 5. PR believed that White City's leasing of space to Chair 5 violated Section 4.07 of the Lease. Specifically, PR believed, and later asserted that tacos, burritos, and quesadillas fell within meaning of "sandwiches" and therefore, White City was prohibited from leasing to Chair 5 under the Lease. White City refused to provide the requested assurance when PR's attorney contacted it about the pending Chair 5 lease. On or around August 22, 2006, White City executed a lease with Chair 5 for 2,100 square feet of retail space in the Shopping Center. On September 28, 2006, White City filed an action against PR, seeking a declaratory judgment that it did not breach its lease with PR.

Since the execution of the Chair 5 lease, Chair 5 has spent over $85,000 in planning costs, and it is further contractually obligated to spend over $300,000 for the construction of a Qdoba restaurant in the Shopping Center. According to Chair 5, it has yet to schedule an opening date for its restaurant.

DISCUSSION

Under the well-established test of Packaging Industries Group v. Cheney, 380 Mass. 609, 617, 405 N.E.2d 106 (1980), a preliminary injunction is warranted only when the moving party establishes both a likelihood of success on the merits of the claim, and a substantial risk of irreparable harm in the absence of an injunction. Once these factors are established, the Court must balance them against the harm that an injunction will inflict on the opposing party, and must also consider the impact on the public interest.

See T & D Video, Inc. v. City of Revere, 423 Mass. 577, 580, 670 N.E.2d 162 (1996).

A. LIKELIHOOD OF SUCCESS ON THE MERITS

To demonstrate a likelihood of success on the merits, PR must establish as a reasonable interpretation that the Mexican-style food products which Qdoba sells fall within the Lease's restrictions. Absent an explicit and broad definition of "sandwiches" in the Lease itself, PR has not shown a likelihood of success to establish a right to injunctive relief under relevant contract principles.

The interpretation of a contract is question of law for the court. Sarvis v. Cooper, 40 Mass.App.Ct. 471, 475, 665 N.E.2d 119 (1996). A contract is construed to be given reasonable effect to each of its provisions. Id. "The object of the court is to construe the contract as a whole in a reasonable and practical way, consistent with its language, background and purpose." USM Corp. v. Arthur D. Little Systems, Inc., 28 Mass.App.Ct. 108, 166, 546 N.E.2d 888 (1989). The starting point must be the actual words chosen by the parties to express their agreement. Id. If the words of the contract are plain and free from ambiguity, they must be construed in accordance with their ordinary and usual sense. See Ober v. National Casualty Co., 318 Mass. 27, 39, 60 N.E.2d 90 (1945).

Given that the term "sandwiches" is not ambiguous and the Lease does not provide a definition of it, this court applies the ordinary meaning of the word. The New Webster Third International Dictionary describes a "sandwich" as "two thin pieces of bread, usually buttered, with a thin layer (as of meat, cheese, or savory mixture) spread between them." Merriam-Webster, 2002. Under this definition and as dictated by common sense, this court finds that the term "sandwich" is not commonly understood to include burritos, tacos, and quesadillas, which are typically made with a single tortilla and stuffed with a choice filling of meat, rice, and beans. As such, there is no viable legal basis for barring White City from leasing to Chair 5. Further, PR has not proffered any evidence that the parties intended the term "sandwiches" to include burritos, tacos, and quesadillas. As the drafter of the exclusivity clause, PR did not include a definition of "sandwiches" in the lease nor communicate clearly to White City during lease negotiations that it intended to treat burritos, tacos, quesadillas, and sandwiches the same. Another factor weighing against PR's favor is that it was aware that Mexican-style restaurants near the Shopping Center existed which sold burritos, tacos, and quesadillas prior to the execution of the Lease yet, PR made no attempt to define, discuss, and clarify the parties' understanding of the term "sandwiches." Accordingly, based on the record before the court, PR has not shown a likelihood of success on the merits.

B. IRREPARABLE HARM

Irreparable harm occurs when a loss of rights cannot be remedied even though the party seeking an injunction prevails after a full hearing on the merits. Planned Parenthood League of Massachusetts, Inc. v. Operation Rescue, 406 Mass. 701, 710, 550 N.E.2d 1361 (1990). Economic loss alone, however, does not usually rise to the level of irreparable harm which a party must establish to obtain a preliminary injunction. See Hull Mun. Lighting Plant v. Mass. Mun. Wholesale Elec., 399 Mass. 640, 643, 506 N.E.2d 140 (1987).

Here, PR has alleged irreparable harm on the basis that money damages will be difficult to quantify. However, this allegation is unsupported by any data showing that the profitability of Panera will disappear once Qdoba opens. Absent a showing by PR that Panera's survival is dependent upon enjoining the opening of Qdoba and where both parties sell distinct and different food products, preliminary injunctive relief is inappropriate.

C. BALANCE OF THE HARMS

This court further finds that the potential harm to the plaintiffs is outweighed by the harm to the defendant where plaintiffs have expended considerable time and money to plan and develop a Qdoba restaurant at the Shopping Center, in light of the fact that this court finds that White City did not breach its lease with PR. Even though PR vigorously argues for a broad definition of "sandwiches" under § 4.07 to include food products sold by Qdoba, this argument does not change the fact that burritos, quesadillas, and tacos are not commonly understood to mean "sandwiches." Because PR failed to use more specific language or definitions for "sandwiches" in the Lease, it is bound to the language and the common meaning attributable to "sandwiches" that the parties agreed upon when the Lease was drafted.

Having heard the parties and reviewing their filings, this court is not convinced that defendant, PR, has carried its burden in showing a likelihood of success on the merits; that it will suffer irreparable harm if the injunctive relief sought is not granted; or that its harm, without the injunction, outweighs any harm to plaintiffs from being enjoined in the operation of its restaurant.

ORDER

For the foregoing reasons stated, it is hereby ORDERED that the Defendant's motion for preliminary injunction be denied.

NOTES AND QUESTIONS

*A. **Principles Guiding the Interpretation of Contracts.*** The Restatement (Second) of Contracts provides a useful summary of the principles governing the interpretation of contracts in its sections 202 and 203. In White City Shopping Center L.P., the court does not explicitly reference the Restatement. Is the court's reasoning nonetheless consistent with the principles set forth in sections 202 and 203 of the Restatement?

*B. **Sandwiches and burritos.*** Can you think of any other arguments for why a burrito is or is not a sandwich?

*C. **Negotiations.*** The court mentions that the parties' negotiations took several months. Does the court mention whether this fact is relevant to the lease's interpretation. Should it be deemed relevant?

*D. **Drafting the lease.*** Which party drafted paragraph 4.07 of the lease agreement? Should the question who drafted the clause factor into its interpretation?

CHAPTER 17
IMPRACTICABILITY AND FRUSTRATION OF PURPOSE

I. Introduction

As a general rule, liability arising from contractual obligations is strict.[1] Upon making an enforceable promise, a party is expected to fulfill that promise, and failure to do so may result in liability, irrespective of fault.

There are exceptions to the principle of strict liability such as the rules on mutual and bilateral mistakes: sometimes, we allow a party to avoid a contract—and hence escape liability for failure to perform—because one or both parties were mistaken regarding certain basic assumptions. However, the law rarely allows contracts to be avoided based on mistakes. For example, even assuming that all the other requirements of the mistake doctrine are met, this doctrine only applies if the party holds an erroneous belief related to facts

1. CITGO Asphalt Refining Co. v. Frescati Ship. Co., Ltd., 140 S. Ct. 1081, 1089 (2020); Johnson v. Johnson, No. 2014-479, 2015 WL 3756807, at *2 (Vt. June 12, 2015); Laborers Combined Funds of W. Pennsylvania v. Mattei, 518 A.2d 1296, 1300 n.4 (Pa. Super. 1986); 476 Grand, LLC v. Dodge of Englewood, Inc., No. A-2048-10T1, 2012 WL 670020, at *3 (N.J. Super. App. Div. Mar. 2, 2012); MNS Wind Co., LLC v. U.S., No. 04-1569C, 2010 WL 2640141, at *2 (Fed. Cl. June 25, 2010); Restatement (Second) of Contracts, ch. 11, introductory note.

existing at the time of the contract.[2] By contrast, events occurring *after* the contract's conclusion cannot justify applying the mistake doctrine.

There are, however, other doctrines that may allow a party to escape liability for a promise she has made. In this chapter, we focus on three particularly significant events that may potentially discharge a party's duty to perform: impracticability, impossibility, and frustration of purpose.

The following sections will discuss the rules governing these events. As a preliminary matter, though, it should be noted that impossibility is just a particular type of impracticability. A performance is impracticable if it is outright impossible, but a performance can be impracticable even if it is not impossible. For example, a still possible performance can nonetheless be impracticable because rendering it has become unreasonably difficult or costly. The frustration of purpose doctrine, by contrast, has independent significance. A party's duty to perform can be discharged due to frustration of purpose even though the performance has not become impracticable.

II. Impracticability and Impossibility

A party's duty to perform is discharged under the impracticability doctrine if several requirements are met.

First, the party's performance must have been impracticable.[3] Impracticability requires that a party's performance becomes so difficult, costly, or dangerous that one cannot reasonably understand the contract to demand such a performance. If the performance is impossible, it is impracticable. However, the concept of impracticability is broader than that of impossibility.[4] Conversely, the "[p]erformance of a contractual duty is not impracticable merely because it has become inconvenient or more expensive."[5]

Second, the non-occurrence of the event that made the performance

---

2. E.g., Midland Mut. Life Ins. v. Robison, No. 185868, 1997 WL 33353689, at *2 (Mich. App. Feb. 21, 1997); U.S. v. Heatley, 39 F. Supp. 2d 287, 309 (S.D.N.Y. 1998); Hicks v. Sparks, 89 A.3d 476 (Del. 2014); Ryan v. Ryan, 640 S.E.2d 64, 69 (W. Va. 2006).
3. E.g., Le Ft. Enterprises, Inc. v. Lantern 18, LLC, 199 N.E.3d 1257, 1266 (Mass. 2023); Lewis and Clark Cnty. v. Wirth, 510 P.3d 1206, 1217 (Mont. 2022), holding modified by Tai Tam, LLC v. Missoula Cnty. by and Through Bd. of Cnty. Commissioners, 520 P.3d 312 (Mont. 2022); Restatement (Second) of Contracts § 261.
4. Le Ft. Enterprises, Inc. v. Lantern 18, LLC, 199 N.E.3d 1257, 1265 (Mass. 2023).
5. Armstrong v. Clarkson College, 901 N.W.2d 1, 21 (Neb. 2017).

impracticable must have been a basic assumption of the contract.[6] The term "basic assumption" is understood in the same way as under the mistake doctrine. It precludes certain types of changes from undermining the bargain. Most importantly, changes to a party's financial situation or shifts in market conditions do not qualify as basic assumptions. The general intuition here is that for our market economy to work, we cannot allow certain types of changes to impact contractual duties.

Third, a party's duty to perform can only be discharged by impracticability if that party is not at fault.[7]

Fourth, impracticability will not discharge a party's duty if the contract or the circumstances indicate that the party must bear the relevant risk.[8] In particular, courts have routinely held that unless the contract provides otherwise, each party bears the risk of foreseeable obstacles to their performance.[9]

Depending on whether the impracticability arises before or after the contract was formed, we speak of "pre-existing" and "supervening" impracticability.[10] If the party seeks to escape their duty by invoking the pre-existing impracticability of their performance, they also have to meet a fifth condition. That is, they must show that they neither knew nor had reason to know of the impracticability when the contract was made.[11]

III. Objective v. Subjective Impracticability

Impracticability typically means "objective" impracticability rather than "subjective" impracticability: the mere fact that the individual party is unable to render their performance is not enough; rather, it must be impracticable for

---

6. E.g., Le Ft. Enterprises, Inc. v. Lantern 18, LLC, 199 N.E.3d 1257, 1266 (Mass. 2023); Lewis and Clark Cnty. v. Wirth, 510 P.3d 1206, 1217 (Mont. 2022), holding modified by Tai Tam, LLC v. Missoula Cnty. by and Through Bd. of Cnty. Commissioners, 520 P.3d 312 (Mont. 2022); Pellet v. Pellet, 510 P.3d 388, 399 (Wyo. 2022); AGW Sono Partners, LLC v. Downtown Soho, LLC, 273 A.3d 186, 198 (Conn. 2022); Restatement (Second) of Contracts § 261.

7. E.g., Le Ft. Enterprises, Inc. v. Lantern 18, LLC, 199 N.E.3d 1257, 1266 (Mass. 2023); Lewis and Clark Cnty. v. Wirth, 510 P.3d 1206, 1217 (Mont. 2022), holding modified by Tai Tam, LLC v. Missoula Cnty. by and Through Bd. of Cnty. Commissioners, 520 P.3d 312 (Mont. 2022); Pellet v. Pellet, 510 P.3d 388, 399 (Wyo. 2022); AGW Sono Partners, LLC v. Downtown Soho, LLC, 273 A.3d 186, 198 (Conn. 2022); Restatement (Second) of Contracts § 261.

8. Pellet v. Pellet, 510 P.3d 388, 399 (Wyo. 2022); Restatement (Second) of Contracts § 261.

9. See, e.g., U.S. v. Winstar Corp., 518 U.S. 839, 905 (1996); Pellet v. Pellet, 510 P.3d 388, 399 (Wyo. 2022).

10. Restatement (Second) of Contracts § 261, 266(1).

11. Restatement (Second) of Contracts § 266(1).

anybody to render the performance.[12] For example, suppose you promise to build a bridge. In that case, the fact that you suffer an accident and have to abandon your job as a general contractor does not make the performance impracticable. After all, the performance owed—i.e., the bridge's construction—remains entirely feasible, even if you personally are unable to render it. The exception to this rule is that sometimes, the identity of the person rendering the performance is part of what defines the performance owed.

To determine if the party's identity defines the performance in a certain scenario, ask yourself the following question: could the party have sent someone else to perform in her stead without breaching the contract? If the answer is no, then the party's identity defines the performance. For example, if an actor is hired to star in a movie and an injury makes it impossible for him to act, the performance has become impracticable. The fact that some other actor can play the part does not preclude the application of the impracticability doctrine because only the original actor could render the performance owed.

IV. Frustration of Purpose

Some events do not render performance impracticable but make it pointless. Such events may discharge a party's duties under the so-called frustration of purpose doctrine.[13]

For example, in *Krell v. Henry*, a party had rented a room for the explicit purpose of observing a coronation procession at a price that reflected this purpose.[14] When the coronation was canceled, access to the room became pointless, and the party no longer had to pay. Note that the impracticability doctrine does not apply in this scenario. It is still practicable for the tenant to pay the price of the room, just as it is still practicable for the landlord to give the tenant access to the room. However, given that both parties understood that the purpose of the rental was to allow the tenant to observe the coronation and that the rent reflected this purpose, it would seem unfair if the tenant had to pay even though the rental is now pointless. Thus, the frustration of purpose doctrine applies.

---

12. Meng v. Rahimi, 505 P.3d 926, 929 (Okla. 2022); Restatement (Second) of Contracts § 261 cmt. e.
13. Chicago, M., St. P. & P. R. Co. v. Chicago & N. W. Transp. Co., 263 N.W.2d 189, 193 (Wis. 1978).
14. Krell v. Henry, C.A., 1903, 2 K.B. 740.

The requirements for invoking the frustration of purpose doctrine are equivalent to those of the impracticability doctrine, except that frustration of purpose takes the place of impracticability: the contract's purpose must have been frustrated;[15] the frustration must be due to an event the non-occurrence of which was a basic assumption;[16] the party must not be at fault;[17] and neither the contract nor the circumstances indicate that the party bears relevant risk.[18] Moreover, if the frustration already existed at the time the contract was made, a party can only invoke the frustration doctrine if they had no reason to know of the frustration. [19]

Like the impracticability doctrine, the frustration of purpose doctrine is a risk allocation mechanism. Its scope of application is much narrower than it may seem at first glance. As a general rule, it is incumbent on each party to determine whether or not a contract is useful to them. The frustration of purpose doctrine is a narrow exception from this principle and must be applied sparingly.[20] In particular, as with the impracticability doctrine, if a

---

15. Water Dev. Co. v. Lankford, 506 N.W.2d 763, 766 (Iowa 1993); O'Hara v. State, 590 A.2d 948, 954 n.7 (Conn. 1991); Chicago, M., St. P. & P. R. Co. v. Chicago & N. W. Transp. Co., 263 N.W.2d 189, 193 (Wis. 1978); Inland Com. Real Est. Services, LLC v. ASA EWC, LLC, 213 N.E.3d 604, 607 (Mass. App. 2023), review denied, 220 N.E.3d 100 (Mass. 2023); Restatement (Second) of Contracts § 265.

16. Water Dev. Co. v. Lankford, 506 N.W.2d 763, 766 (Iowa 1993); O'Hara v. State, 590 A.2d 948, 954 n.7 (Conn. 1991); Groseth Intern., Inc. v. Tenneco, Inc., 410 N.W.2d 159, 165 (S.D. 1987); J.J. Brooksbank Co., Inc. v. Budget Rent-A-Car Corp., 337 N.W.2d 372, 377 (Minn. 1983); Chicago, M., St. P. & P. R. Co. v. Chicago & N. W. Transp. Co., 263 N.W.2d 189, 193 (Wis. 1978); Inland Com. Real Est. Services, LLC v. ASA EWC, LLC, 213 N.E.3d 604, 607 (Mass. App. 2023), review denied, 220 N.E.3d 100 (Mass. 2023); Restatement (Second) of Contracts § 265.

17. Water Dev. Co. v. Lankford, 506 N.W.2d 763, 766 (Iowa 1993); O'Hara v. State, 590 A.2d 948, 954 n.7 (Conn. 1991); Groseth Intern., Inc. v. Tenneco, Inc., 410 N.W.2d 159, 165 (S.D. 1987); Chicago, M., St. P. & P. R. Co. v. Chicago & N. W. Transp. Co., 263 N.W.2d 189, 193 (Wis. 1978); Inland Com. Real Est. Services, LLC v. ASA EWC, LLC, 213 N.E.3d 604, 607 (Mass. App. 2023), review denied, 220 N.E.3d 100 (Mass. 2023); Restatement (Second) of Contracts § 265.

18. Water Dev. Co. v. Lankford, 506 N.W.2d 763, 766 (Iowa 1993); Chicago, M., St. P. & P. R. Co. v. Chicago & N. W. Transp. Co., 263 N.W.2d 189, 193 (Wis. 1978); Inland Com. Real Est. Services, LLC v. ASA EWC, LLC, 213 N.E.3d 604, 607 (Mass. App. 2023), review denied, 220 N.E.3d 100 (Mass. 2023); Restatement (Second) of Contracts § 265.

19. Restatement (Second) of Contracts § 265.

20. See, e.g., Inland Com. Real Est. Services, LLC v. ASA EWC, LLC, 213 N.E.3d 604, 607 (Mass. App. 2023), review denied, 220 N.E.3d 100 (Mass. 2023) (holding that "[t]he doctrine is construed narrowly 'so as to preserve the certainty of contracts'") (internal citation omitted); Godfrey v. Commr. of Correction, 246 A.3d 1032, 1039 (Conn. App. 2021), cert. denied, 248 A.3d 2 (Conn. 2021) ("'The doctrine of frustration of purpose is given a narrow construction so as to preserve the certainty of contracts ....") (internal citation omitted).

risk is foreseeable and the contract fails to allocate the risk, each party bears the risk that the purpose they pursued is frustrated.[21]

> **Example.** Alpha wants to work as a driver for rideshare services. Beta owns and operates a car dealership. Alpha tells Beta about his plan, and Beta recommends a particular vehicle. After the parties enter into a sales contract, Alpha discovers, as part of his annual medical exam, that he suffers from a spine deformity that will make it impossible for him to work as a rideshare driver. In this case, Alpha's duty to pay is not discharged under the impracticability doctrine because paying for the car is still practicable. Moreover, Alpha cannot invoke the frustration of purpose doctrine. The buyer must generally bear the risk of not being able to use purchased goods, or else sellers can no longer rely on the contracts they formed. Moreover, the risk of being unable to use a purchased good due to sickness or injury is foreseeable. Finally, Alpha is much better positioned than Beta to control and monitor his health.

V. Temporary Impracticability or Frustration of Purpose

Both impracticability and frustration of purchase discharge a party's duty to perform. However, if the circumstances causing the impracticability or frustration of frustration of purpose are merely temporary, the duty to perform is only suspended, meaning that the performance is not yet due.[22]

---

21. Lloyd v. Murphy, 153 P.2d 47, 50 (Cal. 1944) (holding that "[i]f it was foreseeable there should have been provision for it in the contract, and the absence of such a provision gives rise to the inference that the risk was assumed.").

22. Regarding the temporary frustration of purpose, see, e.g., Le Ft. Enterprises, Inc. v. Lantern 18, LLC, 199 N.E.3d 1257, 1266 (Mass. 2023); Inland Com. Real Est. Services, LLC v. ASA EWC, LLC, 213 N.E.3d 604, 609 (Mass. App. 2023), review denied, 220 N.E.3d 100 (Mass. 2023); Restatement (Second) of Contracts § 269. Regarding the temporary impracticability see, e.g., Nora Springs Co-op. Co. v. Brandau, 247 N.W.2d 744, 747 (Iowa 1976); Restatement (Second) of Contracts § 269.

Highlands Broadway Opco, LLC v. Barre Boss LLC et al.

Colorado Court of Appeals, 528 P.3d 517, 522 (Colo. App. 2023)

OPINION BY JUDGE LIPINSKY

"It is difficult to overstate the adverse economic effects of the COVID-19 pandemic." *Buzzell v. Walz*, 974 N.W.2d 256, 258 (Minn. 2022). The public's concerns about the spread of the virus in public settings, coupled with governmental shutdown orders, exacted a particular economic toll on small businesses. . . .

As a consequence of the financial impact of the pandemic, including "government orders restricting consumer access," numerous businesses that leased space fell behind on their rental obligations or stopped paying rent altogether. . . . *Tenants'* legal efforts to obtain relief from their contractual duties to their landlords flooded the courts. . . .

In this case, we consider the argument of defendant, Barre Boss LLC (tenant), that it should be relieved from its lease obligations because of the financial impact of the pandemic and the Governor's related shutdown order on its fitness business. Specifically, tenant and the guarantors of its lease obligations, defendants Suzanne Dipentino and Daniel Dipentino, argue that they are not liable to the tenant's landlord, plaintiff Highlands Broadway OPCO, LLC (landlord), because the COVID-19 pandemic and the executive order were unanticipated events that made it illegal, and thus impossible, for the business to operate. (We refer to the defendants collectively as "the Barre Boss parties,". . . .) We disagree with this interpretation of the lease and therefore affirm the trial court's judgment in favor of landlord.

I. BACKGROUND

In May 2017, tenant and landlord entered into an agreement (the lease) for tenant's lease of commercial property (the premises), at which Barre Boss planned to operate a fitness facility. The lease term was eighty-four months. The individual defendants personally guaranteed tenant's obligations to landlord. . . .

The lease contains a force majeure clause, which excuses a party's delay in performing under the lease by reason of acts of God, ... restrictive governmental laws or regulations[,] or by other cause without fault and beyond the control of the party obligated (financial inability excepted) ... provided, however, [that] nothing contained in this Section ... shall excuse Tenant from the prompt payment of any Rent or other charge required of Tenant hereunder....

On March 25, 2020, in response to the COVID-19 pandemic, the Governor of Colorado issued an executive order, effective March 26, 2020, requiring "all businesses other than those qualified as 'Critical Businesses'... to close temporarily, except as necessary to engage in minimum basic operations needed to protect assets and maintain personnel functions."... Tenant's business was not deemed "critical."...

Tenant continued to pay rent to landlord through November 2020. In December 2020, however, tenant provided landlord with notice of its "immediate surrender of possession of the premises." Tenant asserted in the notice that its business "ha[d] ceased to operate since the March 16, 2020 government mandated shut down associated with the Coronavirus outbreak"; that it had "sought, without success, to obtain a viable tenant for potential assignment and/or transfer of the lease"; and that, although it had obtained an "Economic Injury Disaster Loan," it had depleted the proceeds of that loan. For these reasons, tenant said it was "no longer able to remit monthly payments in accordance with the provisions of the Lease Term."

After tenant stopped making payments under the lease, landlord filed suit against the Barre Boss parties for breach of contract. In their answer, the Barre Boss parties pleaded, among other affirmative defenses, impossibility [and] frustration of purpose.... The trial in this case focused on those affirmative defenses and the amount of landlord's damages. (The Barre Boss parties do not appeal the amount of damages awarded to landlord.) After a one-day bench trial, the court held that the affirmative defenses were unsupported, adjudicated the amount of landlord's damages, and entered judgment against the Barre Boss parties.

II. ANALYSIS

On appeal, the Barre Boss parties argue that the trial court erred by holding that (1) the Barre Boss parties' defenses of impossibility and frustration of purpose fail because tenant's performance under the lease was not impossible for an unforeseeable and indefinite period of time; and (2) landlord took reasonable steps to mitigate its damages.

A. The Affirmative Defenses of Impossibility and Frustration of Purpose

The Barre Boss parties contend that tenant was not liable to landlord because the COVID-19 pandemic was not foreseeable and the executive order made tenant's performance under the lease "illegal," and thus impossible. We disagree.

1. Applicable Law and Standard of Review

Impossibility or impracticability of performance is a defense to a breach of contract claim when "an unanticipated circumstance has made performance of the promise vitally different from what should reasonably have been within the contemplation of both parties when they entered into the contract." City of Littleton v. Emps. Fire Ins. Co., 169 Colo. 104, 108, 453 P.2d 810, 812 (1969) (quoting 6 Samuel Williston & George J. Thompson, A Treatise on the Law of Contracts § 1931 (rev. ed. 1938)). Similarly, a party may be excused from performance under a contract when the "party's principal purpose is substantially frustrated without his fault by a fact of which he has no reason to know and the non-existence of which is a basic assumption on which the contract is made." Town of Fraser v. Davis, 644 P.2d 100, 101 (Colo. App. 1982) (quoting Restatement (Second) of Conts. § 266(2) (Am. L. Inst. 1981)).

Because the affirmative defenses of impossibility and frustration of purpose are premised on the occurrence of an unanticipated event, neither defense applies when, through their contract, the parties allocated the risk of such an event. See City of Littleton, 169 Colo. at 113, 453 P.2d at 814; Town of Fraser, 644 P.2d at 101. A force-majeure clause can manifest such an intent. See Black's Law Dictionary 788 (11th ed. 2019) (defining a force-majeure clause as a "contractual provision allocating the risk of loss if performance becomes impossible or impracticable, [especially] as a result of an event or effect that the parties could not have anticipated or controlled"); 1600 Walnut Corp. v. Cole Haan Co. Store, 530 F. Supp. 3d 555, 558–59 (E.D. Pa. 2021) (holding that, because the "COVID-19 pandemic is an event covered in the [parties'] force majeure clause[,] ... the common law doctrines of frustration of purpose [and] impossibility/impracticability of performance ... are inapplicable").

"The interpretation of a contract is a question of law that we review de novo," but we "defer to the trial court's factual findings unless they are clearly erroneous." French v. Centura Health Corp., 2022 CO 20, ¶ 24, 509 P.3d 443, 449. "[A]n unambiguous agreement must be enforced according to its express terms." Magnetic Copy Servs., Inc. v. Seismic Specialists, Inc., 805 P.2d 1161, 1163 (Colo. App. 1990).

2. Analysis

The force-majeure clause in the lease manifested a clear intent to allocate to tenant the economic risks associated with the payment of rent and related sums due under the lease, notwithstanding "acts of God, ... restrictive governmental laws or regulations[,] or ... other cause without fault and beyond the control of the party obligated." In light of this language, the Barre Boss parties' defenses of impossibility and frustration of purpose cannot defeat landlord's claims. Tenant and landlord expressly agreed in the lease that no such event would excuse tenant from "the prompt payment of any Rent or other charge required." . . . Finally, the executive order did not make it illegal for the Barre Boss parties to pay rent, which is the only contractual duty that landlord alleged tenant breached. . . .

We hold parties to the terms of their bargains "to encourage parties to confidently allocate risks and costs during their bargaining without fear that unanticipated [events] may ... effectively negat[e] the parties' efforts to build these cost considerations into the contract." Town of Alma v. AZCO Constr., Inc., 10 P.3d 1256, 1262 (Colo. 2000).

Our holding that the impossibility and frustration of purpose affirmative defenses do not relieve tenant of its contractual duties to landlord is consistent with decisions in similar cases from other jurisdictions. See Gap Inc. v. Ponte Gadea N.Y. LLC, 524 F. Supp. 3d 224, 234 (S.D.N.Y. 2021) (rejecting frustration of purpose and impossibility defenses arising from the state's blanket prohibition of nonessential business at the beginning of the pandemic because the force-majeure clause in the parties' lease agreement demonstrated that the parties foresaw that the government might enact "controls in connection with a national or other public emergency") (emphasis omitted); AGW Sono Partners, LLC v. Downtown Soho, LLC, 343 Conn. 309, 273 A.3d 186, 201, 204 (2022) (holding that the defendants did not establish the defenses of impossibility or frustration of purpose based on executive orders barring indoor dining because "the language of the lease agreement suggests that events of the magnitude of the COVID-19 pandemic were not entirely unforeseeable") . . .

In sum, the court correctly held, based on the unambiguous language of tenant's agreements with landlord, that the Barre Boss parties' affirmative defenses of impossibility and frustration of purpose do not relieve them of their contractual obligations to landlord.

III. CONCLUSION

The judgment is affirmed and the case is remanded for the determination and award of landlord's reasonable attorney fees and costs incurred on appeal.

Judge FOX and Judge SCHOCK concur.

NOTES AND QUESTIONS

*A. **Supervening impracticability.*** According to the Restatement (Second) of Contracts, the doctrine of supervening impracticability governs cases in which a party's performance becomes impracticable after the contract has been formed.[23] Supervening impracticability discharges the duty to perform, but only if a few additional conditions are satisfied. First, the party whose performance becomes impractical must not have been at fault.[24] Second, the impracticability must be due to an event whose non-occurrence was a basic assumption of the contract.[25] Third, discharging the relevant duty does is not inconsistent with the contract or unjustified by the circumstances.[26] The doctrine of supervening impracticability is one of several doctrines by which the common law allocates risks between the parties. In the case at hand, the tenant argues that its duty has become impracticable. What was the tenant's duty, and does the court agree that it has become impracticable?

*B. **Supervening frustration of purpose.*** According to section 265 of the Restatement (Second) of Contracts, a contractual duty can be discharged due to frustration of purpose. The court concludes that the tenant cannot invoke the frustration of purpose doctrine. Do you agree?

*C. **Force-majeure clauses.*** In the absence of transaction costs, informational asymmetries, and other obstacles to perfect bargaining, we expect the parties to negotiate a Kaldor-Hicks efficient contract. Can we expect the parties to bargain over force-majeure provisions?

*D. **Hypothetical variation.*** Should the court in *Highlands* have reached a different conclusion if the contract had not contained a force-majeure clause? Courts have generally been reluctant to allow commercial tenants to invoke the frustration of purpose doctrine due to the Covid-19 Pandemic even if the contract did not contain a force-majeure clause.[27]

---

23. Restatement (Second) of Contracts § 261.
24. Restatement (Second) of Contracts § 261.
25. Restatement (Second) of Contracts § 261.
26. Restatement (Second) of Contracts § 261.
27. See, e.g., 9795 Perry Highway Mgmt., LLC v. Bernard, 273 A.3d 1098, 1105 (Pa. Super. Ct.

E. Interpreting contracts. How would you describe the court's philosophy on the interpretation of contracts? Does the court's approach to interpretation match the Restatement's?

F. Economic impact. Assume that courts had been willing to allow commercial tenants to invoke the frustration of purpose doctrine in the case of the Covid-19 pandemic, despite force-majeure clauses. Would that have benefited the economy overall? What would the long-term consequences of such an approach have been?

2022) (rejecting tenant's attempt to invoke the frustration of purpose doctrine in the case of Covid induced closure); 1140 Broadway LLC v. Bold Food, LLC, 2020 WL 7137817, at *2 (N.Y.Sup. 2020) (rejecting the application of the frustration of purpose doctrine in a case involving the lease of office space). Cf. also A&R Real Est., Inc. v. Dorian New York LLC, 2023 WL 6257267, at *12 (S.D.N.Y. 2023) ("In the period following the pandemic, New York courts have rejected countless frustration of purpose defenses by commercial tenants claiming the COVID-19 pandemic excused them from paying rent."). For a detailed discussion of the relationship between the COVID-19 pandemic and the frustration of purpose doctrine, see Andrew A. Schwartz, Frustration, the Mac Clause, and Covid-19, 55 U. CAL. DAVIS L. REV. 1771 (2022).

CHAPTER 18
RECIPROCITY

I. Introduction

As we have already seen, there are circumstances where one party's performance does not go as planned. Specifically, we have studied circumstances in which a duty is discharged due to impracticability or frustration of purpose. But what happens to the other party's duty?

One answer might require the other party to perform as though nothing had happened. However, such a solution would disregard that a contract requires a bargain in which each promise is given so that the other is given. In other words, the promises are reciprocal ("synallagmatic"). Therefore, it would be patently unfair if a party were required to render their performance despite not receiving the other party's performance. Accordingly, the law intertwines the fates of the parties' synallagmatic promises even after the contract has been formed: if one party does not perform—even due to a valid reason such as impracticability—then, as a general rule, the other party does not have to perform either.[1]

---

1. See, e.g., Facto v. Pantagis, 915 A.2d 59, 63 (N.J. Super. App. Div. 2007) ("Where one party to a contract is excused from performance as a result of an unforeseen event that makes performance impracticable, the other party is also generally excused from performance."); Hollis v. Lubrizol Corp. Long Term Disability Plan, No. 4:06-CV-3691, 2008 WL 11503946, at *2 (S.D. Tex. July 8, 2008) ("Where one party to a contract is excused from performance as a result of an unforeseen event that makes performance impracticable, the other party is also generally excused from perfor-

Below, we will look at the rules that implement this general principle. These rules rely heavily on the order in which the parties' performances are due. Fortunately, the principles governing the order of performances are simple. First, we look at the contract.[2] If the contract is silent, we can apply the general principle that if one performance takes time and the other can be rendered instantaneously, the performance that takes time is due first.[3] If both parties can perform simultaneously, their performances are due at the same time.[4]

Example. Alpha and Beta agree that Alpha will cut Beta's hair for $20. Alpha's performance takes time and is therefore due first, whereas Beta's duty to pay can be performed instantaneously and is therefore due after Alpha has performed.

Now that we have clarified in which order the parties' performances are due, we can analyze how one party's duty being discharged by impracticability or frustration of purpose impacts the other party's duty to perform.

II. The Performance Due First Becomes Impracticable

Let us begin with the scenario in which the performance due first becomes impracticable. Given the reciprocal character of the parties' duties, requiring the other party to perform would generally be unfair.

Question. On January 1, Alpha and Beta contract for Alpha to paint Beta's house by March 31 for $10,000. On January 2, the house burns down due to

---

mance.") (internal citation omitted); see also Tresman Steel Industries, Ltd. v. N. Steel Co., No. C6-90-215, 1990 WL 81407, at *2 (Minn. App. June 19, 1990) (noting that "[i]mpracticability excuses performance by both parties.") (emphasis in original).

2. Intl. Ass'n of Firefighters Loc. 1596 v. City of Lawrence, 798 P.2d 960, 969 (Kan. App. 1990); Restatement (Second) of Contracts § 234.

3. Opus Group, LLC v. Intl. Gourmet Corp., No. 1:11-CV-23803-UU, 2013 WL 12383483, at *3 (S.D. Fla. Mar. 12, 2013); Intl. Ass'n of Firefighters Loc. 1596 v. City of Lawrence, 798 P.2d 960, 969 (Kan. App. 1990); Winning v. Winning, 2012-Ohio-1448, ¶ 32; Restatement (Second) of Contracts § 234 (2).

4. U-Save Auto Rental of Am., Inc. v. Merit Associates, Inc., No. 3:14CV792HTW-LRA, 2016 WL 3896365, at *4 (S.D. Miss. June 17, 2016), report and recommendation adopted sub nom. U-Save Auto Rental of Am. v. Merit Associates, Inc., No. 3:14-CV-792 HTW-LRA, 2016 WL 3896518 (S.D. Miss. July 14, 2016); Intl. Ass'n of Firefighters Loc. 1596 v. City of Lawrence, 798 P.2d 960, 969 (Kan. App. 1990); Pullman, Comley, Bradley and Reeves v. Tuck-it-away, Bridgeport, Inc., 611 A.2d 435, 439 (Conn. App. 1992); Winning v. Winning, 2012-Ohio-1448, ¶ 32; Restatement (Second) of Contracts § 234 (1).

arson, without either party being at fault. Assume that the applicable common law corresponds exactly to the Restatement (Second) of Contracts. Does Alpha still have to paint Beta's house? Can Beta still demand payment?

Partial Answer. Alpha's duty to paint the house is discharged due to impracticability when Beta's house burns down. But what happens to Beta's duty to pay? Surely, it would be unfair to make Beta pay for a performance that Beta will never receive.

The law uses the doctrine of implied conditions to protect the party whose performance is due last against having to pay for a performance they never received. If one party has to perform first, the other party's duty is subject to an implied condition that the first party has substantially performed.[5]

Example. On January 1, Alpha and Beta contract for Alpha to paint Beta's house by March 31 for $10,000. Since Alpha's performance takes time, whereas Beta's performance can be rendered instantaneously, Alpha's performance is due first. By law, since Alpha's performance is due first, Beta's duty to pay is conditional on Alpha having substantially performed.

What happens if the performance due first becomes impracticable? In that case, the implied condition to which the other party's duty is subject can no longer occur.

Example. Same facts as in the previous example. On January 2, the house burns down due to arson, without either party being at fault. In light of the house's destruction, it has become impracticable for Alpha to paint the house. This means that Alpha cannot substantially perform.

Why does it matter that the implied condition can no longer occur? Under the general rules governing conditions, if a duty is conditional, the condition has not occurred, is not excused, and can no longer occur, then the duty is discharged.[6] This means that if the performance that is due first becomes

5. Restatement (Second) of Contracts §§ 237, 267.
6. Warner Bros. Intern. TV Distrib. v. Golden Channels & Co., 522 F.3d 1060, 1070 (9th Cir. 2008);

impracticable, the other party's duty to perform is discharged unless the implied condition is excused.

> **Question.** Same facts as the previous example. Assume that the applicable common law corresponds exactly to the Restatement (Second) of Contracts. What happens to Beta's duty to pay?

> **Answer.** Alpha's performance is due first because Alpha's performance takes time, whereas Beta's performance can be rendered instantaneously.[7] Therefore, Beta's duty to pay is subject to an implied condition that Alpha has substantially performed. If that condition is not excused and cannot be met, Beta's duty to pay is discharged.[8] Since Alpha has not substantially performed, the implied condition has not been met. Moreover, the condition can no longer be satisfied since Beta's house no longer exists. Thus, the key question is whether the condition can be deemed excused. As a general rule, impracticability does not excuse a condition.[9] An exception applies if satisfying the condition has become impracticable, the condition is a non-material part of the bargain, and upholding the condition would cause the party burdened by the condition to suffer forfeiture.[10] In the case at hand, these requirements are not satisfied. First, substantial performance by Alpha is a central part of the exchange. Second, Alpha has not yet performed, so he is not at risk of forfeiture, which is the risk of not being compensated for one's efforts. Therefore, the condition is not excused, and since it can no longer occur, Beta's duty to pay is discharged.

> **Question.** On January 1, Alpha and Beta contract for Alpha to paint Beta's house by March 31 for $10,000. On January 2, Beta willfully burns down their own house. Assume that the applicable common law corresponds exactly to the Restatement (Second) of Contracts. Does Alpha still have to paint Beta's house? Can Beta still demand payment?

Hollis v. Lubrizol Corp. Long Term Disability Plan, No. 4:06-CV-3691, 2008 WL 11503946, at *2 (S.D. Tex. July 8, 2008); Facto v. Pantagis, 915 A.2d 59, 63 (N.J. Super. App. Div. 2007); Restatement (Second) of Contracts § 225(2).

7. See Restatement (Second) of Contracts § 234.
8. See Restatement (Second) of Contracts § 225(2).
9. Restatement (Second) of Contracts § 267.
10. Restatement (Second) of Contracts § 271.

Answer. Alpha's duty to paint the house has been discharged under the impracticability doctrine. But what happens to Beta's duty to pay? Because Alpha's performance takes time, whereas Beta's performance can be rendered instantaneously, Alpha's performance is due first.[11] Therefore, Beta's duty to pay is conditional on Alpha having substantially performed. If that condition is not excused and can no longer be met, Beta's duty to perform is discharged.[12] The condition has not occurred since Alpha has not yet painted the house. Furthermore, the condition can no longer occur since the house has burned down. However, a condition is excused if the party benefited by the condition has prevented the condition's occurrence in bad faith.[13] Some courts even dispense with the bad faith requirement.[14] Beta has acted in bad faith by burning down their house, so the condition's non-occurrence is excused. Therefore, Beta still has to pay.

III. The Performances Are Due Simultaneously

Now, let us focus on the scenario where both parties' performances occur simultaneously. In this scenario, too, it would be unfair if one of the parties had to perform despite not receiving the other party's performance. The law again uses the doctrine of implied conditions to address this issue. If both parties' performances are due simultaneously, each party's duty is subject to an implied condition that the other party is ready, willing, and able to perform.[15]

---

11. See Restatement (Second) of Contracts § 234.
12. See Restatement (Second) of Contracts § 225(2).
13. See, e.g., Khadka v. Am. Home Mortg. Servicing, Inc., 964 N.Y.S.2d 60 (N.Y. Sup. Ct. 2012) (holding that "if defendant acted in bad faith by delaying [the condition's occurrence], defendant cannot rely upon plaintiff's failure to satisfy the condition precedent"); Preka v. Vermont Mut. Ins. Co., No. CV156024492S, 2017 WL 6947747, at *5 (Conn. Super. Dec. 11, 2017) (holding that the occurrence of a condition in an insurance contract is excused if "the insurer prevents or hinders the condition's occurrence through a breach of the duty of good faith and fair dealing"); Restatement (Second) of Contracts § 225 ct. b; see Little v. Real Living HER, 2014 WL 7274227 ("A promisor "may excuse a condition of its duty by committing a breach that causes the nonoccurrence of the condition.")
14. See, e.g., Armstrong v. Clarkson College, 901 N.W.2d 1, 22 (Neb. 2017) ("A promisor's duty to perform will be excused if it is the other party's conduct that makes performance impossible or impracticable.").
15. Facto v. Pantagis, 915 A.2d 59, 63 (N.J. Super. App. Div. 2007); Restatement (Second) of Contracts §§ 238, 267

Question. Alpha and Beta are neighbors. On January 1, they enter into a contract whereby on January 15, Alpha will paint Alpha's house, and, in exchange, Beta will paint Beta's house. On January 5, Beta's house burns down without either party being at fault. Assume that the applicable common law corresponds exactly to the Restatement (Second) of Contracts. What happens to the parties' duties in this case?

Answer. Beta's duty to paint Beta's house is discharged under the impracticability doctrine. Alpha's performance has not become impracticable. However, note that both parties' duties were to be performed simultaneously. Therefore, the duties of each party were subject to an implied condition that the other party was ready, willing, and able to perform. If a duty is conditional, not excused, and no longer capable of occurring, the duty is discharged. Given that Beta was unable to perform, the implied condition to which Alpha's duty is subject is not satisfied. Moreover, because Beta's house has burned down, the condition is no longer capable of occurring. Also, the condition is not excused. As a general rule, impracticability does not excuse a condition.[16] An exception applies if satisfying the condition has become impracticable, the condition is a non-material part of the bargain, and upholding the condition would cause the party burdened by the condition to suffer forfeiture.[17] In the case at hand, these requirements are not satisfied. First, substantial performance by Beta is a substantial part of the exchange. Second, Beta has not yet performed, so they are not at risk of forfeiture, which is the risk of not being compensated for one's efforts. In sum, Alpha's duty to pay Beta is discharged as well.

IV. The Performance Due Last Becomes Impracticable

What if the performance that becomes due last becomes impracticable? The question of which party has to perform first does not fundamentally alter the equities of the situation. Regardless of which party has to perform first, it would not be fair to make a party perform even though they are not receiving the other party's performance. However, the doctrine of implied conditions

16. Restatement (Second) of Contracts § 267.
17. Restatement (Second) of Contracts § 271.

does not help the party who must perform first. Therefore, the law instead relies on two additional legal principles.

First, suppose the party who has to perform last claims impracticability or frustration of purpose or even voluntarily causes such impracticability or frustration of purpose. In that case, the duties of the party who has to perform first are discharged.[18]

Question. On January 1, Alpha and Beta contract for Alpha to paint Beta's house between March 1 and March 31 for $10,000. According to the contract, Beta's payment is due on February 28. On January 2, Beta willfully burns down their own house. Assume that the applicable common law corresponds exactly to the Restatement (Second) of Contracts. Does Alpha still have to paint Beta's house? Can Alpha still demand payment?

Answer. Alpha's duty to paint is discharged due to impracticability. Is the same true for Beta's duty to pay? The doctrine of implied conditions does not help Beta because Beta's duty to perform first is not subject to an implied condition. However, the law nonetheless protects Beta. Alpha's duty is discharged because Beta voluntarily made their own performance impracticable.

Question. On January 1, Alpha and Beta contract for Alpha to paint Beta's portrait between March 1 and March 31 for $10,000. According to the contract, Beta's payment is due on February 28. On January 3, Alpha is injured, through no fault of their own, in a hit-and-run accident that forces them to abandon painting. On January 4, Alpha informs Beta that Alpha will not be able to paint Beta's portrait. Assume that the applicable common law corresponds exactly to the Restatement (Second) of Contracts. What happens to the parties' duties?

---

18. See Restatement (Second) of Contracts §§ 268, 253(2); see also G. W. Andersen Constr. Co. v. Mars Sales, 210 Cal. Rptr. 409, 415 (Cal. App. 2d Dist. 1985) (embracing the Restatement's rules on this issue); Little Canada Charity Bingo Hall Ass'n v. Movers Warehouse, Inc., 498 N.W.2d 22, 25 (Minn. App. 1993) (regarding frustration of purpose); Juarez v. Hamner, 674 S.W.2d 856, 861 (Tex. App.—Tyler 1984) (regarding prospective impracticability); Voit v. Mertz, 346 P.3d 1132 (Mont. 2014) (regarding prospective inability to perform).

Answer. Alpha's duty to paint Beta's portrait is discharged due to impracticability. Can the same be said of Beta's duty to pay? The doctrine of implied conditions does not help Beta because Beta's duty to perform first is not subject to an implied condition. However, because Alpha has made it clear that they will not be able to paint Beta's portrait, Beta's duty to pay is discharged

Second, if the party who must perform first knows or has reasonable grounds to think that the other party's duty to perform will be discharged due to impracticability or frustration of purpose, the party who has to perform first can suspend their own performance and demand adequate assurance of performance.[19] If such assurance is not provided within a reasonable time, the party whose performance is due first can treat their own duty as discharged.[20]

Question. On January 1, Alpha and Beta contract for Alpha to paint Beta's portrait between March 1 and March 31 for $10,000. According to the contract, Beta's payment is due on February 28. On January 3, Alpha is injured, through no fault of their own, in a hit-and-run accident that may force them to abandon painting. Assume that the applicable common law corresponds exactly to the Restatement (Second) of Contracts. What are Beta's options?

Answer. Beta's duty is not discharged. However, Beta has reasonable grounds to believe that Alpha's duty will be discharged due to impracticability. Therefore, Beta can suspend their payment and demand adequate assurance of performance.[21] If Alpha does not provide such assurance within a reasonable time, Beta can treat their own duty to perform as discharged.[22]

It is possible that the party who had to perform first has already performed by the time that the other party's performance becomes impracticable or by the time that the contract's purpose is frustrated. In that case, the law grants the party who has already performed the remedy of restitution.[23]

---

19. Restatement (Second) of Contracts §§ 268, 251, 253(2).
20. Restatement (Second) of Contracts §§ 268, 251, 253(2).
21. See Restatement (Second) of Contracts §§ 268, 251, 253(2).
22. Restatement (Second) of Contracts §§ 268, 253(2).
23. Facto v. Pantagis, 915 A.2d 59, 63 (N.J. Super. App. Div. 2007) (granting a quantum meruit claim

Question. On January 1, Alpha and Beta contract for Alpha to paint Beta's house between March 1 and March 31 for $10,000. According to the contract, Beta's payment is due on February 28. On February 27, Beta pays the $10,000. On February 28, the house burns down due to arson, without either party being at fault. Assume that the applicable common law corresponds exactly to the Restatement (Second) of Contracts. Does Alpha still have to paint Beta's house? Can Beta demand their money back?

Answer. Alpha's duty to paint the house has been discharged due to impracticability. Beta is entitled to restitution regarding the $10,000 because Alpha's synallagmatic duty to paint the house was discharged under the impracticability doctrine.

---

regarding any benefits already performed where other party's performance became impracticable); Restatement (Second) of Contracts §§ 272, 377.

CHAPTER 19
EXPRESS CONDITIONS

I. Introduction

The parties to a contract are free to stipulate that one or more contractual duties shall be subject to one or more conditions.[1] Such conditions are called "express conditions." The term "express condition" distinguishes contractually agreed upon conditions from so-called "implied conditions," which are imposed by law.

> **Example.** Alpha is a violinist. Alpha and Beta contract for Alpha to play the violin at Beta's outdoor wedding in exchange for $500. The contract provides that Alpha does not have to perform if it rains on the day of the wedding but also notes that even if it rains, Alpha will still get paid. In this case, Alpha's duty to play the violin is subject to an express condition.

Courts frequently distinguish between duties subject to "conditions precedent" and duties subject to "conditions subsequent." If a duty is subject to a condition precedent, the duty does not arise until the condition occurs.[2] In

---

1. See, e.g., Massachusetts Mun. Wholesale Elec. Co. v. Town of Danvers, 577 N.E.2d 283, 288 (Mass. 1991) ("Parties to a contract, of course, are free to create whatever conditions precedent they choose.").
2. See, e.g., Village Beer and Bev., Inc. v. Vernon D. Cox and Co., Inc., 475 A.2d 117, 122 (Pa. Super. 1984) (holding that "a condition precedent and a condition subsequent are fundamentally differ-

contrast, if a duty is subject to a condition subsequent, the duty is extinguished if the condition occurs.[3] The Restatement (Second) of Contracts abandoned this approach and uses the term "condition" only for conditions precedent.[4] Instead of using the term "condition subsequent," the Restatement refers to events whose non-occurrence discharges a duty.[5] Nonetheless, given courts' continuing use of the distinction between conditions precedent and conditions subsequent,[6] it is worth being familiar with this terminology.

According to the traditional view, express conditions require strict compliance.[7] In recent years, some courts have deviated from this principle and have held that substantial compliance may be sufficient for some types of express conditions. In particular, some courts have applied the substantial compliance doctrine to contractual provisions conditioning a party's duty to perform on the other party having provided notice of particular events ("notice condi-

---

ent: a condition precedent must occur before performance under a contract arises, while a condition subsequent acts to discharge a contractual duty after it has already occurred"); see also Gulf Const. Co., Inc. v. Self, 676 S.W.2d 624, 627 (Tex. App. 1984), writ refused NRE (Mar. 20, 1985) ("Conditions precedent to an obligation to perform are those acts or events, which occur subsequently to the making of the contract, that must occur before there is a right to immediate performance and before there is a breach of contractual duty."); Wells Fargo Bank, N.A. v. Lorson, 267 A.3d 1, 11 (Conn. 2021) (holding that "the nonoccurrence of a condition precedent limits a right by preventing it from coming into existence . . . whereas the nonoccurrence of a condition subsequent limits the right by extinguishing it"); Barrington Mgt. Co., Inc. v. Paul E. Draper Fam. Ltd. Partn., 695 N.E.2d 135, 141 (Ind. App. 1998) ("A condition precedent is either a condition which must be performed before the agreement of the parties becomes binding, or a condition which must be fulfilled before the duty to perform an existing contract arises. A condition subsequent is a condition which, if performed or violated (as the case may be), defeats the contract.") (internal citation omitted).

3. Id.

4. Restatement (Second) of Contracts § 224 cmt. e.

5. E.g. Restatement (Second) of Contracts § 227.

6. E.g., Wells Fargo Bank, N.A. v. Lorson, 267 A.3d 1, 11 (Conn. 2021); Paul E. Draper Fam. Ltd. Partn., 695 N.E.2d 135, 141 (Ind. App. 1998).

7. Midwest Builder Distribg., Inc. v. Lord and Essex, Inc., 891 N.E.2d 1, 23 (Ill. App. 1st Dist. 2007); Regency Com. Associates, LLC v. Lopax, Inc., 869 N.E.2d 310, 321 (Ill. App. 4th Dist. 2007). See Snyder v. Chester Cnty. Mut. Ins. Co., 264 F. Supp. 2d 332, 337 (D. Md. 2003) (holding that under Maryland law, express conditions in insurance contract require strict compliance).

[8] Some courts have even made statements suggesting that the doctrine of substantial compliance may apply to contractual conditions in general.[9]

II. Conditions and Contractual Duties

Within a contract, the same conduct can become the subject of both a duty and a condition.[10] For example, assume that a homeowner and a painter enter into a contract in which the painter promises to paint the owner's house within two weeks and the owner promises to pay once the painter has completed his work. In that case, both parties have incurred duties, but neither duty is subject to an express condition. Now imagine that the contract also states: "The painter loses the right to be paid if he does not finish his work exactly on time." This provision conditions the owner's duty to pay on the painter's punctual performance. If the condition is not satisfied, the owner no longer has to pay the painter. This means that painting the house within a two-week deadline is both a contractual duty and an express condition.

Whether the contract contains an express condition is a question of contractual interpretation. Given the potentially harsh consequences of express conditions, in case of doubt, courts tend to interpret contracts as

8. See James Constr. Group, LLC v. Westlake Chem. Corp., 650 S.W.3d 392, 406 (Tex. 2022), reh'g denied (Sept. 2, 2022) (holding that "Texas law generally recognizes substantial compliance as a proper standard by which to evaluate satisfaction of contractual notice conditions"); Wells Fargo Bank, N.A. v. Fitzpatrick, 210 A.3d 88, 96 (Conn. App. 2019) (holding that the substantial compliance doctrine applies to "contract notice provisions"); but see Chesapeake Bank of Maryland v. Monro Muffler/Brake, Inc., 891 A.2d 384, 397 (Md. Spec. App. 2006) (holding that contractual notice conditions require strict compliance).

9. See, e.g., Allstate Floridian Ins. Co. v. Farmer, 104 So. 3d 1242, 1246 (Fla. 5th Dist. App. 2012) ("Courts require there to be at least substantial compliance with conditions precedent in order to authorize performance of a contract.").

10. E.g., Weber v. N. Loup River Pub. Power and Irrigation Dist., 854 N.W.2d 263, 273 (Neb. 2014); Restatement (Second) of Contracts § 229(2)(c).

containing mere duties rather than express conditions.[11] Read section 227 of the Restatement (Second) of Contracts.[12]

III. Conditions and Forfeiture

Express conditions can lead to severe consequences. For example, in *Acme*, a carrier's duty to reimburse robbery-induced losses was conditional upon the carrier or its employees having issued a receipt.[13] As a result, the mere fact that the customer's employee failed to insist on a receipt during a robbery may have cost Acme its right to be reimbursed. A party's loss of the right to be compensated after the party has already performed or has incurred expenses in preparation for their performance is known as "forfeiture."[14]

Courts have developed various mechanisms to reduce the risk of forfeiture. As already noted, if a contractual provision can be interpreted as either a contractual duty or as a condition, courts tend to interpret it as a duty.[15] Moreover, even if a duty is conditional and the condition has not occurred, the non-occurrence of a condition can be excused.[16] Which circumstances excuse the

---

11. See, e.g., Holland v. Holland, No. M199902791COAR3CV, 2001 WL 585107, at *3 (Tenn. App. June 1, 2001) ("Courts do not favor conditions precedent and will construe doubtful language to impose a duty rather than create a condition precedent."); Navarro v. F.D.I.C., 371 F.3d 979, 981 (7th Cir. 2004) ("Conditions precedent are generally disfavored; in resolving doubts about whether a contract contains a condition precedent, interpretations that reduce the risk of forfeiture are favored."); Harmon Cable Commun. of Nebraska Ltd. Partn. v. Scope Cable TV, Inc., 468 N.W.2d 350, 359 (Neb. 1991) ("Where the intent of the parties is not clear, the disputed language is generally deemed to be promissory rather than conditional."); Prichard v. Clay, 780 P.2d 359, 362 (Alaska 1989) ("Conditions are not favored, and will not be construed as such unless they are "expressed in plain, unambiguous language or arise by clear implication.").

12. Gresham, Smith and Partners v. Middleburg Real Est. Partners, LLC, No. M202101459-COAR3CV, 2023 WL 6210983, at *5 (Tenn. App. Sept. 25, 2023) ("Courts do not favor conditions precedent and will construe doubtful language to impose a duty rather than create a condition precedent"); Navarro v. F.D.I.C., 371 F.3d 979, 981 (7th Cir. 2004) ("Conditions precedent are generally disfavored; in resolving doubts about whether a contract contains a condition precedent, interpretations that reduce the risk of forfeiture are favored.").

13. Acme Markets, Inc. v. Fed. Armored Exp., Inc., 648 A.2d 1218, 1219 (Pa. Super. 1994).

14. Restatement (Second) of Contracts § 229 cmt. b.

15. See, e.g., Holland v. Holland, No. M199902791COAR3CV, 2001 WL 585107, at *3 (Tenn. App. June 1, 2001) ("Courts do not favor conditions precedent and will construe doubtful language to impose a duty rather than create a condition precedent."); Navarro v. F.D.I.C., 371 F.3d 979, 981 (7th Cir. 2004) ("Conditions precedent are generally disfavored; in resolving doubts about whether a contract contains a condition precedent, interpretations that reduce the risk of forfeiture are favored.").

16. Restatement (Second) of Contracts § 224.

occurrence of a condition? Without offering an exhaustive list,[17] we want to mention a few scenarios that are of particular importance:

First and most importantly, if the condition is not a material part of the bargain, courts can excuse the occurrence of a condition to avoid disproportionate forfeiture.[18]

Second, if the condition is not a material part of the bargain and excusing the condition is necessary to avoid forfeiture, its non-occurrence is excused if the occurrence of the condition becomes impracticable.[19] For example, suppose a construction contract makes the owner's duty to pay the general contractor subject to an express condition that the architect named in the contract certifies the work. If the architect dies, that condition will be excused due to impracticability.[20]

Third, courts will excuse the occurrence of a condition if the other party has prevented the condition from occurring in a way that violates the general duty of good faith and fair dealing.[21] Some courts have even held that a condition is excused if the party protected by the condition prevented its occurrence, regardless of whether that party acted in bad faith.[22]

---

17. For a more comprehensive list, see Restatement (Second) of Contracts § 225 ct. b.

18. In re Wansdown Properties Corp. N.V., 626 B.R. 165, 168 (Bankr. S.D.N.Y. 2021); Restatement (Second) of Contracts § 229.

19. E.g., Grenier v. Compratt Const. Co., 454 A.2d 1289, 1292 (Conn. 1983); Restatement (Second) of Contracts § 271.

20. Grenier v. Compratt Const. Co., 454 A.2d 1289, 1292 (Conn. 1983).

21. See, e.g., Khadka v. Am. Home Mortg. Servicing, Inc., 964 N.Y.S.2d 60 (N.Y. Sup. Ct. 2012) (holding that "if defendant acted in bad faith by delaying [the condition's occurrence], defendant cannot rely upon plaintiff's failure to satisfy the condition precedent"); Preka v. Vermont Mut. Ins. Co., No. CV156024492S, 2017 WL 6947747, at *5 (Conn. Super. Dec. 11, 2017) (holding that the occurrence of a condition in an insurance contract is excused if "the insurer prevents or hinders the condition's occurrence through a breach of the duty of good faith and fair dealing"); Restatement (Second) of Contracts § 225 ct. b; see Little v. Real Living HER, 2014 WL 7274227 ("A promisor "may excuse a condition of its duty by committing a breach that causes the nonoccurrence of the condition.").

22. See, e.g., D & S Realty, Inc. v. Markel Ins. Co., 816 N.W.2d 1, 15 (Neb. 2012) (holding that a condition can be excused if the promisor hinders or prevents its occurrence, even if the promisor does not act in bad faith); see also Bailey v. Farmers Union Co-op. Ins. Co. of Nebraska, 498 N.W.2d 591, 598 (Neb. App. 1992) ("A condition is excused if the occurrence of the condition is prevented by the party whose performance is dependent upon the condition"); Rastek Constr. & Dev. Corp. v. Gen. Land Com. Real Est. Co., LLC, 806 S.E.2d 740, 745 (Va. 2017) ("'The prevention doctrine is the well-recognized "principle of contract law that if one party to a contract hinders, prevents or makes impossible performance by the other party, the latter's failure to perform will be excused.'") (internal citation omitted); Bradford Dyeing Ass'n, Inc. v. J. Stog Tech GmbH, 765 A.2d 1226, 1237–38 (R.I. 2001) ("It is further both elementary as well as fundamental contract law that if one party

Furthermore, a condition can be waived.[23] As a general rule, waiving a condition constitutes a contractual amendment, which requires mutual assent and consideration. However, if the condition is not a material part of the exchange, the party protected by the condition can waive the condition unilaterally, and the waiver does not need to be supported by consideration.[24]

IV. Conditions and Consequences

What happens if a duty is conditional, the condition has not occurred, and its non-occurrence is neither waived nor excused? That depends on whether the condition can still occur. If the condition can still occur, the relevant party's performance is not yet due.[25] If the condition can no longer occur, the conditional duty is discharged.[26]

V. Conditional Duties v. Conditional Contracts

So far, we have discussed cases in which the contract makes one or more *duties* conditional. However, the parties can also make the entire contract subject to a condition. In this case, the non-occurrence of a condition renders the contract non-existent.[27]

---

to the contract prevents the happening or performance of a condition precedent that is part of the contract, that action eliminates the condition precedent").

23. E.g., Indiana State Hwy. Commn. v. Curtis, 704 N.E.2d 1015, 1019 (Ind. 1998); Preka v. Vermont Mut. Ins. Co., No. CV156024492S, 2017 WL 6947747, at *5 (Conn. Super. Dec. 11, 2017); Restatement (Second) of Contracts § 84.

24. Grigoleit Co. v. Whirlpool Corp., No. 05-CV-2126, 2010 WL 1881992, at *5 (C.D. Ill. May 10, 2010), aff'd, 769 F.3d 966 (7th Cir. 2014); Restatement (Second) of Contracts § 84.

25. E.g., Rastek Constr. & Dev. Corp. v. Gen. Land Com. Real Est. Co., LLC, 806 S.E.2d 740, 745 (Va. 2017); Anchorage Chrysler Ctr., Inc. v. DaimlerChrysler Corp., 129 P.3d 905, 911 (Alaska 2006); R. G. Pope Const. Co., Inc. v. Guard Rail of Roanoke, Inc., 244 S.E.2d 774, 778 (Va. 1978) ("The performance of Guard Rail's duty, subject to such conditions, did not become due unless the conditions occurred, or unless their nonoccurrence was excused . . . ") (internal citation omitted); Restatement (Second) of Contracts § 225(1).

26. E.g., Rastek Constr. & Dev. Corp. v. Gen. Land Com. Real Est. Co., LLC, 806 S.E.2d 740, 745 (Va. 2017); Grigoleit Co. v. Whirlpool Corp., No. 05-CV-2126, 2010 WL 1881992, at *5 (C.D. Ill. May 10, 2010), aff'd, 769 F.3d 966 (7th Cir. 2014); Davis v. Dawson, Inc., 15 F. Supp. 2d 64, 118 (D. Mass. 1998); Restatement (Second) of Contracts § 225(1).

27. See e.g., Davidson v. Barstad, 435 P.3d 640, 646 (Mont. 2019) ("The failure or non-satisfaction of a condition precedent to contract formation renders the contemplated contract non-existent as never formed and thus non-binding and unenforceable. . . ."); Sharifi v. Steen Automotive, LLC, 370 S.W.3d 126, 143–44 (Tex. App.—Dallas 2012) ("A condition precedent may be either a condition to the formation of a contract or a condition to an obligation to perform an existing agreement. . .

Acme Markets, Inc. v. Federal Armored Express, Inc.

Superior Court of Pennsylvania, 648 A.2d 1218 (Pa. Super 1994)

HESTER, JUDGE.

Acme Markets, Inc., appeals from the order entered in the Court of Common Pleas of Montgomery County on December 21, 1993, which granted Federal Armored Express, Inc. ("Federal") summary judgment. For the reasons set forth below, we reverse that order and remand the matter for further proceedings.

[According to the appellant (Acme Markets Inc), the parties had entered into a contract under which Federal Armored Express ("Federal") had to provide armored car services. The contract, following an amendment, provided that the defendant had to replace any "service-related losses," a term that both the parties and the court understood to cover losses from robberies. However, the contract also provided, in paragraph five, that "[r]esponsibility of Federal under this contract shall begin when said [cash]bags or packages have been accepted and receipted for by Federal or its authorized employees . . . ."]

. . . [A]ppellant averred that a Federal employee was robbed on May 19, 1990, after accepting possession of one of appellant's cashbags. . . . [A]ppellant asserted that even though it had notified Federal promptly of the $62,544.32 loss, Federal had not made the reimbursement required by the agreement. Consequently, appellant requested, among other things, an award of damages equivalent to the amount of the loss. . . . Federal noted that neither party disputed the fact that the employee in question had not provided a receipt for the bag prior to its loss. . . . [Both parties filed for summary judgment.] . . . [T]he court denied appellant's summary judgment motion and granted Federal relief. This timely appeal followed. . . .

In reviewing an order granting a motion for summary judgment, we must view the record in the light most favorable to the non-moving party. . . . All

---

. Thus, conditions precedent may relate to either the formation of contracts or to the liability under them. Id. If there is a condition precedent to the formation of a contract, then no binding contract will arise until the specified condition has occurred or been performed.").

doubts as to the existence of a genuine issue of material fact must be resolved against the moving party. Marks v. Tasman, 527 Pa. 132, 589 A.2d 205 (1991). Moreover, in summary judgment proceedings, it is not the court's function to determine the facts, but only to determine if an issue of material fact exists. . . . Summary judgment should only be granted in those cases which are free and clear from doubt. . . .

Appellant asserts that the trial court erroneously concluded that the fifth paragraph of the agreement constituted a condition precedent to Federal's liability for the lost bag. Specifically, appellant argues that since the paragraph was not labelled a condition precedent and does not contain other language normally associated with such a condition, "[t]here is no means by which to state with the certainty required by Pennsylvania law that it creates a condition precedent." Appellant's brief at 13. We find appellant's claim devoid of merit.

Initially, we note that a condition precedent may be defined as a condition which must occur before a duty to perform under a contract arises. . . . While the parties to a contract need not utilize any particular words to create a condition precedent, an act or event designated in a contract will not be construed as constituting one unless that clearly appears to have been the parties' intention. See Estate of Barilla, . . . 535 A.2d 125 (1987) . . . In addition, we note that the purpose of any condition set forth in a contract must be determined in accordance with the general rules of contractual interpretation. . . . Those rules may be summarized as follows.

When construing agreements involving clear and unambiguous terms, this Court need only examine the writing itself to give effect to the parties ['] understanding. . . . The court must construe the contract only as written and may not modify the plain meaning of the words under the guise of interpretation. . . . When the terms of a written contract are clear, this Court will not rewrite it to give it a construction in conflict with the accepted and plain meaning of the language used. . . . Conversely, when the language is ambiguous and the intention of the parties cannot be reasonably ascertained from the language of the writing alone, the parol evidence rule does not apply to the admission of oral testimony to show both the intent of the parties and the circumstances attending the execution of the contract. . . .

In the present case, the contested paragraph indicates that Federal's responsibility under the contract "shall begin when ... bags or packages have been accepted and receipted for by Federal or its employees....". . . Our reading of this plain language demonstrates that it clearly and unambiguously conditions Federal's performance under the contract upon both the acceptance of bags or packages and the granting of a receipt for them. Thus, it unquestionably delineates a condition precedent involving those requirements.

Since we have found that Federal's liability under the contract was subject to a condition precedent and neither party disputes that the receipt portion of the condition remained unfulfilled at the time of the robbery, we must determine whether satisfaction of that requirement may be excused. Apparently arguing that strict application of the condition would be unfair, appellant asserts that the receipt requirement was immaterial and could only be seen as incidental to the far more significant satisfied requirement of possession and acceptance by Federal's employee of appellant's property....

Restatement (Second) of Contracts § 229 discusses the excuse of a condition to avoid unfairness in connection with its strict enforcement. More specifically, that section relates to the excuse of a condition leading to a forfeiture, a term referring to "the denial of compensation that results when the obligee loses his right to the agreed exchange after he has relied substantially, as by preparation or performance on the expectation of that exchange." Restatement (Second) of Contracts § 229, comment b. Section 229 provides, "To the extent that the non-occurrence of a condition would cause disproportionate forfeiture, a court may excuse the non-occurrence of that condition unless its occurrence was a material part of the agreed exchange." Restatement (Second) of Contracts § 229. Since Pennsylvania law "abhors forfeitures and penalties and enforces them with the greatest reluctance when a proper case is presented[,]" Fogel Refrigerator Co. v. Oteri, 391 Pa. 188, 195, 137 A.2d 225, 231 (1958), section 229 is consistent with the law of this Commonwealth. . . . Consequently, we will apply it in the present case.

There can be little doubt that the operation of the condition in question will lead to a forfeiture since the condition's nonoccurrence results in the denial of compensation for the loss of a cashbag possessed by Federal for transportation in accordance with the contract. Thus, the question becomes whether the forfeiture would be disproportionate.

In determining whether the forfeiture is "disproportionate," [the] court must weigh the extent of the forfeiture by the obligee against the importance to the obligor of the risk from which he sought to be protected and the degree to which that protection will be lost if the nonoccurrence of the condition is excused to the extent required to prevent forfeiture.

Restatement (Second) of Contracts § 229, comment b.

In the present case, appellant obviously entered into the armored car service contract so that it would have a secure method of transporting cash and checks to the bank. Strict application of the condition precedent would result in the loss of appellant's ability to recover from Federal for the theft of the bag entrusted to Federal's care. Moreover, we believe that the receipting requirement was intended to provide Federal with proof that it accepted, at a specific time, a certain number of cashbags for shipment. Thus, in our opinion, the requirement probably was little more than an accounting device designed to track bags picked up in accordance with the agreement. Under such circumstances, the receipt primarily would serve to protect Federal rather than Acme from, among other things, theft by its own employees and disputes regarding the number of bags accepted. Those are two risks not at issue herein.

While we believe that the receipt requirement probably was an accounting device which had little impact upon the situation presently at issue, our examination of the certified record reveals that it is devoid of any evidence demonstrating the requirement's actual purpose. Thus, even though we have speculated on the matter, the record is inadequate to determine whether our speculation is accurate. In view of the inadequate record, we may not conduct the critical weighing analysis required by the Restatement or determine whether fulfillment of the condition may be excused. Indeed, we note that the trial court erroneously believed that its analysis ended upon concluding that a receipt was required to fulfill the condition precedent. Thus, the court did not consider whether the forfeiture would be disproportionate, decide if the receipt requirement constituted a material part of the exchange, or require the parties to provide an adequate record either for resolving those issues or deciding whether summary judgment in favor of Federal would be appropriate. Accordingly, we must reverse the trial court's grant of summary judgment and remand the matter for further proceedings.

On remand, the trial court should conduct an evidentiary hearing to determine the purpose of the receipt requirement and engage in the necessary weighing analysis. In addition, the court should determine whether the contested requirement constituted a material part of the agreement. While this determination rests to a large extent on the analysis of the requirement's purpose, it also involves a consideration of the negotiations of the parties along with all other circumstances relevant to the formation of the contract or to the requirement itself, including the circumstances surrounding the theft.

ORDER REVERSED. CASE REMANDED FOR FURTHER PROCEEDINGS. JURISDICTION RELINQUISHED.

NOTES AND QUESTIONS

A. Express Condition. In *Acme,* the court concluded that Federal's duty to reimburse Acme was subject to an express condition. Do you agree?

B. Waiver. Can you argue that Federal waived the express condition?

C. Excuse. Can the occurrence of the condition be excused?

CHAPTER 20
BREACH BY NONPERFORMANCE

I. Introduction

A breach of contract can occur in different ways. In this chapter, we will focus on "breach by non-performance." A party breaches by non-performance if the party's performance is due and the party either does not perform at all or does not perform as required.[1] By contrast, if a party announces before their performance is due that they will not honor the contract, we speak of a breach by anticipatory repudiation (or, "repudiation").[2]

Contrary to what its common meaning may suggest, the term "non-performance" is not limited to cases where the party fails to render any performance ("absence of performance"). Instead, it also covers scenarios where a party renders a performance that does not satisfy the terms of the contract ("defective performance").[3]

---

1. Restatement (Second) of Contracts § 235 (2); see also Lincicome v. Sables, LLC as Tr. of Deed of Tr. Given by Vicenta Lincicome and Dated 5/23/2007, 523 P.3d 1100 (Nev. 2022) ("Failure by the promisor to perform at the time indicated for performance in the contract establishes an immediate breach"); Franconia Associates v. U.S., 536 U.S. 129, 142–43 (2002) ("Failure by the promisor to perform at the time indicated for performance in the contract establishes an immediate breach.").
2. See Restatement (Second) of Contracts §§ 250 et seq.
3. Cf. Restatement (Second) of Contracts § 236 cmt. a (dividing all breaches into breaches by nonperformance and breaches by anticipatory repudiation).

For a breach to qualify as a breach by non-performance (as opposed to a breach by anticipatory repudiation), the relevant party's performance must be due.[4] Generally, performance is due at the time specified in the contract or, if the contract is silent with regard to timing, within a reasonable time.[5] However, if a duty to perform is subject to a condition, the performance is not due until the condition has occurred or is excused.[6]

In the following sections, we will discuss the injured party's rights and duties when a breach of contract occurs. To understand the consequences of a breach, you must distinguish carefully between two questions. First, what rights does the injured party have in case of a breach? For example, can the injured party demand damages? And second, how does the breach impact the injured party's duties to perform? For example, does the injured party still have to perform, or can they suspend their performance?

II. Non-Material vs. Material Breach

When one of the parties has committed a breach by non-performance, the first question to ask is whether the breach is material or non-material. The type of breach determines the injured party's rights and whether the injured party must still perform. A breach is material if it "substantially limits the non-breaching party from receiving the benefit of [their] bargain."[7] In other

4. E.g., Restatement (Second) of Contracts § 235 (2).

5. E.g., Lake Steel Erection, Inc. v. Egan, 403 N.Y.S.2d 387, 389 (N.Y. App. Div. 4th Dept. 1978).

6. E.g., Rastek Constr. & Dev. Corp. v. Gen. Land Com. Real Est. Co., LLC, 806 S.E.2d 740, 745 (Va. 2017); Anchorage Chrysler Ctr., Inc. v. DaimlerChrysler Corp., 129 P.3d 905, 911 (Alaska 2006); R. G. Pope Const. Co., Inc. v. Guard Rail of Roanoke, Inc., 244 S.E.2d 774, 778 (Va. 1978) ("The performance of Guard Rail's duty, subject to such conditions, did not become due unless the conditions occurred, or unless their nonoccurrence was excused . . . ") (internal citation omitted); Restatement (Second) of Contracts § 225(1).

7. AFA Priv. Eq. Fund 1 v. Miresco Inv. Services, No. 02-74650, 2006 WL 680857, at *4 (E.D. Mich. Mar. 16, 2006). This is just one of many different tests that differ in their wording but not so much in substance. See, e.g., Watkins & Eager, PLLC v. Lawrence, 326 So. 3d 988, 991 (Miss. 2021) ("A breach is material when there is 'a failure to perform a substantial part of the contract or one or more of its essential terms or conditions, or if there is such a breach as substantially defeats [the purpose of the contract].'"); Thomas v. Dept. of Hous. and Urb. Dev., 124 F.3d 1439, 1442 (Fed. Cir. 1997) ("A breach is material when it relates to a matter of vital importance, or goes to the essence of the contract."); 44 Associates Ltd. Partn. v. Capital Fitness, L.L.C., 731 N.W.2d 382 (Wis. App. 2007) (holding that "A breach is material when it is 'so serious ... as to destroy the essential objects of the contract.'") (internal citation omitted); Bakery Bling v. Matrix Packaging Mach., LLC, No. 21-CV-1399-JPS-JPS, 2023 WL 4933913, at *12 (E.D. Wis. Aug. 2, 2023) (holding that "[a] breach of contract is material when it is so serious as to destroy the essential object of the contract.'")

words, the distinction between material and non-material breaches depends on whether the breaching party has substantially performed. A breach is material if and only if the breaching party has not substantially performed.[8] Conversely, a breach is non-material if and only if the breaching party has substantially performed.[9] Whether a breach is material or non-material depends on the circumstances of the individual case. Section 241 of the Restatement (Second) of Contracts lists various factors that are helpful in distinguishing between a material and a non-material breach.[10]

III. Non-Material Breach

In case of a non-material breach, the injured party can demand damages for

(internal citation omitted); cf. Barufaldi v. Ocean City, Chamber of Com., Inc., 7 A.3d 643, 656 (Md. Spec. App. 2010) (holding that "[a] breach is material when it 'is such that further performance of the contract would be 'different in substance from that which was contracted for''") (internal citation omitted).

8. MD Helicopters Inc. v. Boeing Co., No. CV-17-02598-PHX-JAT, 2019 WL 3840974, at *12 (D. Ariz. Aug. 15, 2019); ESPN, Inc. v. Off. of Com'r of Baseball, 76 F. Supp. 2d 383, 401 (S.D.N.Y. 1999); see Contl. Dredging, Inc. v. De-Kaizered, Inc., 120 S.W.3d 380, 394 (Tex. App.—Texarkana 2003) ("If there is a material breach of the contract, the contract has not been substantially performed."); Patel v. Ambassador Drycleaning Co., Inc., 86 S.W.3d 304, 309 (Tex. App.—Eastland 2002) ("If a party has committed a material breach of a contract, his performance cannot be substantial.").

9. MD Helicopters Inc. v. Boeing Co., No. CV-17-02598-PHX-JAT, 2019 WL 3840974, at *12 (D. Ariz. Aug. 15, 2019); ESPN, Inc. v. Off. of Com'r of Baseball, 76 F. Supp. 2d 383, 401 (S.D.N.Y. 1999); see

Clean Harbors, Inc. v. Union P. Corp., No. CVN15C07081MMJCCLD, 2017 WL 5606953, at *4 (Del. Super. Nov. 15, 2017), aff'd, 201 A.3d 1161 (Del. 2019) (holding that "where there is a substantial performance, there can be no material breach").

10. Restatement (Second) of Contracts § 241. Courts often apply the factors listed in section 241 of the Restatement (Second) to distinguish between material and non-material breaches. E.g., Van Oort Constr. Co., Inc. v. Nuckoll's Concrete Serv., Inc., 599 N.W.2d 684, 693 (Iowa 1999); Burgess v. N. Bend Sch. Dist. #£13, 173 P.3d 1271, 1273 (Or. App. 2007); Casarez v. Alltec Const. Co., Inc., No. 14-07-00068-CV, 2007 WL 3287933, at *4 (Tex. App.—Hous. [14th Dist.] Nov. 6, 2007); Frazier v. Mellowitz, 804 N.E.2d 796, 805 (Ind. App. 2004).

any loss the breach has caused.[11] However, the injured party cannot suspend their own performance.[12]

> **Example.** A general contractor and an owner agree that the general contractor shall build a house according to the owner's specifications in exchange for $1,000,000. The general contractor follows the specifications to the letter, except that one of the interior walls is half an inch thicker than it should be. Barring exceptional circumstances, this breach is non-material. Accordingly, the owner cannot suspend their payment, though the owner is entitled to damages for any loss in value caused by the breach.

IV. Material Breaches

A. Curable vs. Incurable Material Breaches

When a material breach occurs, the injured party's rights and obligations depend on whether the breach is curable or incurable. Sometimes, a party has committed a material breach, but the breach is curable.[13] In other words, it is still possible for the party to substantially perform. Whether a breach is curable depends on whether the injured party can reasonably be expected to give the breaching party a shot at curing the breach. If it is physically impos-

---

11. Restatement (Second) of Contracts § 236. See Caraballo v. U.S., 691 Fed. Appx. 613, 621 (Fed. Cir. 2017) (unpublished) ("A breach need not be material in order to support a claim for breach of contract."); Waypoint Mgt. Consulting, LLC v. Krone, No. CV ELH-19-2988, 2022 WL 2528465, at *43 (D. Md. July 6, 2022) (holding that "'[e]very breach [of contract] gives rise to a claim for damages'") (internal citation omitted); Jay Dee/Mole Jt. Venture v. Mayor and City Council of Baltimore, 725 F. Supp. 2d 513, 526 (D. Md. 2010) (holding that "any breach of contract may give rise to a cause of action for damages") (citation omitted); Alliant Energy Corp. v. Alltel Corp., 344 F. Supp. 2d 1176, 1191 (S.D. Iowa 2004) (holding that even a non-material breach entitles the injured party to damages); TMT Bear Creek Shopping Ctr., Inc. v. Petco Animal Supplies, Inc., 165 P.3d 1271, 1282 (Wash. App. Div. 1 2007) (holding that even a non-material breach entitles the injured party to damages).

12. See, e.g., Solar Applications Engr., Inc. v. T.A. Operating Corp., 327 S.W.3d 104, 108 (Tex. 2010) (holding that "[b]reach of a covenant may give rise to a cause of action for damages, but does not affect the enforceability of the remaining provisions of the contract unless the breach is a material or total breach"); Burgess v. N. Bend Sch. Dist. #£13, 173 P.3d 1271, 1274 (Or. App. 2007) (holding that non-material breach did not excuse injured party from performing their duties).

13. E.g., Jorgensen v. United Commun. Group Ltd. Partn., No. 8:10-CV-00429-AW, 2011 WL 3821533, at *5 (D. Md. Aug. 25, 2011); Anacapa Tech., Inc. v. ADC Telecomm., Inc., 241 F. Supp. 2d 1016, 1021 n.3 (D. Minn. 2002); O'Connell Mgt. Co., Inc. v. Carlyle-XIII Managers, Inc., 765 F. Supp. 779, 784 (D. Mass. 1991).

to cure the breach, it is an incurable breach. However, a breach may also be incurable because the breaching party does not deserve another attempt to cure it in light of the circumstances. Section 242 of the Restatement (Second) of Contracts lists a variety of factors that are helpful in distinguishing between a curable and a non-curable breach.[14]

Example. Alpha is a cosmetic surgeon. Alpha and Beta have contracted for Alpha to straighten Beta's nose in exchange for $2,000. During the operation, Alpha is drunk and, as a result, botches the surgery leaving Beta with visible scars. In theory, Alpha might be able to fix the situation through a second surgery. But, in light of Alpha's intoxication during the first surgery, Beta cannot reasonably be expected to give Alpha another shot.

Example. Alpha is a painter. On January 1, Alpha and Beta contract for Alpha to paint Beta's house by March 31. When March 31 arrives, Alpha has completed only half of the work. In this case, Alpha has committed a material breach. However, since nothing suggests that time was of the essence and delays are quite common for this type of work, Alpha can still cure the breach.

Because the curability of a breach depends on what can reasonably be expected of the injured party, an originally curable breach can become incurable over time, e.g., the breaching party waits too long to cure the breach or repeated attempts to cure fail.

Example. Alpha owns and operates a garage. On January 1, Alpha and Beta contract for Alpha to fix the windshield wipers on Beta's car, which do not function properly. On January 3, Alpha notifies Beta that Alpha has fixed the problem and Beta picks up the car, only to find that the windshield wipers still do not function properly. Subsequently, Beta brings in their car three more times to allow Alpha to fix the problem, but none of the attempts yield the desired result. When Beta picked up their car on January 3, Alpha's breach was material but curable. However, after three failed repair attempts, Alpha's

14. Restatement (Second) of Contracts § 242. Courts often rely on the factors listed in section 242. See, e.g., Dolly Investments, LLC v. MMG Sioux City, LLC, 984 N.W.2d 168, 177 (Iowa 2023); Querencia Properties, S. de R.L. de C.V. v. New Querencia Capital Partners, L.L.C., 224 S.W.3d 348, 351 (Tex. App.—Dallas 2006).

breach is no longer curable because Beta cannot be expected to give Alpha another shot.

B. Curable Material Breaches

What are the consequences of a material but curable breach? As long as a material breach is curable, it does not (yet) discharge the injured party's duties to perform.[15] However, the curable material breach allows the injured party to suspend their own performance.[16] Moreover, the injured party is entitled to damages for any loss that will remain even if the breach is cured.[17]

Question. A general contractor and a hotel owner enter into a contract under which the general contractor must renovate a particular room by noon, January 1, for $5,000. However, as of January 5, the room still lacks windows, the walls have not been painted, and no fixtures have been attached. Explain the hotel owner's rights.

---

15. Triad Packaging, Inc. v. Supplyone, Inc., 597 Fed. Appx. 734, 741 (4th Cir. 2015); Frazier v. Mellowitz, 804 N.E.2d 796, 803 (Ind. App. 2004); Busch Marine Group, Inc. v. Calumet River Fleeting, Inc., 617 F. Supp. 3d 809, 818 (E.D. Mich. 2022). Courts are not always clear on this issue. Many cases have held that a material breach will discharge the injured party's duty to perform. See, e.g., Weiss v. Smulders, 96 A.3d 1175, 1197 (Conn. 2014) ("Under contract law, it is well settled that a material breach by one party discharges the other party's subsequent duty to perform on the contract."); Polyglycoat Corp. v. Holcomb, 591 P.2d 449, 451 (Utah 1979) (holding that "[a]s a general proposition, a party to a contract has a right of rescission and an action for restitution as an alternative to an action for damages where there has been a [m]aterial breach of the contract by the other party."). However, a closer inspection of the relevant case law typically reveals that the courts had incurable material breaches in mind. See, e.g., Weiss v. Smulders, 96 A.3d 1175, 1197 (Conn. 2014) (concluding that the injured party's duties had not been discharged because the injured party had not given the breaching party the opportunity to cure the breach). Cf. Mrs. Fields Fran., LLC v. MFGPC, Inc., No. 2:15-CV-00094-JNP, 2018 WL 3972924, at *9 (D. Utah Aug. 20, 2018) ("The Utah Supreme Court has used "material breach" to refer to a breach that allows the non-breaching party to terminate, or rescind, a contract as well as a breach that allows the non-breaching party to suspend performance."); Provident Life & Accident Ins. Co. v. Nassif, 221 F.3d 1335 (6th Cir. 2000) (holding that a material failure to perform will discharge the injured party's duties while also making it clear that a curable delay does not constitute a material failure to perform).

16. Dolly Investments, LLC v. MMG Sioux City, LLC, 984 N.W.2d 168, 177 (Iowa 2023) (holding that "a material breach temporarily suspends the injured party's duty to perform"); Van Oort Constr. Co., Inc. v. Nuckoll's Concrete Serv., Inc., 599 N.W.2d 684, 691 (Iowa 1999) (holding that one party's material breach justified other party's suspension of performance).

17. Restatement (Second) of Contracts § 346.

Answer. As of January 5, the breach is material but curable. The hotel owner can suspend their own performance and demand damages for the losses they have suffered due to being unable to use the room between January 1 and January 5.

The injured party's right to suspend their own subsequent performance follows directly from the implied conditions doctrine. Recall that if one party has to perform first, the other party's duty to perform is subject to the implied condition that the first party has substantially performed.[18] Moreover, under the general rules governing conditions, if a duty to perform is conditional, and the condition is not excused and has not occurred, then the performance is not due.[19] By definition, if a party has committed a material breach, that party has not substantially performed. Accordingly, the implied condition to which the other party's duty is subject has not occurred, meaning that the injured party's duty is not due. Saying that the injured party's performance is not due is just another way of saying that the injured party can suspend their performance.

Question. Alpha is a painter. On January 1, Alpha and Beta enter into a contract whereby Alpha is required to paint Beta's house by January 31. In exchange, Beta promises to pay Alpha $10,000 on February 1. As of February 2, Alpha has only painted half of Beta's house, and Beta has not yet paid Alpha. Has Alpha committed a material breach by non-performance? Has Beta committed a material breach by non-performance?

Answer. Once a party's performance is due, any failure to render the performance precisely as required by the contract constitutes a breach by non-performance.[20] Alpha's performance was due on January 31, and their failure to paint the entire house by that date constitutes a breach by non-perfor-

18. Restatement (Second) of Contracts § 237.
19. E.g., Rastek Constr. & Dev. Corp. v. Gen. Land Com. Real Est. Co., LLC, 806 S.E.2d 740, 745 (Va. 2017); Anchorage Chrysler Ctr., Inc. v. DaimlerChrysler Corp., 129 P.3d 905, 911 (Alaska 2006); R. G. Pope Const. Co., Inc. v. Guard Rail of Roanoke, Inc., 244 S.E.2d 774, 778 (Va. 1978) ("The performance of Guard Rail's duty, subject to such conditions, did not become due unless the conditions occurred, or unless their nonoccurrence was excused . . . ") (internal citation omitted); Restatement (Second) of Contracts § 225(1).
20. Cf. Restatement (Second) of Contracts § 235(2).

> The breach is material since it deprives Beta of a substantial part of the benefit of the bargain.
>
> For Beta to have committed a material breach by non-performance, Beta's performance would have had to be due. According to the contract, Beta had to pay Alpha on February 1. However, by law, since Alpha's performance was due first, Beta's duty to perform was subject to an implied condition that Alpha had substantially performed.[21] That condition was not excused or satisfied since Alpha committed an uncured material breach. Therefore, under section 225(1) of the Restatement (Second) of Contracts, Beta's performance was not yet due. This means that Beta could suspend their payment without breaching the contract. In sum, Beta has not breached the contract.

An equivalent outcome occurs if both performances are due at the same time. In this case, each party's performance is subject to the implied condition that the other party is ready, willing, and able to perform.[22] Under the general rules on conditions, the performance does not become due until the condition has occurred or its non-occurrence is excused.[23] It follows that if one party is not ready, willing, and able to perform without a material breach, the other party's performance is not due.

> **Question**. Alpha and Beta are neighbors. Both of their houses are painted gray. On January 1, Alpha and Beta enter into a contract under which each party promises to paint the front of their own house yellow on January 10. On January 10, Alpha stands in their own front yard with paint, paintbrushes, and a ladder, ready, willing, and able to perform. By contrast, Beta has not obtained any painting supplies. In addition, Beta partied hard the previous night and would therefore be unable to climb a ladder even if they tried. Because Beta is not ready to paint, Alpha abstains from painting their own house since Alpha is concerned that if Alpha paints their own house that day,

---

21. Restatement (Second) of Contracts § 237.
22. Restatement (Second) of Contracts § 238.
23. If a duty is conditional, the condition has not occurred and is not excused, the performance is not due. E.g., Rastek Constr. & Dev. Corp. v. Gen. Land Com. Real Est. Co., LLC, 806 S.E.2d 740, 745 (Va. 2017); Anchorage Chrysler Ctr., Inc. v. DaimlerChrysler Corp., 129 P.3d 905, 911 (Alaska 2006); R. G. Pope Const. Co., Inc. v. Guard Rail of Roanoke, Inc., 244 S.E.2d 774, 778 (Va. 1978); Restatement (Second) of Contracts § 225(1).

Beta will not make good on their promise to paint Beta's house. Have the parties breached the contract?

Answer. Once a party's performance is due, any failure to render the performance precisely as required by the contract constitutes a breach by non-performance.[24] Alpha has not breached the contract. Under the contract, the parties' duties were due simultaneously. This means that Alpha's duty was subject to an implied condition that Beta was ready, willing, and able to perform. Given Beta's lack of painting supplies and physical inability to paint the house, Beta was neither ready nor able to perform. Accordingly, the implied condition for Alpha's duty to perform was not satisfied, and, under the rule in section 225(1) of the Restatement (Second) of Contracts, Alpha's performance was not due. In other words, Alpha could suspend their performance without breaching the contract.

Beta, on the other hand, has breached the contract. Like Alpha's duty to perform, Beta's duty was subject to an implied condition that the other party, Alpha, was ready, willing, and able to perform. However, that condition was satisfied since, unlike Beta, Alpha was ready, willing, and able to paint their own house yellow. Therefore, Beta's performance was due on the agreed-upon date (January 10), and Beta's failure to perform constituted a breach.

C. Incurable Material Breaches

If the breaching party has committed an incurable material breach, the injured party's remaining duties to perform are discharged.[25] Moreover, the injured party is generally entitled to damages for total breach.[26]

---

24. Cf. Restatement (Second) of Contracts § 235(2).

25. Dolly Investments, LLC v. MMG Sioux City, LLC, 984 N.W.2d 168, 177 (Iowa 2023) (holding that once it is too late for the breaching party to cure their material breach, the injured party's duties are discharged); Mustang Pipeline Co., Inc. v. Driver Pipeline Co., Inc., 134 S.W.3d 195, 200 (Tex. 2004) (holding that material breach discharged injured party's duties to perform where breaching party could not be expected to cure the breach); Murphy Farrell Dev., LLP v. Sourant, 272 P.3d 355, 364 (Ariz. App. 1st Div. 2012), as amended (June 29, 2012) (holding that "an uncured material breach of contract relieves the non-breaching party from the duty to perform and can discharge that party from the contract").

26. See, e.g., Allied Capital Partners, LP v. Proceed Tech. Resources, Inc., 313 S.W.3d 460, 465 (Tex. App.—Dallas 2010) (holding that "the general rule is that an uncured material breach before the injured party has fully performed his duties with respect to the expected exchange, will discharge

D. The Restatement (Second) of Contracts

Under the Restatement (Second) of Contracts, the discharge of the injured party's remaining duties to perform is based on the doctrine of implied conditions. Recall that a conditional duty is discharged under the general rules on conditions if a condition is not excused, has not occurred, and can no longer occur.[27] If the breaching party had to perform first, the injured party's duty to perform is conditional on the breaching party having substantially performed.[28] But, by definition, a party who has committed an incurable breach has not substantially performed and, because the breach is incurable, cannot substantially perform. It follows that the implied condition of substantial performance can no longer occur so that the injured party's duty is discharged. Similarly, if both parties had to perform simultaneously, each party's duty was subject to the implied condition that the other party was willing, ready, and able to perform.[29] If the breaching party was not ready, willing, and able to perform without committing a material breach, and if that breach is incurable, the condition can no longer occur, and the injured party's duty is discharged.

Damages for total breach mean that the injured party can demand damages based on their remaining rights to performance.[30] We will discuss the various ways of calculating damages later when we cover remedies. However, two simple examples may illustrate the importance of damages for total breach.

> **Question.** Alpha and Beta enter into a contract that requires Alpha to paint Beta's house a particular shade of blue by March 1 in exchange for $10,000 to be paid on March 2. Alpha paints Beta's house by the due date but uses a

---

that party's remaining duties of performance and give rise to a claim for damages for total breach.").

27. E.g., Rastek Constr. & Dev. Corp. v. Gen. Land Com. Real Est. Co., LLC, 806 S.E.2d 740, 745 (Va. 2017); Grigoleit Co. v. Whirlpool Corp., No. 05-CV-2126, 2010 WL 1881992, at *5 (C.D. Ill. May 10, 2010), aff'd, 769 F.3d 966 (7th Cir. 2014); Davis v. Dawson, Inc., 15 F. Supp. 2d 64, 118 (D. Mass. 1998); Restatement (Second) of Contracts § 225(2).

28. Restatement (Second) of Contracts § 237.

29. Restatement (Second) of Contracts § 238.

30. Infousa.com, Inc. v. Berj, Inc., No. A-04-303, 2005 WL 2648955, at *13 (Neb. App. Oct. 18, 2005) ("A claim for damages for total breach is one for damages based on all of the injured party's remaining rights to performance") (internal citation omitted); Restatement (Second) of Contracts § 236(1).

slightly different shade of blue. On March 2, Beta seeks legal counsel. Beta wants to know if Alpha has breached the contract, whether Alpha is still entitled to the $10,000, and whether Beta is entitled to damages, assuming that the market value of the house is the same as it would be if Alpha had used the contractually specified color.

Answer. Beta has asked three different questions, which we will address in turn.

First, Alpha committed a breach by non-performance since their performance was due and deviated from what the contract required.

Second, Beta's duty to pay was conditional on Alpha having substantially performed. Even though Alpha has breached the contract, Alpha's deviation from the contract was minor, and Beta obtained most of what they were entitled to. Therefore, Alpha's breach was non-material, meaning that Alpha has substantially performed. Accordingly, the implied condition to which Beta's duty to pay is subject is met. It follows that Alpha is still entitled to the promised compensation.

Third, because Alpha has committed a breach, albeit a non-material one, Beta is entitled to damages. However, since the market value of the house has not changed meaning Beta has not suffered a loss, Beta will be awarded nominal damages, typically $1.

Question. Alpha and Beta enter into a contract whereby Alpha is required to paint Beta's house in a particular shade of blue by March 1 in exchange for $10,000 to be paid on March 2. Alpha paints Beta's house by the due date but uses pink paint and then decorates the house with large blue dots. When Beta asks Alpha to repaint the house in the contractually agreed-upon shade of blue, Beta points out that they are an artist and will not, under any circumstances, compromise the integrity of their work by repainting the house. On March 2, Beta hires the cheapest painter they can find, Gamma, to repaint the house in the desired color. Gamma charges Beta $11,000 for their work. The next day, Beta seeks legal counsel. Beta wants to know if Alpha has breached the contract, whether Alpha is still entitled to the $10,000, and whether Beta is entitled to damages, assuming that the market value of the house is the same as it would be if Alpha had used the contractually specified color.

Answer. Beta has asked three different questions, which we will address in turn.

First, Alpha committed a breach by non-performance since their performance was due and deviated from what the contract required.

Second, Beta's duty to pay was conditional on Alpha having substantially performed. Alpha's breach was material, given that the chosen performance differed dramatically from what the contract specified and deprived Beta of most of the benefit of the bargain. It was theoretically possible for Alpha to repaint the house. Still, because of Alpha's stout refusal to do so, Beta cannot be expected to give Alpha another shot at curing the breach. Therefore, Alpha's breach is both material and incurable. It follows that the condition for Beta's duty to perform can no longer occur, so Beta's duty to pay Alpha is discharged.

Third, because Alpha has committed a breach, Beta is entitled to damages. Moreover, since the breach was both material and incurable, Beta can demand damages for total breach. In the case of breach, the injured party is typically entitled to expectation damages.[31] Expectation damages include the loss in value due to the breaching party's performance and any other consequential or incidental loss minus expenses saved.[32] In case of a non-curable material breach, the injured party can enter into a reasonable alternative transaction to obtain the benefits to which the injured party was entitled under the contract, as long as the relevant costs are not disproportionate.[33] The costs of a reasonable substitute transaction determine the loss in value that the injured party has suffered. Hiring Gamma was a reasonable substitute transaction, especially given that Gamma was the cheapest alternative that Beta could find. In these circumstances, Beta's loss in value is determined by the reasonable substitute transaction and hence amounts to $11,000. The hypothetical does not mention consequential or incidental damages. However, Beta saved expenses of $10,000 because they did not have to pay Alpha. In sum, Beta can demand expectation damages of $1,000. Note that this outcome is quite intuitive: By paying Beta $1,000, Alpha makes Beta as well off as Beta would have been if Alpha had not breached.

31. Restatement (Second) of Contracts § 347.
32. Restatement (Second) of Contracts § 347.
33. Restatement (Second) of Contracts § 348 cmt. c.

E. A Note on the Restatement (Second) of Contracts

The Restatement (Second) of Contracts embraces the principle that an incurable material breach will also generally lead to damages for total breach but obtains this outcome through a complex combination of different rules.

Suppose the breaching party must perform first and commits an incurable material breach. In that case, the principle that an incurable material breach leads to damages for total breach follows based on sections 225(2), 237, and 243(1) of the Restatement (Second) of Contracts. Under section 243(1), a breach by non-performance that will cause the injured party's remaining duties to be discharged gives the injured party a claim for damages for total breach.

If the breaching party had to perform first, under section 237, the injured party's remaining duties to perform are subject to the implied condition that the breaching party has substantially performed. If the breaching party has committed an incurable breach, the implied condition can no longer occur, and the injured party's duties are therefore discharged under section 225(2). And the injured party has a right to damages for total breach under section 243(1).

Next, suppose that both parties must perform simultaneously and the breaching party commits an incurable material breach. In this case, the reasoning is relatively similar, with the injured party's right to damages for total breach stemming from sections 225(2), 238, and 243(1). Again, section 243(1) grants a right to damages for total breach if the breach discharges the injured party's remaining duties to perform. Section 238 makes the injured party's duties to perform subject to an implied condition that the breaching party is ready, willing, and able to perform. But if the breaching party has committed an incurable material breach, that condition can no longer occur, meaning that the injured party's duties are discharged under section 225(2). It follows that the injured party has a right to damages for total breach under section 243(1).

Finally, suppose that the injured party had to perform first, and, after the injured party has done so, the breaching party commits an incurable material breach. In that case, the injured party's right to damages for total breach can be based on section 243(4). According to that provision, the injured party can demand damages for total breach if the breach so substantially impairs the contract's value to the injured party that granting damages for total breach is justified.[34]

Both Section 243(3) of the Restatement (Second) of Contracts and many courts recognize one exception to the principle that an incurable material breach gives rise to damages for total breach.[35] This exception concerns cases where the injured party has fully performed, and all that the breaching party remains obligated to do is make payments in installments. The reason underlying this exception is that granting damages for total breach in this scenario would effectively mean that missing one of several payments would cause the breaching party's entire debt to come due (in the form of damages for total breach).

Question. On January 1, Alpha and Beta enter into a contract whereby Alpha repairs Beta's car by January 15, and, in exchange, Beta makes ten monthly payments of $100, due on the first of each month, starting on February 1. Alpha repairs Beta's car. Beta makes the first three payments but misses the fourth payment and subsequently informs Alpha that Beta does not have the money to make the fourth payment but will continue with the other remaining payments as scheduled. Can Alpha demand damages for total breach?

Answer. As a general rule, an incurable material breach will lead to damages for total breach. Missing a payment is a material breach, and with Beta's subsequent announcement that Beta had no intention of making that payment, that breach became incurable. However, under section 243(3) of the Restatement (Second) of Contracts, if the injured party has fully performed, and all that the breaching party remains obligated to do is make payments in installments, committing an incurable material breach concerning only some of these payments will not allow the injured party to demand damages for total breach. This rule does not prevent Alpha from demanding damages

34. Restatement (Second) of Contracts § 243. Numerous courts have cited this principle with approval. See, e.g. Alaska Energy Auth. v. Fairmont Ins. Co., 845 P.2d 420, 424 (Alaska 1993) (holding that "[a] breach by non-performance gives rise to a claim for total breach only if it substantially impairs the value of the contract to the injured party") (internal citation omitted).

35. Restatement (Second) of Contracts § 243(3). See also Greguhn v. Mut. of Omaha Ins. Co., 461 P.2d 285, 287 (Utah 1969) (holding that "[i]n unilateral contract for the payment in installments after default of one or more, no repudiation can amount to an anticipatory breach of the rest of the installments not yet due").

regarding Beta's missed payment. However, and this is the point of the rule, Alpha cannot demand damages with respect to all of Beta's remaining duties, which would require Alpha to pay the entire outstanding amount.

Jacobs & Youngs, Inc. v. Kent

Court of Appeals of New York, 230 N.Y. 239 (1921)

CARDOZO, J.

The plaintiff built a country residence for the defendant at a cost of upwards of $77,000, and now sues to recover a balance of $3,483.46, remaining unpaid. The work of construction ceased in June, 1914, and the defendant then began to occupy the dwelling. There was no complaint of defective performance until March, 1915. One of the specifications for the plumbing work provides that——

'All wrought-iron pipe must be well galvanized, lap welded pipe of the grade known as 'standard pipe' of Reading manufacture.'

The defendant learned in March, 1915, that some of the pipe, instead of being made in Reading, was the product of other factories. The plaintiff was accordingly directed by the architect to do the work anew. The plumbing was then encased within the walls except in a few places where it had to be exposed. Obedience to the order meant more than the substitution of other pipe. It meant the demolition at great expense of substantial parts of the completed structure. The plaintiff left the work untouched, and asked for a certificate that the final payment was due. Refusal of the certificate was followed by this suit.

The evidence sustains a finding that the omission of the prescribed brand of pipe was neither fraudulent nor willful. It was the result of the oversight and inattention of the plaintiff's subcontractor. Reading pipe is distinguished from Cohoes pipe and other brands only by the name of the manufacturer stamped upon it at intervals of between six and seven feet. Even the defendant's architect, though he inspected the pipe upon arrival, failed to notice the discrepancy. The plaintiff tried to show that the brands installed, though made by other manufacturers, were the same in quality, in appearance, in market value, and in cost as the brand stated in the contract—that they were, indeed, the same thing, though manufactured in another place. The evidence was excluded, and a verdict directed for the defendant. The Appellate Division reversed, and granted a new trial.

We think the evidence, if admitted, would have supplied some basis for the inference that the defect was insignificant in its relation to the project. The courts never say that one who makes a contract fills the measure of his duty by less than full performance. They do say, however, that an omission, both trivial and innocent, will sometimes be atoned for by allowance of the resulting damage, and will not always be the breach of a condition to be followed by a forfeiture. Spence v. Ham, 163 N. Y. 220. . . . The distinction is akin to that between dependent and independent promises, or between promises and conditions. . . . Some promises are so plainly independent that they can never by fair construction be conditions of one another. . . . Others are so plainly dependent that they must always be conditions. Others, though dependent and thus conditions when there is departure in point of substance, will be viewed as independent and collateral when the departure is insignificant. . . . Considerations partly of justice and partly of presumable intention are to tell us whether this or that promise shall be placed in one class or in another. The simple and the uniform will call for different remedies from the multifarious and the intricate. The margin of departure within the range of normal expectation upon a sale of common chattels will vary from the margin to be expected upon a contract for the construction of a mansion or a 'skyscraper.' There will be harshness sometimes and oppression in the implication of a condition when the thing upon which labor has been expended is incapable of surrender because united to the land, and equity and reason in the implication of a like condition when the subject-matter, if defective, is in shape to be returned. From the conclusion that promises may not be treated as dependent to the extent of their uttermost minutiae without a sacrifice of justice, the progress is a short one to the conclusion that they may not be so treated without a perversion of intention. Intention not otherwise revealed may be presumed to hold in contemplation the reasonable and probable. If something else is in view, it must not be left to implication. There will be no assumption of a purpose to visit venial faults with oppressive retribution.

Those who think more of symmetry and logic in the development of legal rules than of practical adaptation to the attainment of a just result will be troubled by a classification where the lines of division are so wavering and blurred. Something, doubtless, may be said on the score of consistency and certainty in favor of a stricter standard. The courts have balanced such considerations against those of equity and fairness, and found the latter to be the weightier. The decisions in this state commit us to the liberal view, which is making its way, nowadays, in jurisdictions slow to welcome it. Dakin & Co. v. Lee, 1916, 1 K. B. 566, 579. Where the line is to be drawn between the important and the trivial cannot be settled by a formula. 'In the nature of the case precise boundaries are impossible.' 2 Williston on Contracts, § 841. The same omission may take on one aspect or another according to its setting. Substitution of equivalents may not have the same significance in fields of art on the one side and in those of mere utility on the other. Nowhere will change be tolerated, however, if it is so dominant or pervasive as in any real or substantial measure to frustrate the purpose of the contract. Crouch v. Gutmann, 134 N. Y. 45, 51. . . . There is no general license to install whatever, in the builder's judgment, may be regarded as 'just as good.' Easthampton L. & C. Co., Ltd., v. Worthington, 186 N. Y. 407, 412, 79 N. E. 323. The question is one of degree, to be answered, if there is doubt, by the triers of the facts (Crouch v. Gutmann; Woodward v. Fuller, supra), and, if the inferences are certain, by the judges of the law (Easthampton L. & C. Co., Ltd., v. Worthington, supra). We must weigh the purpose to be served, the desire to be gratified, the excuse for deviation from the letter, the cruelty of enforced adherence. Then only can we tell whether literal fulfillment is to be implied by law as a condition. This is not to say that the parties are not free by apt and certain words to effectuate a purpose that performance of every term shall be a condition of recovery. That question is not here. This is merely to say that the law will be slow to impute the purpose, in the silence of the parties, where the significance of the default is grievously out of proportion to the oppression of the forfeiture. The willful transgressor must accept the penalty of his transgression. . . . For him there is no occasion to mitigate the rigor of implied conditions. The transgressor whose default is unintentional and trivial may hope for mercy if he will offer atonement for his wrong. Spence v. Ham, supra.

In the circumstances of this case, we think the measure of the allowance is not the cost of replacement, which would be great, but the difference in value, which would be either nominal or nothing. Some of the exposed sections might perhaps have been replaced at moderate expense. The defendant did not limit his demand to them, but treated the plumbing as a unit to be corrected from cellar to roof. In point of fact, the plaintiff never reached the stage at which evidence of the extent of the allowance became necessary. The trial court had excluded evidence that the defect was unsubstantial, and in view of that ruling there was no occasion for the plaintiff to go farther with an offer of proof. We think, however, that the offer, if it had been made, would not of necessity have been defective because directed to difference in value. It is true that in most cases the cost of replacement is the measure. Spence v. Ham, supra. The owner is entitled to the money which will permit him to complete, unless the cost of completion is grossly and unfairly out of proportion to the good to be attained. When that is true, the measure is the difference in value. Specifications call, let us say, for a foundation built of granite quarried in Vermont. On the completion of the building, the owner learns that through the blunder of a subcontractor part of the foundation has been built of granite of the same quality quarried in New Hampshire. The measure of allowance is not the cost of reconstruction. 'There may be omissions of that which could not afterwards be supplied exactly as called for by the contract without taking down the building to its foundations, and at the same time the omission may not affect the value of the building for use or otherwise, except so slightly as to be hardly appreciable.' Handy v. Bliss, 204 Mass. 513, 519. . . . The rule that gives a remedy in cases of substantial performance with compensation for defects of trivial or inappreciable importance has been developed by the courts as an instrument of justice. The measure of the allowance must be shaped to the same end.

The order should be affirmed, and judgment absolute directed in favor of the plaintiff upon the stipulation, with costs in all courts.

McLaughlin, J.

I dissent. The plaintiff did not perform its contract. Its failure to do so was either intentional or due to gross neglect which, under the uncontradicted facts, amounted to the same thing, nor did it make any proof of the cost of compliance, where compliance was possible.

Under its contract it obligated itself to use in the plumbing only pipe (between 2,000 and 2,500 feet) made by the Reading Manufacturing Company. The first pipe delivered was about 1,000 feet and the plaintiff's superintendent then called the attention of the foreman of the subcontractor, who was doing the plumbing, to the fact that the specifications annexed to the contract required all pipe used in the plumbing to be of the Reading Manufacturing Company. They then examined it for the purpose of ascertaining whether this delivery was of that manufacture and found it was. Thereafter, as pipe was required in the progress of the work, the foreman of the subcontractor would leave word at its shop that he wanted a specified number of feet of pipe, without in any way indicating of what manufacture. Pipe would thereafter be delivered and installed in the building, without any examination whatever. Indeed, no examination, so far as appears, was made by the plaintiff, the subcontractor, defendant's architect, or anyone else, of any of the pipe except the first delivery, until after the building had been completed. Plaintiff's architect then refused to give the certificate of completion, upon which the final payment depended, because all of the pipe used in the plumbing was not of the kind called for by the contract. After such refusal, the subcontractor removed the covering or insulation from about 900 feet of pipe which was exposed in the basement, cellar, and attic, and all but 70 feet was found to have been manufactured, not by the Reading Company, but by other manufacturers, some by the Cohoes Rolling Mill Company, some by the National Steel Works, some by the South Chester Tubing Company, and some which bore no manufacturer's mark at all. The balance of the pipe had been so installed in the building that an inspection of it could not be had without demolishing, in part at least, the building itself.

I am of the opinion the trial court was right in directing a verdict for the defendant. The plaintiff agreed that all the pipe used should be of the Reading Manufacturing Company. Only about two-fifths of it, so far as appears, was of that kind. If more were used, then the burden of proving that fact was upon the plaintiff, which it could easily have done, since it knew where the pipe was obtained. The question of substantial performance of a contract of the character of the one under consideration depends in no small degree upon the good faith of the contractor. If the plaintiff had intended to, and had, complied with the terms of the contract except as to minor omissions, due to inadvertence, then he might be allowed to recover the contract price, less the amount necessary to fully compensate the defendant for damages caused by such omissions. Woodward v. Fuller, 80 N. Y. 312 . . . . But that is not this case. It installed between 2,000 and 2,500 feet of pipe, of which only 1,000 feet at most complied with the contract. No explanation was given why pipe called for by the contract was not used, nor that any effort made to show what it would cost to remove the pipe of other manufacturers and install that of the Reading Manufacturing Company. The defendant had a right to contract for what he wanted. He had a right before making payment to get what the contract called for. It is no answer to this suggestion to say that the pipe put in was just as good as that made by the Reading Manufacturing Company, or that the difference in value between such pipe and the pipe made by the Reading Manufacturing Company would be either 'nominal or nothing.' Defendant contracted for pipe made by the Reading Manufacturing Company. What his reason was for requiring this kind of pipe is of no importance. He wanted that and was entitled to it. It may have been a mere whim on his part, but even so, he had a right to this kind of pipe, regardless of whether some other kind, according to the opinion of the contractor or experts, would have been 'just as good, better, or done just as well.' He agreed to pay only upon condition that the pipe installed were made by that company and he ought not to be compelled to pay unless that condition be performed. Schultze v. Goodstein, 180 N. Y. 248, 73 N. E. 21. . . . The rule, therefore, of substantial performance, with damages for unsubstantial omissions, has no application. Crouch v. Gutmann, 134 N. Y. 45. . . .

What was said by this court in Smith v. Brady, supra, is quite applicable here:

'I suppose it will be conceded that everyone has a right to build his house, his cottage or his store after such a model and in such style as shall best accord with his notions of utility or be most agreeable to his fancy. The specifications of the contract become the law between the parties until voluntarily changed. If the owner prefers a plain and simple Doric column, and has so provided in the agreement, the contractor has no right to put in its place the more costly and elegant Corinthian. If the owner, having regard to strength and durability, has contracted for walls of specified materials to be laid in a particular manner, or for a given number of joists and beams, the builder has no right to substitute his own judgment or that of others. Having departed from the agreement, if performance has not been waived by the other party, the law will not allow him to allege that he has made as good a building as the one he engaged to erect. He can demand payment only upon and according to the terms of his contract, and if the conditions on which payment is due have not been performed, then the right to demand it does not exist. To hold a different doctrine would be simply to make another contract, and would be giving to parties an encouragement to violate their engagements, which the just policy of the law does not permit.' (17 N. Y. 186, 72 Am. Dec. 422).

I am of the opinion the trial court did not err in ruling on the admission of evidence or in directing a verdict for the defendant.

For the foregoing reasons I think the judgment of the Appellate Division should be reversed and the judgment of the Trial Term affirmed.

HISCOCK, C. J., and HOGAN and CRANE, JJ., concur with CARDOZO, J.

NOTES AND QUESTIONS

A. Implied conditions v. express conditions. Contract law distinguishes between express conditions and implied conditions. Express conditions are conditions that the parties have agreed on in their contract, whereas implied conditions are imposed by law.[36] Which type of condition does *Jacobs & Youngs* involve?

B. Order of performances. To determine when each party's performance is due, we look to the rules expressed in section 234 of the Restatement (Second) of Contracts. The parties can determine the order of performances in the contract. To the extent that the contract is silent, if one performance takes time and the other does not, the performance that takes time is due first.[37] If both performances can be rendered simultaneously, they are due at the same time.[38] Which party had to perform first in *Jacobs & Youngs*?

C. Synallagmatic and implied conditions. To understand the role of implied conditions, one has to take into account that bilateral contracts involve a bargain in the form of a quid-pro-quo: each party promises so that the other party promises. When there are quid-pro-quo promises, the parties' contractual obligations are reciprocal or "synallagmatic." Because of the reciprocal nature of the parties' obligations, the fates of the parties' duties remain intertwined. If party A has to perform first, then party B's duty to perform is subject to the implied condition that party A has substantially performed.[39] Similarly, if both parties' performances are due at the same time, then, by law, each party's duty is subject to an implied condition that the other party is will-

36. See, e.g., Oppenheimer & Co., Inc. v. Oppenheim, Appel, Dixon & Co., 660 N.E.2d 415, 418 (N.Y. 1995) (holding that "[e]xpress conditions are those agreed to and imposed by the parties themselves" whereas "[i]mplied or constructive conditions are those 'imposed by law to do justice'") (citations omitted); In re NextMedia Group, Inc., 440 B.R. 76, 80 (Bankr. D. Del. 2010), af'd sub nom. In re NextMedia Group Inc., No. BR 09-14463 PJW, 2011 WL 4711997 (D. Del. Oct. 6, 2011) (holding that "[e]xpress conditions are those agreed to by the parties and implied/constructive conditions are those imposed by a court").

37. Restatement (Second) of Contracts § 234(2).

38. Restatement (Second) of Contracts § 234(1).

39. Restatement (Second) of Contracts § 237.

ready, and able to substantially perform.[40] Which, if any, duties were subject to an implied condition in *Jacobs & Youngs*?

D. Substantial performance and material breach. Substantial performance is the flip-side of a non-material breach. If a party's breach is non-material, then the party has substantially performed. By contrast, if a party's breach is material, then the party has not substantially performed. Was the breach in *Jacobs & Youngs* material or non-material? Why or why not?

E. Strict compliance v. substantial performance. According to the traditional view, substantial performance is sufficient for implied conditions, but express conditions require strict compliance.[41] What would be the consequence if courts generally demanded strict compliance with implied conditions? In particular, how would this impact the construction industry?

F. Protecting the injured party. In *Jacobs & Youngs*, if the use of a particular brand of pipe was of paramount importance to the defendant (Kent), what, if anything, could he have done to protect his interests?

40. Restatement (Second) of Contracts § 238.

41. Midwest Builder Distribg., Inc. v. Lord and Essex, Inc., 891 N.E.2d 1, 23 (Ill. App. 1st Dist. 2007); Regency Com. Associates, LLC v. Lopax, Inc., 869 N.E.2d 310, 321 (Ill. App. 4th Dist. 2007).

CHAPTER 21
BREACH BY REPUDIATION

I. Introduction

Non-performance is not the only way to breach a contract. A breach by non-performance requires that the performance is due.[1] Yet, sometimes, a party makes it clear that they will not perform even before their performance is due. In that case, the party has "repudiated" the contract. When repudiation occurs, it would be overly formalistic to expect the prospective injured party to wait until the relevant performance becomes due before terminating the contract or demanding damages. Therefore, the repudiation itself is treated as a breach of contract. Consequently, there are two ways to breach a contract—breach by non-performance and breach by repudiation.

II. Repudiation Defined

There are three ways for a party to repudiate a contract before their performance is due: repudiation by statement, repudiation by voluntary act, and repudiation by failure to provide adequate assurance of performance.

---

1. Restatement (Second) of Contracts § 235 (2).

A. Repudiation by Statement

A PARTY CAN REPUDIATE by making a statement. That statement must imply that once the party's performance becomes due, they will commit a breach giving rise to damages for total breach.[2] For example, the party can state that they will not perform at all.[3] Alternatively, the party can communicate that they will perform in so defective a manner as to give rise to a claim for damages for total breach.[4]

Crucially, the breach implied must be sufficiently severe to give rise to damages for total breach.[5] A party has not repudiated the contract if they state that they will commit a non-material breach or that they will commit a curable material breach and subsequently cures that breach.

Example. Alpha and Beta have formed a contract under which Beta is required to paint Alpha's house by June 5. On May 31, Beta calls Alpha and tells him that he will only be able to commence his work on June 6 and that he will finish his work on June 7. In this case, Beta has not repudiated the contract. The failure to paint the house is a material breach, but Beta has clarified that he will cure the breach before it becomes incurable. Therefore, Beta's actions do not give rise to damages for total breach.

Example. Alpha and Beta have formed a contract under which Beta is required to paint Alpha's house. The contract provides that the house shall be painted in a particular shade of light blue. Before Beta's performance is due, he contacts Alpha and tells him that he will paint the house in a very slightly different shade of light blue. In this case, Beta has stated that he will commit a breach of contract, but because the breach is non-material, it will not give rise

---

2. E.g., Trumble v. Farm Bureau Mut. Ins. Co. of Idaho, 456 P.3d 201, 215 (Idaho 2019); Pavone v. Kirke, 807 N.W.2d 828, 833 (Iowa 2011); Norcon Power Partners, L.P. v. Niagara Mohawk Power Corp., 705 N.E.2d 656, 659 (N.Y. 1998); Rec. v. Kempe, 928 A.2d 1199, 1206 (Vt. 2007); Essex Holding, LLC v. Basic Properties, Inc., 427 P.3d 708, 726 (Wyo. 2018); Restatement (Second) of Contracts § 250.
3. E.g., Homeland Energy Sols., LLC v. Retterath, 938 N.W.2d 664, 697 (Iowa 2020)
4. E.g., Norcon Power Partners, L.P. v. Niagara Mohawk Power Corp., 705 N.E.2d 656, 659 (N.Y. 1998).
5. Trumble v. Farm Bureau Mut. Ins. Co. of Idaho, 456 P.3d 201, 216 (Idaho 2019); Restatement (Second) of Contracts § 250.

to damages for total breach. Therefore, Beta's statement does not amount to a repudiation.

B. Repudiation by Voluntary Act

A party can also repudiate by taking voluntary actions that make the party unable to avoid a breach, giving rise to damages for total breach.[6]

Example. Alpha, a violinist, contracts with Beta to play the violin at Beta's wedding on June 1 for $500. On May 31, Alpha embarks on a flight to Japan, making it impossible for him to be back in time to perform at Beta's wedding. Alpha's conduct constitutes a repudiation by voluntary action.

Example. Alpha and Beta have entered into a contract to sell a particular parcel of land owned by Alpha. Before the land is due to be conveyed to Beta, Alpha conveys the land to a third party, Gamma. Because Alpha's action renders him unable to avoid a breach of his contract with Beta that gives rise to damages for total breach, Alpha's conduct constitutes a repudiation by voluntary act.

C. Repudiation by Failure to Provide Adequate Assurance of Performance

A party can also repudiate by failing to provide adequate assurance of performance where such assurance is required.[7] For background, a party can demand adequate assurance of performance if that party has reasonable grounds to think that the other party will breach the contract in such a way as to give rise to a claim for damages for total breach.[8] Until the prospective

---

6. Pavone v. Kirke, 807 N.W.2d 828, 833 (Iowa 2011); Paul v. Bogle, 484 N.W.2d 728, 736 (Mich. App. 1992); Norcon Power Partners, L.P. v. Niagara Mohawk Power Corp., 705 N.E.2d 656, 659 (N.Y. 1998); Griffin v. Zapata, 570 A.2d 659, 662 (R.I. 1990); Thompson v. Thompson, 495 A.2d 678, 682 (R.I. 1985); Rec. v. Kempe, 928 A.2d 1199, 1206 (Vt. 2007); Essex Holding, LLC v. Basic Properties, Inc., 427 P.3d 708, 726 (Wyo. 2018); Downtown Barre Dev. v. GU Markets of Barre, LLC, 22 A.3d 1174, 1178 (Vt. 2011); Restatement (Second) of Contracts § 250.
7. Bitzes v. Sunset Oaks, Inc., 649 P.2d 66, 70 (Utah 1982); Drinkwater v. Patten Realty Corp., 563 A.2d 772, 776 (Me. 1989); Jessup v. Five Star Fran. LLC, 515 P.3d 466, 475 (Utah App. 2022); Smargon v. Grand Lodge Partners, LLC, 288 P.3d 1063, 1069 (Utah App. 2012); AGS Contracting LLC v. Outside the Box, LLC, No. 7:20-CV-255 (WLS), 2023 WL 6064732, at *9 (M.D. Ga. Sept. 18, 2023).
8. McNeal v. Lebel, 953 A.2d 396, 401 (N.H. 2008); Drinkwater v. Patten Realty Corp., 563 A.2d 772,

breacher provides such assurance, the prospective injured party can suspend any parts of her own performance for which the agreed equivalent has not yet been rendered.[9] Moreover, if the required assurance is not provided within a reasonable time, the prospective injured party can treat the failure to provide such assurance as a repudiation.

> **Example.** On May 1, Alpha, a violinist, contracts with Beta to play the violin at Beta's wedding on June 1 for $500. The $500 is to be paid one day before the wedding. On May 10, Alpha contracts with Gamma to play the violin at Gamma's wedding for $2,000. Alpha cannot play at both weddings because they occur simultaneously and in different cities. Beta can demand adequate assurance that Alpha will honor his contract and can suspend his payment to Alpha until Alpha provides such assurance. Furthermore, if Alpha fails to provide such assurance within a reasonable time, Beta can treat this failure as a repudiation.

III. Retracting A Repudiation

Can a party who has repudiated a contract change her mind and retract the repudiation later on? As a general rule, a repudiation is retractable.[10]

In the case of a repudiation by statement, the retraction also requires a statement. In the case of repudiation by voluntary act, the retraction occurs through a change in circumstances such that the repudiating party is no longer unable to perform without a breach that gives rise to damages for total breach. Similarly, in the case of a repudiation by failure to provide adequate assurance of performance, the repudiation is retracted if the repudiating party provides the required assurance or if the circumstances change so that demanding assurance is no longer justified.

However, in all these cases, retraction is no longer possible once the injured party has materially relied on the repudiation.[11] Moreover, a retrac-

---

776 (Me. 1989); Jessup v. Five Star Fran. LLC, 515 P.3d 466, 475 (Utah App. 2022); Smargon v. Grand Lodge Partners, LLC, 288 P.3d 1063, 1069 (Utah App. 2012); AGS Contracting LLC v. Outside the Box, LLC, No. 7:20-CV-255 (WLS), 2023 WL 6064732, at *9 (M.D. Ga. Sept. 18, 2023).

9. Julian v. Montana State U., 747 P.2d 196, 200 (Mont. 1987); Jessup v. Five Star Fran. LLC, 515 P.3d 466, 475 (Utah App. 2022).

10. In re WBZE, Inc., 220 B.R. 568, 572 (D. Md. 1998); Infousa.com, Inc. v. Berj, Inc., No. A-04-303, 2005 WL 2648955, at *12 (Neb. App. Oct. 18, 2005); Restatement (Second) of Contracts § 256.

11. BioVeris Corp. v. Meso Scale Diagnostics, LLC, No. CV 8692-VCMR, 2017 WL 5035530, at *8

is impossible after the injured party has informed the repudiating party that they deem the repudiation to be final.[12]

IV. Effects

If a party repudiates the contract before her performance is due, the injured party can demand damages for total breach.[13] Moreover, the injured party's remaining duties to perform are discharged.[14]

However, the injured party no longer has a claim to damages for total breach if, following the repudiation, it becomes clear that the repudiated duty would have been discharged by impracticability or frustration of purpose. Moreover, the injured party's claim to damages for total breach is also discharged if, following the repudiation, it becomes clear that the injured party would have failed to render their performance.[15]

> **Example.** On January 1, Alpha and Beta enter into a contract under which Beta will rent Alpha's ski lodge between February 1 and February 7 for $2,000. On January 12, Beta informs Alpha that Beta no longer has the funds to pay the $2,000 and will not go through with the contract. On January 20, an avalanche destroys the ski lodge. Beta's January 12 statement constitutes a repudiation because Beta announced that he would commit a breach giving rise to damages for total breach. Due to Beta's repudiation, Alpha was entitled to damages for total breach. However, once the avalanche destroyed the ski

---

(Del. Ch. Nov. 2, 2017), aff'd, 202 A.3d 509 (Del. 2019); Pavone v. Kirke, 807 N.W.2d 828, 834 (Iowa 2011); Infousa.com, Inc. v. Berj, Inc., No. A-04-303, 2005 WL 2648955, at *12 (Neb. App. Oct. 18, 2005); In re WBZE, Inc., 220 B.R. 568, 572 (D. Md. 1998).

12. Pavone v. Kirke, 807 N.W.2d 828, 834 (Iowa 2011); In re WBZE, Inc., 220 B.R. 568, 572 (D. Md. 1998); Infousa.com, Inc. v. Berj, Inc., No. A-04-303, 2005 WL 2648955, at *12 (Neb. App. Oct. 18, 2005); Restatement (Second) of Contracts § 256(1).

13. E.g., Smargon v. Grand Lodge Partners, LLC, 288 P.3d 1063, 1069 (Utah App. 2012); C. Valley Gen. Hosp. v. Smith, 75 Cal. Rptr. 3d 771, 781 (Cal. App. 5th Dist. 2008).

14. E.g., Homeland Energy Sols., LLC v. Retterath, 938 N.W.2d 664, 697 (Iowa 2020); Margolis v. Daily Direct LLC, 297 A.3d 144, 148 (Vt. 2023); In re Stand. Jury Instructions-Contract and Bus. Cases, 116 So. 3d 284, 306 (Fla. 2013); Downtown Barre Dev. v. GU Markets of Barre, LLC, 22 A.3d 1174, 1178 (Vt. 2011); Beauchamp v. Coastal Boat Storage, LLC, 4 So. 3d 443, 451 (Ala. 2008); Rec. v. Kempe, 928 A.2d 1199, 1206 (Vt. 2007).

15. Thomas v. Montelucia Villas, LLC, 302 P.3d 617, 620 (Ariz. 2013); Beauchamp v. Coastal Boat Storage, LLC, 4 So. 3d 443, 451 (Ala. 2008); Skyco Resources, LLP v. Fam. Tree Corp., 512 P.3d 11, 23 (Wyo. 2022); Ingalls v. Keene, 496 A.2d 1051, 1052 (Me. 1985); Hosp. Mortg. Group v. First Prudential Dev. Corp., 411 So. 2d 181, 182 (Fla. 1982); HIFN, Inc. v. Intel Corp., No. CIV.A. 1835-VCS, 2007 WL 1309376, at *16 (Del. Ch. May 2, 2007); Gonzalez v. Denning, 394 F.3d 388, 394 (5th Cir. 2004).

lodge it became clear that Alpha would have failed to perform. Therefore, Beta's duty to pay damages is discharged.

Example. The annual Carnival parade through High Street is scheduled for February 18. On January 1, in anticipation of this parade, Alpha contracts with Beta to let Beta use a room in Alpha's house facing High Street to watch the parade. In exchange, Beta promises to pay $500, which is only justified because both parties assume that the room will offer an excellent view of the parade. On January 5, Beta informs Alpha that he (Beta) has decided to go on a cruise between February 15 and February 20 and therefore will not go through with the contract. On January 10, the organizers cancel the parade due to the threat of a terrorist attack. In this case, Beta's January 5 announcement constituted a repudiation, allowing Alpha to demand damages for total breach. However, when the parade's organizers canceled it, it became clear that Beta's duty to pay would have been discharged due to frustration of purpose. Accordingly, Beta's duty to pay damages is discharged.

Sackett v. Spindler

Court of Appeal, First District, Division 1, California, 56 Cal Rptr. 435 (Cal. App. 1st Dist. 1967)

MOLINARI, Presiding Justice.

Plaintiff and cross-defendant, Sheldon Sackett, appeals from the judgment of the trial court determining that he take nothing on his complaint . . . and further awarding defendant and cross-complainant, Paul Spindler, $34,575.74 plus interest on his cross-complaint against Sackett for breach of contract. . . .

THE RECORD

As of July 8, 1961 Spindler was the owner of a majority of the shares of S & S Newspapers, a corporation which, since April 1, 1959, had owned and operated a newspaper in Santa Clara known as the Santa Clara Journal. In addition, Spindler, as president of S & S Newspapers, served as publisher, editor, and general manager of the Journal. On July 8, 1961 Spindler entered into a written agreement with Sackett whereby the latter agreed to purchase 6,316 shares of stock in S & S Newspapers, this number representing the total number of shares outstanding. The contract provided for a total purchase price of $85,000 payable as follows: $6,000 on or before July 10, $20,000 on or before July 14, and $59,000 on or before August 15. In addition the agreement obligated Sackett to pay interest at the rate of 6 percent on any unpaid balance. And finally, the contract provided for delivery of the full amount of stock to Sackett free of encumbrances when he made his final payment under the contract.

Sackett paid the initial $6,000 installment on time and made an additional $19,800 payment on July 21. On August 10 Sackett gave Spindler a check for the $59,200 balance due under the contract; however, due to the fact that the account on which this check was drawn contained insufficient funds to cover the check, the check was never paid. Meanwhile, however, Spindler had acquired the stock owned by the minority shareholders of S & S Newspapers, had endorsed the stock certificates, and had given all but 454 shares to Sackett's attorneys to hold in escrow until Sackett had paid Spindler the $59,200 balance due under the contract. However, on September 1, after the $59,200 check had not cleared, Spindler reclaimed the stock certificates held by Sackett's attorney.

Thereafter, on September 12 Spindler received a telegram from Sackett to the effect that the latter 'had secured payments our transaction and was ready, willing and eager to transfer them' and that Sackett's new attorney would contact Spindler's attorney. In response to this telegram Spindler, by return telegram, gave Sackett the name of Spindler's attorney. Subsequently, Sackett's attorney contacted Spindler's attorney and arranged a meeting to discuss Sackett's performance of the contract. At this meeting, which was held on September 19 at the office of Sackett's attorney, in response to Sackett's representation that he would be able to pay Spindler the balance due under the contract by September 22, Spindler served Sackett with a notice to the effect that unless the latter paid the $59,200 balance due under the contract plus interest by that date, Spindler would not consider completing the sale and would assess damages for Sackett's breach of the agreement. Also discussed at this meeting was the newspaper's urgent need for working capital. Pursuant to this discussion Sackett on the same date paid Spindler $3,944.26 as an advance for working capital. However, Sackett failed to make any further payments or to communicate with Spindler by September 22, and on that date the latter, by letter addressed to Sackett, again extended the time for

Sackett's performance until September 29. Again Sackett failed to tender the amount owing under the contract or to contact Spindler by that date, the next communication between the parties occurring on October 4 in the form of a telegram by which Sackett advised Spindler that Sackett's assets were now free as a result of the fact that his wife's petition to impress a receivership on his assets had been dismissed by the trial court in which divorce proceedings between Sackett and his wife were pending; that he was 'ready, eager and willing to proceed to . . . consummate all details of our previously settled sale and purchase'; and that the decision of the trial court dismissing his wife's petition for receivership 'will clear way shortly for full financing any unpaid balance.' Accordingly, Sackett, in this telegram, urged Spindler to have his attorney contact Sackett's attorney 'regarding any unfinished details.' In response to this telegram Spindler's attorney, on October 5, wrote a letter to Sackett's attorney stating that as a result of Sackett's delay in performing the contract and his unwillingness to consummate the agreement, 'there will be no sale and purchase of the stock . . . .' Following this letter Sackett's attorney, on October 6, telephoned Spindler's attorney and offered to pay the balance due under the contract over a period of time through a 'liquidating trust.' This proposal was rejected by Spindler's attorney, who, however, informed Sackett's attorney at that time that Spindler was still willing to consummate the sale of the stock provided Sackett would pay the balance in cash or its equivalent. No tender or offer of cash or its equivalent was made and Sackett thereafter failed to communicate with Spindler until shortly before the commencement of this action.

Beginning during the period scheduled for Sackett's performance of the contract Spindler found it increasingly difficult to operate the paper at a profit, particularly due to the lack of adequate working capital. In an attempt to remedy this situation Spindler obtained a loan of approximately $4,000 by mortgaging various items of personal property owned by him. In addition, in November, Spindler sold half of his stock in S & S Newspapers for $10,000. Thereafter, in December, in an effort to minimize the cost of operating the newspaper, Spindler converted the paper from a daily to a weekly. Finally, in July 1962 Spindler repurchased for $10,000 the stock which he had sold the previous November and sold the full 6,316 shares for $22,000, which sale netted Spindler $20,680 after payment of brokerage commission.

BREACH OF CONTRACT

Sackett contends that the evidence reveals no 'actionable breach' on his part. The basis of his argument is that despite his failure to tender over half of the purchase price for the stock of S & S Newspapers, his duty to consummate the contract was discharged by Spindler's conduct in two respects, namely, Spindler's 'rescission' of the purchase agreement as a result of his reclamation of the stock certificates from Sackett's attorney on September 1 and Spindler's 'repudiation' of the contract on October 5.

To begin with, the undisputed evidence shows that of the $85,000 due from Sackett to Spindler under the purchase agreement the total amount which the former paid to the latter up to the time of trial was $29,744.26. Moreover, the purchase agreement reveals that Sackett's promise to pay Spindler $85,000 was an unconditional one once the respective dates on which the payments were due had arrived. Accordingly, since the trial court found that it was not impossible for Sackett to perform the subject contract either by virtue of his illness and hospitalization or his pending divorce litigation, it is clear that his failure to tender the balance due under the contract constituted a breach of the agreement, a breach being defined as an unjustified or unexcused failure to perform all or any part of what is promised in a contract. (Rest., Contracts, ss 312, 314, pp. 462, 465.) The question remains, therefore, as to whether Sackett's duty to consummate the contract or to respond to Spindler in damages for the former's failure to perform the subject contract was in any way discharged by Spindler's conduct.

With regard first to Spindler's reclaiming of the stock which he had previously delivered to Sackett's attorney to hold in escrow until Sackett paid the balance due under the contract, Sackett argues that under the Uniform Stock Transfer Act . . . , which was in effect at the time of the transactions involved in this action, Spindler's delivery of the endorsed shares of stock to Sackett's attorney served to transfer title to these shares . . . , and that by subsequently reclaiming the shares of stock Spindler effected a rescission of the purchase agreement and thus barred himself from being able to recover damages for Sackett's breach of the contract.

In response to this contention we note initially that although former Corporations Code s 2466 provided that 'Title to a certificate and to the shares represented thereby can be transferred . . . (a) By delivery of the certificate endorsed either in blank or to a specified person by the person appearing by the certificate to be the owner of the shares represented thereby,' it is apparent that delivery of such endorsed stock certificates into escrow does not constitute a transfer of title to the stock within the purview of this section.

Moreover, even if such delivery did constitute a transfer of title to the stock, a subsequent reclaiming of the stock certificates would not work a rescission of the contract pursuant to which the stock certificates were delivered into escrow. The procedure by which a unilateral rescission of a contract is effected is set forth in Civil Code s 1691, as follows: '* * * to effect a rescission a party to the contract must, promptly * * * (a) Give notice of rescission to the party as to whom he rescinds; and (b) Restore to the other party everything of value which he has received from him under the contract or offer to restore the same upon condition that the other party do likewise * * *.' Spindler did neither of these acts in connection with his withdrawal of the stock certificates from escrow on September 1. Rather, even after that date he continued to affirm the contract and to urge Sackett to perform it. Thus, it is clear that Spindler neither intended to rescind the contract as of September 1 nor took any action which could effect such a rescission.3 Secondly, with regard to Sackett's claim that Spindler 'repudiated' the contract on October 5, it is clear that the letter which Spindler's attorney wrote to Sackett's attorney on that date informing the latter that as a result of the 'many delays' on the part of Sackett 'there will be no sale and purchase of the (newspaper) stock' constituted notification to Sackett that Spindler considered his own duty of performance under the contract discharged as a result of Sackett's breach of the contract and that Spindler was thereby terminating the contract and substituting his legal remedies for his contractual rights. Such action was justifiable on Spindler's part if, but only if, Sackett's breach could properly be classified as a total, rather than a partial, breach of the contract. . . . If, on the other hand, Sackett's breach at that time was not total so that Spindler was not entitled to consider himself discharged under the contract, then Spindler's action would constitute an unlawful repudiation of the contract, which would in turn be a total breach of the contract sufficient to discharge Sackett from any further duty to perform the contract. . . .

Whether a breach of contract is total or partial depends upon its materiality. (Rest., Contracts, s 317, p. 471.) In determining the materiality of a failure to fully perform a promise the following factors are to be considered: (1) The extent to which the injured party will obtain the substantial benefit which he could have reasonably anticipated; (2) the extent to which the injured party may be adequately compensated in damages for lack of complete performance; (3) the extent to which the party failing to perform has already partly performed or made preparations for performance; (4) the greater or less hardship on the party failing to perform in terminating the contract; (5) the wilful, negligent, or innocent behavior of the party failing to perform; and (6) the greater or less uncertainty that the party failing to perform will perform the remainder of the contract. (Rest., Contracts, s 275, pp. 402—403.) In the instant case, although Sackett had paid part of the purchase price for the newspaper stock and although his delay in paying the balance due under the contract could probably be compensated for in damages, we are of the opinion that Spindler was justified in terminating the contract on October 5 on the basis that despite Sackett's 'offers' to perform and his assurances to Spindler that he would perform, it was extremely uncertain as to whether in fact Sackett intended to complete the contract. In addition, in light of Spindlers' numerous requests of Sackett for the balance due under the contract, the latter's failure to perform could certainly not be characterized as innocent; rather it could be but ascribed to gross negligence or wilful conduct on his part.

The facts in the instant case are similar to those in Coughlin v. Blair, 41 Cal.2d 587, 262 P.2d 305. There the plaintiffs purchased a lot from the defendants, who, in the deposit receipt evidencing the sale, agreed to install utilities and to pave the road to the subject lot within one year from the date of the agreement. On May 30, 1949, the date that performance was due under the contract, the utilities had not been installed nor had the road been paved. During the following year the plaintiffs wrote several letters to the defendants demanding performance. The defendants, however, did not perform their obligations nor did they repudiate the contract. Ultimately, on May 24, 1950, the work still not having been done, the plaintiffs brought an action for general damages based on the difference in value of the property with and without the performance promised in the contract and for special damages. In affirming the judgment of the trial court insofar as it awarded the plaintiffs general damages, the Supreme Court considered whether, in view of the defendants' assertion that they intended to perform their obligations under the contract in the future, the trial court's award of damages to the plaintiffs allowed them a double recovery, that is, both the improvements and damages for failure to secure the improvements. In this context the Supreme Court pointed out that if the defendants' breach was total, the plaintiffs could recover all their damages, past and prospective, in one action and that a judgment for the plaintiffs in such an action would absolve the defendants from any duty to perform the contract. The Supreme Court then proceeded to consider whether the plaintiffs were entitled to treat the defendants' breach as total as of the date of the commencement of the action and concluded that 'Although defendants had not expressly repudiated the contract, their conduct clearly justified plaintiffs' belief that performance was either unlikely or would be forthcoming only when it suited defendants' convenience.' Under these circumstances it was held that the plaintiffs were not required to endure that uncertainty or to await the defendants' convenience but were justified in treating the defendants' nonperformance as a total breach of the contract. (Pp. 599—600, 262 P.2d p. 312; see also Gold Mining & Water Co. v. Swinerton, 23 Cal.2d 19, 29—30, 142 P.2d 22; Walker v. Harbor Business Blocks Co., 181 Cal. 773, 780—781, 186 P. 356.)

Similarly, in the instant case although Sackett at no time repudiated the contract and although he frequently expressed willingness to perform, the evidence was such as to warrant the inference that he did not intend to perform the subject contract. Certainly, the state of the record was such as to justify the conclusion either that it was unlikely that Sackett would tender the balance due or that he would do so at his own convenience. Spindler was not required to endure the uncertainty or to await Sackett's convenience and was therefore justified in treating the latter's nonperformance as a total breach of the contract. Accordingly, we conclude that the letter which Spindler's attorney wrote to Sackett's attorney on October 5 did not constitute an unlawful repudiation of the contract on Spindler's part, was therefore not a breach of the contract by him, and thus did not discharge Sackett's duty to perform the contract or, alternatively, to respond to Spindler in damages.

In any event, even if Spindler was not justified in treating Sackett's breach as total as of October 5, the latter's contention that his duty to perform was discharged by Spindler's repudiation of the contract as of that date is untenable. Since Spindler was not obligated to perform his promise at that time due to Sackett's failure to tender the balance due under the contract, Spindler's repudiation was, at best, anticipatory in nature. Its effect was nullified by Sackett's disregard of it and his treating the contract as still in force as evidenced by his attempt, through his attorney, to arrange an alternative method of financing the balance due under the agreement. . . . Moreover, Spindler's repudiation was itself retracted by his attorney who, on Spindler's behalf, told Sackett's attorney in the same conversation at which the latter suggested an alternative method of financing that Spindler was still willing to consummate the sale provided Sackett would pay the balance due in cash or its equivalent. Such a retraction constitutes a nullification of the original effectiveness of the repudiation. (Rest., Contracts, s 319, p. 481.) . . .

SIMS and BRAY,* JJ., concur.

Hearing denied; SULLIVAN, J., not participating.

NOTES AND QUESTIONS

*A. **Material v. non-material breach.*** Why was Sackett's breach material as opposed to non-material?

*B. **Partial and total breach.*** The court distinguishes between a partial breach of contract and a total breach of contract. Does the Restatement (Second) of Contracts use that distinction as well? According to the court, what are the consequences of a total breach of contract?

*C. **Type of breach.*** Did Sackett's breach constitute a breach by nonperformance or a breach by anticipatory repudiation?

*D. **Spindler.*** Did Spindler breach the contract? Why or why not?

*E. **Hypothetical variation?*** Suppose the court had found Sackett's breach to be non-material. How would such a finding have impacted the outcome of the case?

CHAPTER 22
INTRODUCTION TO REMEDIES

I. Introduction

What does it mean for a contract to be enforced? In other words, what will the court do for the plaintiff? The law of remedies answers that question. A remedy is, in essence, the means for enforcing rights or redressing wrongs.

Before addressing different types of remedies, it is helpful to ask what they are supposed to achieve. A partial answer to that question is given in section 344 of the Restatement, which defines the various interests that judicial remedies in contract law seek to protect. These include the promisee's expectation interest, their reliance interest, and their restitution interest.[1]

The *expectation interest* is the promisee's interest in obtaining the benefit of the bargain: the promisee is put in a position that is as good, at least financially, as the one they would be in had the promisor kept their promise.[2]

The *reliance interest* is the promisee's interest in being put in a position that is as good, at least financially, as the one they would be in if the contract had not been formed.[3]

---

1. Restatement (Second) of Contracts § 344.
2. Restatement (Second) of Contracts § 344.
3. Restatement (Second) of Contracts § 344.

The *restitution interest* is the promisee's interest in getting back any benefits they have conferred on the promisor.[4]

Whereas the restitution interest is quite intuitive, the expectation and reliance interests invite further explanation. To determine the expectation interest, we compare the world in which the promisor has committed a breach with the hypothetical world without a breach. To determine the reliance interest, we compare the world where the promisor has relied on the contract (e.g., by making payments to the promisor or incurring expenses) with a world where the promisor has not relied on the contract.

Question. Alpha is a publisher, and Beta is a writer. On January 1, Alpha and Beta enter into a contract whereby Beta will write a spy thriller for Alpha by June 1. In exchange, Alpha will pay Beta $10,000 in advance and another $40,000 upon the thriller's completion. As agreed, Alpha pays Beta the $10,000 once the parties have signed the contract. Moreover, Alpha incurs advertising costs of $5,000. On May 31, Beta informs Alpha that Beta has not written a word and will never write the thriller. If Alpha had published the thriller, Alpha would have incurred additional expenses for printing and distribution of $20,000. At the same time, Alpha would have received revenues of $100,000. Calculate Alpha's expectation interest, reliance interest, and restitution interest.

Answer. To calculate Alpha's expectation interest, we compare the world with Beta's breach to the hypothetical world without a breach. In the world with the breach, Alpha has paid $10,000 to Beta and $5,000 for advertising, and Alpha's revenues are $0. Accordingly, Alpha has a net loss of $15,000. Meanwhile, in a world without breach, Alpha would also have paid the advance of $10,000 and the $5000 for advertising. Additionally, Alpha would have had to pay the $40,000 due on the novel's completion and the printing and distribution costs of $20,000. On the other hand, Alpha would have received revenues of $100,000. Accordingly, Alpha would have made a net profit of $25,000 since $100,000 – $10,000 – $5000 – $40,000 – $20,000 = $25,000. In other words, Alpha would have a profit of $25,000 in the world without a breach, whereas in a world with breach, Alpha has incurred a net loss of $15,000. To make Alpha as well off as they would be in a world without breach, Beta must pay

4. Restatement (Second) of Contracts § 344.

Alpha $25,000 – (-$15,000) = $40,000. Thus, Alpha's expectation interest is $40,000.

What is Alpha's reliance interest? In the actual world, in which Alpha has relied on the contract with Beta, Alpha has incurred costs of $15,000 (namely, the advance of $10,000 and the advertising costs of $5,000). In a hypothetical world without the contract, Alpha would not have incurred any costs. Note that the hypothetical does not mention any other projects that Alpha would have pursued in the absence of a contract with Beta. Therefore, to make Alpha as well off as they would be in a world without reliance, we would have to pay them $15,000. That is Alpha's reliance interest.

Alpha's restitution interest simply consists of the benefits they have conferred on Beta, which is the advance of $10,000. In other words, Alpha's restitution interest is $10,000.

II. Damages versus Specific Performance

As a general rule, when a contract is breached, the law seeks to protect the promisee's expectation interest. That is, the law tries to put the promisee in the same position that they would be in had the promisor fully performed their duties under the contract. However, there are two different ways of achieving this goal.

First, the plaintiff can be awarded damages so that they are in as good a *financial* position as they would be in if the contract had not been breached.

Example. Alpha promises to paint Beta's house for $100. Beta promptly pays Alpha the $100. However, Alpha refuses to paint Beta's house. Despite Beta's best efforts to find a cheaper option, the least expensive alternative painter charges $100 for painting Beta's house. In that case, Beta's expectation interest is $200. Accordingly, one way of protecting Beta's expectation interest is to award Beta damages in the amount of $200.

Second, we may mean that the other party is forced to render the promised performance. We refer to this remedy as "specific performance."

Example. Same facts as the previous example. An alternative way of protecting Beta's expectation interest would be for the court to issue an injunction forcing Alpha to paint Beta's house.

The general remedy for breach of contract is damages,[5] with specific performance available only if damages are inadequate and if certain other conditions are met.[6]

III. Availability of Specific Performance

Granting specific performance lies within the court's discretion if the requirements for specific performance are satisfied.[7]

The most essential requirement is that specific performance will only be granted if damages are inadequate to protect the injured party's expectation interest.[8] There are various reasons why damages may be inadequate. The injured party may find it challenging to prove their loss, to collect damages, or to procure a substitute performance.[9] In practice, the main case in which damages are considered inadequate involves duties to transfer interests in land.

Even if damages are inadequate, there are various reasons why specific performance may be unavailable. For example, the contract may be too indefinite to enforce through specific performance.[10] Additionally, specific performance may impose an undue burden on the court in terms of enforcement or supervision.[11]

IV. Expectation damages

As a general rule, the injured party can demand expectation damages.[12] According to section 347 of the Restatement (Second) of Contracts, expectation damages are calculated in three steps. First, one has to ascertain the value that the injured party was deprived of because the breaching party's performance was not rendered at all or was rendered defectively. Second, one has to

5. Restatement (Second) of Contracts § 346(1).
6. Restatement (Second) of Contracts §§ 359 et seq.
7. Restatement (Second) § 357(1).
8. Restatement (Second) § 359.
9. Restatement (Second) § 360.
10. Restatement (Second) of Contracts § 362.
11. Restatement (Second) of Contracts § 366.
12. See Restatement (Second) of Contracts § 346 (providing that the injured party is entitled to damages for any breach of contract), § 347 (providing that the injured party is entitled to damages based on their expectation interest).

add any other losses, in particular, any incidental or consequential losses. Third, one must deduct any losses or costs that the injured party has managed to avoid as a result of not having to render their own performance. This rule may sound complex, but it matches the injured party's expectation interest, albeit in a roundabout way.

Question. Alpha enters into a contract with Beta, whereby Alpha promises Beta a specific parcel of real estate for $100,000. Beta plans to resell the property later and has already found a buyer, Gamma, willing to pay $150,000. Alpha refuses to convey the land. Selling the land to Gamma would have caused Beta to incur transaction costs in the amount of $2,000. Beta has not yet paid the $100,000 for the land. Assume that the applicable common law corresponds exactly to the Restatement (Second) of Contracts. Is Beta entitled to expectation damages, and if so, in what amount?

Answer. Beta is entitled to expectation damages. If you were to apply the general principle that the injured party has to be paid the amount of money necessary to put them in the position that they would have been in had the contract been performed, then you would presumably start by asking: "How much more money would Beta have, had the contract been performed?" Beta would have spent $2,000 in transaction costs and $100,000 in paying Alpha, leaving Beta with a net profit of $48,000. Accordingly, you would conclude that Beta needs to be paid $48,000 to be in the position they would have been in had the contract been performed.

The same result is reached by applying the rule in section 347 of the Restatement (Second) of Contracts. You start by applying section 347(a) of the Restatement. What is the loss that Alpha's performance experiences due to its failure or deficiency? Answering that question involves three steps. First, you ask what value Beta has been deprived of because Alpha's performance was not rendered correctly. In this case, the answer is $148,000 because, due to the opportunity to sell the land to Gamma, having the land would have been worth $148,000 to Beta.[13] Second, you ask: What was the performance worth to Beta as it was rendered? Here, the answer is zero. Getting no real estate was

13. Note that in calculating the loss in value, we focus on the net profits. See, e.g., Restatement (Second) of Contracts § 347 cmt. b.

> worth nothing to Beta. Third, you compare the two, and you know the loss in value, namely $148,000.
>
> Then you proceed to section 347(b) of the Restatement. In other words, you ask if Alpha's breach caused any other losses, such as incidental or consequential losses. Here, Beta experienced no such other losses. (But it is easy to imagine a scenario where Beta would have suffered other losses. Assume, for example, that Beta had already resold the land to Gamma for $150,000. If Gamma does not receive the land from Beta and, as a result, cannot fulfill their subsequent sale to Delta for $160,000, Gamma might not only withhold the $150,000 payment from Beta but also be entitled to damages of $10,000 against Beta. In this scenario, Beta's additional losses would amount to $10,000.)
>
> Finally, you proceed to section 347(c) of the Restatement and ask whether Beta managed to avoid any losses or costs by not having to perform. Because Beta did not have to perform the transaction, Beta did not have to pay Alpha the $100,000. Therefore, Beta has avoided costs of $100,000.
>
> In sum, under section 347 of the Restatement, too, the expectation damages amount to $48,000. That is because we add the loss in value [here: $148,000] to other loss [here: $0] and then deduct the costs avoided [here: $100,000] and obtain $48,000.

Often, it will be difficult to ascertain the facts that are relevant to determining the amount owed as expectation damages. For example, if Alpha fails to convey a piece of land to Beta, it may be challenging to determine for what amount Beta could have resold that land. The injured party can only recover damages for losses established with reasonable certainty.[14] In other words, the injured party bears the risk that the actual losses cannot be proven.

V. Reliance Damages

Given the need to prove losses with reasonable certainty, there are bound to be cases where the injured party cannot obtain their expectation interest. To protect the injured party in such cases, the law provides the injured party with an alternative measure of their damages. Instead of demanding their

14. Restatement (Second) of Contracts § 352.

expectation interest, the injured party can demand their reliance interest.[15] However, this alternative measure comes with a significant limitation. Any loss the injured party would have incurred in a world without breach that the breaching party can prove with reasonable certainty must be deducted from the reliance interest.[16] In simple terms, if the injured party's expectation interest is established with reasonable certainty, it serves as the upper limit for the injured party's reliance interest. Consequently, for the injured party, reliance damages are a valuable alternative to expectation damages only if the expectation interest cannot be proven with reasonable certainty.

Example. Beta is a publisher, and Alpha is a writer. On January 1, Alpha and Beta enter into a contract whereby Alpha will write a spy thriller for Beta by June 1. In exchange, Beta will pay Alpha $10,000 in advance and another $40,000 upon completing the thriller. As agreed, Beta pays Alpha the $10,000 once the parties have signed the contract. Moreover, Beta incurs advertising costs of $5,000. On May 31, Alpha informs Beta that Alpha has not written a word and will never write the thriller. If Beta had published the thriller, Beta would have incurred additional expenses for printing and distribution of $20,000. However, Beta would only have received revenues from the sale of the thriller in the amount of $20,000. Assume that the applicable common law corresponds exactly to the Restatement (Second) of Contracts. Calculate the expectation and reliance damages to which Beta is entitled.

Answer. Let us calculate the expectation damages first. Using the approach in section 347 of the Restatement (Second) of Contracts, the expectation damages are calculated as follows: The loss in value due to the failure to perform is $0 because that is the net profit Beta would have made from selling the novel, disregarding any payment owed to Alpha. At the same time, Beta saved the $40,000 that Beta would have had to pay Alpha upon the novel's completion. Therefore, Beta has not suffered any loss and is not entitled to expectation damages. Incidentally, you may find it easier to calculate the expectation interest by comparing the world with breach to the world without breach. In a world without breach, Beta would have ended up with a net loss of $55,000. That is because -$5000 - $10,000 - $40,000 - $20,000 + $20,000 = -55,000. In a

15. Restatement (Second) of Contracts § 349.
16. Restatement (Second) of Contracts § 349.

world with breach, Beta ended up with a net loss of $15,000, because -$5000 - $10,000 = -$15,000. In other words, Beta is $40,000 richer than Beta would be in a world without breach.

To calculate reliance damages, we compare the world with reliance to the world without reliance. In the world with reliance, Beta has had expenses of $15,000 consisting of the advance and the advertising costs. In a world without reliance, Beta would have had no expenses. Therefore, Beta's reliance interest is $15,000. But we also know that if Alpha had properly performed, Beta would have incurred a loss of $55,000. Therefore, Beta is better off in the world in which he has relied on the contract and hence cannot demand reliance damages. Note, though, that if Beta's expectation interest could not be proven in this example, then Beta's expectation interest would not cap Beta's reliance interest, and Beta would be entitled to reliance damages of $15,000.

Siam v. Mountain Vista Builders

Court of Appeals of Texas, El Paso, 544 S.W.3d 504 (2018)

CRAWFORD MCCLURE, Chief Justice

. . . On August 6, 2005, the Siams, both of whom were California residents, signed a written contract with Mountain Vista to purchase a home to be built by Mountain Vista in a subdivision it was developing in El Paso, for the sales price of $145,450.[2] . . . The Siams paid a $500 deposit on the home, as well as an additional $2,510 for custom changes to the home.

In January of 2006, the Siams paid for an appraisal on the property and secured a title commitment from a title company. In addition, in April of 2006, the Siams, who had previously been pre-approved for a loan from an independent lender in September of 2005, received a good faith estimate from their lender, indicating that they had been approved for a loan in the amount of $131,159.

In the meantime, for reasons that are not clear from the record, Mountain Vista believed the Siams were having difficulty securing a loan, and were not "strong" buyers, and therefore began taking back-up offers from other buyers in March of 2006. In addition, in April of 2006, Mountain Vista received a new appraisal on the home, indicating that the home's value had gone up to

$161,000. For reasons that are again unclear from the record, Mountain Vista "cancelled" the contract with the Siams sometime in April or May of 2006, apparently without notifying the Siams of the cancellation.

Unaware that Mountain Vista was considering cancelling their contract, the Siams traveled to El Paso to conduct a move-in inspection of the home on May 1, 2006. After inspecting the home, Jose Siam signed a move-in inspection report, noting certain unsatisfactory conditions with the home, including the fact that the custom changes they had paid for had not been made. On that same date, a representative from Mountain Vista, who was apparently also unaware of the cancellation, signed the report and provided the Siams with a copy of a warranty manual for the home. Shortly thereafter, on May 3, 2006, the City of El Paso issued a certificate of occupancy for the home. The Siams traveled to El Paso to close on the home on two separate occasions, first on May 8, 2006 and later on May 12, 2006. However, pursuant to instructions from Mountain Vista, the title company refused to close on the sale. Mountain Vista thereafter signed a contract with another buyer on May 15, 2006, for a total sales price of $166,950, approximately $21,000 over the original sales price in the Siams' contract.

THE SIAMS' LAWSUIT

The Siams thereafter retained an attorney and filed their lawsuit against Mountain Vista on September 15, 2006, raising claims of breach of contract, fraud, and unjust enrichment. . . . [T]he trial court entered a . . . judgment on February 19, 2015, finding that Mountain Vista had breached its contract with the Siams, and awarding the Siams damages in the amount of $24,835. . . . The Siams filed . . . a motion for new trial, in which they alleged that they were entitled to an award of attorney's fees, and that they were also entitled to be reimbursed for their travel expenses. . . . .

THE SIAMS' TRAVEL EXPENSES

. . . [T]he Siams argue that the trial court erred in refusing to award damages for the travel expenses, which they allegedly incurred in attempting to perform the contract, in an amount totaling $3,879.89.10 The Siams contend that they presented uncontroverted evidence of those expenses, and that the trial court was therefore required to award them those expenses as reliance damages. Because we believe that awarding travel expenses to the Siams in this instance would result in a double recovery, we disagree.

Double Recovery Prohibited

The universal rule for measuring damages for the breach of a contract is just compensation for the loss or damage actually sustained. See Abraxas Petroleum Corp. v. Hornburg, 20 S.W.3d 741, 760 (Tex.App.—El Paso 2000, no pet.) (citing Stewart v. Basey, 150 Tex. 666, 245 S.W.2d 484, 486 (1952); Stamp–Ad, Inc. v. Barton Raben, Inc., 915 S.W.2d 932, 936 (Tex.App.—Houston [1st Dist.] 1996, no writ)). Under this rule, a party generally should be awarded neither less nor more than his actual damages. Id. (citing Stewart, 245 S.W.2d at 486).

"American law has traditionally recognized three damages measures for breach of contract: expectancy, reliance, and restitution." See Quigley v. Bennett, 227 S.W.3d 51, 56 (Tex. 2007); see also Abraxas Petroleum Corp., 20 S.W.3d at 760 ("Damages for breach of contract protect three interests: a restitution interest, a reliance interest, and an expectation interest."). Reliance damages entitle a plaintiff to be reimbursed for the out-of-pocket expenditures that were caused by his reliance on the contract, in order to put him in the same position he would have been in if the contract had not been made. Quigley, 227 S.W.3d at 56 n.1 (Brister, J., concurring in part & dissenting in part) (citing Restatement (Second) of Contracts § 344 (1981)); Sharifi v. Steen Auto., LLC, 370 S.W.3d 126, 149 (Tex.App.—Dallas 2012, no pet.) (reliance damages reimburse a plaintiff for expenditures made towards the execution of the contract in order to restore the status quo before the contract). Under this measure of damages, plaintiffs are entitled recover the "expenditures made in preparation for performance or in performance, less any loss that the party in breach can prove with reasonable certainty the injured party would have suffered had the contract been performed." Mistletoe Exp. Serv. of Oklahoma City, Okl. v. Locke, 762 S.W.2d 637, 638 (Tex.App.—Texarkana 1988, no writ) (allowing for the recovery of capital expenditures plaintiff made as reliance damages, which included purchases of vehicles, in furtherance of contract to provide freight services to the defendant, less the amounts the plaintiff recouped by selling the trucks). On the other hand, expectancy damages, similar to benefit-of-the-bargain damages, award damages "for the reasonably expected value of the contract." Sharifi, 370 S.W.3d at 148 (citing Foley v. Parlier, 68 S.W.3d 870, 884 (Tex.App.—Fort Worth 2002, no pet.)); see also SAVA gumarska in kemijska industria d.d. v. Advanced Polymer Sci., Inc., 128 S.W.3d 304, 317 n.6 (Tex.App.—Dallas 2004, no pet.) (benefit-of-the-bargain damages seek to restore the non-breaching party to the same economic position it would have been in had the contract been performed).

However, a plaintiff may not receive both forms of damages; thus, if a plaintiff chooses to recover his reliance damages for his out-of-pocket expenses, he may not also recover damages for his expectancy damages, i.e., for the profits or benefits he would have received if the contract had been performed, as allowing for both forms of damages would result in an impermissible double recovery. See Sharifi, 370 S.W.3d at 151; Mistletoe Exp. Serv. of Oklahoma City, Okl., 762 S.W.2d at 638 (citing The Restatement (Second) of Contracts § 349 (1981)). For example, in Sharifi, the plaintiff had entered into a contract with the defendant to purchase an automotive repair business, and in reliance on the contract, the plaintiff incurred expenses for undergoing a training program to prepare him to run the business. Sharifi, 370 S.W.3d at 151-52. The trial court found that the defendant had breached the contract, and awarded the plaintiff the equivalent of the profits he would have received for a year if the contract had been performed, i.e., his lost profits, as well as his out-of-pocket expenses made in reliance on the contract, including his training expenses. Id. at 139. The Dallas Court of Appeals, however, concluded that the plaintiff could not receive compensation for both, as a "party cannot both 'retain all the benefits of the transaction and escape all of the obligations.' " Id. at 151 (citing Foley v Parlier, 68 S.W.3d 870, 885 (Tex.App.—Fort Worth 2002, no pet.)). As the court explained, a "party is entitled to sue and seek damages on alternative theories but is not entitled to recover on both theories; to do so is considered equivalent to a 'double recovery.' " Id.; see also Mistletoe Exp. Serv., 762 S.W.2d at 638 (recognizing that a nonbreaching party may recover capital investments she made in furtherance of performing a contract, but may not also recover her lost profits under the contract); Foley, 68 S.W.3d at 884-85 (recognizing that a plaintiff seeking damages for breach of contract could not recover both his lost profits for a breach of contract, as well as his reliance damages, such as the moving expenses he had incurred in performing the contract, as doing so would result in an impermissible "double recovery").

In the present case, the trial court's judgment was based primarily on the Siams' lost profits, or benefit-of-the-bargain damages, i.e., the difference in the price set forth in their contract with Mountain Vista for the purchase of the home, and the price that Mountain Vista received from the third-party who ultimately purchased the home. Therefore, the Siams were not entitled to also recover the travel expenses they incurred in reliance on the contract, as doing so would allow them to retain all of the benefits of the contract, yet escape all of its obligations, thereby leading to an impermissible double recovery....

We affirm the trial court's judgment denying the Siams their travel expenses ... The judgment of the trial court is affirmed ....

HUGHES, J., not participating

NOTES AND QUESTIONS

A. The different interests. Section 346 of the Restatement (Second) of Contracts defines the expectation interest, the reliance interest, and the restitution interest.

B. The relationship between expectation interest and reliance interest. As a general rule, the injured party can demand damages based on the expectation interest.[17] Alternatively, the injured party can demand damages based on reliance interest.[18] However, if the breaching party can prove with reasonable certainty that the injured party would have suffered a loss under the contract, then the court will deduct that loss from the reliance interest.[19] In simple terms, this means that if the breaching party can prove the injured party's expectation interest with reasonable certainty, then the expectation interest caps the injured party's reliance interest claim.

C. Restitution Interest. The injured party's restitution interest is governed by section 370 et seq. of the Restatement (Second) of Contracts. Under section 373 of the Restatement, an injured party is entitled to restitution if: (a) the party has conferred benefits on the breaching party; and (b) the injured party is entitled to damages for total breach. However, the right to restitution is excluded if the injured party has fully performed, and the breaching party's only remaining duty is to pay the injured party for its performance. In the case at hand, could the Siams have demanded restitution under these rules? What would their restitution interest have been?

D. Travel Expenses. According to the court, the Siams' travel expenses are not part of their expectation interest. Do you agree? Should the court have distinguished between the expenses incurred on May 8, 2006 and the expenses incurred on May 12, 2006?

---

17. Restatement (Second) of Contracts § 347

18. Id. § 349.

19. Id.

E. Double Recovery. The court's key holding is that the injured party cannot demand *both* expectation damages and reliance damages. This is consistent with the wording of section 349 of the Restatement (Second) of Contracts, which states that reliance damages are available "[a]s an alternative" to expectation damages. The court emphasizes the need to avoid "double recovery." Is that an apt description of the problem?

F. Policy. Can you think of efficiency or other policy arguments for why the injured party should not be able to recover both reliance and expectation damages?

CHAPTER 23
DUTY TO MITIGATE

Forbes v. Prime General Contractors, Inc

District Court of Appeal of Florida, Second District, 255 So.3d 448 (2018)

SALARIO, Judge.

This is an appeal from a final judgment on a claim for breach of contract. James and Fay Forbes sued Prime General Contractors, Inc. for breach after Prime walked off a home construction job. . . . The Forbeses and Prime signed a written contract under which Prime agreed to renovate the Forbeses' home in accord with plans drawn up by an architect. In exchange, the Forbeses agreed to pay Prime a total of $276,000 in five separate draws. Under the draw schedule, the Forbeses were to pay (a) 25% of the contract price upon signing, (b) 25% upon completion of demolition, (c) 25% upon completion of the "dry-in" stage of construction,1 (d) 15% after roofing and siding installation, and (e) the remaining 10% upon completion of the job. The contract provided that "any alteration or deviation from this agreement must be made in writing and signed by the Parties." Prime began the job as agreed, and the Forbeses paid the first two contract draws—totaling $138,000. They also paid an additional $6000 for updated architectural plans.

Under the contract, the Forbeses should not have had to pay anything more until the dry-in phase of the project was done. Unfortunately, things hit a snag before then. Prime said that the cost of the materials it needed to do the job had gone up. It told the Forbeses that the work would now cost at least $550,000—almost twice the original contract price—and demanded that the Forbeses immediately pay the third draw plus an additional $31,450 for work Prime had already done and for which the Forbeses had already paid. Prime presented the Forbeses with a written change order making these adjustments. The Forbeses refused to sign it and told Prime that they were prepared to move forward at the contract price. Prime refused and walked off the job, leaving the Forbeses' home unfinished and uninhabitable.

Because they could not live in their home, the Forbeses began renting a house nearby so that they had somewhere to stay. In the meantime, they looked for another contractor to finish the work on their home—ultimately talking with five potential candidates to perform the service—but none was willing to handle the job. After five months of living in a rental with no luck getting the work on their house finished, the Forbeses bought a new house and moved into it. They were unable, however, to pay a mortgage on their new house and another mortgage on the home that Prime left uninhabitable. So they let the uninhabitable home go into foreclosure. At the time they contracted with Prime, the Forbeses had about $45,000 in equity in the house. That equity was lost in the foreclosure.

The Forbeses sued Prime for breach of contract, and the case went to a bench trial at which the evidence was consistent with the facts related above. The Forbeses argued that Prime materially breached the contract by demanding payments to which it was not entitled under the contract and thereafter walking off the job. Prime contended, among other things, that the Forbeses also failed to perform under the contract, to which the Forbeses answered that they were entitled to suspend performance due to Prime's material breach. The Forbeses requested the following items of damages: $138,000 in payments made pursuant to their contract with Prime, $6000 for updated architectural plans, $45,000 of lost equity in their home, $5600 in rent, and various other expenses incurred in reliance on their contract with Prime. It is clear from the damages the Forbeses requested that they were asking to be put in the position they would have occupied had they not contracted with Prime in the first place. Prime asserted and litigated at trial an affirmative defense that the Forbeses failed to mitigate their damages.

About a month after the bench trial wrapped, the trial court entered a final judgment. It found that Prime had materially breached the contract as the Forbeses argued. However, it awarded the Forbeses as damages only the

$5600 in rent they paid while searching for a new contractor. The trial court explained that "[t]he purpose of contract damages is to put the injured party in as good a position as that in which full performance would have put him" and concluded that the Forbeses failed to offer persuasive or credible evidence at trial of the difference between the market value of the home had it been completed, less such part of the contract price that has not been paid, and the value of the construction that has been furnished by [Prime] thus far.

The court also found, without elaboration, that the Forbeses "made a financial decision not to engage in reasonable mitigation efforts" with respect to their damages.

This is the Forbeses' timely appeal of the final judgment. They argue two points: (1) by looking to place them in the position they would have occupied had Prime fully performed instead of the position they would have occupied had they never contracted with Prime, the trial court used an incorrect method of calculating damages; and (2) the trial court's finding that the Forbeses failed to mitigate their damages is unsupported by the evidence.... Both points have merit.

Method of calculating damages. . . . . When one party to a contract commits a material breach, the nonbreaching party has the option to treat the breach "as a breach of the entire contract—in other words, an entire or total breach." Hyman v. Cohen, 73 So.2d 393, 397 (Fla. 1954) . . . . From the perspective of the nonbreaching party, there are two main consequences of that decision: (1) the nonbreaching party may suspend his or her own performance of the contract, see Rector v. Larson's Marine, Inc., 479 So.2d 783, 785 (Fla. 2d DCA 1985), and (2) the nonbreaching party can elect one of two damage remedies in a suit for breach, see City of Miami Beach v. Carner, 579 So.2d 248, 251 (Fla. 3d DCA 1991).

When a party seeks damages for a total breach, "[h]e may treat the contract as void and seek the damages that will restore him to the position he was in immediately prior to entering the contract." Rector, 479 So.2d at 785; see also McCray v. Murray, 423 So.2d 559, 561 (Fla. 1st DCA 1982). Or, in the alternative, he may instead "affirm the contract, 'insist upon the benefit of his bargain, and seek the damages that would place him in the position he would have been in had the contract been completely performed.' " Tubby's Customs, 225 So.3d at 407 (quoting Citizen's Prop. Ins. Corp. v. Amat, 198 So.3d 730, 734 (Fla. 2d DCA 2016)). In the case of a breached construction contract like Prime's contract with the Forbeses, the benefit-of-the-bargain remedy is "either the reasonable cost of completion, or the difference between the value the construction would have had if completed and the value of the construction that has been thus far performed." Rector, 479 So.2d at 785 (citing Grossman Holdings Ltd. v. Hourihan, 414 So.2d 1037 (Fla. 1982) (adopting section 346(1)(a) of the Restatement (First) of Contracts (Am. Law Inst. 1932), to cases involving breach of a construction contract)).

Here, the final judgment on its face shows that the trial court believed that the Forbeses were entitled only to the benefit-of-the-bargain remedy. As reflected in the language from its final judgment quoted above, the trial court concluded that the Forbeses were entitled to be put in the position they would have occupied had Prime fully performed and that they had failed to present evidence to establish the key factors that go into that remedy in a construction contract case.

But the reason the Forbeses did not produce that evidence was because they did not seek benefit-of-the-bargain damages. They sought to be put in the position they would have occupied had they never contracted with Prime. It was clear at trial that the Forbeses regarded the breach as total; indeed, they were explicit that they were entitled to suspend their own performance under the contract. And the damages they asked the court to award—return of payments made under the contract and the equity in their home at the time of contracting—were of a type that regarded the contract as void and attempted to restore the Forbeses to their precontractual situation. Those damages were inconsistent with an affirmance of the contract and request for damages approximating full performance. Cf. Sec. & Inv. Corp. of the Palm Beaches v. Droege, 529 So.2d 799, 802 (Fla. 4th DCA 1988) ("If the two remedies are inconsistent or mutually exclusive, ... then the mere choice of one remedy and ... pursuit of one remedy to judgment ... operates as an election."); McCray, 423 So.2d at 561 (holding that a trial court did not err in failing to instruct a jury on benefit-of-the-bargain damages where the evidence supported damages to restore plaintiff to his original condition). In the final analysis, then, the remedy the Forbeses chose and pursued was not the remedy the trial court either considered or awarded.

Mitigation of damages. We agree with the Forbeses that the trial court's finding that they failed to mitigate damages was mistaken. The concept of mitigation is often used, as it appears to have been in this case, to refer to the doctrine of avoidable consequences. In contract cases, there is really no "duty to mitigate" because the claimant "is not compelled to undertake any ameliorative efforts"; rather, he is merely prevented from recovering damages he "could have reasonably avoided." Sys. Components Corp. v. Fla. Dep't of Transp., 14 So.3d 967, 982 (Fla. 2009). . . . The word "reasonably" is important. See Fla. Std. Jury Instr. (Contract & Bus.) 504.9 (requiring a jury to consider which damages could have been avoided through the plaintiff's reasonable efforts). The doctrine of avoidable consequences does not allow a trial court to reduce damages "based on what 'could have been avoided' through Herculean efforts." Sys. Components, 14 So.3d at 982. It applies only where a claimant fails to undertake measures to avoid damages that are available to him without undue effort or expense. Id.

Here, there is no competent substantial evidence that the Forbeses could have taken any measure without undue effort or expense to avoid the damages they sought. When Prime walked off the job, the Forbeses were left with an uninhabitable home that no other contractor would finish. At that point, the money they paid for Prime's work and updated plans was sunk; to avoid that loss they would have had to have been able to finish the home, and there was no evidence that they could have done that with another contractor at the price at which Prime was contractually required to do it.

With respect to the lost equity, the Forbeses spent five months living in a rental property as they searched for someone to finish the renovations. After that proved futile, they used their remaining resources to buy a new home rather than continue to make rent payments indefinitely. On the evidence here, had the Forbeses not bought the new house and instead continued paying rent without end, they still would have found themselves unable to continue paying the mortgage on the home that Prime left uninhabitable. This record establishes no course of action available to the Forbeses without undue effort or expense to avoid their damages. Thus, there was no competent substantial evidence to support a damage reduction based on the doctrine of avoidable consequences here. See, e.g., Graybar Elec. Co. v. Stratton of Fla., Inc., 509 So.2d 1133, 1134 (Fla. 2d DCA 1987) (reversing a final judgment in which the trial court erroneously applied the doctrine of avoidable consequences despite "insufficient evidence to support the application of that doctrine").

In sum, the trial court's use of the wrong method for calculating damages together with its erroneous application of the doctrine of avoidable consequences denied the Forbeses the full amount of damages to which they were entitled. We reverse the damages award and remand this case to the trial court for entry of an amended final judgment awarding those damages it finds, after hearing any arguments the parties decide to make, are necessary to place the Forbeses in the position they occupied immediately before they contracted with Prime. In all other respects, the final judgment is affirmed.

Affirmed in part; reversed in part; remanded with instructions.

NORTHCUTT and ROTHSTEIN-YOUAKIM, JJ., Concur.

NOTES AND QUESTIONS

A. ***Interests.*** Judicial remedies can protect the injured party's expectation interest, reliance interest, or restitution interest.[1] Which of these interests is at stake in *Forbes*?

B. ***Choosing between different interests.*** If the injured party is entitled to damages for total breach, can they choose freely between expectation damages, reliance damages, and restitution? Read sections 347, 349, and 373 of the Restatement (Second) of Contracts.

C. ***The mitigation doctrine.*** According to the mitigation doctrine, the injured party cannot demand damages for losses that the injured party could have avoided through reasonable efforts. Read section 350 of the Restatement (Second) of Contracts. The injured party can recover the costs of reasonable mitigation efforts as incidental loss.[2]

D. ***Efforts to mitigate.*** The *Forbes* court emphasizes that the mitigation doctrine does not require "Herculean" efforts. Similarly, section 350 of the Restatement (Second) of Contracts limits the mitigation doctrine to losses that the injured party can avoid without "undue risk, burden, or humiliation."[3] Courts take this limitation very seriously. For example, "before projected earnings from other employment opportunities not sought or accepted by the discharged employee can be applied in mitigation, the employer must show that the other employment was comparable, or substantially similar, to that of which the employee has been deprived; the employee's rejection of or failure to seek other available employment of a different or inferior kind may not be resorted to in order to mitigate damages."[4]

E. ***Unsuccessful mitigation efforts.*** Sometimes, an injured party takes

---

1. See Restatement (Second) of Contracts § 344 (defining these different interests).
2. Restatement (Second) of Contracts § 350 ct. h.
3. See Restatement (Second) of Contracts § 350.
4. Parker v. Twentieth Cent.-Fox Film Corp., 474 P.2d 689, 692 (Cal. 1970).

reasonable but unsuccessful steps to mitigate their loss. In that case, the injured party has fulfilled their duty to mitigate.[5]

F. Voluntary mitigation. If the injured party manages to mitigate their loss, the damages to which they are entitled are reduced accordingly, even if the injured party was not *required* to mitigate.[6]

G. Equal opportunity to mitigate. A few courts have held that if both parties had an equal opportunity to mitigate the injured party's loss, the breaching party is precluded from invoking the injured party's failure to mitigate.[7] However, Richard Posner, writing for the Seventh Circuit, wrote on this view: "We need not try to guess whether Illinois would recognize the 'equal opportunity' doctrine (if so recent and rarely applied and, as we are about to see, questionable a legal idea can be called a doctrine) in a suitable case. The doctrine is discordant with common law principles, which demand a reason for not letting losses lie where they fall. If a plaintiff can avoid a loss at a cost no greater than the defendant would bear, one might have thought that he would have to incur the cost (for which of course he could seek reimbursement from the defendant) and thereby avoid the loss."[8]

H. Landlords. A particularly thorny question within the mitigation doctrine emerges in the realm of landlord-tenant law. If a tenant breaches their lease and leaves the premises, is the landlord obligated to find a new tenant as part of their duty to mitigate damages? Historically, courts have rejected such a duty.[9] According to this view, "[o]nce the tenant abandoned the premises prior to the expiration of the lease . . . [the landlord has the option of doing] nothing and collect[ing] the full rent due under the lease."[10] However, for residential leases, most states now reject this traditional view and recognize the landlord's duty to mitigate damages by making reasonable

---

5. Restatement (Second) of Contracts § 350(2).

6. Cf. Community Health Choice, Inc. v. U.S., 970 F.3d 1364, 1376 (Fed. Cir. 2020) (holding that "there must be a reduction in damages equal to the amount of benefit that resulted from the mitigation efforts that the non-breaching party in fact undertook."); Citizens Fed. Bank, FSB v. U.S., 59 Fed. Cl. 507, 526 (2004) (holding that "as a matter of law, the benefits of mitigation must be credited" to the breaching party).

7. E.g., Ecksel v. Orleans Const. Co., 519 A.2d 1021, 1028 (Pa. Super. 1987); Loyal Christian Ben. Ass'n v. Bender, 493 A.2d 760, 763 (Pa. Super. 1985).

8. Cates v. Morgan Portable Bldg. Corp., 780 F.2d 683, 688-689 (1985) (footnotes omitted)

9. Holy Properties Ltd., L.P. v. Kenneth Cole Productions, Inc., 661 N.E.2d 694, 696 (N.Y. 1995); Miller v. Burnett, 397 P.3d 448, 452 (Kan. App. 2017).

10. Holy Properties Ltd., L.P. v. Kenneth Cole Productions, Inc., 661 N.E.2d 694, 696 (N.Y. 1995).

efforts to relet the vacated premises.[11] And even regarding commercial leases, the clear trend among states is to recognize such a duty.[12] Some states even ban contractual provisions that eliminate the landlord's duty to mitigate.[13]

---

11. See, e.g., 29 Holding Corp. v. Diaz, 775 N.Y.S.2d 807, 814 (N.Y. Sup. Ct. 2004) (holding that "landlord [of residential tenant] should be prepared to demonstrate reasonable and diligent efforts to re-rent the premises"); Sommer v. Kridel, 378 A.2d 767, 772 (N.J. 1977); see also CONN. GEN. STAT. ANN. § 47A-11A (West) (imposing duty to mitigate damages on the landlord if tenant abandons "dwelling unit"); N.D. CENT. CODE ANN. § 47-16-13.5 (West) (imposing duty to mitigate in case of residential leases); TEX. PROP. CODE ANN. § 91.006 (Vernon) (providing that contractual provisions negating the landlord's duty to mitigate are void); MD. REAL PROP. CODE ANN. § 8-207 (d) (voiding contractual clauses that waive landlord's duty to mitigate where tenant vacates premises prematurely); but see, Alsup v. Banks, 9 So. 895, 895 (Miss. 1891) (rejecting the landlord's duty to mitigate in case of a residential lease).

12. Frenchtown Square Partn. v. Lemstone, Inc., 791 N.E.2d 417, 422 (Ohio 2003); New Towne L.P. v. Pier 1 Imports (U.S.), Inc., 680 N.E.2d 644, 646 (Ohio App. 6th Dist. 1996); Fanarjian v. Moskowitz, 568 A.2d 94, 97 (N.J. Super. App. Div. 1989); O'Brien v. Black, 648 A.2d 1374, 1376 (Vt. 1994); Dover Mall, LLC v. Tang, No. K22C-07-013 JJC, 2023 WL 6536975, at *6 (Del. Super. Oct. 5, 2023), amended, No. K22C-07-013 JJC, 2023 WL 7903639 (Del. Super. Nov. 16, 2023). In some states, this duty is imposed by statutory law. See Tex. PROP. CODE ANN. § 91.006 (Vernon) (providing that "[a] landlord has a duty to mitigate damages if a tenant abandons the leased premises in violation of the lease"); MD. REAL PROP. CODE ANN. § 8-207 (a) (3) (providing that landlord has a duty to mitigate if tenant vacates premises prematurely); 735 Ill. Comp. Stat. Ann. 5/9-213.1 (imposing duty on landlord to mitigate damages); Mont. Code Ann. § 70-24-401 (imposing a duty to mitigate on landlords).

13. See Tex. PROP. CODE ANN. § 91.006 (Vernon) (providing that contractual provisions negating the landlord's duty to mitigate are void); MD. REAL PROP. CODE ANN. § 8-207 (d) (voiding contractual clauses that waive landlord's duty to mitigate where tenant vacates premises prematurely). In contrast, some courts have enforced contractual provisions that waive the landlord's duty to mitigate. New Towne L.P. v. Pier 1 Imports (U.S.), Inc., 680 N.E.2d 644, 646 (Ohio App. 6th Dist. 1996); Sylva Shops Ltd. Partn. v. Hibbard, 623 S.E.2d 785, 792 (N.C. App. 2006); Dover Mall, LLC v. Tang, No. K22C-07-013 JJC, 2023 WL 6536975, at *6 (Del. Super. Oct. 5, 2023), amended, No. K22C-07-013 JJC, 2023 WL 7903639 (Del. Super. Nov. 16, 2023).

CHAPTER 24
LIQUIDATED DAMAGES

Lloyd v. Niceta

Supreme Court of Maryland, 485 Md. 422 (2023)

HOTTEN, J.

... Petitioner and Respondent were married on March 25, 2006 in the District of Columbia. Both parties have college degrees. Respondent was employed as an event planner and served as the White House Social Secretary between February 2017 and January 2021, earning between $130,000 and $200,000 per year. Petitioner was a wealth manager who earned between $70,000 and $122,000 per year. Petitioner has a wealthy family, including his paternal grandmother, Rachel Mellon, who left him a substantial inheritance after she passed away in March 2014.

In April 2015, Respondent forwarded a draft of the Agreement to Petitioner. The Agreement contained, in relevant part, a lump sum clause that would require Petitioner to pay Respondent a sum of $5 million if he engaged in adultery and related acts. On June 16, 2015 and July 16, 2015, the parties and their attorneys reviewed the draft "line by line[ ]" during extensive meetings. Petitioner proposed a $2 million increase to the lump sum provision to demonstrate "his good faith toward" Respondent and because he anticipated that he would inherit approximately $12 million from his father's estate. Respondent agreed to the change, and the parties signed the finalized Agreement on September 18, 2015. The lump sum provision provides, in relevant part:

10. LUMP SUM MONETARY AWARD.

A. This provision shall only be effective only in the limited situation that any one of the following conditions are satisfied:

(i) If Husband is found by a preponderance of the evidence to have committed adultery....

B. If Wife proves by a preponderance of the evidence that Husband has engaged in any of the conduct as set forth above in subparagraph 10.A, Husband shall make a tax-free transfer to Wife of SEVEN MILLION AND 00/100 DOLLARS ($7,000,000.00) within ninety (90) days of such findings. If the parties remained married, said transfer shall be a permanent gift between husband and wife; if the parties divorce, this transfer shall constitute a lump sum monetary award not subject to taxation under the terms of the Internal Revenue Code. The transfer shall be made from Husband's 50% share of the Column B Assets.... [Column B contained a list of assets.]

After the parties entered into the Agreement, Petitioner engaged in another extramarital affair in October 2018. The parties separated on April 14, 2019, after Petitioner advised Respondent that he no longer wished to remain married to her.

II. Proceeding in the Circuit Court for Montgomery County.

On October 23, 2019, Respondent filed a Complaint for Absolute Divorce in the Circuit Court for Montgomery County on the grounds of adultery. She requested that the circuit court incorporate the Agreement into the divorce decree and enforce, among other things, the lump sum provision. Petitioner filed an Answer and Counterclaim, arguing that the Agreement was void because it was unconscionable and against public policy. Petitioner also asserted that the lump sum provision constituted an unenforceable penalty because it was an excessive liquidated damages clause....

On January 15, 2021, the circuit court determined that the lump sum provision constituted a penalty, but was enforceable. ... The Appellate Court of Maryland affirmed the circuit court's decision ...

ANALYSIS

I. Postnuptial Agreements in Maryland.

... Under Maryland law, spouses "may make a valid and enforceable deed or agreement that relates to alimony, support, property rights, or personal rights." Fam. Law § 8-101(a). A postnuptial agreement is a type of marital contract "that sets forth the rights, duties and responsibilities of the parties during and upon termination of the marriage through death or divorce." McGeehan, . . . 167 A.3d at 596. . . . Spouses generally enter a postnuptial agreement "at a time when separation or divorce is not imminent." Postnuptial Agreement, Black's Law Dictionary (11th ed. 2019). Postnuptial agreements "encourage the private resolution of family issues[,]" because "they may allow couples to eliminate a source of emotional turmoil--usually, financial uncertainty--and focus instead on resolving other aspects of the marriage that may be problematic." Bedrick v. Bedrick, 300 Conn. 691, 698, 17 A.3d 17, 24 (2011).

A postnuptial agreement is valid and enforceable, unless the agreement is unconscionable or the byproduct of fraud, duress, mistake, or undue influence. McGeehan, 455 Md. at 298, 167 A.3d at 597. . . . Postnuptial agreements allow spouses to alter their default rights under the Family Law Article, subject to the court's equitable authority. See Nouri v. Dadgar, 245 Md. App. 324, 359–60, 226 A.3d 797, 818 (2020) (noting that spouses may enter into a postnuptial agreement that relinquishes their default statutory rights to marital property). . . . Absent countervailing equitable considerations, courts will enforce the terms of a marital agreement to the extent they concern spouses and not children. See Fam. Law § 8-103(a) ("The court may modify any provision of a[n] ... agreement ... with respect to the care, custody, education, or support of any minor child of the spouses, if the modification would be in the best interests of the child.").

II. The Appropriate Framework for the Lump Sum Provision.

A. The doctrine of liquidated damages is inapplicable to postnuptial agreements.

Petitioner characterizes the lump sum provision as a penalty because, in his view, it is an excessive liquidated damages provision. We reject Petitioner's interpretation because the principles governing liquidated damages provisions are incongruent with divorce law and, therefore, provide an inadequate framework for evaluating the lump sum provision. As we explain in the next section, the lump sum provision is better viewed as an allocation of marital assets based on a party's conduct that led to the estrangement of the parties. See Fam. Law § 8-205(b)(4) (permitting courts to consider "the circumstances that contributed to the estrangement of the parties[ ]" when fashioning a monetary award following divorce).

Liquidated damages provisions, as applied in non-marital contracts, provide for "a specific sum stipulated to and agreed upon by the parties at the time they entered into a contract, to be paid to compensate for injuries in the event of a breach of that contract." Barrie Sch. v. Patch, 401 Md. 497, 507, 933 A.2d 382, 388 (2007) (citation omitted). A valid liquidated damages clause: (1) must unambiguously provide for a specified sum; (2) must reasonably compensate a party "for the damages anticipated by the breach[;]" and (3) "may not be altered to correspond to actual damages determined after the fact[.]" Bd. of Educ. of Talbot Cnty. v. Heister, . . . 896 A.2d 342, 352 (2006). . . . A liquidated damages provision will be construed as a penalty when the parties intend for the sum to punish the breaching party or when the sum is "grossly excessive and out of all proportion to the damages that might reasonably have been expected to result from such breach of the contract." Patch, . . . A.2d at 389. . . . Contract law rejects penalties because "[t]he central objective behind the system of contract remedies is compensatory, not punitive." Restatement (Second) of Contracts § 356 cmt. a (1981).

We agree with Petitioner that the lump sum provision would constitute an unenforceable penalty had the Agreement been a traditional common law contract, rather than a marital contract. The Agreement arose following Petitioner's infidelity, which established a backdrop for negotiations. The Agreement provided that any further act of infidelity would require payment of the $7 million lump sum, thus deterring Petitioner from engaging in conduct that was repugnant to the marriage. Ms. Day's testimony supports this interpretation because she stated that the lump sum provision "was intended to [ ] be prohibitive ... so that [Petitioner] would not" commence another extramarital affair. Additionally, Ms. Day and Mr. Delvecchio both referred to the lump sum provision as the "bad boy clause." That phrase implied that the operation of the lump sum provision would compel Petitioner to comport himself or face a consequence. Therefore, the record demonstrates that the parties intended for the lump sum provision to deter Petitioner from engaging in adultery again and, if the deterrent did not work, to reallocate marital assets to reflect his responsibility for the breakdown of the marriage.

Petitioner contends that this Court's inquiry should end here because marital agreements are governed by the same principles as common law contracts, which prohibit penalties. We disagree. We recognize that "[t]he general principles governing other types of contracts apply to" marital agreements. Bruce v. Dyer, 309 Md. 421, 439, 524 A.2d 777, 786 (1987) (citations omitted). This approach, however, does not prohibit this Court from deviating from common law contract principles when they are incongruent with principles governing marital contracts. See, e.g., McGeehan, 455 Md. at 294, 167 A.3d at 594 ("Unlike other contracts, ... a confidential relationship exists between the parties, as a matter of law[,] in an antenuptial agreement." (cleaned up) (emphasis added)). Indeed, marital "agreements are necessarily infused with equitable considerations and are construed in light of salient legal and policy concerns[,]" which may occasionally render "normal tenets of contract interpretation" inapplicable. Holtham v. Lucas, . . . A.3d 1226, 1232 (App. Div. 2019). . .

Petitioner's position presumes that the doctrine of liquidated damages and, by extension, the rule against penalties, apply to marital agreements. This is because liquidated damages provisions and penalties exist on a spectrum of enforceability, and one doctrine cannot be imported into family law without the other. See Patch, 401 Md. at 510, 933 A.2d at 390 (noting that the boundary between liquidated damages clauses and penalties is "one of the most difficult and perplexing inquiries encountered in the construction of written agreements[.]" (cleaned up)). We hold that such a framework is ill-suited for marital agreements.

In non-marital agreements, liquidated damages operate as "a sum that will compensate the nonbreacher for any harm caused by the breach, in lieu of the compensatory contract damage[s] to which the nonbreacher would otherwise be entitled[.]" Id. at 513, 933 A.2d at 392 (cleaned up) (emphasis added). In divorce proceedings, parties are not entitled to compensatory damages. Instead, the primary monetary sums available to an aggrieved spouse are alimony, child support, and a division of marital assets, including a potential monetary award, attendant to divorce, which are statutory remedies and subject to the court's equitable authority. . . . None of those monetary sums serve as compensatory damages for which liquidated damages may substitute. Additionally, liquidated damages cannot serve as a substitute for non-monetary relief, such as annulment, divorce, custody, or visitation. See Fam. Law § 1-201(b)(3)–(6). Marital agreements may "alter the presumptive consequences of" divorce, but this Court has never held that provisions in a marital agreement may substitute for the statutory remedy of divorce. See Nouri, 245 Md. App. at 359, 226 A.3d at 818 (citations omitted). We decline to do so in this case.

Additionally, as a practical matter, applying a liquidated damages framework would place this Court in the untenable position of assigning a dollar value to a marriage for purposes of evaluating when a liquidated damages provision becomes a penalty. . . . Even if this Court were inclined to try to make such a calculation, any measure of damages would be speculative. The speculative nature of damages undermines a liquidated damages framework because liquidated damages must "provide a fair estimate of potential damages[.]" See Patch, 401 Md. at 510, 933 A.2d at 390 (citations omitted). Accordingly, we decline to apply a liquidated damages framework in evaluating the lump sum provision in this case.

Treating provisions in marital agreements as penalties under a liquidated damages framework would also undermine the goals of marital agreements. Courts in other jurisdictions have rejected doing so even when faced with provisions that more clearly resemble traditional contract penalties. The Superior Court of New Jersey, Appellate Division's decision in Holtham is instructive. In that case, a husband challenged a marital settlement agreement that required him to pay off an automobile loan and transfer title of that automobile to his wife. Holtham, 460 N.J. Super. at 314, 214 A.3d at 1229. The agreement imposed a $150 fee for each day that the husband failed to comply. Id., 214 A.3d at 1229. The trial court incorporated the agreement into the parties' divorce decree and ordered the husband to pay $18,450 pursuant to the agreement. Id., 214 A.3d at 1229. On appeal, the Superior Court of New Jersey, Appellate Division "agree[d] that $18,450 would constitute an unenforceable penalty under traditional contract law principles," but held that "the penalty rule does not apply with equal force to marital settlement agreements embodied in final divorce judgments." Id., 214 A.3d at 1229.

The court considered the policies underlying the penalty rule, which "protect[ed] against both oppression and ... recovery that far exceed[ed] the economic losses normally recoverable for breach of contract." Id. at 320, 214 A.3d at 1232–33 (citations omitted). In the court's view, the penalty rule was incompatible with marital contracts because it "fail[ed] to account for non-market-based 'idiosyncratic value' " or "recognize the premium that the court and parties place on post-divorce peace." Id. at 321, 214 A.3d at 1233 (citations omitted). The court explained that "[t]he penalty rule also does not account for the fact that parties to matrimonial agreements may behave far differently than the rational economic actors presumed to participate in typical contractual relationships." Id. at 322, 214 A.3d at 1233. The court observed that, unlike common law contracts, marital agreements "are necessarily infused with equitable considerations and are construed in light of salient legal and policy concerns." Id. at 319, 214 A.3d at 1232 (cleaned up). The court concluded that "a per diem fee that may fail as a penalty under traditional contract principles may reasonably deter or remedy the emotional harm caused by a breach of post-marital peace." Id. at 322, 214 A.3d at 1233.

Similarly, the Appellate Court of Connecticut upheld a penalty provision in a separation agreement that required a husband to pay his wife an additional 10% annual interest if he failed to timely pay her approximately $15 million over two installments. Dougan v. Dougan, . . . 970 A.2d 131, 134 (2009). . . . The court declined to apply the rule against penalties because the state had an interest in spouses entering into agreements that "conserve[ ] judicial resources and encourage private resolution of family issues." Id. at 385, 970 A.2d at 136–37. The court noted that "the parties were both represented by counsel, [ ] reached an agreement after a long negotiation period, ... participated actively in the negotiations[,] and found the agreement fair, reasonable[,] and in line with their expectations." Id. at 387–88, 970 A.2d at 138.

Unlike economic and arms-length transactions between business entities, transactions between spouses involve a marriage, which "is a coming together for better or for worse, hopefully enduring, and intimate to the degree of being sacred." Obergefell v. Hodges, 576 U.S. 644, 667 ... (2015). . . The intimacy of marriage and the equitable considerations in divorce proceedings undermine the economic-based rationale of the rule against penalties because spouses have an emotional stake in ensuring their marriage endures or, in the alternative, securing their future following divorce. See Holtham, 460 N.J. Super. at 322, 214 A.3d at 1233 (noting that parties to a marital agreement "may behave far differently than the rational economic actors presumed to participate in typical contractual relationships.").

Postnuptial agreements offer a vehicle through which spouses may: (1) memorialize their commitment to each other by deterring conduct that is repugnant to their marriage; (2) resolve their marital disputes without judicial intervention; and (3) financially secure their post-divorce future, particularly where one spouse is culpable for the failure of the marriage. See McGeehan, 455 Md. at 298, 167 A.3d at 596–97 (noting that postnuptial agreements may incorporate "financial rewards and penalties to create incentives during a marriage that constrain the behavior of both spouses." (citation omitted)); see also Bedrick, 300 Conn. at 698, 17 A.3d at 24 ("Postnuptial agreements may also encourage the private resolution of family issues[,]" thereby "eliminat[ing] a source of emotional turmoil ... and [allowing spouses to] focus instead on resolving other aspects of the marriage that may be problematic.").

Assuming, arguendo, that the lump sum provision was akin to a traditional contractual penalty provision, we would not agree that it should be governed by principles of liquidated damages. As we explain further in the next section, the term "penalty," as used in a liquidated damages framework, is inapplicable to postnuptial agreements. Accordingly, the issue before this Court is best framed as whether a provision in a postnuptial agreement may allocate marital assets based on one party committing adultery, thereby being primarily responsible for the breakdown of the marriage. Maryland statutory law enshrines the ability of spouses to mold their marriage, as well as the consequences of any divorce, through agreements. See Fam. Law § 8-101(a). Embedded in that statutory right is the power for spouses to include interspousal transfers of marital assets based on adultery in their postnuptial agreements. . . . .

The lump sum provision is properly understood as an interspousal distribution of marital assets that is contingent upon infidelity as the cause of the breakdown of the marriage. We note that the Agreement describes the provision as either a "permanent gift" or "a lump sum monetary award[,]" depending on whether the parties divorced. . . .

IV. The Public Policy of Maryland.

We hold that the public policy in Maryland currently supports spouses negotiating in good faith to condition a transfer of marital assets upon the dissolution of the marriage when a spouse commits adultery. . . . "[T]he declaration of public policy is normally the function of the legislative branch[,]" but "[c]ourts may [also] rely on prior judicial opinions, legislative enactments, or administrative regulations as the chief sources of public policy[.]" . . . Given the dearth of case law regarding postnuptial agreements in Maryland, we consider decisions from other jurisdictions to ascertain the public policy that is relevant to distributions of assets based on adultery. . . .

Some of our sister jurisdictions have rejected provisions in marital agreements that are similar to the lump sum provision in this case on the grounds that they undermine no-fault divorce laws. In Diosdado v. Diosdado, the Court of Appeal of California declined to enforce a liquidated damages clause in a marital settlement agreement that imposed a $50,000 penalty for adultery because the "penalty [was] in direct contravention of the public policy underlying no-fault divorce." 97 Cal.App.4th 470, 118 Cal. Rptr. 2d 494, 496

(2002). In In re Marriage of Cooper, the Supreme Court of Iowa invalidated a postnuptial agreement that would have required a husband to pay $2,600 in temporary monthly spousal support if he committed adultery. 769 N.W.2d 582, 583–84 (Iowa 2009). The court "reject[ed] the idea of injecting the courts into the complex web of interpersonal relationships[,]" because Iowa's "no-fault divorce law [was] designed to limit acrimonious proceedings[ ]" and "a contrary approach would empower spouses" to contractually circumvent those laws. Id. at 586–87. In Crofford v. Adachi, the Supreme Court of Hawai'i found the reasoning in Cooper persuasive in a case involving a postnuptial agreement that would award a wife most of the parties' marital assets if the husband either engaged in an extramarital affair or physically harmed her. 150 Haw. 518, 519, 506 P.3d 182, 183 (2022). The court held that the agreement violated "Hawai'i's no-fault divorce policy and must be voided[,]" because it "require[d] the family court to evaluate the parties' fault[.]" Id. at 526, 506 P.3d at 190.

The Supreme Court of Hawai'i stated that the reasoning of cases supporting the transfer of marital assets based on adultery from jurisdictions that permit fault-based divorce was "less persuasive in a no-fault state such as Hawai'i." Id. at 527, 506 P.3d at 191. The same is true for the persuasive force of Diosdado, Cooper, and Crofford in Maryland, because this State currently permits divorce based on fault, including adultery. Fam. Law § 7-103(a)(1). Further indicia of this State's public policy lies in Fam. Law § 8-205(b)(4), which requires courts to "determine the amount and the method of payment of a monetary award[ ]" based on several factors, including "the circumstances that contributed to the estrangement of the parties[.]" Those "circumstances" may include adultery. Ohm v. Ohm, 49 Md. App. 392, 410, 431 A.2d 1371, 1381 (1981) ("[A]dultery is a factor to be considered ... in making a monetary award."). In light of these statutes, the General Assembly has recognized that adultery is repugnant to a marriage and courts should consider adultery, to the extent it contributed to the breakdown of a marriage, as a factor when fashioning a monetary award during divorce proceedings. As the Appellate Court observed, Maryland's public policy, at a minimum, "generally frowns on adultery[.]" Lloyd, 255 Md. App. at 698, 284 A.3d at 829. Permitting spouses to allocate marital assets upon divorce based on adultery comports with that public policy.

Petitioner argues that it "is a dangerous idea[ ]" for this Court to "dabbl[e]" with adultery penalties in marital agreements. In his view, penalties will exacerbate spousal abuse and become "instruments of fear and coercion[.]" Petitioner's policy arguments would be more appropriate for the General Assembly. Furthermore, Petitioner's contentions belie the record in this case, which reflects that he recommended the $2 million increase to the lump sum provision and subsequently entered into the Agreement against the advice of counsel following months of negotiation. Regarding infidelity provisions that follow this Court's decision, we encourage trial courts to exercise their equitable authority to address the specter of abuse whenever it invades the negotiations or language of postnuptial agreements. See Holtham, 460 N.J. Super. at 325, 214 A.3d at 1235 (holding that "the family court, in exercising its broad authority, may reform a penalty provision to achieve fairness and equity.").

Based on the above principles, we conclude that Maryland's public policy currently permits spouses to transfer assets to each other based on adultery that leads to the dissolution of a marriage. The Court is not holding that spouses may impose on each other monetary penalties unrelated to marital assets or unrelated to the division of such assets during a divorce; rather, the Court is narrowly holding that spouses may allocate marital assets in the event of divorce based on adultery. We have not decided whether the above principles apply to prenuptial agreements....

V. The $7 Million Lump Sum Provision in the Case at Bar.

With the above principles in mind, we hold that the $7 million lump sum provision in this case is valid and enforceable. Petitioner argues that the provision is overly broad because it imposed the same $7 million "penalty" to conduct ranging from trivial physical contact to sexual relations. Petitioner also claims that the $7 million lump sum is excessive because it "awarded [Respondent] more than 100% of the marital estate." These arguments are unpersuasive.

... The lump sum provision did not restrict Petitioner's ability to foster his platonic relationships. Respondent's mere suspicions were insufficient to trigger the provision because she was required to establish "by a preponderance of the evidence" that Petitioner had engaged in adultery. Petitioner alone controlled whether the provision would trigger. The lump sum provision did not require the parties to remain married. Indeed, nothing prevented Petitioner from divorcing Respondent, thereby rendering the provision inoperative, and subsequently pursuing a romantic or sexual relationship with another person. In essence, the lump sum provision required Petitioner to remain faithful to Respondent. We reject the contention that remaining faithful to a spouse is too onerous of an obligation.

There is no dispute that Petitioner could have transferred $7 million to Respondent had the transfer not been conditioned upon his infidelity. As the *Laudig* court observed, this broad power to contract allows parties to place conditions upon those transfers based "on the occurrence of a specified type of conduct[,]" such as adultery. 425 Pa. Super. at 236, 624 A.2d at 655. Like the spouses in Dougan, Petitioner and Respondent entered into the Agreement after consulting attorneys, participating in lengthy negotiations, and thoroughly reviewing the terms. . . . As with the husband in Holtham, Petitioner's access to counsel establishes that "he understood the nature of the [adultery] provision and was prepared to abide by it[.]" 460 N.J. Super. at 325, 214 A.3d at 1235. We note that Petitioner proposed the $2 million increase to the lump sum provision and thereafter entered into the Agreement against the advice of counsel. It is immaterial that the provision applied exclusively to Petitioner because he could have negotiated for it to apply to Respondent as well. Additionally, that limitation was logical because Petitioner was the only party who had previously been unfaithful. Petitioner's promise to remain faithful was part of his consideration for Respondent agreeing to remain married to him.

Regarding whether the sum was too severe, we recognize, as Petitioner states, that monetary awards under Fam. Law § 8-205(a)(1) "cannot exceed the value of the marital [estate]."... We need not address whether this limitation applies to interspousal transfers in postnuptial agreements because the Agreement already provides a limitation to the $7 million transfer. . . . By identifying a source, i.e., marital property, for the $7 million, the Agreement limits the transfer to the cumulative value of those assets....

By limiting its scope to marital assets, the lump sum provision "eliminate[d] a source of emotional turmoil––[specifically], financial uncertainty––and [allowed the spouses to] focus instead on resolving other aspects of the marriage that may be problematic." ... Therefore, we hold that the lump sum provision was valid and enforceable...

. . . For the foregoing reasons, we affirm the decision of the Appellate Court of Maryland.

JUDGMENT OF THE APPELLATE COURT OF MARYLAND IS AFFIRMED. COSTS TO BE PAID BY PETITIONER.

. . .

NOTES AND QUESTIONS

A. No-fault divorce v. fault-based divorce. In the realm of divorce proceedings, the United States distinguishes between no-fault and fault-based divorce. All states permit some form of no-fault-divorce,[1] but not all states permit fault-based divorce. "No-fault divorce states" grant divorces solely on no-fault grounds. Conversely, other states offer the flexibility of filing for divorce based on either fault or no-fault grounds. Pursuing a fault-based divorce may allow the party to receive a larger portion of assets.[2]

B. Liquidated damages. Section 356 of the Restatement (Second) of Contracts allows liquidated damages but only within strict limits. The damages specified in the contract must be reasonable either in light of the anticipated loss or in consideration of the actual loss incurred. Liquidated damages clauses are impermissible if they impose payment obligations exceeding both the actual and the anticipated loss.

C. Policy. What could be the policy rationale for disallowing penalty clauses in contract law?

D. Comparative Law. Many other countries are more permissive regarding contractual penalty clauses. For example, civil law jurisdictions such as Brazil, France, and Germany all allow penalty clauses.[3] What might be the reason for this divide?

E. Penalty clauses and divorce regimes. In *Lloyd*, the court acknowledges that allowing penalty clauses may undermine the purpose of true no-fault divorce regimes in no-fault divorce states. In what ways could this be true?

---

1. For a recent survey of divorce regimes in the various states see Jessica Pacwa, Marriage and Divorce, 24 GEO. J. GENDER & L. 671, 725 (2023).

2. See, e.g., Matter of Marriage of Mena and Fernandez, No. 06-21-00088-CV, 2022 WL 3907926, at *2 (Tex. App.—Texarkana Aug. 31, 2022) (noting that because the defendant pled a fault-based divorce, 'the court may consider the conduct of the errant spouse in making a disproportionate distribution of the marital estate.'") (quoting In re Marriage of Hultquist, 2021 WL 2252129, at *3 (Tex. App. 2021)).

3. Mariana Pargendler, The Role of the State in Contract Law: The Common-Civil Law Divide, 43 YALE J. INTL. L. 143, 189 n. 65 (2018).

CHAPTER 25
RESTITUTION AS A REMEDY FOR BREACH

U.S. v. Algernon Blair, Inc

United States Court of Appeals, Fourth Circuit, 479 F.2d 638 (1973)

CRAVEN, Circuit Judge:

May a subcontractor, who justifiably ceases work under a contract because of the prime contractor's breach, recover in quantum meruit the value of labor and equipment already furnished pursuant to the contract irrespective of whether he would have been entitled to recover in a suit on the contract? We think so, and, for reasons to be stated, the decision of the district court will be reversed.

The subcontractor, Coastal Steel Erectors, Inc., brought this action under the provisions of the Miller Act, 40 U.S.C.A. § 270a et seq., in the name of the United States against Algernon Blair, Inc., and its surety, United States Fidelity and Guaranty Company. Blair had entered a contract with the United States for the construction of a naval hospital in Charleston County, South Carolina. Blair had then contracted with Coastal to perform certain steel erection and supply certain equipment in conjunction with Blair's contract with the United States. Coastal commenced performance of its obligations, supplying its own cranes for handling and placing steel. Blair refused to pay for crane rental, maintaining that it was not obligated to do so under the subcontract. Because of Blair's failure to make payments for crane rental, and after completion of approximately 28 percent of the subcontract, Coastal terminated its performance. Blair then proceeded to complete the job with a new subcontractor. Coastal brought this action to recover for labor and equipment furnished.

The district court found that the subcontract required Blair to pay for crane use and that Blair's refusal to do so was such a material breach as to justify Coastal's terminating performance. This finding is not questioned on appeal. The court then found that under the contract the amount due Coastal, less what had already been paid, totaled approximately $37,000. Additionally, the court found Coastal would have lost more than $37,000 if it had completed performance. Holding that any amount due Coastal must be reduced by any loss it would have incurred by complete performance of the contract, the court denied recovery to Coastal. While the district court correctly stated the " 'normal' rule of contract damages,"1 we think Coastal is entitled to recover in quantum meruit.

In United States for Use of Susi Contracting Co. v. Zara Contracting Co., 146 F.2d 606 (2d Cir. 1944), a Miller Act action, the court was faced with a situation similar to that involved here–the prime contractor had unjustifiably breached a subcontract after partial performance by the subcontractor. The court stated:

For it is an accepted principle of contract law, often applied in the case of construction contracts, that the promisee upon breach has the option to forego any suit on the contract and claim only the reasonable value of his performance.

146 F.2d at 610. The Tenth Circuit has also stated that the right to seek recovery under quantum meruit in a Miller Act case is clear. Quantum meruit recovery is not limited to an action against the prime contractor but may also be brought against the Miller Act surety, as in this case. Further, that the complaint is not clear in regard to the theory of a plaintiff's recovery does not preclude recovery under quantum meruit. Narragansett Improvement Co. v. United States, 290 F.2d 577 (1st Cir. 1961). A plaintiff may join a claim for quantum meruit with a claim for damages from breach of contract.

In the present case, Coastal has, at its own expense, provided Blair with labor and the use of equipment. Blair, who breached the subcontract, has retained these benefits without having fully paid for them. On these facts, Coastal is entitled to restitution in quantum meruit.

The "restitution interest," involving a combination of unjust impoverishment with unjust gain, presents the strongest case for relief. If, following Aristotle, we regard the purpose of justice as the maintenance of an equilibrium of goods among members of society, the restitution interest presents twice as strong a claim to judicial intervention as the reliance interest, since if A not only causes B to lose one unit but appropriates that unit to himself, the resulting discrepancy between A and B is not one unit but two. Fuller & Perdue, The Reliance Interest in Contract Damages, 46 Yale L.J. 52, 56 (1936).

The impact of quantum meruit is to allow a promisee to recover the value of services he gave to the defendant irrespective of whether he would have lost money on the contract and been unable to recover in a suit on the contract. Scaduto v. Orlando, 381 F.2d 587, 595 (2d Cir. 1967). The measure of recovery for quantum meruit is the reasonable value of the performance, Restatement of Contracts § 347 (1932); and recovery is undiminished by any loss which would have been incurred by complete performance. 12 Williston on Contracts § 1485, at 312 (3d ed. 1970). While the contract price may be evidence of reasonable value of the services, it does not measure the value of the performance or limit recovery.7 Rather, the standard for measuring the reasonable value of the services rendered is the amount for which such services could have been purchased from one in the plaintiff's position at the time and place the services were rendered.

Since the district court has not yet accurately determined the reasonable value of the labor and equipment use furnished by Coastal to Blair, the case must be remanded for those findings. When the amount has been determined, judgment will be entered in favor of Coastal, less payments already made under the contract. Accordingly, for the reasons stated above, the decision of the district court is

Reversed and remanded with instructions.

NOTES AND QUESTIONS

*A. **The Miller Act.*** The Miller Act protects subcontractors and suppliers in cases involving the construction, alteration, or repair of federal buildings. Under the Miller Act, primary contractors hired for such project are required to furnish a so-called payment bond if the contract with the subcontractor or supplier is for more than $100,000.[1] For amounts between $25,000 and

---

1. 40 U.S.C.A. § 3131 (West).

$100,000, other methods of protection can be provided.[2] If the primary contractor fails to pay the subcontractor or supplier, the subcontractor or supplier can sue the primary contractor in the name of the United States. That is why the United States is named as the plaintiff in *U.S. v. Algernon Blair.*

B. The injured party's right to restitution. When does a breach give the injured party a right to restitution? The Restatement (Second) of Contracts addresses this question in section 373. Under this section, the injured party can demand restitution in only two situations.[3] Restitution is available if the breaching party has committed a breach by anticipatory repudiation.[4] Alternatively, restitution is available if the breaching party has committed a breach by nonperformance that entitles the injured party to damages for total breach, which typically means that the breaching party has committed a non-curable material breach.[5] Do the facts in *Algernon Blair* fit into either of these categories?

C. Restitution in case of full performance. Section 373(2) of the Restatement (Second) of Contracts limits the injured party's right to restitution in a significant way. Under this provision, restitution is not available if the only unperformed obligation left is the breaching party's obligation to pay a definite amount of money for performance received.[6] At first glance, this rule may seem odd. It punishes a conscientious party since, under this rule, an injured party who has fully performed is worse off than an injured party who has only partially performed. What might be the policy reason underlying this rule?

---

2. 40 U.S.C.A. § 3132 (West).
3. Restatement (Second) of Contracts, § 373(1). See Mobil Oil Expl. and Producing S.E., Inc. v. U.S., 530 U.S. 604, 614 (2000)(holding that "a contracting party [is entitled] to restitution if the other party 'substantially' breached a contract or communicated its intent to do so"); MC Baldwin Fin. Co. v. DiMaggio, Rosario & Veraja, LLC, 845 N.E.2d 22, 30 (Ill. App. 1st Dist. 2006)(holding that "where a defendant has committed a total breach or a repudiation of a contract, a plaintiff may alternatively seek restitution"); Abdul v. Subbiah, 735 N.Y.S.2d 29, 30 (N.Y. App. Div. 1st Dept. 2001) (holding that "[s]ince the breach of contract by non-performance was a total breach, plaintiff was entitled to obtain restitution"); Midwest Prop. Mgt. LP v. DesignWise, Inc., 2023 IL App (4th) 230120-U, ¶ 30(holding that "when a defendant has committed a total breach or a repudiation of a contract, a plaintiff may alternatively seek restitution").
4. Restatement (Second) of Contracts, § 373(1).
5. Restatement (Second) of Contracts, § 373(1).
6. Restatement (Second) of Contracts, § 373(2). See Com. Recycling Ctr., Ltd. v. Hobbs Industries, Inc., 228 P.3d 93, 100 (Alaska 2010) (following section 373(2) of the Restatement (Second) of Contracts); Fair Oaks Phase II v. Fox & Proffitt, No. 101388., 1991 WL 834841, at *3 (Va. Cir. Mar. 11, 1991) (following section 373(2) of the Restatement (Second) of Contracts).

D. Measuring the injured party's restitution interest. How does one quantify the injured party's restitution interest? Section 371 of Restatement (Second) of Contracts provides two alternative measures: the first is the price that the recipient of the benefit would have had to pay a third party for the received benefit;[7] the second is the increase in value that the recipient has experienced as a result of receiving the benefit.[8] To illustrate, let's consider a scenario where the injured party is a builder who constructed a mansion for the party in breach based on plans that the party in breach provided. Additionally, assume that even though other builders would have charged $10,000,000 to build the mansion, the mansion's construction only augmented the property value by $5,000,000 because of the mansion's unattractive design. In such a scenario, the first criterion results in a restitution interest of $10,000,000, while the second yields a restitution interest of $5,000,000. The question then arises: which criterion prevails? As a general principle, if the injured party seeks restitution, she can rely on the higher of the two criteria.[9]

E. Unprofitable contracts. In *Algernon v. Blair*, the court allows the injured party to recover their restitution interest even though the injured party would have lost money on the contract in the absence of a breach. The Restatement (Second) takes the same view,[10] as do a number of courts.[11] By contrast, the Restatement (Third) of Restitution, which also addresses this issue, explicitly limits the injured party's restitution interest to the contract price,[12] and this position, too, has persuaded various courts.[13] Which approach seems more equitable?

---

7. Restatement (Second) of Contracts § 371(a).
8. Restatement (Second) of Contracts § 371(b).
9. Restatement (Second) of Contracts § 371 ct. b.
10. Restatement (Second) of Contracts, § 373(1) ct. d (discussing the application of section 373 to losing contracts).
11. See, e.g., U.S. ex rel. Asphalt Contractors, & Site Work, Inc. v. KAR Contracting, LLC, 2015 WL 3651279, at *4 (S.D.W. Va. June 11, 2015) (allowing plaintiff to recover for quantum meruit); Window Specialists, Inc. v. Forney Enterprises, Inc., 106 F. Supp. 3d 64, 93 (D.D.C. 2015) (holding that "a subcontractor can recover in quantum meruit without regard to its ability to recover on the contract.").
12. Restatement (Third) of Restitution and Unjust Enrichment (2011) § 38 (2).
13. See, e.g., Admiral Fin. Corp. v. U.S., 378 F.3d 1336, 1345 (Fed. Cir. 2004) (holding that "even if the remedy of restitution would otherwise be appropriate, . . . restitution should not be awarded if it would result in a windfall to the nonbreaching party"); GuestHouse Intern., LLC v. Shoney's N.A. Corp., 330 S.W.3d 166, 207 n.58 (Tenn. App. 2010) ("Rescission and restitution for breach of a valid and enforceable contract does not seek to punish the party who breached or bestow a windfall on the nonbreaching party.").

F. Efficiency. What are the efficiency consequences of the court's holding in *Algernon Blair*? Does the rule embraced by the court threaten to deter some parties from breaching the contract even though a breach of contract would maximize the parties' joint payoffs from the breach?

CHAPTER 26
FORESEEABILITY

Hadley v. Baxendale

Court of Exchequer Chamber, 156 Eng. Rep. 145 (1854)

[*The plaintiffs owned and operated a mill in Gloucester. The mill relied on a steam engine. When a component (the crank shaft) of that steam engine broke, the plaintiffs ordered a new crank shaft from W. Joyce & Co. in Greenwich. For the latter company to manufacture the new crank shaft, the plaintiffs had to send in the old, broken crank shaft. Therefore, the plaintiffs contracted with the defendant, a carrier, to transport the old crank shaft to W. Joyce & Co. in Greenwich. According to the contract, the crankshaft was to be delivered to W. Joyce & Co. on the day after it was sent.*]

The delivery of the shaft at Greenwich was delayed by some neglect; and the consequence was, that the plaintiffs did not receive the new shaft for several days after they would otherwise have done, and the working of their mill was thereby delayed, and they thereby lost the profits they would otherwise have received.

On the part of the defendants, it was objected that these damages were too remote, and that the defendants were not liable with respect to them. The learned Judge left the case generally to the jury, who found a verdict with 25l. damages beyond the amount paid into Court. Whateley . . . obtained a rule . . . for a new trial, on the ground of misdirection. . .

The judgment of the Court was now delivered by ALDERSON, B.

We think that there ought to be a new trial in this case; but, in so doing, we deem it to be expedient and necessary to state explicitly the rule which the Judge, at the next trial, ought, in our opinion, to direct the jury to be governed by when they estimate the damages. . . .

Now we think the proper rule is such as the present is this: Where two parties have made a contract which one of them has broken, the damages which the other party ought to receive in respect of such breach of contract should be such as may fairly and reasonably be considered either arising naturally, i.e., according to the usual course of things, from such breach of contract itself, or such as may reasonably be supposed to have been in the contemplation of both parties, at the time they made the contract, as the probable result of the breach of it. Now, if the special circumstances under which the contract was actually made where communicated by the plaintiffs to the defendants, and thus known to both parties, the damages resulting from the breach of such a contract, which they would reasonably contemplate, would be the amount of injury which would ordinarily follow from a breach of contract under these special circumstances so known and communicated. But, on the other hand, if these special circumstances were wholly unknown to the party breaking the contract, he, at the most, could only be supposed to have had in his contemplation the amount of injury which would arise generally, and in the great multitude of cases not affected by any special circumstances, from such a breach of contract. For such loss would neither have flowed naturally from the breach of this contract in the great multitude of such cases occurring under ordinary circumstances, nor were the special circumstances, which, perhaps, would have made it a reasonable and natural consequence of such breach of contract, communicated to or known by the defendants. The Judge ought, therefore, to have told the jury, that, upon the fats then before them, they ought not to take the loss of profits into consideration at all in estimating the damages. There must therefore be a new trial in this case.

Rule absolute.

NOTES AND QUESTIONS

A. The Restatement. The court's holding in *Hadley v. Baxendale* regarding the foreseeability of loss is now a firm rule of common law.[1] Read section 351 of the Restatement (Second) of Contracts.

B. Mandatory rules and default rules. Contract law consists, for the most part, of so-called default rules as opposed to mandatory rules. Mandatory rules are rules that the parties cannot opt out of in their contract. In contrast, parties can opt out of default rules in their contract. Put differently, default rules are the rules that apply if the parties' agreement does not address a particular issue. For example, if both parties to a contract are required to render a performance, but only one party's performance requires a certain amount of time, that performance is due first. This norm is a mere default rule, which only applies "unless the language or the circumstances indicate the contrary."[2]

C. Designing default rules. A central question in contract law is how courts and lawmakers should design default rules. The traditional answer to this question is the so-called hypothetical bargain approach. According to this approach, default rules should reflect what most parties would have agreed on in the absence of transaction costs.[3] A key advantage of this approach is that it can reduce transaction costs by making it unnecessary for most parties to opt out of the default. Moreover, it will not always be practical for parties to opt out of the default. The hypothetical bargain approach is likely to reduce the costs of such accidental opt-out failures because it reflects the solution that most parties would have chosen anyway.

However, the hypothetical bargain approach is not the only way of designing default rules. Ian Ayres and Robert Gertner have suggested that it can sometimes be efficient to design default rules to make them unattractive to one or even both of the parties.[4] Such "penalty defaults" may improve efficiency in certain scenarios. First, if it is costly for the court to formulate a reasonable rule, a penalty default rule can incentivize the parties to negotiate a reasonable solution instead of relying on the courts to fulfill that task.[5]

---

1. See Restatement (Second) of Contracts § 351.
2. Id. § 234(2).
3. See, e.g., Charles J. Goetz, The Mitigation Principle: Toward A General Theory of Contractual Obligation, 69 VA. L. REV. 967, 971 (1983) ("Ideally, the preformulated rules supplied by the state should mimic the agreements contracting parties would reach were they costlessly to bargain out each detail of the transaction.").
4. Robert Gertner & Ian Ayres, Filling Gaps in Incomplete Contracts: An Economic Theory of Default Rules, 99 YALE L.J. 87, 93–94 (1989).
5. Id.

Second, one party will often be better informed than the other, creating informational asymmetry. This information asymmetry may prevent the parties from negotiating a contract that maximizes the parties' joint payoff from the contract because the less-informed party cannot negotiate effectively. By choosing a legal default that is particularly burdensome for the better-informed party, the law can incentivize the better-informed party to try to negotiate an opt-out. Crucially, the attempt to negotiate an opt-out may force the better-informed party to reveal its superior information, eliminating the informational asymmetry and thereby leading to a more efficient contract.[6] Can the theory of penalty defaults explain the holding in *Hadley v. Baxendale*?

D. Cheapest cost avoider. In *Evra Corp. v. Swiss Bank Corp.*, Judge Posner argues that "the animating principle of *Hadley v. Baxendale* . . . is that the costs of the untoward consequence of a course of dealings should be borne by that party who was able to avert the consequence at least cost and failed to do so."[7] Posner provides the following reasons for this interpretation: "In *Hadley* the untoward consequence was the shutting down of the mill. The carrier could have avoided it by delivering the engine shaft on time. But the mill owners, as the court noted, could have avoided it simply by having a spare shaft. Prudence required that they have a spare shaft anyway, since a replacement could not be obtained at once even if there was no undue delay in carting the broken shaft to and the replacement shaft from the manufacturer. The court refused to imply a duty on the part of the carrier to guarantee the mill owners against the consequences of their own lack of prudence, though of course if the parties had stipulated for such a guarantee the court would have enforced it. The notice requirement of *Hadley v. Baxendale* is designed to assure that such an improbable guarantee really is intended."[8] Do you agree with this reasoning?

---

6. Id.
7. Evra Corp. v. Swiss Bank Corp., 673 F.2d 951, 957 (7th Cir. 1982).
8. Id. (internal citation omitted).

TABLE OF CASES

ACA Galleries Inc. v. Kinney, 928 F. Supp.2d 699 (S.D.N.Y. 2013)
Acme Markets v. Federal Armored Express, 648 A.2d 1218 (Pa. Super. 1994)
Berryman v. Kmoch, 221 Kan. 304 (1977)
Boswell v. Panera Bread Company, 879 F.3d 296 (8th Cir. 2018)
Brown Machine, Division of John Brown, Inc. v. Hercules, 770 S.W.2d 416 (Mo. App. E. Dist. 1989)
Cadillac Rubber & Plastics v. Tubular Metal Systems, 952 N.W.2d 576 (Mich. App. 2020)
Coburn v. Rhodig, 2019 WL 1530298 (Ariz. App. 1st Div. 2019)
Crabtree v. Elizabeth Arden Sales Corp., 110 N.E.2d 551 (N.Y. App. 1953)
Daitom Inc. v. Pennwalt Corp., 741 F.2d 1569 (10th 1984)
Dodson v. Shrader, 824 S.W.2d 545 (Tenn. 1992)
Forbes v. Prime General Contractors, Inc., 255 So.3d 448 (Fla. 2nd DCA 2018)
Hadley v. Baxendale, 156 Eng. Rep. 145 (1854)
Hamer v. Sidway, 27 N.E. 256 (N.Y. App. 1891)
Highlands Broadway Opco, LLC v. Barre Boss LLC, 528 P.3d 517 (Colo. App. 2023)
Jacobs & Youngs, Inc. v. Kent, 230 N.Y. 239 (App. 1921)
James Baird Co. v. Gimbel Bros. Inc., 64 F.2d 344 (2nd Cir. 1933)
Lloyd v. Niceta, 485 Md. 422 (2023)
Lonergan v. Scolnick, 129 Cal.App.2d 179 (1955)
Lower Kuskokwim School District v. Alaska Diversified Contractors, 734 P.2d 62 (Alaska 1987)

Mills v. Wyman, 3 Pick. 207 (Mass. 1825)
Normile v. Miller, 313 N.C. 98 (1985)
Plowman et al. v. Indian Refining Co., 20 F. Supp. 1 (E.D. Ill. 1937)
ProCD, Inc. v. Zeidenberg, 86 F.3d 1447 (7th Cir. 1996)
Sackett v. Spindler, 56 Ca. Rptr. 435 (Cal. App. 1st Dist. 1967)
Siam v. Mountain Vista Builders, S.W.3d 504 (Tex.App. El Paso 2018)
U.S. v. Algernon Blair, Inc., 479 F.2d 638 (4th Cir. 1973)
Webb v. McGowin, 168 So. 196 (Ala. Ct. App. 1935)
White City Shopping Center L.P. v. PR Restaurants, LLC, 21 Mass. L. Rptr. 565 (Sup. Ct. Worcester 2006)
William A. Drennan v. Star Paving Company, 51 Cal.2d 409 (1958)

www.ingramcontent.com/pod-product-compliance
Lightning Source LLC
LaVergne TN
LVHW060026210926
848481LV00013B/3793